JOHN DONNE'S
POETRY

AUTHORITATIVE TEXTS

CRITICISM

⇛ NORTON CRITICAL EDITIONS ⇚

JOHN DONNE'S POETRY

AUTHORITATIVE TEXTS
CRITICISM

➤➤⫷⫷

Selected and Edited by

A. L. CLEMENTS

STATE UNIVERSITY OF NEW YORK AT BINGHAMTON

➤➤ ⫷⫷

W · W · NORTON & COMPANY · INC · *New York*

⇛ ⇚

⇛ W. W. Norton & Company, Inc. is also the publisher of *The Norton Anthology of English Literature*, edited by M. H. Abrams, Robert M. Adams, David Daiches, E. Talbot Donaldson, George H. Ford, Samuel Holt Monk, and Hallett Smith; *The American Tradition in Literature*, edited by Sculley Bradley, Richmond Croom Beatty, and E. Hudson Long; *World Masterpieces*, edited by Maynard Mack, Kenneth Douglas, Howard E. Hugo, Bernard M. W. Knox, John C. McGalliard, P. M. Pasinetti, and René Wellek; and *The Norton Reader*, edited by Arthur M. Eastman, Caesar R. Blake, Hubert M. English, Jr., Alan B. Howes, Robert T. Lenaghan, Leo F. McNamara, and James Rosier.

Contents

Criticism

Contents · ix

Preface

"If you would teach a scholar in the highest form
how to *read*, take Donne. . . . When he has learnt
to read Donne, with all the force and meaning which
are involved in the words, then send him to Milton,
and he will stalk on like a master *enjoying* his walk."

SAMUEL TAYLOR COLERIDGE

Excepting the four poems published in Donne's lifetime, the first
edition of his poetry appeared in 1633, two years after his death.
Six other editions were printed in the seventeenth century. Of all
of these, modern scholars, following Sir Herbert Grierson's monu-
mental work and Helen Gardner's valuable edition of *The Divine
Poems*, are generally agreed that the edition of 1633 is the most
reliable. Though subject to some correction from the other editions and the manuscripts, it provides, they believe, a better text
than could be provided by any single extant manuscript or than
could be constructed by taking the extant manuscripts together;
and they agree that it must be the basis of any critical edition.
The edition of 1635 adds some new poems by Donne, rearranges
the order of the poems more satisfactorily, and makes many
changes in the 1633 text. Although the 1635 edition does not
have greater authority, it is especially useful for its new poems
(nine of which are included in this volume), for its order, and
for its corrections of the misprints and some of the punctuation
of the 1633 edition. Of the remaining seventeenth-century editions, which are significant mainly for their new poems, only the
1650 and 1669 editions are here notable. The 1650 edition is
the text for two of the Songs and Sonnets: "Sonnet. The
Token" and "Self-Love," poems which only doubtfully can be
ascribed to Donne. (Although "Sonnet. The Token" was first
printed in 1649, the texts of the poem in 1649 and 1650 are
identical; it appears that the edition of 1649 was not actually
issued and that the sheets of most of the copies were incorporated in the 1650 volumes, edited by the younger John Donne.)
The 1669 edition is, as Grierson says, "the last which affords
evidence of access to independent manuscript sources"; it adds two
elegies, one of which, Elegy XIX, considerably corrected by the
manuscripts, is included in this selection. The Westmoreland manu-

script, now in the New York Public Library, and of high textual value, is the sole authority for several poems not printed in the early editions, most notably Holy Sonnets XVII, XVIII, and XIX. Of the poems printed in Donne's lifetime, the most significant are *The Anniversaries*, published in 1611 and 1612. Recently, Frank Manley has demonstrated that the 1611 edition, which Donne may have seen through the press, furnishes, with some correction from 1633 and from the 1612 edition with its "unique" errata slip, the only authoritative text of *The First Anniversary*.

The text of this edition, therefore, is substantially that of 1633; sixteen poems are included for which the Westmoreland manuscript and the editions of 1611, 1635, 1650 and 1669 have authority. That is, the text is based upon the first edition of each poem or, in the case of three Holy Sonnets, upon the Westmoreland manuscript. Effort has been made throughout to take into account the many important contributions of modern scholars and editors of Donne. For example, while retaining in parentheses Grierson's numbering of the Holy Sonnets, by which they are usually referred to, this volume adopts the sequence suggested by Helen Gardner, based on her study of the editions and manuscripts. The annotations are intended chiefly to compensate for some of the changes in language and knowledge effected by the passage of more than three centuries and to suggest some of the rewarding complexities of Donne's poetry. On occasion, the annotations also refer the reader to helpful critical articles and record some of the editor's debts. Accidentals of spelling, capitalization, and punctuation have been carefully updated; when the updating might obscure a possible alternative reading, I have printed the original or have indicated editorial changes in the Textual Notes, which contain further prefatory remarks on my principles for updating. The Notes also record substantive departures from the authoritative text (as corrected by the other editions and manuscripts) and significant variants. The aim throughout has been reliability.

The essays in criticism range from the seventeenth century to the twentieth century, from sharply critical accounts to highly favorable evaluations, from close analyses of individual poems to general considerations of Donne and metaphysical poetry. The division of the essays into three sections should be almost self-explanatory. The first section, "Donne and Metaphysical Poetry," contains introductory and background material and provides an historical range of opinion by outstanding critics. The second section, "Donne's Love Poetry," begins with the dispute between C. S. Lewis and Joan Bennett; and Theodore Redpath continues and elaborates the discussion of critical issues raised. The articles by Cleanth Brooks, Clay Hunt, and R. A. Durr not only present sensitive, illuminating explications, but also afford some transition from the love poetry to the divine poems. In the third section, "Donne's Divine Poems and *The Anniversaries*," Helen Gardner offers some comprehensive considerations of Donne's religious poetry. Helen Gardner, in the second part of her essay, and Louis Martz discuss the meditative element in the Holy Sonnets and in "Good Friday, 1613," and Stanley Archer raises objections to their approach. The short "Readings of Holy Sonnet XIV" provide, again, differing views and yet also illustrate how criticism may contribute, over a period of time, to a fuller and more exact understanding of literature. Finally, Frank Manley summarizes criticism of *The Anniversaries* over the centuries and then considers these poems in terms of the complex and inchoate Renaissance tradition of Wisdom. Thus, each of these interrelated sections contains controversy and varying and divergent opinions, yet also displays some continuity and development of particular critical ideas on Donne's poetry. The abundance of excellent writing on Donne makes it impossible to represent here every point of view, but the Selected Bibliography at the end of this book will direct the reader to sources helpful in the further study of Donne.

Indeed, the abundance of excellent work on Donne in this century puts any modern editor of Donne under heavy debt. I am especially conscious of indebtedness to Sir Herbert Grierson, Helen Gardner, and Frank Manley, all of whom have contributed greatly to establishing and illuminating the text of Donne's poetry. Special expression of my gratefulness must go also to the other scholars whose work is represented in the critical essays of this book. I am grateful also to Professor John Hagopian, who generously put in my hands his published and unpublished materials on Donne; to Professor David Novarr, who offered many thoughtful suggestions, some of which I have incorporated; to Mr. Josiah Newcomb, Director of Libraries, State University of New York at Binghamton, who helped me to obtain the numerous books, photostats, and microfilms I needed; to members of the staffs of the Huntington Library, the New York Public Library, Princeton University Library, and Yale University Library, who extended many courtesies; and, finally, to my wife, Irma, who helped with typing and proofreading and who made all of my tasks much easier by her thoughtfulness and encouragement.

A. L. CLEMENTS

The Text of
The Poems

Songs and Sonnets

The Good-Morrow

I wonder, by my troth, what thou and I
Did, till we loved? were we not weaned till then?
But sucked on country pleasures, childishly?
Or snorted we in the Seven Sleepers' den?[1]
'Twas so; but this,[2] all pleasures fancies be.   5
If ever any beauty I did see,
Which I desired, and got, 'twas but a dream of thee.

And now good-morrow to our waking souls,
Which watch not one another out of fear;
For love, all love of other sights controls,   10
And makes one little room an everywhere.
Let sea-discoverers to new worlds have gone,
Let maps to others, worlds on worlds have shown,[3]
Let us possess one world, each hath one, and is one.[4]

My face in thine eye, thine in mine appears,   15
And true plain hearts do in the faces rest;
Where can we find two better hemispheres,
Without sharp north, without declining west?
Whatever dies was not mixed equally;[5]
If our two loves be one, or, thou and I   20
Love so alike that none do slacken, none can die.

Song

Go and catch a falling star,
    Get with child a mandrake root,[6]
Tell me where all past years are,

1. Legend tells of seven Christian youths who, fleeing from Roman persecution, took refuge in a cave and slept unharmed for two centuries.
2. Except for this.
3. Let maps reveal to other people many worlds.
4. According to the theory of Donne's time, every man was thought to be a little world in himself, a microcosm, paralleling the great world, the macrocosm.
5. Scholastic doctrine held that decay will eventually occur when a thing is composed of unequal or dissimilar elements.
6. The mandrake root's forked shape roughly resembles the human body. But the mandrake was also thought to be a soporific, an aphrodisiac, and a cause of fruitfulness in women. See D. C. Allen, *Modern Language Notes*, 74 (1959), 393-97, and cf. "Twickenham Garden," line 17.

Or who cleft the Devil's foot,
Teach me to hear mermaids singing,   5
Or to keep off envy's stinging,
    And find
    What wind
Serves to advance an honest mind.

If thou be'st born to strange sights,   10
   Things invisible to see,
Ride ten thousand days and nights,
   Till age snow white hairs on thee,
Thou, when thou return'st, wilt tell me
   All strange wonders that befell thee,   15
    And swear
    Nowhere
Lives a woman true, and fair.

If thou findst one, let me know,
   Such a pilgrimage were sweet.   20
Yet do not; I would not go,
   Though at next door we might meet;
Though she were true, when you met her,
   And last, till you write your letter,
    Yet she   25
    Will be
False, ere I come, to two, or three.

Woman's Constancy

Now thou hast loved me one whole day,
Tomorrow when thou leav'st, what wilt thou say?
Wilt thou then antedate some new-made vow?
    Or say that now
We are not just those persons which we were?   5
Or, that oaths made in reverential fear
Of Love, and his wrath, any may forswear?
Or, as true deaths true marriages untie,
So lovers' contracts, images of those,
Bind but till sleep, death's image, them unloose?   10
    Or, your own end to justify,
For having purposed changed, and falsehood, you
Can have no way but falsehood to be true?
Vain lunatic,[7] against these 'scapes I could
    Dispute, and conquer, if I would,   15
    Which I abstain to do,
For by tomorrow, I may think so too.

---

7. Under sway of the moon, and thus changeable, inconstant, as well as madly foolish person; " 'scapes" means "excuses," "evasions."

The Undertaking

I have done one braver thing
    Than all the Worthies[8] did,
And yet a braver thence doth spring,
    Which is, to keep that hid.

It were but madness now to impart   5
    The skill of specular stone,[9]
When he which can have learned the art
    To cut it can find none.

So, if I now should utter this,
    Others (because no more   10
Such stuff to work upon there is)
    Would love but as before.

But he who loveliness within
    Hath found, all outward loathes,
For he who color loves, and skin,   15
    Loves but their oldest clothes.

If, as I have, you also do
    Virtue attired in woman see,
And dare love that, and say so too,
    And forget the He and She,   20

And if this love, though placed so,
    From profane men you hide,
Which will no faith on this bestow,
    Or, if they do, deride:

Then you have done a braver thing   25
    Than all the Worthies did.
And a braver thence will spring,
    Which is, to keep that hid.

The Sun Rising

    Busy old fool, unruly sun,
      Why dost thou thus,
Through windows, and through curtains, call on us?
Must to thy motions lovers' seasons run?
    Saucy pedantic wretch, go chide   5
    Late schoolboys, and sour prentices,

8. Outstanding heroes of antiquity.
9. The technique or craft of cutting old selenite, an ancient transparent material used for glazing, but no longer available in Donne's time.

Go tell court-huntsmen that the King will ride,
    Call country ants to harvest offices;
Love, all alike, no season knows, nor clime,
Nor hours, days, months, which are the rags of t...me.   10

        Thy beams, so reverend and strong
        Why shouldst thou think?
I could eclipse and cloud them with a wink,
But that I would not lose her sight so long:
        If her eyes have not blinded thine,   15
        Look, and tomorrow late, tell me
Whether both the Indias of spice and mine[1]
Be where thou leftst them, or lie here with me.
Ask for those kings whom thou saw'st yesterday,
And thou shalt hear, All here in one bed lay.   20

        She's all states, and all princes I,
        Nothing else is.
Princes do but play us; compared to this,
All honor's mimic, all wealth alchemy.[2]
        Thou, sun, art half as happy as we,   25
        In that the world's contracted thus;
Thine age asks[3] ease, and since thy duties be
To warm the world, that's done in warming us.
Shine here to us, and thou art everywhere;
This bed thy center is, these walls thy sphere.   30

The Indifferent

I can love both fair and brown,
Her whom abundance melts, and her whom want betrays,
Her who loves loneness best, and her who masks and plays,
Her whom the country formed, and whom the town,
Her who believes, and her who tries,   5
Her who still weeps with spongy eyes,
And her who is dry cork, and never cries;
I can love her, and her, and you, and you,
I can love any, so she be not true.

Will no other vice content you?   10
Will it not serve your turn to do as did your mothers?
Or have you all old vices spent, and now would find our others?
Or doth a fear, that men are true, torment you?
Oh we are not, be not you so;
Let me, and do you, twenty know.   15

1. The East Indies, source of spices, and the West Indies, source of precious metals.

2. Alchemy was often regarded as a fraud.

3. Requires.

Rob me, but bind me not, and let me go.
Must I, who came to travail[4] thorough[5] you,
Grow your fixed subject, because you are true?

Venus heard me sigh this song,
And by love's sweetest part, variety, she swore   20
She heard not this till now; and that it should be so no more.
She went, examined, and returned ere long,
And said, "Alas, some two or three
Poor heretics in love there be,
Which think to 'stablish[6] dangerous constancy.   25
But I have told them, 'Since you will be true,
You shall be true to them who are false to you.' "

Love's Usury

For every hour that thou wilt spare me now,
      I will allow,
Usurious God of Love, twenty to thee,
When with my brown, my gray hairs equal be;
Till then, Love, let my body reign, and let   5
Me travel, sojourn, snatch, plot, have, forget,
Resume my last year's relict:[7] think that yet
      We'd never met.

Let me think any rival's letter mine,
      And at next nine[8]   10
Keep midnight's promise; mistake by the way
The maid, and tell the lady of that delay;
Only let me love none, no, not the sport;
From country grass, to comfitures of Court,
Or city's quelque-choses, let report   15
      My mind transport.[9]

This bargain's good: if, when I'm old, I be
      Inflamed by thee,
If thine own honor, or my shame, or pain,
Thou covet, most at that age thou shalt gain.   20
Do thy will then, then subject and degree
And fruit of love, Love, I submit to thee;
Spare me till then, I'll bear it, though she be
      One that loves me.

4. Hardship, suffering; labor; with a pun on travel (as a verb).
5. "Thorough": "through."
6. Establish.
7. The woman loved and left behind last year.

8. Nine A.M.
9. Let reports about the different kinds of women—"country grass"; "comfitures" (literally, "sweetmeats"); "quelque-choses" (literally, "fancy dishes") —turn my fancy from one to the other.

The Canonization

For God's sake, hold your tongue, and let me love,
  Or chide my palsy, or my gout,
My five gray hairs, or ruined fortune flout,
  With wealth your state, your mind with arts improve,
    Take you a course, get you a place,[1]   5
    Observe his honor, or his grace,
Or the King's real, or his stamped[2] face
  Contemplate; what you will, approve,[3]
  So you will let me love.

Alas, alas, who's injured by my love?   10
  What merchant's ships have my sighs drowned?
Who says my tears have overflowed his ground?
  When did my colds a forward spring remove?
    When did the heats which my veins fill
    Add one more to the plaguy bill?[4]   15
Soldiers find wars, and lawyers find out still
  Litigious men, which quarrels move,
  Though she and I do love.

Call us what you will, we are made such by love;
  Call her one, me another fly,   20
We're tapers too, and at our own cost die,[5]
  And we in us find the eagle and the dove.[6]
    The phoenix riddle hath more wit
    By us; we two being one, are it.
So, to one neutral thing both sexes fit.   25
  We die and rise the same, and prove
  Mysterious by this love.[7]

We can die by it, if not live by love,
  And if unfit for tombs and hearse
Our legend be, it will be fit for verse;   30
  And if no piece of chronicle we prove,
    We'll build in sonnets pretty rooms;[8]
    As well a well-wrought urn becomes
The greatest ashes, as half-acre tombs,
  And by these hymns, all shall approve   35
  Us *canonized* for Love.

1. Take a course of action, get yourself a position.
2. Stamped on coins.
3. Try, experience.
4. A list of people who died of the plague.
5. Flies or moths, symbols of the ephemeral and lustful, are attracted to and burned by candles ("tapers"), which are self-consuming. In Donne's time, to "die" was slang for consummating the sexual act, and it was believed that this act reduced one's life span.
6. Symbols of strength and of meekness.
7. Just as the phoenix, a unique mythological bird, is consumed by its own funeral fire, yet rises reborn from the ashes, so the lovers, made one by love, are consumed in their fire of passion but revive; "wit" means "sense," "meaning."
8. Donne uses "sonnets" loosely to mean "love poems"; "stanza" in Italian means "room."

And thus invoke us: "You, whom reverend love
  Made one another's hermitage;
You, to whom love was peace, that now is rage;
    Who did the whole world's soul extract, and drove[9]   40
      Into the glasses of your eyes
      (So made such mirrors, and such spies,
That they did all to you epitomize)
    Countries, towns, courts: beg from above
    A pattern of your love!"   45

The Triple Fool

    I am two fools, I know,
For loving, and for saying so
    In whining poetry;
But where's that wiseman, that would not be I,
    If she would not deny?   5
      Then, as the earth's inward narrow crooked lanes
Do purge sea-water's fretful salt away,
    I thought, if I could draw my pains
Through rhyme's vexation, I should them allay.
Grief brought to numbers[1] cannot be so fierce,   10
For he tames it that fetters it in verse.

    But when I have done so,
Some man, his art and voice to show,
    Doth set[2] and sing my pain,
And, by delighting many, frees again   15
    Grief, which verse did restrain.
To love and grief tribute of verse belongs,
But not of such as pleases when 'tis read;
    Both are increased by such songs:
For both their triumphs so are published,   20
And I, which was two fools, do so grow three;
Who are a little wise, the best fools be.

Lovers' Infiniteness

If yet I have not all thy love,
Dear, I shall never have it all;
I cannot breathe one other sigh to move,
Nor can entreat one other tear to fall;
And all my treasure, which should purchase thee,   5
Sighs, tears, and oaths, and letters, I have spent.

9. Crammed. "Countries, towns courts"
(line 44) are objects of the verb "drove."   1. Verse.
    2. To music.

Yet no more can be due to me,
Than at the bargain made was meant.
If then thy gift of love were partial,
That some to me, some should to others fall,   10
    Dear, I shall never have thee all.

Or if then thou gavest me all,
All was but all which thou hadst then;
But if in thy heart, since, there be or shall
New love created be, by other men,   15
Which have their stocks entire, and can in tears,
In sighs, in oaths, in letters, outbid me,
This new love may beget new fears,
For this love was not vowed by thee.
And yet it was, thy gift being general,   20
The ground, thy heart, is mine; whatever shall
    Grow there, dear, I should have it all.

Yet I would not have all yet;
He that hath all can have no more,
And since my love doth every day admit   25
New growth, thou shouldst have new rewards in store;
Thou canst not every day give me thy heart;
If thou canst give it, then thou never gavest it:
Love's riddles are, that though thy heart depart,
It stays at home, and thou with losing savest it: 30
But we will have a way more liberal
Than changing hearts, to join them, so we shall
    Be one, and one another's All.

Song

Sweetest love, I do not go
    For weariness of thee,
Nor in hope the world can show
    A fitter love for me;
      But since that I   5
Must die at last, 'tis best
To use myself in jest,
    Thus by feigned deaths to die.[3]

Yesternight the sun went hence,
    And yet is here today;   10
He hath no desire nor sense,
    Nor half so short a way:
      Then fear not me,

3. To accustom myself to death by play-   absences.
ing at it through "feigned deaths," *i.e.*,

But believe that I shall make
  Speedier journeys, since I take   15
    More wings and spurs than he.

O how feeble is man's power,
    That if good fortune fall,
Cannot add another hour,
    Nor a lost hour recall!   20
      But come bad chance,
And we join to it our strength,
And we teach it art and length,
    Itself o'er us to advance.

When thou sigh'st, thou sigh'st not wind,   25
    But sigh'st my soul away;
When thou weep'st, unkindly kind,
    My life's blood doth decay.[4]
      It cannot be
That thou lov'st me, as thou say'st,   30
If in thine my life thou waste;
    Thou art the best of me.

Let not thy divining heart
    Forethink me any ill;
Destiny may take thy part,   35
    And may thy fears fulfill;
      But think that we
Are but turned aside to sleep;
They who one another keep
    Alive, ne'er parted be.   40

The Legacy

When I died last (and, dear, I die
  As often as from thee I go),
    Though it be but an hour ago,
And lovers' hours be full eternity,
I can remember yet, that I   5
  Something did say, and something did bestow;
Though I be dead, which sent me, I should be
Mine own executor and legacy.

I heard me say, Tell her anon,
  That my self (that is you, not I)
    Did kill me, and when I felt me die,   10
I bid me send my heart, when I was gone,
But I alas could there find none,

4. Every sigh or tear was supposed to shorten life a little.

When I had ripped me, and searched where hearts did lie;
It killed me again, that I who still was true   15
In life, in my last will should cozen you.

Yet I found something like a heart,
  But colors it, and corners had;[5]
  It was not good, it was not bad,
It was entire to none, and few had part.   20
As good as could be made by art
  It seemed; and therefore, for our losses sad,
I meant to send this heart instead of mine,
But oh, no man could hold it, for 'twas thine.

A Fever

Oh do not die, for I shall hate
  All women so, when thou art gone,
That thee I shall not celebrate,
  When I remember, thou wast one.

But yet thou canst not die, I know;   5
  To leave this world behind, is death,
But when thou from this world wilt go,
  The whole world vapors[6] with thy breath.

Or if, when thou, the world's soul, goest,
  It stay, 'tis but thy carcass then,   10
The fairest woman, but thy ghost,
  But corrupt worms, the worthiest men.

O wrangling schools,[7] that search what fire
  Shall burn this world, had none the wit
Unto this knowledge to aspire,   15
  That this her fever might be it?

And yet she cannot waste by this,
  Nor long bear this torturing wrong,
For much corruption needful is,
  To fuel such a fever long.   20

These burning fits but meteors[8] be,
  Whose matter in thee is soon spent.
Thy beauty and all parts which are thee
  Are unchangeable firmament.

5. It was painted and thus not plain and true; it had corners and thus was imperfect, the circle being a symbol of perfection.
6. Evaporates.
7. Writers of various philosophical and religious schools of thought had written and disputed about the final conflagration which would destroy the world.
8. *I.e.*, passing foreign bodies which will soon burn themselves out and disappear.

Yet 'twas of my mind, seizing thee,   25
   Though it in thee cannot persever:
For I had rather owner be
   Of thee one hour, than all else ever.

Air and Angels

Twice or thrice had I loved thee,
Before I knew thy face or name;
So in a voice, so in a shapeless flame
Angels affect us oft, and worshiped be;
   Still when, to where thou wert, I came,   5
Some lovely glorious nothing I did see.
   But since my soul, whose child love is,
Takes limbs of flesh, and else could nothing do,
   More subtle than the parent is
Love must not be, but take a body too;   10
   And therefore what thou wert, and who,
      I bid Love ask, and now
That it assume thy body, I allow,
And fix itself in thy lip, eye, and brow.

Whilst thus to ballast love, I thought,   15
And so more steadily to have gone,
With wares which would sink admiration
I saw I had love's pinnace overfraught;[9]
   Every thy hair[1] for love to work upon
Is much too much, some fitter must be sought;   20
   For, nor in nothing, nor in things
Extreme, and scatt'ring[2] bright, can love inhere;
   Then as an angel, face, and wings
Of air, not pure as it, yet pure doth wear,[3]
   So thy love may be my love's sphere;[4]   25
      Just such disparity
As is 'twixt air and angels' purity,
'Twixt women's love and men's will ever be.

Break of Day[5]

   'Tis true, 'tis day; what though it be?
   Oh wilt thou therefore rise from me?

9. I had overloaded love's small, light vessel; the pinnace was often used as a scout and the word also meant "a woman" in Donne's time; also, there is a possible pun on "pinnace."
1. Each one of your hairs and even your least hair.
2. Dazzlingly.
3. According to scholastic doctrine, angels, in order to appear to men, assumed bodies of air, which were pure but not as pure as the angelic essence.
4. Each celestial sphere was thought to be inhabited and governed by an angel.
5. The speaker of this poem is a woman. In the 1669 edition and some MSS., a stanza (in a different meter, spoken by a man, and probably not written by Donne) precedes the three stanzas of this poem. See Grierson's *Poems of John Donne*, I, 432.

Why should we rise because 'tis light?
Did we lie down because 'twas night?
Love, which in spite of darkness brought us hither,   5
Should in despite of light keep us together.

Light hath no tongue, but is all eye;
If it could speak as well as spy,
This were the worst that it could say,
That being well, I fain would stay,   10
And that I loved my heart and honor so,
That I would not from him, that had them, go.

Must business thee from hence remove?
Oh, that's the worst disease of love;
The poor, the foul, the false, love can   15
Admit, but not the busied man.
He which hath business, and makes love, doth do
Such wrong, as when a married man doth woo.

The Anniversary

All kings, and all their favorites,
    All glory of honors, beauties, wits,
The sun itself, which makes times,[6] as they pass,
Is elder by a year, now, than it was
When thou and I first one another saw: 5
All other things to their destruction draw,
    Only our love hath no decay;
This, no tomorrow hath, not yesterday;
Running it never runs from us away,
But truly keeps his first, last, everlasting day.   10

    Two graves must hide thine and my corse;[7]
If one might, death were no divorce:
Alas, as well as other princes, we
(Who prince enough in one another be)
Must leave at last in death, these eyes, and ears,   15
Oft fed with true oaths, and with sweet salt tears;
    But souls where nothing dwells but love
(All other thoughts being inmates[8]) then shall prove
This, or a love increased there above,[9]
When bodies to their graves, souls from their graves remove.   20

    And then we shall be throughly[1] blest,
    But we no more than all the rest;

---

6. Days, years; "they" probably refers to "times" rather than to "kings," "favorites," etc.
7. Corpse.

8. Only temporary lodgers; "prove" means "learn," "discover."
9. In heaven.
1. Thoroughly.

Here upon earth, we're kings, and none but we
Can be such kings, nor of such subjects be;
Who is so safe as we, where none can do   25
Treason to us, except one of us two?
    True and false fears let us refrain,
Let us love nobly, and live, and add again
Years and years unto years, till we attain
To write threescore, this is the second of our reign.   30

A Valediction: Of My Name, in the Window

    My name engraved herein
Doth contribute my firmness to this glass,
    Which, ever since that charm, hath been
    As hard as that which graved it was;
Thine eye will give it price enough to mock   5
    The diamonds of either rock.[2]

    'Tis much that glass should be
As all-confessing, and through-shine[3] as I;
    'Tis more, that it shows thee to thee,
    And clear reflects thee to thine eye.   10
But all such rules, love's magic can undo,
    Here you see me, and I am you.[4]

    As no one point, nor dash,
Which are but accessories to this name,
    The showers and tempests can outwash,   15
    So shall all times find me the same;
You this entireness better may fulfill,
    Who have the pattern with you still.[5]

    Or if too hard and deep
This learning be, for a scratched name to teach,   20
    It as a given death's head[6] keep,
    Lovers' mortality to preach,
Or think this ragged bony name to be
    My ruinous anatomy.[7]

    Then, as all my souls[8] be   25
Emparadised in you (in whom alone
    I understand, and grow, and see),

2. Your looking at it will give the glass
(on which the speaker has engraved his
name with a diamond) a value superior
to the diamonds of either India or South
America.
3. Transparent.
4. Because lovers are one.
5. You may complete this unchanging
love by also loving wholeheartedly, and
you may do so more easily for you have
the "pattern" (example) of my enduring
name always with you.
6. A skull, a reminder of mortality.
7. My skeleton.
8. The intellectual ("understand"), veg-
etative ("grow"), and sensitive ("see")
faculties of the soul.

The rafters of my body, bone,[9]
Being still with you, the muscle, sinew, and vein,
   Which tile this house, will come again.   30

     Till my return, repair
And recompact my scattered body so.
   As all the virtuous powers which are
   Fixed in the stars, are said to flow
Into such characters as graved be   35
   When these stars have supremacy:

     So since this name was cut
When love and grief their exaltation had,
   No door 'gainst this name's influence shut;
   As much more loving, as more sad,   40
'Twill make thee; and thou shouldst, till I return,
   Since I die daily,[1] daily mourn.

     When thy inconsiderate hand
Flings ope this casement, with my trembling name,
   To look on one, whose wit or land   45
   New batt'ry to thy heart may frame,
Then think this name alive, and that thou thus
   In it offend'st my Genius.[2]

     And when thy melted maid,
Corrupted by thy lover's gold, and page,   50
   His letter at thy pillow hath laid,
   Disputed it,[3] and tamed thy rage,
And thou begin'st to thaw towards him, for this,
   May my name step in,[4] and hide his.

     And if this treason go   55
To an overt act, and that thou write again,
   In superscribing, this name flow[5]
   Into thy fancy, from the pane.
So, in forgetting, thou rememb'rest right,
   And unaware to me shalt write.   60

     But glass and lines must be
No means our firm substantial love to keep;
   Near death inflicts this lethargy,
   And this I murmur in my sleep;
Impute this idle talk to that I go,   65
   For dying men talk often so.

---

9. Skeleton, *i.e.*, the name.
1. By being absent.
2. Spirit.
3. Argued in its favor.
4. Perhaps by the sunlight's reflecting the name from the window onto the rival's letter.
5. In addressing your reply to the other lover, may the name in the window flow.

Twickenham Garden[6]

Blasted with sighs, and surrounded with tears,
  Hither I come to seek the spring,[7]
  And at mine eyes, and at mine ears,
Receive such balms as else cure everything;
    But oh, self-traitor, I do bring   5
The spider[8] love, which transubstantiates all,
  And can convert manna to gall;
And that this place may thoroughly be thought
True Paradise, I have the serpent[9] brought.

'Twere wholesomer for me, that winter did   10
  Benight the glory of this place,
  And that a grave frost did forbid
These trees to laugh, and mock me to my face;
    But that I may not this disgrace
Endure, nor leave this garden, Love, let me   15
  Some senseless piece of this place be;
Make me a mandrake,[1] so I may groan here,
Or a stone fountain weeping out my year.

Hither with crystal vials, lovers, come,
  And take my tears, which are love's wine,   20
  And try your mistress' tears at home,
For all are false, that taste not just like mine;
    Alas, hearts do not in eyes shine,
Nor can you more judge woman's thoughts by tears,
  Than by her shadow, what she wears.   25
O perverse sex, where none is true but she,
Who's therefore true, because her truth kills me.

A Valediction: Of the Book

I'll tell thee now, dear love, what thou shalt do
  To anger destiny, as she doth us,
  How I shall stay, though she eloign[2] me thus,
And how posterity shall know it too,
    How thine may out-endure   5
    Sibyl's glory, and obscure

6. Twickenham was the home of Lucy, Countess of Bedford, a patroness and friend of Donne.
7. The season; healing waters; the source or cause of the sighs and tears.
8. Believed to be poisonous.
9. The tempter. The serpent is also often a symbol of envy or jealousy; cf. lines 26–27.

1. A plant whose forked shape roughly resembles the human body; it was supposed to shriek or groan when uprooted and was thought to be an aphrodisiac. If he were a mandrake or a fountain, he could groan his sighs or weep his tears inconspicuously.
2. Remove far off.

Her who from Pindar could allure,
And her, through whose help Lucan is not lame,
And her, whose book (they say) Homer did find, and name.[3]

Study our manuscripts, those myriads   10
    Of letters, which have past 'twixt thee and me,
    Thence write our annals, and in them will be,
To all whom love's subliming[4] fire invades,
        Rule and example found;
        There, the faith of any ground[5]   15
        No schismatic will dare to wound,
    That sees how Love this grace to us affords,
To make, to keep, to use, to be these his records.

This book, as long-lived as the elements,
    Or as the world's form, this all-graved tome   20
    In cypher writ, or new-made idiom;
We for Love's clergy only are instruments,
        When this book is made thus,
        Should again the ravenous
        Vandals and Goths inundate us,   25
    Learning were safe; in this our universe
Schools might learn sciences, spheres music,[6] angels verse.

Here Love's divines (since all divinity
    Is love or wonder) may find all they seek,
    Whether abstract spiritual love they like,   30
Their souls exhaled[7] with what they do not see,
        Or, loath so to amuse[8]
        Faith's infirmity, they choose
        Something which they may see and use;
    For, though mind be the heaven, where love doth sit,   35
Beauty a convenient type may be to figure[9] it.

Here, more than in their books, may lawyers find
    Both by what titles mistresses are ours
    And how prerogative these states devours,
Transferred from Love himself, to womankind,   40
        Who, though from heart, and eyes,
        They exact great subsidies,
        Forsake him who on them relies,
    And for the cause, honor, or conscience, give—
Chimeras, vain as they, or their prerogative.   45

3. The Cumaean Sibyl was a legendary
prophetess and authoress; Corinna was
a poetess who five times defeated the
Greek poet Pindar in competition; the
wife of the Latin poet Lucan assisted
him with his poetry; the mythical Egyptian poetess Phantasia was reputed to
have been Homer's source.

4. Purifying.
5. Basic tenet.
6. The movement of the heavenly
spheres was said to produce music.
7. Drawn out.
8. Bewilder.
9. Represent.

Here statesmen (or of them, they which can read)
 May of their occupation find the grounds:
 Love and their art alike it deadly wounds,
If to consider what 'tis, one proceed;
  In both they do excel   50
  Who the present govern well,
  Whose weakness none doth or dares tell;
 In this thy book, such will their nothing see,
As in the Bible some can find out alchemy.

Thus vent thy thoughts; abroad I'll study thee,[1] 55
 As he removes far off, that great heights takes;
 How great love is, presence best trial makes,
But absence tries how long this love will be;
  To take a latitude,
  Sun, or stars, are fitliest viewed   60
  At their brightest, but to conclude
 Of longitudes, what other way have we,
But to mark when and where the dark eclipses be?

Community

Good we must love, and must hate ill,
For ill is ill, and good good still,
 But there are things indifferent,
Which we may neither hate, nor love,
But one, and then another prove,[2]   5
 As we shall find our fancy bent.

If then at first wise Nature had
Made women either good or bad,
 Then some we might hate, and some choose;
But since she did them so create,   10
That we may neither love, nor hate,
 Only this rests:[3] All, all may use.

If they were good it would be seen,
Good is as visible as green,
 And to all eyes itself betrays;   15
If they were bad, they could not last,
Bad doth itself, and others, waste;
 So, they deserve nor blame, nor praise.

But they are ours as fruits are ours,
He that but tastes, he that devours, 20
 And he that leaves all, doth as well;

1. Thus express your thoughts; while I'm away I'll read what you have written.
2. Try, experience.
3. Remains.

Changed loves are but changed sorts of meat,
And when he hath the kernel eat,
Who doth not fling away the shell?

Love's Growth

I scarce believe my love to be so pure
    As I had thought it was,
    Because it doth endure
Vicissitude, and season, as the grass;
Methinks I lied all winter, when I swore   5
My love was infinite, if spring make it more.

But if this medicine, love, which cures all sorrow
With more, not only be no quintessence,[4]
But mixed of all stuffs paining soul or sense,
And of the sun his working vigor borrow,   10
Love's not so pure, and abstract, as they use
To say, which have no mistress but their muse,
But as all else, being elemented[5] too,
Love sometimes would contemplate, sometimes do.

And yet no greater, but more eminent,[6]   15
    Love by the spring is grown;
    As, in the firmament,
Stars by the sun are not enlarged, but shown,[7]
Gentle love deeds, as blossoms on a bough,
From love's awakened root do bud out now.   20
If, as in water stirred more circles be
Produced by one, love such additions take,
Those, like so many spheres, but one heaven make,
For they are all concentric unto thee;[8]
And though each spring do add to love new heat,   25
As princes do in times of action get
New taxes, and remit them not in peace,
No winter shall abate the spring's increase.

4. A pure essense, which could cure all ills.
5. Composed of various elements; *i.e.,* not a pure essence.
6. *I.e.,* outstanding, perceptible; etymologically, standing out, projecting.
7. Referring to the phenomenon that as the sun rises and the sky becomes lighter the definite dark background of the sky gradually recedes and the stars thus gradually *seem* larger. Such a "growing" appearance is similar to the gradual budding out of a blossom.
8. According to Ptolemaic astronomy, the heavenly spheres were concentric to the earth. By "love's growth," Donne might also be referring to the physical appearance of a woman's pregnancy; esp. cf. lines 15–20. If so, the asymmetrical, "growing" stanzas of the editions and some MSS. may have an added significance and may have been quite deliberate.

Love's Exchange

Love, any devil else but you
Would for a given soul give something too.
At Court your fellows every day
Give the art of rhyming, huntsmanship, or play,[9]
For them which were their own before;   5
Only I have nothing which gave more,
But am, alas, by being lowly, lower.

I ask no dispensation now
To falsify a tear, or sigh, or vow,
I do not sue from thee to draw   10
A *non obstante*[1] on nature's law;
These are prerogatives, they inhere
In thee and thine; none should forswear
Except that he Love's minion were.

Give me thy weakness, make me blind,   15
Both ways, as thou and thine, in eyes and mind;
Love, let me never know that this
Is love, or, that love childish is.
Let me not know that others know
That she knows my pains, lest that so   20
A tender shame make me mine own new woe.

If thou give nothing, yet thou art just,
Because I would not thy first motions[2] trust;
Small towns which stand stiff till great shot[3]
Enforce them, by war's law *condition* not.[4]   25
Such in love's warfare is my case;
I may not article[5] for grace,
Having put Love at last to show this face—

This face, by which he could command
And change the idolatry of any land;   30
This face, which, wheresoe'er it comes,
Can call vowed men from cloisters, dead from tombs,
And melt both poles at once, and store
Deserts with cities, and make more
Mines in the earth, than quarries were before.   35

For this,[6] Love is enraged with me,
Yet kills not. If I must example be
To future rebels, if the unborn
Must learn by my being cut up and torn,

9. Gambling.
1. Exception.
2. Impulses.
3. Heavy artillery.

4. *I.e.*, they must surrender unconditionally.
5. Negotiate, arrange.
6. See esp. lines 23, 28.

Kill, and dissect me, Love; for this 40
Torture against thine own end is:
Racked carcasses make ill anatomies.[7]

Confined Love

Some man unworthy to be possessor
Of old or new love, himself being false or weak,
  Thought his pain and shame would be lesser,
If on womankind he might his anger wreak;
    And thence a law did grow, 5
    One might but one man know;
    But are other creatures so?

Are sun, moon, or stars by law forbidden
To smile where they list, or lend away their light?
  Are birds divorced, or are they chidden 10
If they leave their mate, or lie abroad a night?
    Beasts do no jointures[8] lose
    Though they new lovers choose,
    But we are made worse than those.

Who e'er rigged fair ship to lie in harbors, 15
And not to seek new lands, or not to deal withal?[9]
  Or built fair houses, set trees, and arbors,
Only to lock up, or else to let them fall?
    Good is not good, unless
    A thousand it possess, 20
    But doth waste with greediness.

The Dream

Dear love, for nothing less than thee
Would I have broke this happy dream;
    It was a theme
For reason, much too strong for phantasy,
Therefore thou wak'dst me wisely; yet 5
My dream thou brok'st not, but continued'st it,
Thou art so truth, that thoughts of thee suffice
To make dreams truths, and fables histories;
Enter these arms, for since thou thought'st it best
Not to dream all my dream, let's do the rest. 10

As lightning, or a taper's light,
  Thine eyes, and not thy noise, waked me;

7. Tortured bodies make bad corpses for dissection.
8. Joining, union; also, joint holding of an estate by husband and wife for life.
9. Trade with.

Yet I thought thee
(For thou lovest truth) an angel, at first sight,
But when I saw thou sawest my heart,   15
And knew'st my thoughts, beyond an angel's art,[1]
When thou knew'st what I dreamt, when thou knew'st when
Excess of joy would wake me, and cam'st then,
I must confess, it could not choose but be
Profane to think thee anything but thee.   20

Coming and staying showed thee, thee,
But rising makes me doubt,[2] that now
        Thou art not thou.
That love is weak, where fear's as strong as he;
'Tis not all spirit, pure, and brave,   25
If mixture it of *fear, shame, honor* have.
Perchance, as torches which must ready be,
Men light and put out, so thou deal'st with me,
Thou cam'st to kindle, goest to come; then I
Will dream that hope again, but else would die.[3]   30

A Valediction: Of Weeping

        Let me pour forth
My tears before thy face, whilst I stay here,
For thy face coins them, and thy stamp they bear,
And by this mintage they are something worth,
        For thus they be   5
        Pregnant of thee;
Fruits of much grief they are, emblems of more,
When a tear falls, that thou falls which it bore,[4]
So thou and I are nothing then, when on a diverse shore.

        On a round ball   10
A workman that hath copies by, can lay
An Europe, Afric, and an Asia,
And quickly make that, which was nothing, *All*;[5]
        So doth each tear
        Which thee doth wear,[6]   15
A globe, yea world, by that impression grow,
Till thy tears mixed with mine do overflow
This world, by waters sent from thee, my heaven dissolved so.

1. Church doctrine held that only God, not angels, could see into the heart and thoughts of man.
2. Fear.
3. With a possible play on the slang meaning of "die": to consummate the sexual act.
4. The imminent separation of the lovers causes the speaker's tears, in which the woman's face is reflected; hence when a tear falls, the woman's image (the "thou" which the tear bore) also falls.
5. By pasting his maps onto a blank globe ("round ball"), a mapmaker makes "that which was nothing" (the blank globe) into (a representation of) "All" the world.
6. *I.e.*, which bears your image.

        O more than Moon,
Draw not up seas to drown me in thy sphere,   20
Weep me not dead, in thine arms, but forbear
To teach the sea what it may do too soon;
        Let not the wind
        Example find
To do me more harm than it purposeth;   25
Since thou and I sigh one another's breath,
Whoe'er sighs most is cruellest, and hastes the other's death.[7]

Love's Alchemy

Some that have deeper digged love's mine than I,
Say, where his centric happiness doth lie:
        I have loved, and got, and told,
But should I love, get, tell, till I were old,
I should not find that hidden mystery;   5
        Oh, 'tis imposture all:
And as no chemic yet the elixir got[8]
        But glorifies his pregnant pot,[9]
        If by the way to him befall
Some odoriferous thing, or medicinal,   10
   So, lovers dream a rich and long delight,
   But get a winter-seeming summer's night.

Our ease, our thrift, our honor, and our day,
Shall we for this vain bubble's shadow pay?
        Ends love in this, that my man[1]   15
Can be as happy as I can, if he can
Endure the short scorn of a bridegroom's play?
        That loving wretch that swears
'Tis not the bodies marry, but the minds,
        Which he in her angelic finds,   20
        Would swear as justly, that he hears,
In that day's rude hoarse minstrelsy, the spheres.[2]
        Hope not for mind in women; at their best
        Sweetness and wit, they're but *Mummy*, possessed.[3]

The Flea

Mark but this flea, and mark in this
How little that which thou deny'st me is;

---

7. Sighing was thought to shorten life.
8. As no alchemist has yet obtained the panacean elixir of life.
9. Fruitful crucible.
1. Servant.
2. In the wedding day's raucuous music, the heavenly music of the celestial spheres.

3. The punctuation of lines 23–24 is uncertain. Among possible meanings: even the sweetest and wittiest women are merely dead flesh possessed or animated by an evil demon; or are, when a man possesses them, merely bodies without minds. *Mummy* was also a reputed panacea made from mummies.

It sucked me first, and now sucks thee,
And in this flea our two bloods mingled be;
Thou know'st that this cannot be said   5
A sin, nor shame, nor loss of maidenhead,
    Yet this enjoys before it woo,
    And pampered swells with one blood made of two,[4]
    And this, alas, is more than we would do.

Oh stay, three lives in one flea spare,   10
Where we almost, yea more than married are.
This flea is you and I, and this
Our marriage bed, and marriage temple is;
Though parents grudge, and you, we're met
And cloistered in these living walls of jet.   15
    Though use[5] make you apt to kill me,
    Let not to that, self-murder added be,
    And sacrilege, three sins in killing three.

Cruel and sudden, hast thou since
Purpled thy nail in blood of innocence?   20
Wherein could this flea guilty be,
Except in that drop which it sucked from thee?
Yet thou triumph'st, and say'st that thou
Find'st not thyself, nor me, the weaker now;
    'Tis true; then learn how false, fears be;   25
    Just so much honor, when thou yield'st to me,
    Will waste, as this flea's death took life from thee.

The Curse

Whoever guesses, thinks, or dreams he knows
Who is my mistress, wither by this curse:
    His only, and only his purse
    May some dull heart to love dispose,[6]
And she yield then to all that are his foes;   5
    May he be scorned by one, whom all else scorn,
    Forswear[7] to others, what to her he hath sworn,
    With fear of missing, shame of getting, torn:

Madness his sorrow, gout his cramp, may he
Make by but thinking who hath made him such: 10
    And may he feel no touch
    Of conscience, but of fame,[8] and be
Anguished, not that 'twas sin, but that 'twas she:

4. Medical theory of Donne's time held that in sexual intercourse blood was literally mingled, leading to procreation. The flea symbolizes this mingling.
5. Habit.

6. May his only purse, and nothing but his purse, incline some dull woman to love him.
7. Strongly deny.
8. Public report, reputation.

In early and long scarceness may he rot,
For land which had been his, if he had not   15
Himself incestuously an heir begot:

May he dream treason, and believe that he
Meant to perform it, and confess, and die,
   And no record tell why:
   His sons, which none of his may be,   20
Inherit nothing but his infamy:
   Or may he so long parasites have fed,
   That he would fain be theirs, whom he hath bred,
   And at the last be circumcised for bread:

The venom of all stepdames, gamesters' gall,   25
What tyrants and their subjects interwish,
   What plants, mines, beasts, fowl, fish
   Can contribute, all ill which all
Prophets or poets spake; and all which shall
   Be annexed in schedules[9] unto this by me,   30
   Fall on that man; for if it be a she,
   Nature beforehand hath out-cursed me.

The Message

Send home my long-strayed eyes to me,
Which oh too long have dwelt on thee;
Yet since there they have learned such ill,
   Such forced fashions,
   And false passions,   5
     That they be
     Made by thee
Fit for no good sight, keep them still.

Send home my harmless heart again,
Which no unworthy thought could stain;   10
But if it be taught by thine
   To make jestings
   Of protestings,
     And cross[1] both
     Word and oath,   15
Keep it, for then 'tis none of mine.

Yet send me back my heart and eyes,
That I may know and see thy lies,
And may laugh and joy, when thou
   Art in anguish   20

9. Appended supplementary papers.
1. Cancel, break.

And dost languish
For some one
That will none,[2]
Or prove as false as thou art now.

A Nocturnal upon St. Lucy's Day,
Being the Shortest Day

'Tis the year's midnight, and it is the day's,
Lucy's, who scarce seven hours herself unmasks;[3]
    The sun is spent, and now his flasks[4]
    Send forth light squibs,[5] no constant rays;
        The world's whole sap is sunk;   5
The general balm the hydroptic earth hath drunk,[6]
Whither, as to the bed's-feet, life is shrunk,
Dead and interred; yet all these seem to laugh,
Compared with me, who am their epitaph.

Study me then, you who shall lovers be   10
At the next world, that is, at the next spring:
    For I am every dead thing,
    In whom love wrought new alchemy.
        For his art did express[7]
A quintessence even from nothingness,   15
From dull privations, and lean emptiness;
He ruined me, and I am re-begot
Of absence, darkness, death; things which are not.

All others, from all things, draw all that's good,
Life, soul, form, spirit, whence they being have; 20
    I, by love's limbeck,[8] am the grave
    Of all that's nothing. Oft a flood
        Have we two wept, and so
Drowned the whole world, us two; oft did we grow
To be two chaoses, when we did show   25
Care to aught else; and often absences
Withdrew our souls, and made us carcasses.

But I am by her death (which word wrongs her)
Of the first nothing the elixir[9] grown;
    Were I a man, that I were one   30

2. Will have none of you.
3. St. Lucy's feast day, December 13, thought to be the shortest day of the year in the old calendar.
4. Powder flasks; possibly the stars are intended here.
5. A kind of fireworks, terminated by a slight explosion.

6. The thirsty earth has consumed the general balm, *i.e.*, the healing ointment or the vital sap of all things.
7. Press out.
8. Still, retort.
9. The quintessence of the nothing out of which God created the world.

I needs must know; I should prefer,
    If I were any beast,
Some ends, some means; yea plants, yea stones detest,
And love; all, all some properties invest;
If I an ordinary nothing were,   35
As shadow, a light and body must be here.[1]

But I am none; nor will my Sun renew.
You lovers, for whose sake the lesser sun
    At this time to the Goat[2] is run
      To fetch new lust, and give it you,   40
        Enjoy your summer all;
Since she enjoys her long night's festival,
Let me prepare towards her, and let me call
This hour her Vigil, and her Eve, since this
Both the year's, and the day's deep midnight is.   45

Witchcraft by a Picture

I fix mine eye on thine, and there
    Pity my picture burning in thine eye;
My picture drowned in a transparent tear,
    When I look lower I espy;
      Hadst thou the wicked skill   5
By pictures made and marred, to kill,[3]
How many ways mightst thou perform thy will!

But now I have drunk thy sweet salt tears,
    And though thou pour more I'll depart;
My picture vanished, vanish fears   10
    That I can be endamaged by that art;
      Though thou retain of me
One picture more, yet that will be,
Being in thine own heart, from all malice free.

The Bait[4]

Come live with me, and be my love,
And we will some new pleasures prove
Of golden sands, and crystal brooks:
With silken lines, and silver hooks.

There will the river whispering run   5
Warmed by thy eyes, more than the sun.

1. If I were an ordinary nothing, such as
a shadow, a light and body must exist to
produce it.
2. The zodiacal sign called Capricorn.
Goats were reputed to be lustful.

3. One reputed practice of witchcraft
was the killing of a person by making
and then destroying a picture of him.
4. One of many replies to Marlowe's
"The Passionate Shepherd to his Love."

And there the enamored fish will stay,
Begging themselves they may betray.

When thou wilt swim in that live bath,
Each fish, which every channel hath,   10
Will amorously to thee swim,
Gladder to catch thee, than thou him.

If thou to be so seen be'st loath
By sun, or moon, thou dark'nest both,
And if myself have leave to see,   15
I need not their light, having thee.

Let others freeze with angling reeds,
And cut their legs with shells and weeds,
Or treacherously poor fish beset,
With strangling snare or windowy net: 20

Let coarse bold hands, from slimy nest
The bedded fish in banks out-wrest;
Or curious traitors, sleave-silk[5] flies,
Bewitch poor fishes' wand'ring eyes.

For thee, thou need'st no such deceit,   25
For thou thyself art thine own bait;
That fish that is not catched thereby,
Alas, is wiser far than I.

The Apparition

When by thy scorn, O murd'ress, I am dead,
   And that thou thinkst thee free
From all solicitation from me,
Then shall my ghost come to thy bed,
And thee, fained vestal,[6] in worse arms shall see;   5
Then thy sick taper will begin to wink,[7]
And he, whose thou art then, being tired before,
Will, if thou stir, or pinch to wake him, think
   Thou call'st for more,
And in false sleep will from thee shrink,   10
And then, poor aspen[8] wretch, neglected thou
Bathed in a cold quicksilver sweat wilt lie,
   A verier ghost than I;
What I will say, I will not tell thee now,
Lest that preserve thee; and since my love is spent,   15
I had rather thou shouldst painfully repent,
Than by my threat'nings rest still innocent.

---

5. Untwisted silk.
6. Willing, eager (with a pun on "feigned") virgin.

7. Flicker.
8. Figuratively, tremulous; timorous.

The Broken Heart

He is stark mad, who ever says
    That he hath been in love an hour,
Yet not that love so soon decays,
    But that it can ten in less space devour;
Who will believe me, if I swear   5
That I have had the plague a year?
    Who would not laugh at me, if I should say
    I saw a flask of powder burn a day?

Ah, what a trifle is a heart,
    If once into love's hands it come!   10
All other griefs allow a part
    To other griefs, and ask themselves but some;
They come to us, but us Love draws,
He swallows us, and never chaws:[9]
    By him, as by chained shot, whole ranks do die;   15
    He is the tyrant pike, our hearts the fry.[1]

If 'twere not so, what did become
    Of my heart, when I first saw thee?
I brought a heart into the room,
    But from the room I carried none with me;   20
If it had gone to thee, I know
Mine would have taught thine heart to show
    More pity unto me: but Love, alas,
    At one first blow did shiver it as glass.

Yet nothing can to nothing fall,   25
    Nor any place be empty quite,
Therefore I think my breast hath all
    Those pieces still, though they be not unite;
And now, as broken glasses[2] show
A hundred lesser faces, so   30
    My rags of heart can like, wish, and adore,
    But after one such love, can love no more.

A Valediction: Forbidding Mourning[3]

As virtuous men pass mildly away,
    And whisper to their souls to go,
Whilst some of their sad friends do say,
    "The breath goes now," and some say, "No,"

9. Chews.
1. Small fish (which the pike devours).
2. Mirrors.

3. Izaak Walton says that Donne wrote this poem for his wife before he left for France in 1611.

So let us melt, and make no noise,   5
   No tear-floods, nor sigh-tempests move;
'Twere profanation of our joys
   To tell the laity our love.

Moving of the earth[4] brings harms and fears,
   Men reckon what it did and meant;   10
But trepidation of the spheres,
   Though greater far, is innocent.[5]

Dull sublunary[6] lovers' love
   (Whose soul is sense) cannot admit
Absence, because it doth remove   15
   Those things which elemented[7] it.

But we, by a love so much refined
   That our selves know not what it is,
Inter-assured of the mind,
   Care less, eyes, lips, and hands to miss.   20

Our two souls therefore, which are one,
   Though I must go, endure not yet
A breach, but an expansion,
   Like gold to airy thinness beat.

If they be two, they are two so   25
   As stiff twin compasses are two:
Thy soul, the fixed foot, makes no show
   To move, but doth, if the other do;

And though it in the center sit,
   Yet when the other far doth roam,   30
It leans, and hearkens after it,
   And grows erect, as that comes home.

Such wilt thou be to me, who must,
   Like the other foot, obliquely run;
Thy firmness makes my circle just,   35
   And makes me end where I begun.

The Ecstasy

Where, like a pillow on a bed,
   A pregnant bank swelled up, to rest
The violet's reclining head,
   Sat we two, one another's best.

---

4. Earthquakes.
5. The oscillatory movement of the celestial spheres, though far greater than earthquakes, "is innocent," *i.e.*, causes no "harms and fears."
6. Under the moon, and thus earthly and changeable.
7. Composed.

Our hands were firmly cemented 5
    With a fast balm, which thence did spring;
Our eye-beams twisted, and did thread
    Our eyes, upon one double string;[8]

So to intergraft our hands, as yet
    Was all the means to make us one, 10
And pictures in our eyes to get[9]
    Was all our propagation.

As, 'twixt two equal armies, Fate
    Suspends uncertain victory,
Our souls (which to advance their state 15
    Were gone out) hung 'twixt her and me.

And whilst our souls negotiate there,
    We like sepulchral statues lay;
All day, the same our postures were,
    And we said nothing, all the day. 20

If any, so by love refined
    That he souls' language understood,
And by good love were grown all mind,
    Within convenient distance stood,

He (though he knew not which soul spake, 25
    Because both meant, both spake the same)
Might thence a new concoction[1] take,
    And part far purer than he came.

This Ecstasy doth unperplex,
    We said, and tell us what we love; 30
We see by this it was not sex;
    We see we saw not what did move:[2]

But as all several[3] souls contain
    Mixture of things, they know not what,
Love these mixed souls doth mix again, 35
    And makes both one, each this and that.

A single violet transplant,
    The strength, the color, and the size,
(All which before was poor, and scant)
    Redoubles still, and multiples. 40

8. According to Renaissance theory of perception, the eyes sent out invisible beams which then carried the object's image back to the spectator. Thus the lovers are united by their gazing into one another's eyes as well as by their holding hands.

9. Beget.

1. Purified, perfected state.

2. We now see that we did not before understand what was the cause and source of our love.

3. Separate.

When love, with one another so
 Interinanimates two souls,
That abler soul, which thence doth flow,
 Defects of loneliness controls.

We then, who are this new soul, know   45
 Of what we are composed, and made,
For the atomies[4] of which we grow
 Are souls, whom no change can invade.

But oh, alas, so long, so far
 Our bodies why do we forbear   50
They're ours, though they're not we, we are
 The intelligences, they the sphere.[5]

We owe them thanks because they thus
 Did us to us at first convey,
Yielded their forces, sense, to us,   55
 Nor are dross to us, but allay.[6]

On man heaven's influence works not so,
 But that it first imprints the air;[7]
So soul into the soul may flow,
 Though it to body first repair.   60

As our blood labors to beget
 Spirits[8] as like souls as it can,
Because such fingers need to knit
 That subtle knot which makes us man:

So must pure lovers' souls descend   65
 To affections, and to faculties,
Which sense may reach and apprehend,
 Else a great Prince in prison lies.

To our bodies turn we then, that so
 Weak men on love revealed may look;   70
Love's mysteries in souls do grow,
 But yet the body is his book.

And if some lover, such as we,
 Have heard this dialogue of one,
Let him still mark us, he shall see   75
 Small change, when we're to bodies gone.

4. Atoms.
5. The celestial spheres were thought to be governed by angels or intelligences. So the body is governed by the soul or essential self.
6. Alloy; "dross" is the weakening impurity which is discarded in the process of refining a metal.
7. Astrology held that the stars influenced man through their effect on the air.
8. Vapors produced by the blood and forming a link between body and soul.

Love's Deity

I long to talk with some old lover's ghost,
   Who died before the god of love was born:
I cannot think that he who then loved most
   Sunk so low as to love one which did scorn.
But since this god produced a destiny,   5
And that vice-nature,[9] custom, lets it be,
   I must love her that loves not me.

Sure, they which made him god meant not so much,
   Nor he, in his young godhead, practised it.
But when an even flame two hearts did touch,   10
   His office was indulgently to fit
Actives to passives.[1] Correspondency
Only his subject was; it cannot be
   Love, till I love her that loves me.

But every modern god will[2] now extend   15
   His vast prerogative, as far as Jove.
To rage, to lust, to write to, to commend,
   All is the purlieu of the god of love.
Oh were we wakened by this tyranny
To ungod this child again, it could not be   20
   I should love her who loves not me.

Rebel and atheist too, why murmur I,
   As though I felt the worst that love could do?
Love might make me leave loving, or might try
   A deeper plague, to make her love me too,   25
Which, since she loves before,[3] I'm loth to see;
Falsehood is worse than hate; and that must be,
   If she whom I love should love me.

Love's Diet

To what a cumbersome unwieldiness
And burdenous corpulence my love had grown,
    But that I did, to make it less,
    And keep it in proportion,
Give it a diet, made it feed upon   5
That which love worst endures, *discretion*.

Above one sigh a day I allowed him not,
Of which my fortune and my faults had part;[4]

---

9. Substitute for nature.
1. To join male lovers to corresponding
female lovers.
2. Wants to.

3. Already loves someone else.
4. And a part of that sigh was owing to
my own bad fortune and faults.

And if sometimes by stealth he got
A she-sigh from my mistress' heart,   10
And thought to feast on that, I let him see
'Twas neither very sound, nor meant to me.[5]

If he wrung from me a tear, I brined[6] it so
With scorn or shame, that him it nourished not;
If he sucked hers, I let him know   15
'Twas not a tear which he had got,
His drink was counterfeit, as was his meat;[7]
For eyes which roll towards all, weep not, but sweat.

Whatever he would dictate, I writ that,
But burnt my letters; when she writ to me,   20
And that that favor made him fat,[8]
I said, if any title be
Conveyed by this, ah, what doth it avail
To be the fortieth name in an entail?[9]

Thus I reclaimed my buzzard[1] love, to fly   25
At what, and when, and how, and where I choose;
Now negligent of sport I lie,
And now, as other falconers use,[2]
I spring[3] a mistress, swear, write, sigh and weep:
And the game killed, or lost, go talk, and sleep.   30

The Will

Before I sigh my last gasp, let me breathe,
Great Love, some legacies: Here I bequeath
Mine eyes to Argus,[4] if mine eyes can see;
If they be blind, then, Love, I give them thee;
My tongue to Fame;[5] to ambassadors mine ears;   5
To women or the sea, my tears.
Thou, Love, hast taught me heretofore
By making me serve her who had twenty more,
That I should give to none but such as had too much before.

My constancy I to the planets give;   10
My truth to them who at the Court do live;
Mine ingenuity[6] and openness,

---

5. Neither genuine nor meant for me.
6. Salted.
7. *I.e.*, his sighs.
8. When she wrote to me, and wrote (understood repetition of the preceding verb) that that favor (of writing) made love grow. (See J. V. Hagopian, *Explicator*, XVII, 5.)
9. The fortieth person named in an order of succession for inheriting an estate.

1. A useless species of hawk and a worthless, stupid person. "Reclaim" means "to reduce to obedience, tame."
2. Habitually do.
3. Start, flush (an animal).
4. The mythological figure who had a hundred eyes.
5. Also meaning rumor and evil repute.
6. Frankness; and perhaps also nobility of character.

To Jesuits; to buffoons my pensiveness;
My silence to any who abroad hath been;
    My money to a Capuchin.[7]   15
Thou, Love, taught'st me, by appointing me
To love there where no love received can be,
Only to give to such as have an incapacity.

My faith I give to Roman Catholics;
All my good works unto the Schismatics   20
Of Amsterdam;[8] my best civility
And courtship to an University;
My modesty I give to soldiers bare;
    My patience let gamesters share.
Thou, Love, taught'st me, by making me   25
Love her that holds my love disparity,[9]
Only to give to those that count my gifts indignity.

I give my reputation to those
Which were my friends; mine industry to foes;
To Schoolmen[1] I bequeath my doubtfulness;   30
My sickness to physicians, or excess;[2]
To Nature, all that I in rhyme have writ;
    And to my company my wit.
Thou, Love, by making me adore
Her who begot this love in me before,   35
Taught'st me to make as though I gave, when I do but restore.

To him for whom the passing bell next tolls,
I give my physic[3] books; my written rolls
Of moral counsels, I to Bedlam[4] give;
My brazen medals, unto them which live   40
In want of bread; to them which pass among
    All foreigners, mine English tongue.
Thou, Love, by making me love one
Who thinks her friendship a fit portion
For younger lovers, dost my gifts thus disproportion.   45

Therefore I'll give no more; but I'll undo
The world by dying, because love dies too.
Then all your beauties will be no more worth
Than gold in mines where none doth draw it forth,
And all your graces no more use shall have   50
    Than a sun-dial in a grave.
Thou, Love, taught'st me, by making me
Love her who doth neglect both me and thee,
To invent, and practise, this one way to annihilate all three.

---

7. A Franciscan monk, vowed to poverty.
8. Extreme Puritans, who believed in salvation through faith only, not good works.
9. Of unequal or inferior quality.

1. Medieval philosophers of the universities.
2. Intemperance, a cause of sickness.
3. Medical.
4. The London insane asylum.

The Funeral

Whoever comes to shroud me, do not harm
    Nor question much
That subtle wreath of hair, which crowns my arm;
The mystery, the sign, you must not touch,
    For 'tis my outward Soul,   5
Viceroy to that, which then to heaven being gone,
    Will leave this to control,
And keep these limbs, her provinces, from dissolution.

For if the sinewy thread[5] my brain lets fall
    Through every part   10
Can tie those parts, and make me one of all,
These hairs, which upward grew, and strength and art
    Have from a better brain,
Can better do it; except she meant that I
    By this should know my pain,   15
As prisoners then are manacled, when they're condemned to die.

Whate'er she meant by it, bury it with me,
    For since I am
Love's martyr, it might breed idolatry,
If into others' hands these relics came;   20
    As 'twas humility
To afford to it all that a soul can do,
    So, 'tis some bravery,[6]
That since you would save none of me, I bury some of you.

The Blossom

    Little think'st thou, poor flower,
      Whom I have watched six or seven days,
And seen thy birth, and seen what every hour
Gave to thy growth, thee to this height to raise,
And now dost laugh and triumph on this bough,   5
      Little think'st thou
That it will freeze anon, and that I shall
Tomorrow find thee fal'n, or not at all.

    Little think'st thou, poor heart,
      That labor'st yet to nestle thee,   10
And think'st by hovering here to get a part
In a forbidden or forbidding tree,
And hop'st her stiffness by long siege to bow,
      Little think'st thou

5. The spinal cord and nervous system.
6. Bravado.

That thou tomorrow, ere that Sun[7] doth wake,   15
Must with this sun and me a journey take.

    But thou which lov'st to be
      Subtle to plague thyself, wilt say,
"Alas, if you must go, what's that to me?
Here lies my business, and here I will stay: 20
You go to friends, whose love and means present
      Various content
To your eyes, ears, and tongue, and every part.
If then your body go, what need you a heart?"

    Well then, stay here; but know,   25
      When thou hast stayed and done thy most,
A naked thinking heart, that makes no show,
Is to a woman but a kind of ghost;
How shall she know my heart; or, having none,
      Know thee for one?   30
Practice may make her know some other part,
But take my word, she doth not know a heart.

    Meet me at London, then,
      Twenty days hence, and thou shalt see
Me fresher, and more fat, by being with men,   35
Than if I had stayed still with her and thee.
For God's sake, if you can, be you so too:
      I would give you
There, to another friend, whom we shall find
As glad to have my body, as my mind.   40

The Primrose

    Upon this primrose hill
      Where, if Heav'n would distil
A shower of rain, each several[8] drop might go
To his own primrose, and grow manna so;
And where their form, and their infinity   5
      Make a terrestrial galaxy,
      As the small stars do in the sky,
I walk to find a true love;[9] and I see
That 'tis not a mere woman that is she,
But must or more or less than woman be.   10

    Yet know I not, which flower
      I wish; a six, or four;[1]

---

7. The lady.
8. Separate.

9. Also, "true love" is another name for the primrose.
1. *I.e.*, six- or four-petaled.

For should my true-love less than woman be,
She were scarce anything; and then, should she
Be more than woman, she would get above   15
     All thought of sex, and think to move
     My heart to study her, and not to love;
Both these were monsters; since there must reside
Falsehood in woman, I could more abide
She were by art, than Nature, falsified.   20

     Live, Primrose, then, and thrive
     With thy true number, five;
And women, whom this flower doth represent,
With this mysterious number be content;
Ten is the farthest number;[2] if half ten   25
     Belong unto each woman, then
     Each woman may take half us men;
Or, if this will not serve their turn, since all
Numbers are odd, or even, and they fall
First into this five, women may take us all.   30

The Relic

     When my grave is broke up again
     Some second guest to entertain[3]
     (For graves have learned that woman-head,[4]
     To be to more than one a bed)
     And he that digs it spies   5
A bracelet of bright hair about the bone,
     Will he not let us alone,
And think that there a loving couple lies,
Who thought that this device might be some way
To make their souls, at the last busy day,[5]   10
Meet at this grave, and make a little stay?

     If this fall in a time, or land,
     Where mis-devotion doth command,
     Then he that digs us up will bring
     Us to the Bishop and the King   15
     To make us relics; then
Thou shalt be a Mary Magdalen, and I
     A something else thereby;
All women shall adore us, and some men;
And, since at such time miracles are sought,   20
I would have that age by this paper taught
What miracles we harmless lovers wrought.

2. Highest number; it contains the elements of all other numbers and is thus symbolic of all life.
3. Alludes to the reuse of burial ground.
4. Characteristic of women.

5. Judgment Day, when the risen body must go first to wherever it lost or left a part of itself in order to retrieve it and be whole.

First, we loved well and faithfully,
Yet knew not what we loved, nor why;
Difference of sex no more we knew, 25
Than our guardian angels do;
    Coming and going, we
Perchance might kiss,[6] but not between those meals;
Our hands ne'er touched the seals
Which nature, injured by late law,[7] sets free. 30
These miracles we did; but now, alas,
All measure, and all language, I should pass,
Should I tell what a miracle she was.

The Damp

When I am dead, and doctors know not why,
    And my friends' curiosity
Will have me cut up to survey each part,
When they shall find your picture in my heart,
    You think a sudden damp[8] of love 5
    Will through all their senses move,
And work on them as me, and so prefer[9]
Your murder to the name of massacre.

Poor victories! but if you dare be brave,
    And pleasure in your conquest have, 10
First kill the enormous giant, your *Disdain*,
And let the enchantress *Honor* next be slain,
    And like a Goth and Vandal rise,
    Deface records, and histories,
Of your own arts and triumphs over men, 15
And without such advantage kill me then.

For I could muster up as well as you
    My giants, and my witches too,
Which are vast *Constancy*, and *Secretness*,
But these I neither look for, nor profess; 20
    Kill me as woman, let me die
    As a mere man; do you but try
Your passive valor, and you shall find than,[1]
Naked you've odds enough of any man.

The Dissolution

She's dead; and all which die
    To their first elements resolve;

---

6. The customary kiss of salutation and parting.
7. By the law which came later than nature.

8. Vapor, mist.
9. Promote.
1. Then.

And we were mutual elements to us,
And made of one another.
My body then doth hers involve, 5
And those things whereof I consist, hereby
In me abundant grow, and burdenous,
And nourish not, but smother.
My fire of passion, sighs of air,
Water of tears, and earthly[2] sad despair, 10
Which my materials be
(But near worn out by love's security),
She, to my loss, doth by her death repair;[3]
And I might live long wretched so,
But that my fire doth with my fuel grow. 15
Now, as those active kings
Whose foreign conquest treasure brings,
Receive more, and spend more, and soonest break:
This (which I am amazed that I can speak)
This death, hath with my store 20
My use increased.
And so my soul, more earnestly[4] released,
Will outstrip hers; as bullets flown before
A latter bullet may o'ertake, the powder being more.

A Jet Ring Sent

Thou art not so black as my heart,
Nor half so brittle as her heart, thou art;
What wouldst thou say? Shall both our properties by thee be spoke,
Nothing more endless, nothing sooner broke?

Marriage rings are not of this stuff; 5
Oh, why should aught less precious or less tough
Figure our loves? Except in thy name thou have bid it say,
"I'm cheap, and naught but fashion, fling me away."[5]

Yet stay with me since thou art come,
Circle this finger's top, which didst her thumb. 10
Be justly proud, and gladly safe, that thou dost dwell with me,
She that, oh, broke her faith, would soon break thee.

Negative Love[6]

I never stooped so low, as they
Which on an eye, cheek, lip, can prey;
Seldom to them,[7] which soar no higher

2. Earthy.
3. Restore.
4. Eagerly.
5. Donne puns on "jet" and the French

"jette" (throw away).
6. Some MSS. give "The Nothing" as title; some give both titles.
7. *I.e.*, seldom stooped to them.

Than virtue or the mind to admire,
For sense and understanding may   5
   Know what gives fuel to their fire.
My love, though silly,[8] is more brave,
For may I miss, whene'er I crave,
If I know yet, what I would have.

If that be simply perfectest   10
Which can by no way be expressed
   But *Negatives*,[9] my love is so.
   To All, which all love,[1]I say no.
If any who deciphers best
   What we know not, our selves, can know,   15
Let him teach me that nothing; this
As yet my ease and comfort is:
Though I speed not, I cannot miss.[2]

The Prohibition

   Take heed of loving me;
At least remember, I forbade it thee;
Not that I shall repair[3] my unthrifty waste
Of breath and blood, upon[4] thy sighs and tears,
By being to thee then what to me thou wast;   5
But so great joy our life at once outwears.
Then, lest thy love, by my death, frustrate be,
If thou love me, take heed of loving me.

   Take heed of hating me,
Or too much triumph in the victory;   10
Not that I shall be mine own officer,[5]
And hate with hate again retaliate;
But thou wilt lose the style[6] of conqueror,
If I, thy conquest, perish by thy hate.
Then, lest my being nothing lessen thee,   15
If thou hate me, take heed of hating me.

   Yet, love and hate me too,
So, these extremes shall neither's office do;
Love me, that I may die the gentler way;
Hate me, because thy love's too great for me;   20
Or let these two, themselves, not me, decay;
So shall I live thy stage,[7] not triumph be.
Then, lest thy love, hate, and me thou undo,
Oh let me live, yet love and hate me too.

8. Plain, unsophisticated.
9. Alluding to the idea of the *via negativa* that the perfect Godhead cannot be named, can only be expressed by negative terms, and is therefore an essential Nothing; see line 16.
1. To all positive things, which everybody else loves.
2. *I.e.*, though I succeed not, I cannot fail.
3. Recover.
4. By drawing upon.
5. Agent.
6. Name.
7. For your repeated conquests (rather than a single, unrepeatable triumph).

The Expiration[8]

So, so, break off this last lamenting kiss,
　　Which sucks two souls, and vapors both away;[9]
Turn thou, ghost, that way, and let me turn this,
　　And let ourselves benight our happiest day;
We asked none leave to love; nor will we owe　　　　5
　　Any so cheap a death as saying, "Go";

"Go"; and if that word have not quite killed thee,
　　Ease me with death by bidding me go too.
Or, if it have, let my word work on me,
　　And a just office on a murderer do,　　　　10
Except[1] it be too late to kill me so,
　　Being double dead, going, and bidding go.

The Computation

For the first twenty years, since yesterday,
　　I scarce believed thou couldst be gone away;
For forty more, I fed on favors past,
　　And forty on hopes, that thou wouldst they might last.
Tears drowned one hundred, and sighs blew out two;　　5
A thousand, I did neither think, nor do,
　　Or not divide, all being one thought of you;
　　Or, in a thousand more, forgot that too.
Yet call not this long life; but think that I
Am, by being dead, immortal; can ghosts die?　　　　10

The Paradox

No lover saith, "I love," nor any other
　　Can judge a perfect lover;
He thinks that else none can, nor will agree
　　That any loves but he:
I cannot say I loved, for who can say　　　　5
　　He was killed yesterday?[2]
Love with excess of heat, more young, than old,
　　Death kills with too much cold;
We die but once, and who loved last did die,
　　He that saith twice, doth lie:　　　　10
For though he seem to move, and stir a while,
　　It doth the sense beguile.

8. Entitled "Valediction" in some manuscripts.
9. Causes both to pass away in the form of a vapor.

1. Unless.
2. Here and subsequently, Donne may be playing upon the sexual meaning of "die" and "kill."

Such life is like the light which bideth yet
　　When the light's life[3] is set,
Or like the heat, which fire in solid matter　　　15
　　Leaves behind, two hours after.
Once I loved and died; and am now become
　　Mine epitaph and tomb.
Here dead men speak their last, and so do I:
　　Love-slain, lo, here I lie.[4]　　　　　　　20

Farewell to Love

　　Whilst yet to prove,[5]
I thought there was some deity in love,
　　So did I reverence, and gave
Worship; as atheists at their dying hour
Call, what they cannot name, an unknown power,　　5
　　As ignorantly did I crave:
　　　　Thus when
Things not yet known are coveted by men,
　　Our desires give them fashion,[6] and so
As they wax lesser, fall, as they size,[7] grow.　　10

　　But, from late fair
His Highness sitting in a golden chair[8]
　　Is not less cared for after three days
By children, than the thing which lovers so
Blindly admire, and with such worship woo;　　15
　　Being had, enjoying it decays:
　　　　And thence,
What before pleased them all, takes but one sense,[9]
　　And that so lamely, as it leaves behind
A kind of sorrowing dullness to the mind.　　20

　　Ah, cannot we,
As well as cocks and lions, jocund be
　　After such pleasures? Unless wise
Nature decreed (since each such act, they say,
Diminisheth the length of life a day)　　　　25
　　This; as she would man should despise
　　　　The sport,
Because that other curse of being short,
　　And only for a minute made to be
Eagers desires to raise posterity.[1]　　　　30

3. Sun.
4. *I.e.*, lie prone, dead, and tell a lie.
5. While still inexperienced.
6. Form.
7. Subside, as they increase.
8. *I.e.*, a toy bought at a recent fair.
9. What before pleased all the senses, now pleases only one sense.
1. Various emendations and interpreta-
tions have been suggested for these most difficult lines. Sir Herbert Grierson originally emended "Eager, desires" to "Eagers desire". K. T. Emerson suggests: the brevity of the sex act sharpens man's desire to repeat the act—"to raise posterity" being a cynical euphemism for "to engage in sexual intercourse." *Modern Language Notes*, 72 (1957), 94.

Since so, my mind
Shall not desire what no man else can find;
I'll no more dote and run
To pursue things which had endamaged me.
And when I come where moving beauties be, 35
As men do when the summer's sun
Grows great,
Though I admire their greatness, shun their heat;
Each place can afford shadows. If all fail,
'Tis but applying wormseed[2] to the tail. 40

1635

A Lecture upon the Shadow

Stand still, and I will read to thee
A lecture, love, in love's philosophy.
These three hours that we have spent
In walking here, two shadows went
Along with us, which we ourselves produced; 5
But, now the sun is just above our head,
We do those shadows tread;
And to brave[3] clearness all things are reduced.
So whilst our infant loves did grow,
Disguises did, and shadows, flow 10
From us, and our cares; but now 'tis not so.

That love hath not attained the high'st degree,
Which is still diligent lest others see.

Except our loves at this noon stay,
We shall new shadows make the other way. 15
As the first were made to blind
Others, these which come behind[4]
Will work upon ourselves, and blind our eyes.
If our loves faint, and westwardly decline,
To me thou, falsely, thine, 20
And I to thee mine actions shall disguise.
The morning shadows wear away,
But these grow longer all the day,
But oh, love's day is short, if love decay.

Love is a growing, or full constant light; 25
And his first minute, after noon, is night.

1635

2. A plant used medically against intestinal worms. M. Morillo argues that in an ironic reversal Donne plays upon the bawdy connotations of the last line and that lines 39–40 mean: "if, in spite of my resolution to avoid sex, I succumb, then I shall console myself with the rationalization that the act is committed with purely curative intent." *Tulane Studies in English*, 13 (1963), 39–40. On the other hand, wormseed was also a reputed anaphrodisiac, and "tail" is Latin for "penis."
3. Splendid.
4. Probably meaning "later."

Sonnet. The Token[5]

Send me some token, that my hope may live,
    Or that my easeless thoughts may sleep and rest;
Send me some honey to make sweet my hive,
    That in my passions I may hope the best.
I beg no riband wrought with thine own hands,   5
    To knit our loves in the fantastic strain
Of new-touched youth; nor ring to shew the stands[6]
    Of our affection, that, as that's round and plain,
So should our loves meet in simplicity;
    No, nor the corals which thy wrist enfold,   10
Laced up together in congruity,
    To shew our thoughts should rest in the same hold;
No, nor thy picture, though most gracious,
    And most desired, because best like the best;
Nor witty lines, which are most copious   15
    Within the writings which thou hast addressed.[7]

Send me nor this nor that to increase my store,
But swear thou think'st I love thee, and no more.

1650

Self-Love[8]

He that cannot choose but love,
And strives against it still,
Never shall my fancy move,
For he loves 'gainst his will;
Nor he which is all his own,   5
And can at pleasure choose,—
When I am caught he can be gone,
And, when he list, refuse;
Nor he that loves none but fair,
For such by all are sought;   10
Nor he that can for foul ones care,
For his judgment then is nought;
Nor he that hath wit, for he
Will make me his jest or slave;
Nor a fool, for when others . . . ,   15

5. By reason of its additional four lines and its rhyme scheme, this poem is not actually a sonnet in the strict sense of the term. The poem is not characteristic of Donne, and for various reasons may only dubiously be ascribed to him.
6. Status.
7. Written.
8. This poem, which also may only dubiously be ascribed to Donne, has no title in the early editions and manuscripts. The title "Self-Love" was first given by Sir Edmund Chambers in his edition of 1896 and has since been followed by most subsequent editors, including Grierson. Theodore Redpath's suggestion, "The Rejection," is also an apt title, for the female speaker of the poem rejects various kinds of lovers.

He can neither . . . . ;[9]
Nor he that still his mistress pays,
For she is thralled therefore;
Nor he that pays not, for he says
Within,[1] she's worth no more.
Is there then no kind of men
Whom I may freely prove?[2]
I will vent that humor then
In mine own self-love.

20

1650

9. Lines 15–16 are incomplete in the early editions. One MS. completes line 16 with "want nor crave"; see R. E. Bennett, *The Complete Poems of John Donne*, pp. 51, 297.
1. To himself.
2. Approve; try.

Elegies

Elegy III. Change

Although thy hand and faith, and good works too,
Have sealed thy love, which nothing should undo,
Yea though thou fall back, that apostasy
Confirm thy love; yet much, much I fear thee.
Women are like the Arts, forced unto[1] none,   5
Open to all searchers, unprized, if unknown.
If I have caught a bird, and let him fly,
Another fowler using these[2] means, as I,
May catch the same bird; and, as these things be,
Women are made for men, not him, nor me.   10
Foxes and goats, all beasts, change when they please,
Shall women, more hot, wily, wild than these,
Be bound to one man, and did Nature then
Idly make them apter to endure than men?
They're our clogs,[3] not their own; if a man be   15
Chained to a galley, yet the galley's free;
Who hath a plow-land, casts all his seed corn there,
And yet allows his ground more corn should bear;
Though Danuby into the sea must flow,
The sea receives the Rhine, Volga, and Po.   20
By nature, which gave it, this liberty
Thou lov'st, but oh! canst thou love it and me?
Likeness glues love: and if that thou so do,
To make us like[4] and love, must I change too?
More than thy hate, I hate it; rather let me   25
Allow her change, than change as oft as she,
And so not teach, but force my opinion
To love not any one, nor every one.
To live in one land is captivity,
To run all countries, a wild roguery;[5]   30
Waters stink soon if in one place they bide,
And in the vast sea are more putrefied:[6]
But when they kiss one bank, and leaving this
Never look back, but the next bank do kiss,
Then are they purest; Change is the nursery   35
Of music, joy, life and eternity.

---

1. Compulsory for.
2. The same.
3. Impediments, encumbrances.
4. Alike.
5. Vagrancy.
6. Made salty.

Elegy IV. The Perfume

Once, and but once found in thy company,
All thy supposed escapes[7] are laid on me;
And as a thief at bar is questioned there
By all the men that have been robbed that year,
So am I (by this traitorous means surprised)   5
By thy hydroptic[8] father catechized.
Though he had wont to search with glazed[9] eyes,
As though he came to kill a cockatrice,[1]
Though he hath oft sworn that he would remove
Thy beauty's beauty, and food of our love,   10
Hope of his goods, if I with thee were seen,
Yet close and secret, as our souls, we have been.
Though thy immortal mother, which doth lie
Still buried in her bed, yet will not die,
Takes this advantage to sleep out day-light,   15
And watch thy entries and returns all night,
And, when she takes thy hand and would seem kind,
Doth search what rings and armlets she can find,
And kissing notes the color of thy face,
And fearing lest thou art swol'n doth thee embrace;   20
And to try if thou long, doth name strange meats,
And notes thy paleness, blushing, sighs, and sweats,
And politicly[2] will to thee confess
The sins of her own youth's rank lustiness,
Yet love these sorceries did remove, and move   25
Thee to gull thine own mother for my love.
Thy little brethren, which like faery sprites
Oft skipped into our chamber those sweet nights,
And kissed and ingled[3] on thy father's knee,
Were bribed next day to tell what they did see;   30
The grim eight-foot-high iron-bound serving-man,
That oft names God in oaths, and only than,[4]
He that to bar the first gate doth as wide
As the great Rhodian Colossus[5] stride,
Which, if in hell no other pains there were,   35
Makes me fear hell, because he must be there,
Though by thy father he were hired to this,
Could never witness any touch or kiss.
But oh, too common ill, I brought with me
That which betrayed me to my enemy: 40

---

7. Transgressions, esp. sexual ones.
8. Dropsical; also, insatiably thirsty for information and, as the next line suggests, strong drink.
9. Covered with a film (probably from drinking too much).

1. A fabulous serpent which killed by looking.
2. Craftily.
3. Fondled.
4. Then.
5. The huge statue of Apollo at Rhodes, one of the Seven Wonders.

A loud perfume, which at my entrance cried
Even at thy father's nose; so were we spied.
When, like a tyrant king, that in his bed
Smelt gunpowder, the pale wretch shivered;
Had it been some bad smell, he would have thought   45
That his own feet, or breath, that smell had wrought.
But as we in our Isle[6] imprisoned,
Where cattle only and diverse dogs are bred,
The precious unicorns, strange monsters call,
So thought he good strange, that had none at all.   50
I taught my silks their whistling to forbear,
Even my oppressed shoes dumb and speechless were,
Only, thou bitter-sweet,[7] whom I had laid
Next me, me traitorously hast betrayed,
And unsuspected hast invisibly   55
At once fled unto him and stayed with me.
Base excrement[8] of earth, which dost confound
Sense from distinguishing the sick from sound;
By thee the silly amorous[9] sucks his death
By drawing in a leprous harlot's breath;   60
By thee the greatest stain to man's estate
Falls on us, to be called effeminate;
Though you be much loved in the prince's hall
There, things that seem exceed substantial.[1]
Gods, when ye fumed on altars, were pleased well   65
Because you were burnt, not that they liked your smell;
You're loathsome all, being taken simply alone.
Shall we love ill things joined, and hate each one?
If you were good, your good doth soon decay;
And you are rare, that takes the good away.   70
All my perfumes I give most willingly
To embalm thy father's corpse. What? will he die?

Elegy IX. The Autumnal

No spring, nor summer beauty hath such grace,
    As I have seen in one autumnal face.
Young beauties force our love, and that's a rape,
    This doth but counsel, yet you cannot 'scape.
If 'twere a shame to love, here 'twere no shame,   5
    Affection here takes reverence's name.
Were her first years the Golden Age?[2] That's true,
    But now she's gold oft tried, and ever new.

6. Britain.
7. Lines 53–70 address the perfume; the rest of the poem is addressed, of course, to the speaker's mistress.
8. Growth.

9. Simple lover.
1. Appearances exceed reality, substantial things.
2. The first age of mankind, an age of peace, prosperity, and contentment.

That was her torrid and inflaming time,
    This is her tolerable tropic clime.   10
Fair eyes, who asks more heat than comes from hence,
    He in a fever wishes pestilence.
Call not these wrinkles, graves;[3] if graves they were,
    They were Love's graves; for else he is no where.
Yet lies not Love dead here, but here doth sit   15
    Vowed to this trench, like an anachorite.[4]
And here, till hers, which must be his death, come,
    He doth not dig a grave, but build a tomb.
Here dwells he, though he sojourn ev'rywhere,
    In progress,[5] yet his standing house is here.   20
Here, where still evening is; not noon, nor night;
    Where no voluptuousness, yet all delight.
In all her words, unto all hearers fit,
    You may at revels, you at council, sit.
This is love's timber, youth his underwood;[6]   25
    There he, as wine in June, enrages blood,
Which then comes seasonabliest, when our taste
    And appetite to other things is past. .
Xerxes' strange Lydian love, the platane tree,[7]
    Was loved for age, none being so large as she,   30
Or else because, being young, nature did bless
    Her youth with age's glory, barrenness.
If we love things long sought, age is a thing
    Which we are fifty years in compassing;
If transitory things, which soon decay,   35
    Age must be loveliest at the latest day.
But name not winter-faces, whose skin's slack,
    Lank, as an unthrift's purse, but a soul's sack;
Whose eyes seek light within, for all here's shade;
    Whose mouths are holes, rather worn out, than made;   40
Whose every tooth to a several place is gone,
    To vex their souls at Resurrection;[8]
Name not these living death's-heads unto me,
    For these not ancient, but antique be.
I hate extremes; yet I had rather stay   45
    With tombs than cradles, to wear out a day.
Since such love's natural lation[9] is, may still
    My love descend and journey down the hill,
Not panting after growing beauties, so,
    I shall ebb on with them who homeward go.   50

---

3. French word for wrinkles.
4. Hermit.
5. A visiting tour by royalty; "standing house": fixed residence.
6. Undergrowth.
7. On his march to Greece, Xerxes honored a plane tree in Lydia, decking it with gold and appointing a guard.
8. At the Resurrection, when the body is to rejoin the soul, all of the parts of the body, even though they may be in different places, must be recovered.
9. Motion.

Elegy X. The Dream[1]

Image[2] of her (whom I love, more than she,[3]
    Whose fair impression in my faithful heart
Makes me her medal, and makes her love me
    As Kings do coins to which their stamps impart
The value) go, and take my heart from hence,   5
    Which now is grown too great and good for me.
Honors oppress weak spirits, and our sense
    Strong objects dull; the more, the less we see.

When you are gone, and reason gone with you,
    Then fantasy[4] is queen, and soul, and all;   10
She can present joys meaner than you do,
    Convenient, and more proportional.
So, if I dream I have you, I have you,
    For all our joys are but fantastical.[5]
And so I 'scape the pain, for pain is true;   15
    And sleep, which locks up sense, doth lock out all.

After a such fruition I shall wake,
    And, but the waking, nothing shall repent;
And shall to love more thankful sonnets make
    Than if more honor, tears, and pains were spent.   20
But dearest heart, and dearer image, stay;
    Alas, true joys at best are dream enough;
Though you stay here you pass too fast away,
    For even at first life's taper is a snuff.[6]

Filled with her love, may I be rather grown   25
Mad with much heart than idiot with none.

Elegy XI. The Bracelet

*Upon the loss of his Mistress' Chain, for which he
made satisfaction*

Not that in color it was like thy hair,
For armlets of that thou mayst let me wear:
Nor that thy hand it oft embraced and kissed,
For so it had that good, which oft I missed:
Nor for that silly old morality,[7]   5
That as these links were knit, our love should be:

---

1. Unlike Donne's other elegies, this poem, the title of which is from the 1635 edition, is not written in rhymed couplets. Some *MSS.* include it among the Songs and Sonnets.
2. Probably a "mental picture," which the speaker speaks of as being in his heart.
3. More than she loves it (the image). (The argument for so construing this disputed line is made by E. Schwartz in *Explicator*, XIX, 67.)
4. Imagination or fancy.
5. Products of "fantasy" (line 10).
6. Candle end.
7. Inscription.

Mourn I that I thy sevenfold chain have lost;
Nor for the luck sake, but the bitter cost.
Oh, shall twelve righteous angels,[8] which as yet
No leaven of vile solder did admit;   10
Nor yet by any fault have strayed or gone
From the first state of their creation;
Angels, which heaven commanded to provide
All things to me, and be my faithful guide,
To gain new friends, to appease great enemies,   15
To comfort my soul, when I lie or rise;
Shall these twelve innocents, by thy severe
Sentence (dread judge) my sin's great burden bear?
Shall they be damned, and in the furnace thrown,[9]
And punished for offences not their own?   20
They save not me, they do not ease my pains,
When in that hell they're burnt and tied in chains.
Were they but crowns of France,[1] I cared not,
For most of these their natural country's rot
I think possesseth, they come here to us   25
So pale, so lame, so lean, so ruinous;
And howsoe'er French kings most Christian be,
Their crowns are circumcised most Jewishly,[2]
Or were they Spanish stamps, still travelling,[3]
That are become as Catholic as their king,   30
Those unlicked bear-whelps, unfiled pistolets[4]
That (more than cannon[5] shot) avails or lets;
Which negligently left unrounded, look
Like many-angled figures in the book
Of some great conjurer that would enforce   35
Nature, as these do justice, from her course;
Which, as the soul quickens head, feet and heart,
As streams, like veins, run through the earth's every part,
Visit all countries, and have slyly made
Gorgeous *France*, ruined, ragged, and decayed;   40
Scotland, which knew no state, proud in one day;
And mangled seventeen-headed *Belgia*.[6]
Or were it such gold as that wherewithal
Almighty chemics[7] from each mineral
Having by subtle fire a soul out-pulled,   45
Are dirtily and desperately gulled:
I would not spit to quench the fire they're in,
For they are guilty of much heinous sin.

8. Throughout the poem, Donne plays on two meanings of "angel": (1) spirit; (2) English gold coin.
9. In order to be melted and made into a new chain.
1. French coins.
2. Lines 24–28 refer to the clipping and debasement of the coins.
3. Spanish coins, much used abroad as bribes.
4. Gold coins of an irregular shape; also, small firearms. It was thought that newly born cubs were licked into shape by their mothers.
5. Also, church (canon) laws, which allow or prohibit ("avails or lets").
6. These lines describe the effect of Spanish bribery on France, Scotland, and the seventeen states of the Lowlands.
7. Alchemists.

But shall my harmless angels perish? Shall
I lose my guard, my ease, my food, my all?   50
Much hope which they should nourish will be dead,
Much of my able youth and lustihead
Will vanish; if thou love let them alone,
For thou wilt love me less when they are gone;
And be content that some loud squeaking crier,   55
Well-pleased with one lean threadbare groat, for hire,
May like a devil roar through every street,
And gall the finder's conscience, if they meet.
Or let me creep to some dread conjurer,[8]
That with fantastic schemes fills full much paper;   60
Which hath divided heaven in tenements,[9]
And with whores, thieves, and murderers stuffed his rents,[1]
So full, that though he pass them all in sin,
He leaves himself no room to enter in.
But if, when all his art and time is spent,   65
He say 'twill ne'er be found, yet be content;
Receive from him that doom ungrudgingly,
Because he is the mouth of destiny.
     Thou say'st (alas) the gold doth still remain,
Though it be changed, and put into a chain;   70
So in the first fal'n angels resteth still
Wisdom and knowledge, but 'tis turned to ill:
As these should do good works and should provide
Necessities, but now must nurse thy pride.
And they are still bad angels; mine are none;   75
For form gives being, and their form is gone.
Pity these angels yet; their dignities
Pass Virtues, Powers, and Principalities.[2]
     But thou art resolute; thy will be done!
Yet with such anguish, as her only son   80
The mother in the hungry grave doth lay,
Unto the fire these martyrs I betray.
Good souls (for you give life to everything)
Good angels (for good messages you bring)
Destined you might have been to such an one   85
As would have loved and worshipped you alone,
One that would suffer hunger, nakedness,
Yea, death, ere he would make your number less.
But I am guilty of your sad decay;
May your few fellows longer with me stay.   90
     But oh thou wretched finder whom I hate
So, that I almost pity thy estate:
Gold being the heaviest metal amongst all,
May my most heavy curse upon thee fall:

---

8. Astrologer, magician.
9. Zodiac signs.
1. Fees; holes (in the heavens).

2. Angelic orders; also, ironically, what
money can buy.

Here fettered, manacled, and hanged in chains,   95
First mayst thou be; then chained to hellish pains;
Or be with foreign gold bribed to betray
Thy country, and fail both of that and thy pay.
May the next thing thou stoop'st to reach contain
Poison, whose nimble fume rot thy moist brain,   100
Or libels, or some interdicted thing,
Which negligently kept, thy ruin bring.
Lust-bred diseases rot thee; and dwell with thee
Itchy desire, and no ability.
May all the evils that gold ever wrought,   105
All mischiefs that all devils ever thought,
Want after plenty, poor and gouty age,
The plagues of travellers, love, marriage
Afflict thee, and at thy life's last moment,
May thy swol'n sins themselves to thee present.   110
    But I forgive; repent thee honest man:
Gold is restorative,[3] restore it then:
But if from it thou be'st loath to depart,
Because 'tis cordial, would 'twere at thy heart.

                                                              1635

Elegy XVI. On His Mistress

By our first strange and fatal interview,
By all desires which thereof did ensue,
By our long starving hopes, by that remorse
Which my words' masculine, persuasive force
Begot in thee, and by the memory   5
Of hurts which spies and rivals threatened me,
I calmly beg; but by thy father's wrath,
By all pains which want and divorcement[4] hath,
I conjure thee; and all the oaths which I
And thou have sworn to seal joint constancy,   10
Here I unswear, and overswear them thus,
Thou shalt not love by ways so dangerous.
Temper, O fair love, love's impetuous rage,
Be my true mistress still, not my faigned[5] page;
I'll go, and, by thy kind leave, leave behind   15
Thee, only worthy to nurse in my mind
Thirst to come back; oh, if thou die before,
My soul from other lands to thee shall soar.
Thy (else almighty) beauty cannot move
Rage from the seas, nor thy love teach them love,   20
Nor tame wild Boreas'[6] harshness; thou hast read

3. Gold was used as a medical remedy.
4. Complete separation.
5. Preferred, willing, eager; with a pun
on "feigned." The speaker's mistress
wants to disguise herself as a male page
in order to accompany the speaker on his
imminent journey.
6. The north wind.

How roughly he in pieces shivered
Fair Orithea,[7] whom he swore he loved.
Fall ill or good, 'tis madness to have proved[8]
Dangers unurged; feed on this flattery,   25
That absent lovers one in the other be.
Dissemble nothing, not a boy, nor change
Thy body's habit, nor mind's; be not strange
To thyself only; all will spy in thy face
A blushing, womanly, discovering grace;   30
Richly clothed apes are called apes; and as soon
Eclipsed as bright, we call the moon the moon.
Men of France, changeable chameleons,
Spitals[9] of diseases, shops of fashions,
Love's fuelers, and the rightest company   35
Of players which upon the world's stage be,
Will quickly know thee, and no less, alas![1]
The indifferent Italian, as we pass
His warm land, well content to think thee page,
Will hunt thee with such lust and hideous rage   40
As Lot's fair guests were vexed.[2] But none of these
Nor spongy, hydroptic[3] Dutch shall thee displease
If thou stay here. O stay here; for, for thee
England is only a worthy gallery
To walk in expectation, till from thence   45
Our greatest King call thee to his presence.[4]
When I am gone, dream me some happiness,
Nor let thy looks our long-hid love confess,
Nor praise, nor dispraise me, nor bless, nor curse
Openly love's force, nor in bed fright thy nurse   50
With midnight's startings, crying out, "Oh, oh
Nurse, oh my love is slain, I saw him go
O'er the white Alps alone; I saw him, I,
Assailed, fight, taken, stabbed, bleed, fall, and die."
Augur me better chance, except dread Jove   55
Think it enough for me to have thy love.

                                                            1635

Elegy XIX. To His Mistress Going to Bed

Come, madam, come, all rest my powers defy,
Until labor, I in labor lie.
The foe oft-times having the foe in sight,
Is tired with standing though he never fight.
Off with that girdle, like heaven's zone glistering,   5

---

7. The abducted bride of Boreas.
8. Experienced.
9. Hospitals.
1. Donne plays on the meanings of "know" and puns on "alas": a lass.
2. Genesis xix tells of the angels who, visiting the Hebrew patriarch Lot, were sought by the men of Sodom, city of unnatural vice.
3. Insatiably thirsty; dropsical.
4. England is the only worthy antechamber for you to live in until God calls you.

But a far fairer world encompassing.
Unpin that spangled breastplate which you wear,
That the eyes of busy fools may be stopped there.
Unlace yourself, for that harmonious chime
Tells me from you that now 'tis your bed time.   10
Off with that happy busk,¹ which I envy,
That still can be, and still can stand so nigh.
Your gown, going off, such beauteous state reveals,
As when from flowry meads the hill's shadow steals.
Off with that wiry coronet² and show   15
The hairy diadem which on you doth grow:
Now off with those shoes, and then safely tread
In this love's hallowed temple, this soft bed.
In such white robes, heaven's angels used to be
Received by men; thou, Angel, bring'st with thee 20
A heaven like Mahomet's Paradise; and though
Ill spirits walk in white, we easily know
By this these angels from an evil sprite:
Those set our hairs, but these our flesh upright.

License my roving hands, and let them go   25
Before, behind, between, above, below.
O my America! my new-found-land,
My kingdom, safeliest when with one man manned,
My mine of precious stones, my empery,³
How blest am I in this discovering thee!   30
To enter in these bonds is to be free;
Then where my hand is set, my seal shall be.
Full nakedness!   All joys are due to thee,
As souls unbodied, bodies unclothed must be
To taste whole joys.   Gems which you women use   35
Are like Atlanta's balls,⁴ cast in men's views,
That when a fool's eye lighteth on a gem,
His earthly soul may covet theirs, not them.
Like pictures, or like books' gay coverings made
For lay-men, are all women thus arrayed;   40
Themselves are mystic books, which only we
(Whom their imputed grace will dignify)
Must see revealed.   Then, since that I may know,
As liberally as to a midwife, show
Thyself: cast all, yea, this white linen hence,   45
Here is no penance, much less innocence.⁵
To teach thee, I am naked first; why than,⁶
What needst thou have more covering than a man.

1669

---

1. Corset.
2. Part of a woman's headdress.
3. Empire.
4. The golden apples dropped by a suitor in a foot race with Atalanta, the fleet-footed huntress of Greek myth, in order to distract and delay her. Donne here adapts the myth to his own use.
5. Penance and innocence are both represented by white.
6. Then.

Epithalamion Made at Lincoln's Inn[1]

The sun beams in the east are spread,
Leave, leave, fair bride, your solitary bed,
   No more shall you return to it alone,
It nurseth sadness, and your body's print,
Like to a grave, the yielding down doth dint;[2]   5
     You and your other you meet there anon;
       Put forth, put forth that warm balm-breathing thigh,
Which when next time you in these sheets will smother,
There it must meet another,
     Which never was, but must be, oft, more nigh;   10
Come glad from thence, go gladder than you came,
Today put on perfection, and a woman's name.

Daughters of London, you which be
Our golden mines, and furnished treasury,
   You which are angels, yet still bring with you   15
Thousands of angels[3] on your marriage days,
Help with your presence and devise[4] to praise
     These rites, which also unto you grow due;
       Conceitedly dress her, and be assigned,
By you, fit place for every flower and jewel,   20
Make her for love fit fuel
     As gay as Flora, and as rich as Ind;
So may she fair, rich, glad, and in nothing lame,
Today put on perfection, and a woman's name.

And you frolic patricians,   25
Sons[5] of these senators, wealth's deep oceans,
   Ye painted courtiers, barrels of others' wits,
Ye country men, who but your beasts love none,
Ye of those fellowships whereof he's one,
     Of study and play made strange hermaphrodites,   30
       Here shine; this bridegroom to the temple bring.
Lo, in yon path which store of strewed flowers graceth,
The sober virgin paceth;
     Except my sight fails, 'tis no other thing;
Weep not nor blush, here is no grief nor shame,   35
Today put on perfection, and a woman's name.

---

1. From 1592 to 1594 or 1595, Donne was a student at Lincoln's Inn, one of the Inns of Court, London's law schools. For the argument that the poem celebrates a mock, not a real, wedding, in keeping with the long tradition of Inns of Court reveling, see D. Novarr, "Donne's 'Epithalamion Made at Lincoln's Inn': Context and Date," *Review of English Studies*, VII (1956), 250–63. The poem may have been performed ("Made") by the male law students and may more correctly be regarded as a broadly satiric entertainment rather than as a conventional epithalamion or marriage song.
2. Indent.
3. Also, English gold coins.
4. Device, *i.e.*, fancy, invention.
5. With a pun on "suns."

Thy two-leaved gates, fair temple, unfold,
And these two in thy sacred bosom hold,
   Till, mystically joined, but one they be;
Then may thy lean and hunger-starved womb   40
Long time expect their bodies and their tomb,
   Long after their own parents fatten thee.
      All elder claims, and all cold barrenness,
All yielding to new loves be far for ever,
Which might these two dissever,   45
      All ways all the other may each one possess;
For, the best bride, best worthy of praise and fame,
Today puts on perfection, and a woman's name.

Oh winter days bring much delight,
Not for themselves, but for they soon bring night;   50
   Other sweets wait thee than these diverse meats,
Other disports than dancing jollities,
Other love tricks than glancing with the eyes,
   But that the sun still in our half sphere sweats;
      He flies in winter, but he now stands still,   55
Yet shadows turn: noon point he hath attained,
His steeds will be restrained,
      But gallop lively down the western hill;[6]
Thou shalt, when he hath run the world's half frame,
Tonight put on perfection, and a woman's name.   60

The amorous evening star is rose,
Why then should not our amorous star inclose
   Herself in her wished bed?   Release your strings,
Musicians, and, dancers, take some truce
With these your pleasing labors, for great use   65
   As much weariness as perfection brings;
      You, and not only you, but all toiled beasts
Rest duly; at night all their toils are dispensed;
But in their beds commenced
      Are other labors and more dainty feasts;   70
She goes a maid, who, lest she turn the same,
Tonight puts on perfection, and a woman's name.

Thy virgin's girdle now untie,
And in thy nuptial bed (love's altar) lie
   A pleasing sacrifice; now dispossèss   75
Thee of these chains and robes which were put on
To adorn the day, not thee; for thou, alone,
   Like virtue and truth, art best in nakedness;

---

6. "If line 57 is read with a gradually rising pitch and a momentary pause at the end before beginning line 58, the passage will clearly signify that the sun stands still at noon before the shadows turn, that is, that his horses will be restrained for a moment at the crest of the hill (noon) but will nevertheless gallop down the western slope." J. V. Hagopian, "Some Cruxes in Donne's Poetry," *Notes and Queries*, 202 (1957), 501.

     This bed is only to virginity
A grave, but to a better state, a cradle;   80
Till now thou wast but able
     To be what now thou art; then that by thee
No more be said, *I may be*, but, *I am*,
Tonight put on perfection, and a woman's name.

Even like a faithful man content   85
That this life for a better should be spent,
  So she a mother's rich style doth prefer,
And at the bridegroom's wished approach doth lie
Like an appointed lamb, when tenderly
     The priest comes on his knees to embowel her;   90
     Now sleep or watch with more joy; and O light
Of heaven, tomorrow rise thou hot and early;
This sun will love so dearly
     Her rest, that long, long we shall want her sight;
Wonders are wrought, for she which had no maim,   95
Tonight puts on perfection, and a woman's name.

Satire III

Kind pity chokes my spleen;[1] brave scorn forbids
Those tears to issue which swell my eyelids;
I must not laugh, nor weep sins, and be wise,
Can railing then cure these worn maladies?
Is not our mistress, fair Religion,   5
As worthy of all our soul's devotion,
As virtue was to the first blinded age?[2]
Are not heaven's joys as valiant to assuage
Lusts, as earth's honor was to them? Alas,
As we do them in means, shall they surpass   10
Us in the end, and shall thy father's spirit
Meet blind philosophers[3] in heaven, whose merit
Of strict life may be imputed[4] faith, and hear
Thee, whom he taught so easy ways and near
To follow, damned? O if thou dar'st, fear this;   15
This fear great courage and high valor is.
Dar'st thou aid mutinous Dutch, and dar'st thou lay
Thee in ships, wooden sepulchers, a prey
To leaders' rage, to storms, to shot, to dearth?
Dar'st thou dive seas and dungeons of the earth?   20
Hast thou courageous fire to thaw the ice
Of frozen North discoveries? And thrice
Colder than salamanders,[5] like divine
Children in the oven,[6] fires of Spain, and the line,[7]
Whose countries limbecks[8] to our bodies be,   25
Canst thou for gain bear? And must every he
Which cries not "Goddess!" to thy mistress, draw,[9]
Or eat thy poisonous words? Courage of straw!
O desperate coward, wilt thou seem bold, and
To thy foes and His (Who made thee to stand   30
Sentinel in His world's garrison) thus yield,
And for forbidden wars, leave the appointed field?
Know thy foes: the foul Devil, whom thou
Strivest to please, for hate, not love, would allow
Thee fain his whole realm to be quit;[1] and as   35
The world's all parts[2] wither away and pass,
So the world's self, thy other loved foe, is
In her decrepit wane,[3] and thou, loving this,
Dost love a withered and worn strumpet; last,
Flesh (itself's death) and joys which flesh can taste,   40

1. Regarded, in Donne's time, as the seat of both melancholy and mirth.
2. Pagan antiquity.
3. Pagan philosophers.
4. Accounted as.
5. Reputed to be able to survive fire because they are cold-blooded.
6. For refusing to worship a golden idol, Shadrach, Meshach, and Abednego were cast into the fiery furnace but were miraculously unharmed (Daniel iii).
7. The Inquisition and the equator (objects of "bear," line 26).
8. Distilling retorts.
9. *I.e.*, draw his sword.
1. To be rid of you.
2. All the parts of the world.
3. Decline.

Thou lovest; and thy fair goodly soul, which doth
Give this flesh power to taste joy, thou dost loathe.
Seek true religion.   O where? Mirreus,
Thinking her unhoused here, and fled from us,
Seeks her at Rome; there, because he doth know   45
That she was there a thousand years ago;
He loves her rags so, as we here obey
The statecloth[4] where the Prince sat yesterday.
Crantz to such brave[5] Loves will not be enthralled,
But loves her only, who at Geneva is called   50
Religion, plain, simple, sullen, young,
Contemptuous, yet unhandsome; as among
Lecherous humors, there is one that judges
No wenches wholesome but coarse country drudges.
Graius stays still at home here, and because   55
Some preachers, vile ambitious bawds, and laws,
Still new like fashions, bid him think that she
Which dwells with us is only perfect, he
Embraceth her whom his godfathers will
Tender to him, being tender, as wards still   60
Take such wives as their guardians offer, or
Pay values.[6]   Careless Phrygius doth abhor
All, because all cannot be good, as one,
Knowing some women whores, dares marry none.
Gracchus loves all as one, and thinks that so   65
As women do in diverse countries go
In divers habits, yet are still one kind,
So doth, so is Religion; and this blind-
ness too much light breeds; but unmoved thou
Of force must one, and forced but one allow;   70
And the right; ask thy father which is she,
Let him ask his; though truth and falsehood be
Near twins, yet truth a little elder is;
Be busy to seek her, believe me this,
He's not of none, nor worst,[7] that seeks the best.   75
To adore, or scorn an image, or protest,
May all be bad; doubt wisely; in strange way
To stand inquiring right is not to stray;
To sleep, or run wrong is.   On a huge hill,
Cragged and steep, Truth stands, and he that will   80
Reach her, about must, and about must go;
And what the hill's suddenness resists, win so;
Yet strive so, that before age, death's twilight,
Thy soul rest, for none can work in that night.
To will implies delay, therefore now do.   85
Hard deeds, the body's pains; hard knowledge too

4. We do obeisance to the cloth over the throne.
5. Splendid.
6. Sums paid for refusing an arranged marriage; here compared to fines recusants paid for not attending the national church.
7. Not of no faith, nor the worst faith.

The mind's endeavors reach,[8] and mysteries
Are like the sun, dazzling, yet plain to all eyes.
Keep the truth which thou hast found; men do not stand
In so ill case here that God hath with His hand   90
Signed kings blank charters to kill whom they hate,
Nor are they vicars, but hangmen to fate.
Fool and wretch, wilt thou let thy soul be tied
To man's laws, by which she shall not be tried
At the last day?   Oh, wilt it then boot[9] thee   95
To say a Philip, or a Gregory,
A Harry, or a Martin[1] taught thee this?
Is not this excuse for mere contraries
Equally strong? Cannot both sides say so?
That thou mayest rightly obey power, her bounds know;   100
Those passed, her nature, and name is changed; to be
Then humble to her is idolatry.
As streams are, power is; those blest flowers that dwell
At the rough stream's calm head, thrive and do well,
But having left their roots, and themselves given   105
To the stream's tyrannous rage, alas, are driven
Through mills, and rocks, and woods, and at last, almost
Consumed in going, in the sea are lost:
So perish souls, which more choose men's unjust
Power from God claimed, than God Himself to trust.   110

8. Difficult deeds are accomplished by the body's pains; difficult knowledge is attained by the mind's endeavors.
9. Profit.

1. Philip II of Spain; Pope Gregory XIII or Gregory XIV; Henry VIII of England; Martin Luther.

Verse Letters to
Several Personages

The Storm

TO MR. CHRISTOPHER BROOKE[1]

Thou which art I ('tis nothing to be so),
Thou which art still thyself, by these shalt know
Part of our passage; and a hand, or eye
By *Hilliard*[2] drawn, is worth an history
By a worse painter made; and (without pride)   5
When by thy judgment they are dignified,
My lines are such: 'tis the pre-eminence
Of friendship only to impute excellence.
England to whom we owe what we be and have,
Sad that her sons did seek a foreign grave   10
(For Fate's or Fortune's drifts none can soothsay,
Honor and misery have one face and way),
From out her pregnant entrails sighed a wind
Which at the air's middle marble room did find
Such strong resistance that itself it threw   15
Downward again;[3] and so when it did view
How in the port our fleet dear time did leese,[4]
Withering like prisoners, which lie but for fees,[5]
Mildly it kissed our sails, and, fresh and sweet,
As to a stomach starved, whose insides meet,   20
Meat comes, it came, and swole[6] our sails, when we
So joyed as *Sarah* her swelling joyed to see.[7]
But 'twas but so kind as our countrymen
Which bring friends one day's way, and leave them then.
Then, like two mighty kings which, dwelling far   25
Asunder, meet against a third to war,
The South and West winds joined, and, as they blew,
Waves like a rolling trench before them threw.

1. This poem and "The Calm" describe incidents of the English naval expedition of 1597, the famous "Islands Expedition." "The Calm" was probably also addressed to Christopher Brooke, Donne's close friend and, later, his best man at his wedding.
2. Nicholas Hilliard (1537–1619), English painter.
3. Winds were supposed to be caused by the earth's exhalations and to be driven back upon contact with the hard or frozen middle region of the air.
4. Lose.
5. *I.e.*, fees due to the jailer.
6. Swelled.
7. In old age, Sarah, wife of Abraham, bore him a son, Isaac (Genesis xxi).

Sooner than you read this line, did the gale,
Like shot, not feared till felt, our sails assail;   30
And what at first was called a gust, the same
Hath now a storm's, anon a tempest's name.
Jonas,[8] I pity thee, and curse those men
Who when the storm raged most, did wake thee then;
Sleep is pain's easiest salve, and doth fulfill   35
All offices of death, except to kill.
But when I waked, I saw that I saw not;
Ay, and the sun, which should teach me, had forgot
East, west, day, night, and I could only say,
If the world had lasted, now it had been day.   40
Thousands our noises were, yet we 'mongst all
Could none by his right name, but thunder, call.
Lightning was all our light, and it rained more
Than if the sun had drunk the sea before.
Some coffined in their cabins lie, equally   45
Grieved that they are not dead and yet must die;
And as sin-burdened souls from graves will creep
At the last day, some forth their cabins peep
And tremblingly ask what news, and do hear so,
Like jealous husbands, what they would not know.   50
Some, sitting on the hatches, would seem there
With hideous gazing to fear away fear.
Then note they the ship's sicknesses, the mast
Shaked with this ague, and the hold and waist
With a salt dropsy clogged, and all our tacklings   55
Snapping, like too-high-stretched treble strings.
And from our tattered sails, rags drop down so,
As from one hanged in chains a year ago.
Even our ordnance, placed for our defense,
Strive to break loose and 'scape away from thence.   60
Pumping hath tired our men, and what's the gain?
Seas into seas thrown we suck in again;
Hearing hath deafed our sailors; and if they
Knew how to hear, there's none knows what to say.
Compared to these storms, death is but a qualm,[9]   65
Hell somewhat lightsome, and the Bermudas calm.
Darkness, light's elder brother,[1] his birthright
Claims o'er this world, and to heaven hath chased light.
All things are one, and that one none can be,
Since all forms, uniform deformity   70
Doth cover, so that we, except God say
Another *fiat*, shall have no more day.
So violent, yet long these furies be,
That though thine absence starve me, I wish not thee.

---

8. Jonah, awakened during a storm and later cast into the sea (Jonah i).
9. A feeling of faintness or sickness.

1. Darkness existed before light was created by God's command or *"fiat"* (see line 72 and Genesis i).

The Calm

Our storm is past, and that storm's tyrannous rage,
A stupid calm, but nothing it, doth 'suage.
The fable is inverted, and far more
A block afflicts, now, than a stork before.[2]
Storms chafe, and soon wear out themselves, or us;   5
In calms, Heaven laughs to see us languish thus.
As steady as I can wish that my thoughts were,
Smooth as thy mistress' glass,[3] or what shines there,
The sea is now.   And, as the Isles which we
Seek when we can move, our ships rooted be.   10
As water did in storms, now pitch runs out
As lead when a fired church becomes one spout.[4]
And all our beauty and our trim decays,
Like courts removing, or like ended plays.
The fighting place now seamen's rags supply;   15
And all the tackling is a frippery.[5]
No use of lanterns; and in one place lay
Feathers and dust, today and yesterday.
Earth's hollownesses, which the world's lungs are,
Have no more wind than the upper vault of air.   20
We can nor lost friends nor sought foes recover,
But meteor-like, save that we move not, hover.
Only the calenture[6] together draws
Dear friends, which meet dead in great fishes' jaws.
And on the hatches as on altars lies   25
Each one, his own priest and own sacrifice.
Who live, that miracle do multiply
Where walkers in hot ovens do not die.[7]
If in despite of these, we swim, that hath
No more refreshing than our brimstone bath,   30
But from the sea into the ship we turn
Like parboiled wretches on the coals to burn.
Like *Bajazet* encaged, the shepherds' scoff,[8]
Or like slack-sinewed Samson, his hair off,
Languish our ships.   Now, as a myriad   35
Of ants durst the emperor's loved snake invade,[9]
The crawling galleys, sea-jails, finny chips,

2. In medieval versions of Aesop's fable, when the frogs asked for a king they were given a log of wood, which they scorned; so they were then given a stork, which ate them.
3. Mirror.
4. Pitch was used to caulk the seams of ships; churches were often roofed with lead.
5. A secondhand-clothes shop.
6. A tropical disease which causes sailors deliriously to mistake the sea for green fields and to leap overboard.
7. Three Jews, cast into a fiery furnace, walked on unharmed (see "Satire III," line 24, and Daniel iii).
8. In Marlowe's *Tamburlaine*, the Turkish emperor Bajazeth is captured and kept in a cage by the former shepherd Tamburlaine.
9. Suetonius' *Life of Tiberius* tells of Tiberius' pet snake devoured by ants.

Might brave our pinnaces,[1] now bed-rid ships.
Whether a rotten state and hope of gain,
Or to disuse me from the queasy pain   40
Of being beloved and loving, or the thirst
Of honor or fair death out-pushed me first,
I lose my end: for here as well as I
A desperate may live, and a coward die.
Stag, dog, and all which from, or towards flies,   45
Is paid with life, or prey, or doing dies.
Fate grudges us all, and doth subtly lay
A scourge, 'gainst which we all forget to pray.
He that at sea prays for more wind, as well
Under the poles may beg cold, heat in hell.   50
What are we then? How little more, alas,
Is man now than before he was! he was
Nothing; for us, we are for nothing fit;
Chance or ourselves still disproportion it.
We have no power, no will, no sense; I lie,   55
I should not then thus feel this misery.

To Sir Henry Wotton

Here's no more news, than virtue; I may as well
Tell you *Cales'* or *Saint Michael's* tale[2] for news as tell
That vice doth here habitually dwell.

Yet, as to get stomachs[3] we walk up and down,
And toil to sweeten rest, so may God frown   5
If, but to loathe both, I haunt court or town.

For here no one is from the extremity
Of vice by any other reason free
But that the next to him still is worse than he.

In this world's warfare, they whom rugged Fate   10
(God's commissary[4]) doth so throughly hate
As in the court's squadron to marshal their state,

If they stand armed with silly[5] honesty,
With wishing prayers, and neat integrity,
Like Indians 'gainst Spanish hosts they be.   15

Suspicious boldness to this place belongs,
And to have as many ears as all have tongues;
Tender to know, tough to acknowledge wrongs.

---

1. Because of the calm, the slow galleys,
which were often rowed by prisoners
(hence "sea-jails") and looked small like
chips with fin-like oars, might challenge
the ordinarily quick-sailing pinnaces.
2. Refers to the Cadiz and the Islands
expeditions, on which Donne served in
1596 and 1597. Two MSS. date this letter July 20, 1598.
3. Appetites or relish for food.
4. Deputy; "throughly": thoroughly.
5. Simple.

Believe me, sir, in my youth's giddiest days,
When to be like the court was a play's praise,　　　20
Plays were not so like courts as courts are like plays.

Then let us at these mimic antics jest,
Whose deepest projects and egregious gests[6]
Are but dull morals of a game at chests.[7]

But now 'tis incongruity to smile,　　　25
Therefore I end; and bid farewell a while,
At court, though *from court* were the better style.

To the Countess of Bedford

Madam,
Reason is our soul's left hand, faith her right,
By these we reach divinity, that's you;
Their loves, who have the blessings of your light,
Grew from their reason, mine from fair faith grew.

But as, although a squint lefthandedness　　　5
Be ungracious, yet we cannot want[8] that hand,
So would I, not to increase, but to express
My faith, as I believe, so understand.

Therefore I study you first in your saints,
Those friends whom your election glorifies,　　　10
Then in your deeds, accesses, and restraints,
And what you read, and what yourself devise.

But soon the reasons why you're loved by all
Grow infinite, and so pass reason's reach,
Then back again to implicit faith I fall,　　　15
And rest on what the catholic[9] voice doth teach:

That you are good: and not one heretic
Denies it: if he did, yet you are so.
For rocks which high-topped and deep-rooted stick
Waves wash, not undermine, nor overthrow.　　　20

In everything there naturally grows
A *balsamum*[1] to keep it fresh and new,
If 'twere not injured by extrinsic blows;
Your birth and beauty are this balm in you.

6. Flagrant exploits; with possible puns on "guests" and "jests."
7. Symbolical figures of a game of chess.
8. Lack, do without.
9. Universal.
1. A balm within all things which preserves life and cures wounds.

But you of learning and religion, 25
And virtue, and such ingredients, have made
A mithridate,[2] whose operation
Keeps off or cures what can be done or said.

Yet this is not your physic,[3] but your food,
A diet fit for you; for you are here 30
The first good angel, since the world's frame stood,
That ever did in woman's shape appear.

Since you are then God's masterpiece, and so
His factor[4] for our loves, do as you do,
Make your return home gracious; and bestow 35
This life on that; so make one life of two.
    For so God help me, I would not miss you there
    For all the good which you can do me here.

To Sir Edward Herbert at Juliers[5]

Man is a lump where all beasts kneaded be,
    Wisdom makes him an ark where all agree;
The fool in whom these beasts do live at jar[6]
    Is sport to others, and a theater;
Nor 'scapes he so, but is himself their prey; 5
    All which was man in him is eat away,
And now his beasts on one another feed,
    Yet couple in anger, and new monsters breed.
How happy is he which hath due place assigned
    To his beasts and disafforested his mind! 10
Empaled[7] himself to keep them out, not in;
    Can sow, and dares trust corn, where they have been;
Can use his horse, goat, wolf, and every beast,
    And is not ass himself to all the rest.
Else, man not only is the herd of swine, 15
    But he's those devils, too, which did incline
Them to a headlong rage and made them worse:[8]
    For man can add weight to heaven's heaviest curse.
As souls (they say) by our first touch take in
    The poisonous tincture of Original Sin, 20
So to the punishments which God doth fling,
    Our apprehension contributes the sting.

2. An immunizing medicine. (Mithridates, king of Pontus, is said to have immunized himself by taking poison in gradually increased doses.)
3. Medicine.
4. Agent.
5. Lord Herbert of Cherbury, the brother of the poet George Herbert and himself a poet and philosopher, was with the English army at the seige of Juliers.
6. In discord.
7. Enclosed, fenced in.
8. When Jesus cast out devils into a herd of swine, the herd ran violently down a cliff into the sea (Matthew viii).

To us, as to His chickens, He doth cast
   Hemlock, and we, as men, His hemlock taste;
We do infuse to what He meant for meat,   25
   Corrosiveness, or intense cold or heat.[9]
For, God no such specific poison hath
   As kills we know not how; His fiercest wrath
Hath no antipathy, but may be good
   At least for physic, if not for our food.   30
Thus man, that might be his pleasure, is his rod,
   And is his devil, that might be his God.
Since then our business is to rectify
   Nature to what she was,[1] we're led awry
By them who man to us in little show;[2]   35
   Greater than due, no form we can bestow
On him; for man into himself can draw
   All; all his faith can swallow, or reason chaw.[3]
All that is filled, and all that which doth fill,
   All the round world, to man is but a pill;   40
In all it works not, but it is in all
   Poisonous, or purgative, or cordial,
For, knowledge kindles Calentures[4] in some,
   And is to others icy *Opium*.
As brave as true is that profession than[5]   45
   Which you do use to make: that you know man.
This makes it credible; you have dwelt upon
   All worthy books, and now are such an one.
Actions are authors, and of those in you
   Your friends find every day a mart[6] of new.   50

9. What is harmless to some animals is poison to man, because of what man's own nature infuses or adds to the food.
1. Before the Fall.
2. Show or contend man to be merely a world in little, corresponding to the universe. In *Devotions upon Emergent Occasions*, Donne writes, "It is too little to call Man a little world; Except God, Man is a diminutive to nothing."
3. Chew.
4. A tropical disease, characterized by delirium; fever, burning passion.
5. Then.
6. Market, fair; specifically, the German booksellers' fair, held at Easter.

An Anatomy of the World[1]:

The First Anniversary

The entry into the work.

When that rich soul which to her heaven is gone,
Whom all they celebrate who know they have one,
(For who is sure he hath a soul, unless
It see, and judge, and follow worthiness,
And by deeds praise it? He who doth not this,   5
May lodge an in-mate soul, but 'tis not his);
When that queen ended here her progress[2] time,
And, as to her standing house,[3] to heaven did climb,
Where, loath to make the saints attend[4] her long,
She's now a part both of the choir and song,   10
This world in that great earthquake languished;
For in a common bath of tears it bled,
Which drew the strongest vital spirits[5] out:
But succored then with a perplexed doubt,
Whether the world did lose or gain in this,   15
(Because since now no other way there is
But goodness to see her, whom all would see,
All must endeavor to be good as she,)
This great consumption to a fever turned,
And so the world had fits; it joyed, it mourned.   20
And as men think that agues physic are,
And the ague being spent, give over care,
So thou, sick world, mistak'st thyself to be
Well, when, alas, thou art in a lethargy.
Her death did wound and tame thee then, and than[6]
Thou might'st have better spared the sun, or man;   26
That wound was deep, but 'tis more misery,
That thou hast lost thy sense and memory.
'Twas heavy[7] then to hear thy voice of moan,
But this is worse, that thou art speechless grown.   30
Thou hast forgot thy name, thou hadst; thou wast
Nothing but she, and her thou hast o'erpast.
For as a child kept from the font, until
A prince, expected long, come to fulfill
The ceremonies, thou unnamed had'st laid,   35
Had not her coming, thee her palace made:
Her name defined thee, gave thee form and frame,

1. Following this title in the 1611 edition are the words, "Wherein, by occasion of the untimely death of Mistress Elizabeth Drury the frailty and decay of this whole world is represented." Elizabeth Drury was the younger daughter of Sir Robert Drury, patron and friend of Donne. Although she is the overt subject of this poem and of "The Progress of the Soul: The Second Anniversary," published in 1612, Donne himself told Ben Jonson "that he described the Idea of Woman and not as she was."
2. Visiting tour.
3. Permanent residence.
4. Wait for.
5. Elements in the blood which hold body and soul together.
6. Then.
7. Mournful.

And thou forget'st to celebrate thy name.
Some months she hath been dead (but being dead,
Measures of times are all determined[8]   40
But long she hath been away, long, long, yet none
Offers to tell us who it is that's gone.
But as in states doubtful of future heirs,
When sickness without remedy impairs
The present prince, they're loath it should be said,   45
The prince doth languish, or the prince is dead:
So mankind feeling now a general thaw,
A strong example gone, equal to law,
The cement which did faithfully compact
And glue all virtues, now resolved, and slacked,   50
Thought it some blasphemy to say she was dead,
Or that our weakness was discovered
In that confession; therefore spoke no more
Than tongues, the soul being gone, the loss deplore.
But though it be too late to succor thee,   55
Sick world, yea, dead, yea putrefied, since she,
Thy intrinsic balm and thy preservative,
Can never be renewed, thou never live,
I (since no man can make thee live) will try
What we may gain by thy anatomy.[9]   60
Her death hath taught us dearly that thou art
Corrupt and mortal in thy purest part.
Let no man say, the world itself being dead,
'Tis labor lost to have discovered
The world's infirmities, since there is none   65
Alive to study this dissection;

What life the   For there's a kind of world remaining still,
world hath still. Though she which did inanimate and fill
The world be gone, yet in this last long night,
Her ghost doth walk; that is, a glimmering light.   70
A faint weak love of virtue and of good
Reflects from her on them which understood
Her worth; and though she have shut in all day,
The twilight of her memory doth stay;
Which, from the carcass of the old world, free,   75
Creates a new world; and new creatures be
Produced: the matter and the stuff of this,
Her virtue, and the form our practice is:
And though to be thus elemented, arm
These creatures, from home-born intrinsic harm,   80
(For all assumed[1] unto this dignity,
So many weedless Paradises be,
Which of themselves produce no venomous sin,
Except some foreign serpent bring it in)
Yet, because outward storms the strongest break,   85

8. Ended.   body of the world.
9. By dissecting and analyzing the dead   1. Raised; elected.

And strength itself by confidence grows weak,
This new world may be safer, being told

The sicknesses of the world. The dangers and diseases of the old:
For with due temper men do then forgo,
Or covet things, when they their true worth know.   90

Impossibility of health. There is no health; physicians say that we,
At best, enjoy but a neutrality.
And can there be worse sickness than to know
That we are never well, nor can be so?
We are born ruinous:[2] poor mothers cry   95
That children come not right, nor orderly,
Except they headlong come and fall upon
An ominous precipitation.
How witty's ruin! how importunate
Upon mankind! It labored to frustrate   100
Even God's purpose; and made woman, sent
For man's relief, cause of his languishment.
They were to good ends, and they are so still,
But accessory, and principal in ill.
For that first marriage[3] was our funeral: 105
One woman at one blow then killed us all,
And singly, one by one, they kill us now.
We do delightfully ourselves allow
To that consumption; and profusely blind,
We kill ourselves to propagate our kind.[4]   110
And yet we do not that; we are not men:
There is not now that mankind which was then

Shortness of life. When as the sun and man did seem to strive
(Joint tenants of the world) who should survive;
When stag, and raven,[5] and the long-lived tree,   115
Compared with man, died in minority;
When, if a slow-paced star had stolen away
From the observer's marking, he might stay
Two or three hundred years to see it again,
And then make up his observation plain;   120
When, as the age was long, the size was great;
Man's growth confessed and recompensed the meat;[6]
So spacious and large, that every soul
Did a fair kingdom and large realm control;
And when the very stature, thus erect,   125
Did that soul a good way towards Heaven direct.
Where is this mankind now? who lives to age,
Fit to be made *Methusalah* his page?
Alas, we scarce live long enough to try
Whether a new made clock run right, or lie.   130

2. Falling into ruin.
3. Of Adam and Eve.
4. These lines play on a secondary meaning of "kill" or "die" in the 17th century: to consummate the sexual act; and they refer to the notion that each sexual act shortens life.
5. Thought to be exceedingly long-lived animals.
6. The food of early man was believed to have been much better than it later became.

Old grandsires talk of yesterday with sorrow,
And for our children we reserve tomorrow.
So short is life that every peasant strives,
In a torn house, or field, to have three lives.
And as in lasting, so in length is man   135
Smallness Contracted to an inch, who was a span;[7]
of stature. For had a man at first in forests strayed,
Or shipwrecked in the sea, one would have laid
A wager that an elephant or whale
That met him would not hastily assail   140
A thing so equal to him: now, alas,
The fairies and the pigmies well may pass
As credible; mankind decays so soon,
We're scarce our fathers' shadows cast at noon.
Only death adds to our length: nor are we grown   145
In stature to be men, till we are none.
But this were light,[8] did our less volume hold
All the old text; or had we changed to gold
Their silver; or disposed into less glass
Spirits of virtue, which then scattered was.   150
But 'tis not so: we're not retired, but damped;[9]
And as our bodies, so our minds are cramped:
'Tis shrinking, not close weaving, that hath thus
In mind and body both bedwarfed us.
We seem ambitious, God's whole work to undo;   155
Of nothing He made us, and we strive, too,
To bring ourselves to nothing back; and we
Do what we can to do it so soon as He.
With new diseases on ourselves we war,
And with new physic,[1] a worse engine far.   160
Thus man, this world's vice-emperor, in whom
All faculties, all graces are at home;
And if in other creatures they appear,
They're but man's ministers, and legates there,
To work on their rebellions, and reduce   165
Them to civility, and to man's use.
This man, whom God did woo, and loath to attend[2]
Till man came up, did down to man decend,
This man, so great, that all that is, is his,
Oh what a trifle, and poor thing he is!   170
If man were anything, he's nothing now:
Help, or at least some time to waste, allow
To his other wants, yet when he did depart
With her whom we lament, he lost his heart.
She, of whom the ancients seemed to prophesy   175
When they called virtues by the name of *she*;
She in whom virtue was so much refined

---

7. Nine inches.   1. Medicine.
8. Of small consequence.   2. Wait.
9. Not refined, but deadened.

That for alloy unto so pure a mind
She took the weaker sex; she that could drive
The poisonous tincture, and the stain of *Eve*,   180
Out of her thoughts and deeds; and purify
All, by a true religious alchemy;
She, she is dead; she's dead: when thou knowest this,
Thou knowest how poor a trifling thing man is.
And learn'st thus much by our anatomy,   185
The heart being perished, no part can be free.
And that except thou feed (not banquet) on
The supernatural food, religion,
Thy better growth grows withered and scant;
Be more than man, or thou art less than an ant.   190
Then, as mankind, so is the world's whole frame
Quite out of joint, almost created lame:
For, before God had made up all the rest,
Corruption entered and depraved the best.
It seized the angels, and then first of all   195
The world did in her cradle take a fall,
And turned her brains, and took a general maim,
Wronging each joint of the universal frame.
The noblest part, man, felt it first; and than[3]

Decay of nature in other parts. Both beasts and plants, curst in the curse of man.   200
So did the world from the first hour decay,
That evening was beginning of the day,
And now the springs and summers which we see,
Like sons of women after fifty be.
And new philosophy[4] calls all in doubt,   205
The element of fire is quite put out;[5]
The sun is lost, and the earth, and no man's wit
Can well direct him where to look for it.[6]
And freely men confess that this world's spent,
When in the planets and the firmament   210
They seek so many new; they see that this
Is crumbled out again to his atomies.
'Tis all in pieces, all coherence gone;
All just supply, and all relation:
Prince, subject, father, son, are things forgot,   215
For every man alone thinks he hath got
To be a phoenix, and that there can be
None of that kind, of which he is, but he.[7]
This is the world's condition now, and now
She that should all parts to reunion bow,   220
She that had all magnetic force alone,

3. Then.
4. The new science, esp. astronomy.
5. The new science proved false the notion that the earth was surrounded by fire.
6. The idea of a concentric universe with the earth at its center was disproved by the new astronomy. The following lines also refer to new discoveries of astronomers.
7. These lines refer to social and religious changes and a growing individualism.

To draw, and fasten sundered parts in one;
She whom wise nature had invented then
When she observed that every sort of men
Did in their voyage in this world's sea stray,   225
And needed a new compass for their way;
She that was best, and first original
Of all fair copies, and the general
Steward to Fate; she whose rich eyes and breast
Gilt the West Indies, and perfumed the East;[8]   230
Whose having breathed in this world did bestow
Spice on those Isles, and bade them still smell so,
And that rich Indy which doth gold inter,
Is but as single money, coined from her:
She to whom this world must itself refer,   235
As suburbs, or the microcosm of her,
She, she is dead; she's dead: when thou know'st this,
Thou know'st how lame a cripple this world is.
And learn'st thus much by our anatomy,
That this world's general sickness doth not lie   240
In any humor,[9] or one certain part;
But, as thou sawest it rotten at the heart,
Thou seest a hectic fever hath got hold
Of the whole substance, not to be controlled,
And that thou hast but one way not to admit   245
The world's infection, to be none of it.
For the world's subtlest immaterial parts
Feel this consuming wound, and age's darts.
Disformity   For the world's beauty is decayed or gone;
of parts.   Beauty, that's color and proportion.   250
We think the heavens enjoy their spherical,
Their round proportion embracing all.
But yet their various and perplexed course,
Observed in divers ages, doth enforce
Men to find out so many eccentric parts,[1]   255
Such divers down-right lines, such overthwarts,[2]
As disproportion that pure form. It tears
The firmament in eight and forty shares,
And in those constellations there arise
New stars,[3] and old do vanish from our eyes: 260
As though heav'n suffered earthquakes, peace or war,
When new towns rise, and old demolished are.
They have impaled within a zodiac
The free-born sun, and keep twelve signs awake

8. The West Indies were reputed to be a source of precious metals, and the East Indies were a source of spices and perfumes.
9. There were four bodily fluids or "humors," according to medical theory of the time, which accounted for a man's temperament.
1. The eccentric circles of the old or Ptolemaic astronomy were efforts to reconcile differing and perplexing astronomical observations.
2. Vertical and horizontal lines.
3. Ptolemy had divided the stars into 48 constellations, which were thought to be unchanging—until the discovery of new stars in Donne's lifetime.

To watch his steps; the Goat and Crab control,   265
And fright him back, who else to either pole
(Did not these tropics fetter him) might run:
For his course is not round; nor can the sun
Perfect a circle, or maintain his way
One inch direct; but where he rose today   270
He comes no more, but with a cozening line,
Steals by that point, and so is serpentine:
And seeming weary with his reeling thus,
He means to sleep, being now fall'n nearer us.
So, of the stars which boast that they do run   275
In circle still, none ends where he begun.
All their proportion's lame, it sinks, it swells.
For of meridians and parallels,
Man hath weaved out a net and this net thrown
Upon the heavens, and now they are his own.   280
Loath to go up the hill, or labor thus
To go to heaven, we make heaven come to us.
We spur, we rein the stars, and in their race
They're diversely content to obey our pace.
But keeps the earth her round proportion still?[4]   285
Doth not a Tenerife,[5] or higher hill
Rise so high like a rock, that one might think
The floating moon would shipwreck there and sink?
Seas are so deep that whales being struck today
Perchance tomorrow, scarce at middle way   290
Of their wished journey's end, the bottom, die.
And men, to sound depths, so much line untie,
As one might justly think that there would rise
At end thereof, one of the antipodes:
If under all, a vault infernal be[6]   295
(Which sure is spacious, except that we
Invent another torment, that there must
Millions into a strait hot room be thrust),
Then solidness and roundness have no place.
Are these but warts and pock-holes in the face   300
Of the earth?   Think so: but yet confess, in this
The world's proportion disfigured is,

Disorder in
the world.

That those two legs whereon it doth rely,
Reward and punishment are bent awry.
And, Oh, it can no more be questioned,   305
That beauty's best, proportion, is dead,
Since even grief itself, which now alone
Is left us, is without proportion.
She by whose lines proportion should be
Examined, measure of all symmetry,   310

4. Refers to the notion that the earth
was created perfectly round.
5. The volcanic peak on Tenerife, the
largest of the Canary Islands.

6. Medieval theologians contended that
hell was located in the center of the
earth.

Whom had that ancient seen, who thought souls
    made
Of harmony, he would at next[7] have said
That harmony was she, and thence infer
That souls were but resultances[8] from her,
And did from her into our bodies go,   315
As to our eyes, the forms from objects flow;
She, who if those great doctors truly said
That the ark[9] to man's proportions was made,
Had been a type for that, as that might be
A type of her in this, that contrary   320
Both elements and passions lived at peace
In her, who caused all civil war to cease;
She, after whom, what form soe'er we see,
Is discord, and rude incongruity;
She, she is dead, she's dead; when thou know'st this,
Thou know'st how ugly a monster this world is: 326
And learn'st thus much by our anatomy,
That here is nothing to enamor thee:
And that, not only faults in inward parts,
Corruptions in our brains, or in our hearts,   330
Poisoning the fountains, whence our actions spring,
Endanger us: but that if everything
Be not done fitly and in proportion,
To satisfy wise and good lookers-on
(Since most men be such as most think they be),   335
They're loathsome too, by this deformity.
For good, and well, must in our actions meet:
Wicked is not much worse than indiscreet.
But beauty's other second element,
Color, and luster now, is as near spent.   340
And had the world his just proportion,
Were it a ring still, yet the stone is gone.
As a compassionate turquoise which doth tell
By looking pale the wearer is not well,
As gold falls sick being stung with mercury,   345
All the world's parts of such complexion be.
When nature was most busy, the first week,
Swaddling the new-born earth, God seemed to like
That she should sport herself sometimes and play,
To mingle and vary colors every day.   350
And then, as though she could not make enow,[1]
Himself His various rainbow did allow.
Sight is the noblest sense of any one,
Yet sight hath only color to feed on,
And color is decayed: summer's robe grows   355
Dusky, and like an oft dyed garment shows.

---

7. Immediately.
8. Emanations.

9. Noah's ark, on which ordinarily hostile or "contrary" animals lived in peace.
1. Enough.

Our blushing red, which used in cheeks to spread,
Is inward sunk, and only our souls are red.[2]
Perchance the world might have recovered,
If she whom we lament had not been dead: 360
But she, in whom all white, and red, and blue
(Beauty's ingredients) voluntary grew,
As in an unvexed Paradise; from whom
Did all things verdure, and their luster come,
Whose composition was miraculous,   365
Being all color, all diaphanous
(For air and fire but thick gross bodies were,
And liveliest stones but drowsy and pale to her),
She, she is dead; she's dead: when thou know'st this,
Thou know'st how wan a ghost this our world is: 370
And learn'st thus much by our anatomy,
That it should more affright than pleasure thee.
And that, since all fair color then did sink,
'Tis now but wicked vanity to think

Weakness in
the want of
correspondence
of heaven and
earth.

To color vicious deeds with good pretence,   375
Or with bought colors to illude[3] men's sense.
Nor in aught more this world's decay appears,
Than that her influence the heav'n forbears,
Or that the elements do not feel this,
The father or the mother barren is.   380
The clouds conceive not rain, or do not pour
In the due birth time, down the balmy shower;
The air doth not motherly sit on the earth,
To hatch her seasons and give all things birth;
Springtimes were common cradles, but are tombs; 385
And false conceptions fill the general wombs.
The air shows such meteors[4] as none can see,
Not only what they mean, but what they be.
Earth such new worms[5] as would have troubled much
The Egyptian Mages[6] to have made more such.   390
What artist now dares boast that he can bring
Heaven hither, or constellate anything,
So as the influence of those stars may be
Imprisoned in an herb, or charm, or tree,
And do by touch all which those stars could do?   395
The art is lost, and correspondence too.
For heaven gives little, and the earth takes less,
And man least knows their trade and purposes.
If this commerce 'twixt heaven and earth were not
Embarred, and all this traffic quite forgot,   400
She, for whose loss we have lamented thus,
Would work more fully and pow'rfully on us.
Since herbs and roots by dying lose not all,

---

2. The color of sin.
3. With cosmetics to mock, trick.
4. Any atmospheric phenomenon.

5. Serpents.
6. The Egyptian magicians who changed
their rods into serpents (Exodus vii).

But they, yea ashes too, are medicinal,
Death could not quench her virtue so, but that   405
It would be (if not followed) wondered at:
And all the world would be one dying swan,
To sing her funeral praise, and vanish than.[7]
But as some serpents' poison hurteth not,
Except it be from the live serpent shot,   410
So doth her virtue need her here, to fit
That unto us; she working more than it.
But she, in whom to such maturity
Virtue was grown, past growth, that it must die;
She, from whose influence all impressions came,   415
But, by receivers' impotencies, lame,
Who, though she could not transubstantiate
All states to gold, yet gilded every state,
So that some princes have some temperance,
Some counselers some purpose to advance   420
The common profit, and some people have
Some stay, no more than kings should give, to crave,
Some women have some taciturnity,
Some nunneries some grains of chastity;
She that did thus much, and much more could do,
But that our age was iron,[8] and rusty too,   426
She, she is dead; she's dead: when thou know'st this,
Thou know'st how dry a cinder this world is.
And learn'st thus much by our anatomy,
That 'tis in vain to dew or mollify   430
It with thy tears, or sweat, or blood: nothing
Is worth our travail, grief, or perishing,
But those rich joys, which did possess her heart,
Of which she's now partaker and a part.

Conclusion.   But as in cutting up a man that's dead,   435
The body will not last out to have read
On every part, and therefore men direct
Their speech to parts that are of most effect,
So the world's carcass would not last if I
Were punctual[9] in this anatomy.   440
Nor smells it well to hearers, if one tell
Them their disease, who fain would think they're well.
Here therefore be the end: and, blessed maid,
Of whom is meant whatever hath been said,
Or shall be spoken well by any tongue,   445
Whose name refines coarse lines, and makes prose
    song,
Accept this tribute, and his first year's rent,
Who till his dark short taper's end be spent,
As oft as thy feast sees this widowed earth,

---

7. Then.
8. As contrasted with the earlier (and superior) golden and silver ages.

9. Dealing with a matter point by point; detailed.

Will yearly celebrate thy second birth,   450
That is, thy death. For though the soul of man
Be got when man is made, 'tis born but than[1]
When man doth die; our body's as the womb,
And, as a midwife, death directs it home.
And you, her creatures, whom she works upon,   455
And have your last and best concoction
From her example and her virtue, if you
In reverence to her, do think it due
That no one should her praises thus rehearse,
As matter fit for chronicle, not verse,   460
Vouchsafe to call to mind that God did make
A last, and lasting'st piece, a song.[2]   He spake
To *Moses* to deliver unto all
That song, because He knew they would let fall
The Law, the Prophets, and the History,   465
But keep the song still in their memory.
Such an opinion (in due measure) made
Me this great office boldly to invade.
Nor could incomprehensibleness deter
Me from thus trying to emprison her,   470
Which when I saw that a strict grave could do,
I saw not why verse might not do so too.
Verse hath a middle nature: heaven keeps souls,
The grave keeps bodies, verse the fame enrols.

1611

1. Then.
2. The Song of Moses (Deuteronomy xxxii).

Divine Poems

LA CORONA[1]

1.

Deign at my hands this crown of prayer and praise,
Weaved in my low devout melancholy,
Thou which of good hast, yea, art treasury,
All changing unchanged Ancient of days;
But do not, with a vile crown of frail bays,　　　　　5
Reward my muse's white sincerity,
But what Thy thorny crown gained, that give me,
A crown of Glory, which doth flower always;
The ends crown our works, but Thou crown'st our ends,
For, at our end begins our endless rest;　　　　　10
This first last end,[2] now zealously possessed,
With a strong sober thirst, my soul attends.
'Tis time that heart and voice be lifted high,
Salvation to all that will is nigh.

2. Annunciation

Salvation to all that will is nigh;
That All, which always is All everywhere,
Which cannot sin, and yet all sins must bear,
Which cannot die, yet cannot choose but die,
Lo, faithful Virgin, yields Himself to lie　　　　　5
In prison, in thy womb; and though He there
Can take no sin, nor thou give, yet He'll wear,
Taken from thence, flesh, which death's force may try.
Ere by the spheres time was created, thou
Wast in His mind, who is thy Son, and Brother,　　　　　10
Whom thou conceiv'st, conceived; yea thou art now
Thy Maker's maker, and thy Father's mother;
Thou hast light in dark; and shutst in little room,
Immensity cloistered in thy dear womb.

3. Nativity

Immensity cloistered in thy dear womb,
Now leaves His well-beloved imprisonment,

---

1. These seven sonnets are probably the "Holy Hymns and Sonnets" which Donne sent to Mrs. Magdalen Herbert, along with an introductory sonnet ad-dressed to her, in July 1607. "Corona" means both crown and wreath.
2. The Saviour. "I am*** the first and the last" (Revelation i:11).

There he hath made Himself to His intent
Weak enough, now into our world to come;
But oh, for thee, for Him, hath the Inn no room? 5
Yet lay Him in this stall, and from the Orient,
Stars, and wisemen will travel to prevent[3]
The effect of Herod's jealous general doom.[4]
Seest thou, my soul, with thy faith's eyes, how He
Which fills all place, yet none holds Him, doth lie? 10
Was not His pity towards thee wondrous high,
That would have need to be pitied by thee?
Kiss Him, and with Him into Egypt go,
With His kind mother, who partakes thy woe.

4. Temple

With His kind mother who partakes thy woe,
Joseph turn back; see where your child doth sit,
Blowing, yea blowing out those sparks of wit,
Which Himself on those Doctors did bestow;
The Word but lately could not speak, and lo 5
It suddenly speaks wonders; whence comes it,
That all which was, and all which should be writ,
A shallow seeming child should deeply know?
His Godhead was not soul to His manhood,
Nor had time mellowed Him to this ripeness, 10
But as for one which hath a long task, 'tis good,
With the Sun to begin his business,
He in His age's morning thus began
By miracles exceeding power of man.

5. Crucifying

By miracles exceeding power of man,
He faith in some, envy in some begat,
For, what weak spirits[5] admire, ambitious hate;
In both affections many to Him ran,
But, oh! the worst are most, they will and can, 5
Alas, and do, unto the immaculate,
Whose creature Fate is, now prescribe a Fate,
Measuring self-life's infinity to a span,
Nay to an inch. Lo, where condemned He
Bears His own cross, with pain, yet by and by 10
When it bears Him, He must bear more and die.
Now Thou art lifted up, draw me to Thee,
And at Thy death giving such liberal dole,
Moist, with one drop of Thy blood, my dry soul.

---

3. Precede.
4. *I.e.,* the Massacre of the Innocents; "doom" means "judgment."

5. Cf. Matthew v:3: "Blessed are the poor in spirit: for theirs is the kingdom of heaven."

6. Resurrection

Moist with one drop of Thy blood, my dry soul
Shall (though she now be in extreme degree
Too stony hard, and yet too fleshly) be
Freed by that drop from being starved, hard, or foul,
And life, by this death abled, shall control   5
Death, whom Thy death slew; nor shall to me
Fear of first or last death bring misery,
If in Thy little book my name Thou enroll,
Flesh in that long sleep is not putrefied,
But made that there, of which, and for which 'twas;   10
Nor can by other means be glorified.
May then sin's sleep, and death's, soon from me pass,
That waked from both, I again risen may
Salute the last, and everlasting day.

7. Ascension

Salute the last and everlasting day,
Joy at the uprising of this Sun, and Son,
Ye whose just tears, or tribulation
Have purely washed, or burnt your drossy clay;
Behold the Highest, parting hence away,   5
Lightens the dark clouds, which He treads upon,
Nor doth He by ascending, show alone,
But first He, and He first enters the way.
O strong Ram, which hast battered heaven for me,
Mild Lamb, which with Thy blood hast marked the path;   10
Bright Torch, which shin'st, that I the way may see,
Oh, with Thine own blood quench Thine own just wrath,
And if Thy holy Spirit, my Muse did raise,
Deign at my hands this crown of prayer and praise.

HOLY SONNETS[1]
(1633)

1 (II)

As due by many titles I resign
Myself to Thee, O God, first I was made
By Thee, and for Thee, and when I was decayed

1. The numbering (in Roman numerals) of the Holy Sonnets in the 1635 to 1669 editions and in Sir Herbert Grierson's edition has been retained in parentheses, for the critics have usually referred to the Holy Sonnets by means of these Roman numerals; but the sequence suggested by Helen Gardner in her edition of *The Divine Poems* has been adopted and her renumbering followed. If the sonnets are separate ejaculations, as Grierson thought, the order in which they are printed is not of consequence; however, if they in fact form a sequence, that fact will more readily become apparent by studying them in the proper sequence.

Thy blood bought that the which before was Thine;
I am Thy son, made with Thyself to shine,   5
Thy servant, whose pains thou hast still repaid,
Thy sheep, Thine Image, and, till I betrayed
Myself, a temple of Thy Spirit divine;
Why doth the devil then usurp on² me?
Why doth he steal, nay ravish that's Thy right?   10
Except Thou rise and for Thine own work fight,
Oh I shall soon despair, when I do see
That Thou lov'st mankind well, yet wilt not choose me,
And Satan hates me, yet is loath to lose me.

2 (IV)

Oh my black soul! now thou art summoned
By sickness, death's herald, and champion;
Thou art like a pilgrim, which abroad hath done
Treason, and durst not turn to whence he is fled,
Or like a thief, which till death's doom be read,   5
Wisheth himself delivered from prison;
But damned and haled to execution,
Wisheth that still he might be imprisoned.
Yet grace, if thou repent, thou canst not lack;
But who shall give thee that grace to begin?   10
Oh make thyself with holy mourning black,
And red with blushing, as thou art with sin;
Or wash thee in Christ's blood, which hath this might
That being red,³ it dyes red souls to white.

3 (VI)

This is my play's last scene, here heavens appoint
My pilgrimage's last mile; and my race,
Idly yet quickly run, hath this last pace,
My span's last inch, my minute's last point,
And gluttonous death will instantly unjoint   5
My body and soul, and I shall sleep a space,
But my ever-waking part shall see that face
Whose fear⁴ already shakes my every joint:
Then, as my soul to heaven, her first seat, takes flight,
And earth-born body in the earth shall dwell,   10
So, fall my sins, that all may have their right,
To where they're bred, and would press me, to hell.
Impute me righteous, thus purged of evil,
For thus I leave the world, the flesh, the devil.

2. Claim unjustly; appropriate wrongfully.
3. With a pun on "read" (understood);

red, as applied to man's soul, is the color
of sin.
4. The fear of whom.

4 (VII)

At the round earth's imagined corners,[5] blow
Your trumpets, angels, and arise, arise
From death, you numberless infinities
Of souls, and to your scattered bodies go,
All whom the flood did, and fire shall o'erthrow,   5
All whom war, dearth, age, agues, tyrannies,
Despair, law, chance, hath slain, and you whose eyes
Shall behold God and never taste death's woe.[6]
But let them sleep, Lord, and me mourn a space,
For if above all these my sins abound,   10
'Tis late to ask abundance of Thy grace
When we are there; here on this lowly ground,
Teach me how to repent; for that's as good
As if Thou hadst sealed my pardon with Thy blood.

5 (IX)

If poisonous minerals, and if that tree
Whose fruit threw death on else immortal us,
If lecherous goats, if serpents envious
Cannot be damned, alas, why should I be?
Why should intent or reason, born in me,   5
Make sins, else equal, in me more heinous?
And mercy being easy, and glorious
To God, in His stern wrath why threatens He?
But who am I that dare dispute with Thee?
O God, oh! of thine only worthy blood,   10
And my tears, make a heavenly Lethean[7] flood,
And drown in it my sin's black memory.
That Thou remember them,[8] some claim as debt,
I think it mercy, if Thou wilt forget.

6 (X)

Death be not proud, though some have called thee
Mighty and dreadful, for thou art not so;
For those whom thou think'st thou dost overthrow
Die not, poor death, nor yet canst thou kill me.
From rest and sleep, which but thy pictures be,   5
Much pleasure; then from thee much more must flow,
And soonest our best men with thee do go,
Rest of their bones, and soul's delivery.[9]

---

5. " *** I saw four angels standing on the four corners of the earth," (Revelation vii:1).

6. " *** there be some standing here, which shall not taste of death, till they see the kingdom of God." (Luke ix:27; see also I Corinthians xv:51–57).

7. Inducing forgetfulness.

8. In order to pardon them.

9. Rescue, deliverance; also, the bringing forth or "birth" of the soul.

Thou art slave to fate, chance, kings, and desperate men,
And dost with poison, war, and sickness dwell; 10
And poppy or charms can make us sleep as well,
And better than thy stroke; why swell'st[1] thou then?
One short sleep past, we wake eternally,
And death shall be no more; death, thou shalt die.

7 (XI)

Spit in my face you Jews, and pierce my side,
Buffet, and scoff, scourge, and crucify me,
For I have sinned, and sinned, and only He
Who could do no iniquity hath died:
But by my death cannot be satisfied[2] 5
My sins, which pass the Jews' impiety:
They killed once an inglorious man, but I
Crucify him daily, being now glorified.
Oh let me then His strange love still admire:
Kings pardon, but He bore our punishment. 10
And Jacob came clothed in vile harsh attire
But to supplant, and with gainful intent;[3]
God clothed himself in vile man's flesh that so
He might be weak enough to suffer woe.

8 (XII)

Why are we by all creatures waited on?
Why do the prodigal elements supply
Life and food to me, being more pure than I,
Simple, and further from corruption?[4]
Why brook'st thou, ignorant horse, subjection? 5
Why dost thou, bull and boar, so sillily
Dissemble weakness, and by one man's stroke die,
Whose whole kind you might swallow and feed upon?
Weaker I am, woe is me, and worse than you,
You have not sinned, nor need be timorous. 10
But wonder at a greater wonder, for to us
Created nature doth these things subdue,
But their Creator, whom sin nor nature tied,
For us, His creatures, and his foes, hath died.

9 (XIII)

What if this present were the world's last night?
Mark in my heart, O soul, where thou dost dwell,
The picture of Christ crucified, and tell

1. Puff up with pride.
2. Atoned for.
3. By disguising himself as his older brother, Jacob gained his father's blessing (Genesis xxvii).
4. Being uncompounded, and thus less subject to decay.

Whether that countenance can thee affright,
Tears in His eyes quench the amazing light, 5
Blood fills His frowns, which from His pierced head fell.
And can that tongue adjudge thee unto hell,
Which prayed forgiveness for His foes' fierce spite?
No, no; but as in my idolatry
I said to all my profane mistresses, 10
Beauty, of pity, foulness only is
A sign of rigor:[5] so I say to thee,
To wicked spirits are horrid shapes assigned,
This beauteous form assures a piteous mind.

10 (XIV)

Batter my heart, tnree-personed God; for You
As yet but knock, breathe, shine, and seek to mend;
That I may rise and stand, o'erthrow me, and bend
Your force, to break, blow, burn, and make me new.
I, like an usurped town, to another due, 5
Labor to admit You, but Oh, to no end!
Reason, Your viceroy in me, me should defend,
But is captived, and proves weak or untrue.
Yet dearly I love You, and would be loved fain,
But am betrothed unto Your enemy: 10
Divorce me, untie or break that knot again,
Take me to You, imprison me, for I,
Except You enthrall me, never shall be free,
Nor ever chaste, except You ravish me.

11 (XV)

Wilt thou love God, as He thee? then digest,
My soul, this wholesome meditation,
How God the Spirit, by angels waited on
In heaven, doth make His Temple in thy breast.[6]
The Father, having begot a Son most blest, 5
And still begetting (for he ne'er begun),
Hath deigned to choose thee, by adoption,
Coheir to His glory and sabbath's endless rest;
And as a robbed man which by search doth find
His stol'n stuff sold must lose or buy it again, 10
The Son of glory came down, and was slain,
Us whom He had made, and Satan stol'n,[7] to unbind.
'Twas much that man was made like God before,
But that God should be made like man, much more.

5. Beauty is a sign of pity; ugliness is a sign of strictness, harshness.
6. "Know ye not that ye are the temple of God, and that the Spirit of God dwelleth in you?" (I Corinthians iii:16).
7. And whom Satan had stolen.

12 (XVI)

Father, part of His double interest
Unto Thy kingdom, Thy Son gives to me;
His jointure in the knotty Trinity[8]
He keeps, and gives to me His death's conquest.
This Lamb, whose death with life the world hath blest,   5
Was from the world's beginning slain, and He
Hath made two wills,[9] which with the legacy
Of His and Thy kingdom do Thy Sons invest.
Yet such are those laws that men argue yet
Whether a man those statutes can fulfill;   10
None doth; but all-healing grace and Spirit
Revive again what law and letter kill.[1]
Thy law's abridgment and Thy last command
Is all but love;[2] oh let that last will stand!

HOLY SONNETS
(added in 1635)

1 (I)

Thou hast made me, and shall Thy work decay?
Repair me now, for now mine end doth haste,
I run to death, and death meets me as fast,
And all my pleasures are as yesterday;
I dare not move my dim eyes any way,   5
Despair behind and death before doth cast
Such terror, and my feebled flesh doth waste
By sin in it, which it towards hell doth weigh;
Only Thou art above, and when towards Thee
By Thy leave I can look, I rise again;   10
But our old subtle foe so tempteth me
That not one hour myself I can sustain;
Thy grace may wing me to prevent[3] his art,
And thou like adamant[4] draw mine iron heart.

1635

2 (V)

I am a little world made cunningly
Of elements and an angelic sprite,

---

8. "Jointure": "the holding of an estate by two or more persons in joint-tenancy"; "knotty": "hard to explain" as well as, perhaps, "closely or inextricably tied together."
9. *I.e.*, the Old and New Testaments.
1. " *** the letter killeth, but the spirit giveth life." (II Corinthians iii:6).
2. "This is my commandment, That ye love one another, as I have loved you." (John xv:12)
3. Strengthen me to frustrate.
4. A magnet.

But black sin hath betrayed to endless night
My world's both parts, and, oh, both parts must die.
You which beyond that heaven which was most high   5
Have found new spheres, and of new lands can write,[5]
Pour new seas in mine eyes, that so I might
Drown my world with my weeping earnestly,
Or wash it if it must be drowned no more.[6]
But oh it must be burnt![7] Alas, the fire   10
Of lust and envy have burnt it heretofore,
And made it fouler; let their flames retire,
And burn me, O Lord, with a fiery zeal
Of Thee and Thy house, which doth in eating heal.[8]

1635

3 (III)

O might those sighs and tears return again
Into my breast and eyes, which I have spent,
That I might in this holy discontent
Mourn with some fruit, as I have mourned in vain;
In mine idolatry[9] what showers of rain   5
Mine eyes did waste! What griefs my heart did rent![1]
That sufferance[2] was my sin; now I repent;
'Cause I did suffer I must suffer pain.
The hydroptic[3] drunkard and night-scouting thief,
The itchy lecher and self-tickling proud[4]   10
Have the remembrance of past joys for relief
Of coming ills.   To poor me is allowed
No ease; for long yet vehement grief hath been
The effect and cause, the punishment and sin.

1635

4 (VIII)

If faithful souls be alike glorified
As angels, then my father's soul doth see,
And adds this even to full felicity,
That valiantly I hell's wide mouth o'erstride.
But if our minds to these souls be descried   5
By circumstances and by signs that be
Apparent in us, not immediately,

---

5. Donne addresses the astronomers and explorers who had made new discoveries.
6. After the Flood, God promised Noah that "neither shall there any more be a flood to destroy the earth." (Genesis ix:11).
7. By the fire which, it was believed, would end the world.

8. "For the zeal of thine house hath eaten me up;" (Psalms lxix:9).
9. *I.e.*, when I worshiped a mistress.
1. Tear in pieces.
2. Suffering; also, indulgence in excessive grief.
3. Dropsical; insatiably thirsty.
4. Proud man.

How shall my mind's white truth by them be tried?[5]
They see idolatrous lovers weep and mourn,
And vile blasphemous conjurers to call 10
On Jesus' name, and pharisaical
Dissemblers feign devotion.   Then turn,
O pensive soul, to God, for He knows best
Thy true grief, for He put it in my breast.

1635

HOLY SONNETS
(from the Westmoreland MS.)

1 (XVII)

Since she whom I loved hath paid her last debt
To nature, and to hers, and my good is dead,[6]
And her soul early into heaven ravished,
Wholly in heavenly things my mind is set.
Here the admiring her my mind did whet 5
To seek Thee, God; so streams do show the head;
But though I have found Thee, and Thou my thirst hast fed,
A holy thirsty dropsy melts me yet.
But why should I beg more love, when as Thou
Dost woo my soul, for hers off'ring all Thine: 10
And dost not only fear lest I allow
My love to saints and angels, things divine,
But in Thy tender jealousy dost doubt[7]
Lest the world, flesh, yea devil put Thee out.

W

2 (XVIII)

Show me, dear Christ, Thy spouse, so bright and clear.
What, is it she which on the other shore
Goes richly painted?[8] or which robbed and tore
Laments and mourns in Germany and here?[9]
Sleeps she a thousand, then peeps up one year? 5
Is she self-truth and errs? now new, now outwore?
Doth she, and did she, and shall she evermore

5. Do the faithful souls who have de-
parted this world know our minds by immediate intuition, as angels know, or do
they know our minds by reasoning from
outer circumstances and signs? If the
latter, how can they distinguish between
true grief and the falseness of idolatrous
lovers, of conjurers (who try to effect a
supernatural event by invoking a sacred
name), and of pharisees (self-righteous
hypocrites)?
6. Donne's wife, Anne More, who died
on August 15, 1617, the seventh day
after the birth of her twelfth child.
7. Fear.
8. The Church of Rome.
9. The Protestant Church.

On one, on seven, or on no hill appear?[1]
Dwells she with us, or like adventuring knights
First travail[2] we to seek, and then make love?   10
Betray, kind husband, Thy spouse to our sights,
And let mine amorous soul court Thy mild Dove,
Who is most true and pleasing to Thee then
When she is embraced and open to most men.

                                                                W

3 (XIX)

Oh, to vex me, contraries meet in one;
Inconstancy unnaturally hath begot
A constant habit; that when I would not
I change in vows and in devotion.
As humorous[3] is my contrition   5
As my profane love, and as soon forgot:
As riddlingly distempered, cold and hot;
As praying, as mute; as infinite, as none.
I durst not view heaven yesterday; and today
In prayers and flattering speeches I court God;   10
Tomorrow I quake with true fear of His rod.
So my devout fits come and go away
Like a fantastic ague:[4] save that here
Those are my best days when I shake with fear.

                                                                W

Upon the Annunciation and Passion
Falling upon One Day. 1608[1]

Tamely,[2] frail body, abstain today; today
My soul eats twice, Christ hither and away.
She sees Him man, so like God made in this,
That of them both a circle emblem is,
Whose first and last concur; this doubtful day   5
Of feast or fast, Christ came and went away;
She sees Him nothing twice at once, who's all;
She sees a Cedar[3] plant itself and fall,
Her Maker put to making, and the head
Of life at once not yet alive yet dead;   10
She sees at once the virgin mother stay

---

1. Mt. Moriah, where Solomon's temple stood; the seven hills of Rome; the Genevan Church stood on no hill.
2. Labor; travel.
3. Changeable.
4. A fever, with hot and cold spells and shaking or shivering.

1. In 1608, Good Friday occurred on March 25, the annual date of the feast of the Annunciation, when the Angel Gabriel announced to the Virgin Mary the Incarnation of Christ.
2. Submissively.
3. Symbol of God.

Reclused at home, public at Golgotha;[4]
Sad and rejoiced she's seen at once, and seen
At almost fifty and at scarce fifteen;
At once a Son is promised her, and gone;   15
Gabriel gives Christ to her, He her to John;
Not fully a mother, she's in orbity,[5]
At once receiver and the legacy;
All this, and all between, this day hath shown,
The abridgment of Christ's story, which makes one   20
(As in plain maps, the furthest west is east)
Of the Angels' *Ave* and *Consummatum est*.[6]
How well the Church, God's court of faculties,
Deals in some times and seldom joining these!
As by the self-fixed Pole we never do   25
Direct our course, but the next star[7] thereto,
Which shows where the other is and which we say
(Because it strays not far) doth never stray,
So God by His Church, nearest to Him, we know
And stand firm, if we by her motion go;   30
His Spirit, as His fiery pillar doth
Lead, and His Church, as cloud, to one end both.
This Church, by letting these days join, hath shown
Death and conception in mankind is one:
Or 'twas in Him the same humility   35
That He would be a man and leave to be:
Or as creation He had made, as God,
With the last judgment but one period,
His imitating Spouse would join in one
Manhood's extremes: He shall come, He is gone: 40
Or as though one blood drop, which thence did fall,
Accepted, would have served, He yet shed all;
So though the least of His pains, deeds, or words,
Would busy a life, she all this day affords;
This treasure then, in gross, my soul uplay,   45
And in my life retail it every day.

Good Friday, 1613. Riding Westward

Let man's soul be a sphere, and then, in this,
The intelligence that moves, devotion is,[1]
And as the other spheres, by being grown
Subject to foreign motions,[2] lose their own,
And being by others hurried every day,   5
Scarce in a year their natural form obey,

---

4. The place where Christ was crucified.
5. Bereavement.
6. The first word of Gabriel to Mary was *Ave*, "Hail" (Luke i:28), and Christ's last words before dying on the cross were "It is finished" (John xix:30).
7. The North Star, which guides sailors even though it is not the actual North

Pole, the zenith of which is about one degree distant from the North Star.
1. Each sphere was thought to have a guiding intelligence; so devotion should be the guiding principle or form of a man's soul.
2. *I.e.*, of other spheres.

Pleasure or business, so our souls admit
For their first mover, and are whirled by it.[3]
Hence is 't that I am carried towards the West
This day, when my soul's form bends toward the East.   10
There I should see a Sun, by rising, set,
And by that setting endless day beget;
But that Christ on this cross did rise and fall,
Sin had eternally benighted all.
Yet dare I almost be glad I do not see   15
That spectacle of too much weight for me.
Who sees God's face, that is self life, must die;[4]
What a death where it then to see God die?
It made His own lieutenant, Nature, shrink;
It made His footstool crack, and the sun wink.[5]   20
Could I behold those hands which span the poles,
And tune[6] all spheres at once, pierced with those holes?
Could I behold that endless height which is
Zenith to us, and our antipodes,[7]
Humbled below us? or that blood which is   25
The seat of all our souls, if not of His,
Make dirt of dust, or that flesh which was worn
By God, for His apparel, ragg'd and torn?
If on these things I durst not look, durst I
Upon his miserable mother cast mine eye,   30
Who was God's partner here, and furnished thus
Half of that sacrifice which ransomed us?
Though these things, as I ride, be from mine eye,
They're present yet unto my memory,
For that looks towards them; and Thou look'st towards me,   35
O Saviour, as Thou hang'st upon the tree;
I turn my back to Thee but to receive
Corrections, till Thy mercies bid Thee leave.[8]
O think me worth Thine anger, punish me,
Burn off my rusts and my deformity,   40
Restore Thine image so much, by Thy grace,
That Thou may'st know me, and I'll turn my face.

A Hymn to Christ, at the Author's Last Going into Germany[1]

In what torn ship soever I embark,
That ship shall be my emblem of Thy ark;

3. Our souls are moved or influenced not by devotion to God but by the spheres of pleasure or business.
4. " *** Thou canst not see my face: for there shall no man see me, and live." (Exodus xxxiii:20).
5. The earth is God's footstool (Isaiah lxvi:1); an earthquake and an eclipse attended Christ's crucifixion (Matthew xxvii:51, 45).
6. Give motion and music to.
7. "Zenith": the point in the sky directly overhead; highest point or state. "Antipodes": those who dwell on the opposite side of the globe; exact opposite.
8. Stop.
1. Donne traveled abroad in 1619–20 on a diplomatic mission.

What sea soever swallow me, that flood
Shall be to me an emblem of Thy blood;
Though Thou with clouds of anger do disguise   5
Thy face, yet through that mask I know those eyes,
    Which, though they turn away sometimes,
        They never will despise.

I sacrifice this island[2] unto Thee,
And all whom I loved there, and who loved me;   10
When I have put our seas 'twixt them and me,
Put thou Thy sea[3] betwixt my sins and Thee.
As the tree's sap doth seek the root below
In winter, in my winter now I go
    Where none but Thee, the eternal root   15
        Of true love, I may know.

Nor Thou nor Thy religion dost control[4]
The amorousness of an harmonious soul,
But Thou would'st have that love Thyself; as Thou
Art jealous, Lord, so I am jealous now;   20
Thou lov'st not, till from loving more, Thou free
My soul: whoever gives, takes liberty:
    O, if Thou car'st not whom I love,
        Alas, Thou lov'st not me.

Seal then this bill of my divorce to all   25
On whom those fainter beams of love did fall;
Marry those loves which in youth scattered be
On fame, wit, hopes (false mistresses) to Thee.
Churches are best for prayer that have least light:
To see God only, I go out of sight;   30
    And to 'scape stormy days, I choose
        An everlasting night.

Hymn to God my God, in my Sickness[1]

Since I am coming to that holy room
    Where, with Thy choir of saints forevermore,
I shall be made Thy Music, as I come
    I tune the instrument here at the door,
    And what I must do then, think now before.   5

Whilst my physicians by their love are grown
    Cosmographers, and I their map,[2] who lie
Flat on this bed, that by them may be shown

2. England.
3. Christ's blood.
4. Censure.
1. Izaak Walton dated this poem eight
days before Donne's death on March 31,

1631; but there is other evidence that
the poem may have been written during
Donne's illness in 1623.
2. It was believed that every man was a
"little world."

That this is my South-west discovery
Per fretum febris, by these straits to die,[3]　　　10

I joy, that in these straits, I see my West;
　For, though their current yield return to none,
What shall my West hurt me?　As West and East[4]
　In all flat maps (and I am one) are one,
　So death doth touch the resurrection.　　　15

Is the Pacific Sea my home?　Or are
　The Eastren riches?　Is *Jerusalem?*
Anyan,[5] and *Magellan,* and *Gibraltar,*
　All straits, and none but straits, are ways to them,
　Whether where *Japhet* dwelt, or *Cham,* or *Shem.*[6]　　　20

We think that *Paradise* and *Calvary,*
　Christ's Cross, and *Adam's* tree, stood in one place;
Look, Lord, and find both *Adams* met in me;
　As the first *Adam's* sweat surrounds my face,
　May the last *Adam's*[7] blood my soul embrace.　　　25

So, in His purple[8] wrapped, receive me, Lord,
　By these His thorns give me His other crown;
And as to others' souls I preached Thy word,
　Be this my text, my sermon to mine own,
　Therefore that He may raise, the Lord throws down.　　30

　　　　　　　　　　　　　　　　　　　　　　1635

A Hymn to God the Father[1]

Wilt Thou forgive that sin where I begun,
　Which is my sin, though it were done before?
Wilt Thou forgive those sins through which I run,
　And do them still, though still I do deplore?
　　When Thou hast done, Thou hast not done,　　5
　　For I have more.

Wilt Thou forgive that sin by which I have won
　Others to sin? and made my sin their door?
Wilt Thou forgive that sin which I did shun
　A year or two, but wallowed in a score?
　　When Thou hast done, Thou hast not done,　　10
　　For I have more.

3. As Magellan made a southwest journey through the Straits of Magellan (and
later died in the Philippines), so Donne
will make his last journey "through the
straits of fever" (*per fretum febris*);
south connotes heat, and west, where the
sun sets, connotes death.
4. The east, where the sun (Son) rises,
connotes life, rebirth.
5. Bering Strait.

6. Noah's sons, whose descendants were
said to inhabit, respectively, Europe, Af-
rica, Asia.
7. Christ's.
8. Christ's blood; also, the color of royal
robes and of the garments the soldiers
put on Christ (Mark xv:17).
1. Donne puns on his name throughout
this. poem, which Walton says Donne
wrote in his illness of 1623.

I have a sin of fear, that when I have spun
My last thread, I shall perish on the shore;
Swear by Thyself that at my death Thy Sun   15
Shall shine as it shines now, and heretofore;
And, having done that, Thou hast done,
I have no more.

Textual Notes

With the following exceptions, the text of this edition is that of the 1633 edition:

> 1611 edition: *An Anatomy of the World: The First Anniversary.* (The marginal notes and the sub-title, *The First Anniversary*, are from the 1612 edition of *The Anniversaries*.)
>
> 1635 edition: "Farewell to Love," "A Lecture upon the Shadow," Elegies XI and XVI, Holy Sonnets I, III, V, VIII, "Hymn to God my God, in my Sickness."
>
> 1650 edition: "Sonnet. The Token" and "Self-Love."
>
> 1669 edition: Elegy XIX.
>
> Westmoreland manuscript: Holy Sonnets XVII, XVIII, XIX.

This is to say that the text is based upon the first edition of each poem or, in the case of the three Holy Sonnets not printed in the early editions, upon the Westmoreland manuscript. Some of the poems printed in 1633 did not have titles; the titles for these few poems, titles which have since become standard, are supplied by editions subsequent to 1633 and by manuscripts. In order to avoid needless clutter and to make these textual notes most useful for the student, I have excluded semi-substantive and inconsequential departures and variants and have noted only substantive departures from the authoritative text of any poem and some significant variants in other manuscripts and editions. Excepting the Westmoreland manuscript, manuscript information is obtained from Sir Herbert Grierson's edition of *The Poems of John Donne.* In the following notes, the editions, which almost invariably have some manuscript authority behind them, are indicated by the year of their publication; 1633–69 means all three of the editions of 1633, 1635, and 1669; 1635–69 means the editions of 1635 and 1669; W means the Westmoreland manuscripts; MSS. means "at least some manuscripts"; and *om.* means "omitted in."

An additional word about my principles for updating would seem to be in order. One of the major problems of updating the punctuation is to bring it more in accord with modern practice without losing any of the original meaning and without introducing any new, extraneous meanings. In general, this principle would make for a somewhat lighter punctuation than Donne's. There are, however, numerous complications. For example, the original 1633 punctuation of lines 2 and 3 of "The Sun Rising" permits two readings: line 3 as appositive to "thus"; and "thus" as an adverb modifying "call." Although the second reading is perhaps more likely, to select editorially only one reading over another seems, in this case and many similar ones, unwarranted and arbitrary. Wherever possible, the reader should be presented with the alternatives of the original and be allowed to choose for himself. Thus, although modern practice would call for the removal of the commas after "thus" and "windows," in this instance heavier punctuation (an additional comma after "curtains") is required rather than lighter. In the last stanza of "The Canonization," for another example, modern practice of punctuation calls for the addition of quotation marks, a parenthesis, and an exclamation point. But because such heavier punctuation is in this case interpretive, the Textual Notes indicate what the original punctuation was (as well as the variants "our love" and "your love"), so that a teacher or student may argue for another reading if he chooses. Updating spelling and capitalization is relatively easier, since the great majority of cases offers no difficulties or complications. Nothing significant is lost, for example, by dropping the extra final *e* from two words in the first line of "The Indifferent": "I can love both faire and browne." (Indeed, besides permitting some greater ease of reading, updating can prevent misreadings and save classroom time: one student, zealously looking for hidden meanings, asked, "Might Donne mean 'I can love both fairy and brownie?'") On the other hand, in some instances, Donne's original spelling must stand: to change "thorough" to "through" would affect the meter; to correct "than" to "then" would sometimes spoil a rhyme; to alter "travail" to "travel" would obscure a pun; and so on. In such instances, I have printed the original and glossed the text where necessary. On the interesting and complicated matter of Donne's elision, these principles and practices have been followed: (1) the silent *e* has been inserted before the *d* in such words as "lov'd" and "wean'd." An accent over *ed* has not been inserted even when it seemed likely that the *ed* should be sounded as an extra syllable; instead, following the original text, I have left the decision to the reader. (2) Many of Donne's elisions are like modern practice; or can readily be made so: for example, "oe'r," "return'st," " 'gainst"; "she'is becomes "she's," "I'am" becomes "I'm," and so on. (Sometimes Donne inserts the apostrophe before *st*, sometimes not: "hadst" and "had'st," for example, appear within four lines of each other.) (3) Donne often uses an apostrophe between two words (sometimes eliding a letter, sometimes not) when the first word ends with a vowel and the next begins with a vowel (or *h*). Since this is very unlike modern practice and the student may have some difficulty determining what is intended, the apostrophe has been deleted and the elided letter (if any) restored. With this note (and perhaps even left to his own devices) the student should be able to make most such elisions naturally. (4) For a very few of Donne's spellings it has been necessary to add an apostrophe, with results that are not strictly in accord with modern practice: although such words as "shouldst" and "leftst" remain as they are, "wandring" becomes "wand'ring," "swolne" becomes "swol'n," and so forth. If strict consistency has been sacrificed, it has been, I believe, for the sake of better, special purposes.

The Good-Morrow
14/ our world *MSS.*
21/ Love just alike in all, none of these loves can die. *1635–69.*

Song, "Go and catch *** "
10/ borne *1633–35*; born *1669.*
11/ go see *1669.*

The Sun Rising
12/ Dost thou not think *1635–69.*
14/ long? *1635–69.*

Love's Usury
13/ sport *1633–35*; sport; *1669.*
15/ let not report *1635.*
20/ Thou covet most, *1633, 1669*; Thou covet most *1635*; Thou covet, most *MSS.*

The Canonization
15/ one man *1669.*
37–45/ *no quotations marks, parenthesis, exclamation point 1633–69.*
40/ extract *MSS.*; contract *1633–69.*
45/ our love, *1633–35*; your love. *1669.*

The Legacy
14/ did lie, *1633*; should lie, *1635*; should lie *1669.*

The Anniversary
3/ as these pass, *1635*; (which makes times, as they pass) *1669.*
22/ But now *1633–69*; But we *MSS.*

Twickenham Garden
15/ nor leave this garden, *1635–69*; nor yet leave loving, *1633.*
17/ groan *MSS.*; grow *1633–69.*

A Valediction: Of the Book
18/ Record. *1633, 1669*; Record, *1635.*
25/ Goths inundate us, *MSS*; the Goths invade us, *1633–35*; Goths invade us, *1669.*
53/ their nothing *1635*; there something *1633, 1669.*

Community
3/ there *1635–69*; these *1633.*

Love's Growth
9/ stuffs, paining soul, or sense, *1633*; stuffs, vexing soul, or sense, *1635*; stuffs vexing soul, or sense, *1669.*

Love's Exchange
36/ For, this *1633–69.*

Confined Love
11/ all night *1669.*
16/ with all *1635–69.*

The Dream
10/ do *MSS.*; act *1633–69.*
14/ (Thou lovest truth) but an Angel, *MSS.*

A Valediction: Of Weeping
8/ thou falls *MSS.*; thou falst *1633–69.*

Love's Alchemy
23–24/ *MSS.*; at their best, Sweetness, and wit they'are, but, *Mummy,* possessed. *1633–35*; *no punctuation* 1669.

The Curse
14–16/ Or may he for her virtue reverence
One that hates him only for impotence,
And equal Traitors be she and his sense. *1635–69.*

A Nocturnal upon St. Lucy's Day ***
12/ every *1633*; a very *1635–69.*
16/ emptiness *1633–35*; emptiness, *1669.*

The Broken Heart
8/ flask *1633*; flash *1635–69.*

The Ecstasy
55/forces, sense, *MSS.*; senses force *1633–69.*

Love's Diet
25/ reclaim'd *1635–69*; redeem'd *1633.*

The Will
36/ do *1635–69*; did *1633.*

The Funeral
17/ with me, *1635–69*; by me, *1633.*
24/ save *MSS.*; have *1633–69.*

The Blossom
24/ *MSS.*; need your heart? *1633–69.*

The Damp
24/ Naked *1635–69*; In that *1633.*

The Dissolution
12/ neere *1635–69*; ne'r *1633.*

The Prohibition
5/ *1635–69*; By being to me then that which thou wast; *1633.*
18/ neither's *MSS.*; ne'r their *1633–69.*
22/ Stage, *1635–69*; stay, *1633.*
23–24/ *MSS.*; Then lest thou thy *** too. *1635*;
Lest thou thy love and hate and me undo
To let me live, oh love and hate me too. *1633.*

The Expiration
9/ Or, *1635–69*; Oh, *1633.*

The Paradox
20/ lie *MSS.*; die *1633–69.*

Farewell to Love
30/ Eager, *1635–69.*

A Lecture upon the Shadow
  26/ first *MSS.*; short *1635–69*.

Sonnet. The Token
  14/ desir'd because *** best; *MSS.*;
desired 'cause 'tis like thee best; *1650*;
desired, 'cause 'tis like the best; *1669*.

Self-Love
  6/ *MS.*; And cannot pleasure chose,
1650, 1669.
  17/ *MSS.*; prays, *1650, 1669*.

Elegy IV
  7–8/ *1635–69*; om. *1633*.
  21/ And to try *1635–69*; To try
1633.

Elegy IX
  3/ *1633*; your love *1635*.
  8/ she's *1635–69, MSS.*; they're
1633.
  50/ ebb on *1635–69, MSS.*; ebb out
1633.

Elegy XI
  11/ fault *MSS.*; taint *MSS.*; way
1635–69.
  24/ *MSS.*; their Country's natural
1669, MSS.
  40/ *1669*; ruin'd: ragged and decay'd
1635.
  60/ schemes *MSS.*; scenes *1635–69*.

Elegy XVI
  28/ mind's *MSS.*; mind *1635–69*.
  37/ *1635*; Will quickly know thee,
and know thee, and alas *W*.

Elegy XIX
  5/ glistering *MSS.*; glittering *1669*.
  10/ 'tis your *MSS.*; it is *1669*.
  14/ from *MSS.*; through *1669*.
  16/ on you *MSS.*; on your head
1669.
  17/ safely *MSS.*; softly *1669*.
  20/ Received by *MSS.*; Revealed to
1669.
  28/ *MSS.*; My Kingdom's safest,
1669.
  30/ *MSS.*; How am I blest in thus
1669.
  38/ covet theirs, *MSS.*; court that,
1669.
  41/ *MSS.*; Themselves are only mystic books, which we, *1669*.
  44/ a *MSS.*; thy *1669*.
  46/ *MSS.*; There is no penance due
to innocence: *1669*.

Epithalamion Made at Lincoln's Inn
  23/ *MSS.*; fair and rich, in *1633–69*.
  26/ *W*; Some of these Senators
wealths deep oceans, *1633, MSS.*; Sons
of those Senators, *1635–69, MSS.*
  46/ *W*; Always *1633–69*.
  59/ run *MSS.*; come *1633*.

Satire III
  33–34/ foe, the foul devil h'is, whom
1633; foes the foul devil, he, whom

1635; foes: The foul devil (he, whom
1669; Know thy foes; the foul Devil
whom *MSS.*
  85/ do. *1635–69*; do *1633*.
  90/ here *MSS.*; om. *1633–69*.

The Storm
  38/ I, and the Sun, *1633–69*.

The Calm
  38/ Pinnaces *1635*; venices *1633*.

To Sir Henry Wotton
  2/ Calis *1633–69*.
  14/ wishing prayers, *1633*; wishes,
prayers, *1635*; wishing, prayers, *1669*.

To the Countess of Bedford
  16/ voice *1635–69*; faith *1633*.
  19/ *1633*; high to sense deep-rooted
stick, *1635*; high do seem, deep-rooted
stick, *1669*.
  36/ This *1635–69*; Thy *1633*.

To Sir Edward Herbert ***
  35/ show; *1669*; show, *1633–35*.
  38/ All, All *** chaw. *1633*; All:
All *** chaw, *1635*; All; All *** chaw,
1669.

An Anatomy of the World
  2/ Who all do celebrate *1633*.
  129/ try *1633*; try; *1611–12*.
  130/ new *1611, 1612 errata*; true
1612, 1633.
  153/ close weaving *1633*; close-
weaning *1611–12*.
  217/ there *1612 errata*; then *1611,
1612, 1633*.
  259/ there *1612 errata*; then *1611,
1612, 1633*.
  262/ towns *1612 errata*; towers *1611,
1612 1633*.
  474/ fame *1612 errata, 1633*; same
1611, 1612.

La Corona
3. Nativity
  8/ *MSS., 1669*; effects *1633–35*.

6. Resurrection
  8/ little *1633*; life *1635–69*.
  12/ *MSS.*; death *1633–69*.

Holy Sonnets
3 (VI)
  4/ last point, *MSS.*; latest point,
1633–69.
  7/ *1633*; Or presently, I know not,
see that Face, *MSS.*

4 (VII)
  6/ dearth *W*; death *1633–69, MSS.*

8 (XII)
  1/ am I *W*.

9 (XIII)
  4/ that *MSS.*; his *1633–69*.
  14/ assures *MSS.*; assumes *1633–69*.

12 (**XVI**)
  9/ those *MSS.*; these *1633-69*; thy
MSS.
    11/ None doth, but thy *** Spirit,
        1633;
      None doth; but thy *** Spirit
        1635–69;
      None doth; but all-healing ***
        Spirit *MSS.*
    14/ that *MSS.*; this *1633-69*; thy
MSS.

2 (**V**)
  6/ lands *MSS.*; land *1635–69*.
  11/ have *MSS.*; *om. 1635–69*.

3 (**III**)
  7/ sin, now I repent; *W*; sin I now
repent, *1635*.

4 (**VIII**)
  7/ us, *W*; us *1635–69*.

14/ true *W*; *om. 1635–69*. in *W*; into
1635–69.

1 (**XVII**)
  10/ Dost woe my soul for hers; *W*.

Upon the Annunciation and Passion ***
  10/ and dead; *1635–69*.
  37/ had *MSS.*; hath *1633*.

Good Friday, 1613 ***
  22/ tune *1633–69*; turn *MSS.*
  24/ and *1633–69*; and to' *MSS.*
  27/ Make *MSS.*; Made *1633–69*.

A Hymn to God the Father
  2/ is *MSS.*; was *1633*.
  3/ those sins *MSS.*; that sin; *1633*.
  4/ do them *MSS.*; do run *1633*.
  15/ Swear *** Sun *MSS.*; But swear
*** son *1633*.
  16/ it *MSS.*; he *1633*.
  18/ have *MSS.*; fear *1633*.

Criticism

Donne and Metaphysical Poetry

BEN JONSON

[Conversations on Donne]†

That Done's Anniversarie was profane and full of blasphemies:
that he told Mr. Done, if it had been written of the Virgin Marie it
had been something; to which he answered that he described the Idea
of a Woman, and not as she was. That Done, for not keeping of accent, deserved hanging.***

He esteemeth John Done the first poet in the world in some things:
his verses of the Lost Chaine he heth by heart; and that passage of the
Calme, *That dust and feathers doe not stirr, all was so quiet.* Affirmeth
Done to have written all his best pieces ere he was 25 years old.***

Done's grandfather, on the mother side, was Heywood the Epi-
gramatist. That Done himself, for not being understood, would
perish.***

THOMAS CAREW

An Elegie upon the Death of the Deane of Pauls, Dr. John Donne††

> Can we not force from widdowed Poetry,
> Now thou art dead (Great DONNE) one Elegie
> To crowne thy Hearse? Why yet dare we not trust
> Though with unkneaded dowe-bak't[1] prose they dust,
> Such as the uncisor'd[2] Churchman from the flower   5
> Of fading Rhetorique, short liv'd as his houre,

---

† In 1618-19 Jonson journeyed to Scotland and stayed with William Drummond of Hawthornden, who recorded
Jonson's opinions in a short book, *Ben
Jonson's Conversations with Drummond
of Hawthornden* (published 1833), from
which these extracts were taken.

†† This elegy yas first printed in
Poems (1633).
1. Dough-baked; *i.e.,* inadequately
baked [*Editor*].
2. Unshorn, as a sign of mourning
[*Editor*].

Dry as the sand that measures it, should lay
Upon thy Ashes, on the funerall day?
Have we no voice, no tune? Did'st thou dispense
Through all our language, both the words and sense?   10
'Tis a sad truth; The Pulpit may her plaine,
And sober Christian precepts still retaine,
Doctrines it may, and wholesome Uses frame,
Grave Homilies, and Lectures, But the flame
Of thy brave Soule, that shot such heat and light,   15
As burnt our earth, and made our darknesse bright,
Committed holy Rapes upon our Will,
Did through the eye the melting heart distill;
And the deepe knowledge of darke truths so teach,
As sense might judge, what phansie could not reach;   20
Must be desir'd[3] for ever. So the fire,
That fills with spirit and heat the Delphique quire,[4]
Which kindled first by thy Promethean[5] breath,
Glow'd here a while, lies quench't now in thy death;
The Muses garden with Pedantique weedes   25
O'rspred, was purg'd by thee; The lazie seeds
Of servile imitation throwne away;
And fresh invention planted, Thou didst pay
The debts of our penurious bankrupt age;
Licentious thefts, that make poëtique rage   30
A Mimique fury, when our soules must bee
Possest, or with Anacreons Extasie,
Or Pindars,[6] not their owne; The subtle cheat
Of slie Exchanges, and the jugling feat
Of two-edg'd words, or whatsoever wrong   35
By ours was done the Greeke, or Latine tongue,
Thou hast redeem'd, and open'd Us a Mine
Of rich and pregnant phansie, drawne a line
Of masculine expression, which had good
Old Orpheus[7] seene, Or all the ancient Brood   40
Our superstitious fooles admire, and hold
Their lead more precious, then thy burnish't Gold,
Thou hadst beene their Exchequer, and no more
They each in others dust, had rak'd for Ore.
Thou shalt yield no precedence, but of time,   45
And the blinde fate of language, whose tun'd chime

3. Longed for; the subject of "must be desired" is "flame" (line 14) [*Editor*].
4. The choir of Apollo, god of poetry, whose temple is located in Delphi. [*Editor*].
5. Prometheus was the Titan who took fire from heaven and gave it to man for his use [*Editor*].
6. Anacreon and Pindar were ancient Greek poets [*Editor*].
7. A Thracian singer and lyre-player, son of Apollo [*Editor*].

More charmes the outward sense; Yet thou maist claime
From so great disadvantage greater fame,
Since to the awe of thy imperious wit
Our stubborne language bends, made only fit   50
With her tough-thick-rib'd hoopes to gird about
Thy Giant phansie, which had prov'd too stout
For their soft melting Phrases. As in time
They had the start, so did they cull the prime
Buds of invention many a hundred yeare,   55
And left the rifled fields, besides the feare
To touch their Harvest, yet from those bare lands
Of what is purely thine, thy only hands
(And that thy smallest worke) have gleaned more
Then all those times, and tongues could reape before;   60
But thou are gone, and thy strict lawes will be
Too hard for Libertines in Poetrie.
They will repeale the goodly exil'd traine
Of gods and goddesses, which in thy just raigne
Were banish'd nobler Poems, now, with these
The silenc'd tales o'th' Metamorphoses[8]   65
Shall stuffe their lines, and swell the windy Page,
Till Verse refin'd by thee, in this last Age
Turne ballad rime, Or those old Idolls bee
Ador'd againe, with new apostasie;   70
   Oh, pardon mee, that breake with untun'd verse
The reverend silence that attends thy herse,
Whose awfull solemne murmures were to thee
More then these faint lines, A loud Elegie,
That did proclaime in a dumbe eloquence   75
The death of all the Arts, whose influence
Growne feeble, in these panting numbers lies
Gasping short winded Accents, and so dies:
So doth the swiftly turning wheele not stand
In th'instant we withdraw the moving hand,   80
But some small time maintaine a faint weake course
By vertue of the first impulsive force:
And so whil'st I cast on thy funerall pile
Thy crowne of Bayes, Oh, let it crack a while,
And spit disdaine, till the devouring flashes   85
Suck all the moysture up, then turne to ashes.
   I will not draw the envy to engrosse
All thy perfections, or weepe all our losse;
Those are too numerous for an Elegie,
And this too great, to be express'd by mee.   90

8. Tales by Ovid, ancient Roman poet [*Editor*].

Though every pen should share a distinct part,
Yet art thou Theme enough to tyre all Art;
Let others carve the rest, it shall suffice
I on thy Tombe this Epitaph incise.

> Here lies a King, that rul'd as hee thought fit   95
> The universall Monarchy of wit;
> Here lie two Flamens,[9] and both those, the best,
> Apollo's first, at last, the true Gods Priest.

JOHN DRYDEN
[Donne "Affects the Metaphysics"] †

You [the Earl of Dorset] equal Donne in the variety, multiplicity, and choice of thoughts; you excel him in the manner and the words. I read you both with the same admiration, but not with the same delight. He affects the metaphysics, not only in his satires, but in his amorous verses, where nature only should reign; and perplexes the minds of the fair sex with nice speculations of philosophy, when he should engage their hearts, and entertain them with the softnesses of love.

* * *

Would not Donne's *Satires*, which abound with so much wit, appear more charming, if he had taken care of his words, and of his numbers? But he followed Horace so very close, that of necessity he must fall with him; and I may safely say it of this present age, that if we are not so great wits as Donne, yet certainly we are better poets.

SAMUEL JOHNSON
["The *Metaphysical Poets*"]††

Cowley, like other poets who have written with narrow views, and, instead of tracing intellectual pleasures in the mind of man, paid their court to temporary prejudices, has been at one time too much praised, and too much neglected at another.

Wit, like all other things subject by their nature to the choice of man, has its changes and fashions, and at different times takes differ-

---

9. Priests [*Editor*].
† From *A Discourse Concerning the Original and Progress of Satire* (1693).
†† From *Lives of The Poets* (1779-81), a series of short critical biogra-

phies written by Johnson to preface collections of the work of English poets. "Cowley," from which this extract is taken, was the first of the series.

ent forms. About the beginning of the seventeenth century appeared a race of writers that may be termed the *metaphysical poets*, of whom, in a criticism on the works of Cowley, it is not improper to give some account.

The metaphysical poets were men of learning, and to show their learning was their whole endeavour; but, unluckily resolving to show it in rhyme, instead of writing poetry they only wrote verses, and very often such verses as stood the trial of the finger better than of the ear; for the modulation was so imperfect, that they were only found to be verses by counting the syllables.

If the father of criticism has rightly denominated poetry τέχνη μιμητική, *an imitative art*, these writers will, without great wrong, lose their right to the name of poets, for they cannot be said to have imitated anything; they neither copied nature nor life, neither painted the forms of matter, nor represented the operations of intellect.

Those, however, who deny them to be poets, allow them to be wits. Dryden confesses of himself and his contemporaries, that they fall below Donne in wit, but maintains that they surpass him in poetry.

If wit be well described by Pope, as being "that which has been often thought, but was never before so well expressed," they certainly never attained, nor ever sought it; for they endeavoured to be singular in their thoughts, and were careless of their diction. But Pope's account of wit is undoubtedly erroneous: he depresses it below its natural dignity, and reduces it from strength of thought to happiness of language.

If by a more noble and more adequate conception that be considered as wit which is at once natural and new, that which, though not obvious, is, upon its first production, acknowledged to be just; if it be that which he that never found it wonders how he missed, to wit of this kind the metaphysical poets have seldom risen. Their thoughts are often new, but seldom natural; they are not obvious, but neither are they just; and the reader, far from wondering that he missed them, wonders more frequently by what perverseness of industry they were ever found.

But wit, abstracted from its effects upon the hearer, may be more rigorously and philosophically considered as a kind of *discordia concors*; a combination of dissimilar images, or discovery of occult resemblances in things apparently unlike. Of wit, thus defined, they have more than enough. The most heterogeneous ideas are yoked by violence together; nature and art are ransacked for illustrations, comparisons, and allusions; their learning instructs, and their subtlety surprises; but the reader commonly thinks his improvement dearly bought, and, though he sometimes admires, is seldom pleased.

From this account of their compositions it will be readily inferred that they were not successful in representing or moving the affections.

As they were wholly employed on something unexpected and surprising, they had no regard to that uniformity of sentiment which enables us to conceive and to excite the pains and the pleasure of other minds: they never inquired what, on any occasion, they should have said or done, but wrote rather as beholders than partakers of human nature; as beings looking upon good and evil, impassive and at leisure; as Epicurean deities, making remarks on the actions of men, and the vicissitudes of life, without interest and without emotion. Their courtship was void of fondness, and their lamentation of sorrow. Their wish was only to say what they hoped had been never said before.

Nor was the sublime more within their reach than the pathetic; for they never attempted that comprehension and expanse of thought which at once fills the whole mind, and of which the first effect is sudden astonishment, and the second rational admiration. Sublimity is produced by aggregation, and littleness by dispersion. Great thoughts are always general, and consist in positions not limited by exceptions, and in descriptions not descending to minuteness. It is with great propriety that subtlety, which in its original import means exility of particles, is taken in its metaphorical meaning for nicety of distinction. Those writers who lay on the watch for novelty could have little hope of greatness; for great things cannot have escaped former observation. Their attempts were always analytic; they broke every image into fragments; and could no more represent, by their slender conceits and laboured particularities, the prospects of nature, or the scenes of life, than he who dissects a sunbeam with a prism can exhibit the wide effulgence of a summer noon.

What they wanted however of the sublime, they endeavoured to supply by hyperbole; their amplification had no limits; they left not only reason but fancy behind them; and produced combinations of confused magnificence, that not only could not be credited, but could not be imagined.

Yet great labour, directed by great abilities, is never wholly lost: if they frequently threw away their wit upon false conceits, they likewise sometimes struck out unexpected truth; if their conceits were far-fetched, they were often worth the carriage. To write on their plan, it was at least necessary to read and think. No man could be born a metaphysical poet, nor assume the dignity of a writer, by descriptions copied from descriptions, by imitations borrowed from imitations, by traditional imagery, and hereditary similes, by readiness of rhyme, and volubility of syllables.

In perusing the works of this race of authors, the mind is exercised either by recollection or inquiry; either something already learned is to be retrieved, or something new is to be examined. If their greatness seldom elevates, their acuteness often surprises; if the imagination is not always gratified, at least the powers of reflection and comparison are employed; and in the mass of materials which ingenious absurdity has thrown together, genuine wit and useful knowledge may be sometimes found buried perhaps in grossness of expression, but useful to those who know their value; and such as, when they are expanded to perspicuity, and polished to elegance, may give lustre to works which have more propriety though less copiousness of sentiment.

This kind of writing, which was, I believe, borrowed from Marino and his followers, had been recommended by the example of Donne, a man of a very extensive and various knowledge; and by Jonson, whose manner resembled that of Donne more in the ruggedness of his lines than in the cast of his sentiments.

When their reputation was high, they had undoubtedly more imitators than time has left behind. Their immediate successors, of whom any remembrance can be said to remain, were Suckling, Waller, Denham, Cowley, Cleveland, and Milton. Denham and Waller sought another way to fame, by improving the harmony of our numbers. Milton tried the metaphysic style only in his lines upon Hobson the Carrier. Cowley adopted it, and excelled his predecessors, having as much sentiment and more music. Suckling neither improved versification, nor abounded in conceits. The fashionable style remained chiefly with Cowley; Suckling could not reach it, and Milton disdained it.

SAMUEL TAYLOR COLERIDGE

[Notes on Donne]†

Versification of Donne

To read Dryden, Pope, &c., you need only count syllables; but to read Donne you must measure *Time*, and discover the *Time* of each word by the sense of Passion. I would ask no surer test of a Scotchman's *substratum* (for the turf-cover of pretension they all have) than to make him read Donne's satires aloud. If he made manly metre of them and yet strict metre, then,—why, then he wasn't a Scotchman, or his soul was geographically slandered by his body's first appearing there.

Doubtless, all the copies I have ever seen of Donne's Poems are grievously misprinted. Wonderful that they are not more so, considering that not one in a thousand of his readers have any notion how his lines are to be read—to the many, five out of six appear anti-

† From "Coleridgiana II," *Literary World*, XII (April 30, 1853), 349-50, and *The Literary Remains of Samuel Taylor Coleridge*, ed. H. N. Coleridge, I (London, 1836), 148-49.

metrical. How greatly this aided the compositor's negligence or ignorance, and prevented the corrector's remedy, any man may ascertain by examining the earliest editions of blank verse plays, Massinger, Beaumont and Fletcher, &c. Now, Donne's rhythm was as inexplicable to the many as blank verse, spite of his rhymes—*ergo*, as blank verse, misprinted. I am convinced that where no mode of rational declamation by pause, hurrying of voice, or apt and sometimes double emphasis, can at once make the verse metrical and bring out the sense of passion more prominently, that there we are entitled to alter the text, when it can be done by simple omission or addition of *that, which, and,* and such 'small deer;' or by mere new placing of the same words—I would venture nothing beyond.

> And by delighting many, frees again
> Grief which Verse did restrain.
> > *The Triple Fool,* v. 15.

A good instance how Donne read his own verses. We should write 'The Grief, verse did restrain;' but Donne roughly emphasized the two main words, Grief and Verse, and, therefore, made each the first syllable of a trochee or dactyl:—

> Grief, which | verse did re | strain.

> And we join tō't our strength,
> And we teach it art and length.
> > *Song.*

The anapest judiciously used, in the eagerness and haste to confirm and aggravate. This beautiful and perfect poem proves, by its title "Song," that *all* Donne's Poems are equally *metrical* (misprints allowed for) though smoothness (i.e., the metre necessitating the proper reading) be deemed appropriate to *songs;* but in poems where the writer *thinks,* and expects the reader to do so, the sense must be understood in order to ascertain the metre.

Satire III

If you would teach a scholar in the highest form how to *read,* take Donne, and of Donne this satire. When he has learnt to read Donne, with all the force and meaning which are involved in the words, then send him to Milton, and he will stalk on like a master, *enjoying* his walk.

Notes on "Songs and Sonnets"
On Donne's First Poem [The Flea]

> Be proud as Spaniards. Leap for pride, ye Fleas!
> In Nature's *minim* realm ye're now grandees.

Skip-jacks no more, nor civiller skip-johns;
Thrice-honored Fleas! I greet you all as *Dons.*
In Phoebus's archieves registered are ye,
And this your patent of nobility.

What ever dies is not mixt equally;
If our two loves be one, both thou and I
Love just alike in all; none of these loves can die.

The Good Morrow.

Too good for mere wit. It contains a deep practical truth, this triplet.

To Woman's Constancy

After all, there is but one Donne! and now tell me yet, wherein, in *his own kind,* he differs from the similar power in Shakspeare? Shakspeare was all men, potentially, except Milton; and they differ from him by negation, or privation, or both. This power of dissolving orient pearls, worth a kingdom, in a health to a whore!—this absolute right of dominion over all thoughts, that dukes are bid to clean his shoes, and are yet honored by it! But, I say, in this lordliness of opulence, in which *the* positive of Donne agrees with a positive of Shakspeare, what is it that makes them *homo*iousian, indeed: yet not homoousian?

To Canonization

One of my favorite poems. As late as ten years ago, I used to seek and find out grand lines and fine stanzas; but my delight has been far greater since it has consisted more in tracing the leading thought thro'out the whole. The former is too much like coveting your neighbor's goods; in the latter you merge yourself in the author, you *become He.*

To a Valediction Forbidding Mourning

An admirable poem which none but Donne could have written. Nothing was ever more admirably made out than the figure of the Compass.

To The Extacy

I should never find fault with metaphysical poems, were they all like this, or but half as excellent.

To The Primrose

I am tired of expressing my admiration; else I could not have passed by the Will, the Blossom, and the Primrose, with the Relique.

* * *

With Donne, whose muse on dromedary trots,
Wreathe iron pokers into true-love knots;
Rhyme's sturdy cripple, fancy's maze and clue,
Wit's forge and fire-blast, meaning's press and screw.

The wit of Donne, the wit of Butler, the wit of Pope, the wit of
Congreve, the wit of Sheridan—how many disparate things are here
expressed by one and the same word, Wit!—Wonder-exciting vigour,
intenseness and peculiarity of thought, using at will the almost bound-
less stores of a capacious memory, and exercised on subjects, where
we have no right to expect it—this is the wit of Donne! The four
others I am just in the mood to describe and inter-distinguish;—what
a pity that the marginal space will not let me!

SIR HERBERT GRIERSON

[Donne and Metaphysical Poetry] †

Metaphysical Poetry, in the full sense of the term, is a poetry which,
like that of the *Divina Commedia*, the *De Natura Rerum*, perhaps
Goethe's *Faust*, has been inspired by a philosophical conception of
the universe and the rôle assigned to the human spirit in the great
drama of existence. These poems were written because a definite interpretation of the riddle, the atoms of Epicurus rushing through
infinite empty space, the theology of the schoolmen as elaborated in
the catechetical disquisitions of St. Thomas, Spinoza's vision of life
sub specie aeternitatis, beyond good and evil, laid hold on the mind
and the imagination of a great poet, unified and illumined his comprehension of life, intensified and heightened his personal consciousness
of joy and sorrow, of hope and fear, by broadening their significance,
revealing to him in the history of his own soul a brief abstract of the
drama of human destiny. 'Poetry is the first and last of all knowledge
—it is as immortal as the heart of man.' Its themes are the simplest
experiences of the surface of life, sorrow and joy, love and battle, the
peace of the country, the bustle and stir of towns, but equally the
boldest conceptions, the profoundest intuitions, the subtlest and
most complex classifications and 'discourse of reason', if into these
too the poet can 'carry sensation', make of them passionate experiences communicable in vivid and moving imagery, in rich and varied
harmonies.

It is no such great metaphysical poetry as that of Lucretius and

† From Sir Herbert Grierson, *Metaphysical Lyrics and Poems of the Seventeenth Century*, Copyright 1921, 1959.

Pp. xiii-xxviii. Reprinted by permission
of the publishers, The Clarendon Press,
Oxford.

Dante that the present essay deals with, which this volume seeks to
illustrate. Of the poets from whom it culls, Donne is familiar with the
definitions and distinctions of Mediaeval Scholasticism; Cowley's
bright and alert, if not profound mind, is attracted by the achievements of science and the systematic materialism of Hobbes. Donne,
moreover, is metaphysical not only in virtue of his scholasticism, but
by his deep reflective interest in the experiences of which his poetry
is the expression, the new psychological curiosity with which he writes
of love and religion. The divine poets who follow Donne have each
the inherited metaphysic, if one may so call it, of the Church to which
he is attached, Catholic or Anglican. But none of the poets has for
his main theme a metaphysic like that of Epicurus or St. Thomas
passionately apprehended and imaginatively expounded. Donne, the
most thoughtful and imaginative of them all, is more aware of disintegration than of comprehensive harmony, of the clash between the
older physics and metaphysics on the one hand and the new science
of Copernicus and Galileo and Vesalius and Bacon on the other:

> The new philosophy calls all in doubt,
> The element of fire is quite put out;
> The sun is lost and the earth, and no man's wit
> Can well direct him where to look for it.
> And freely men confess that this world's spent,
> When in the planets and the firmament
> They seek so many new; they see that this
> Is crumbled out again to his atomies.

>   Have not all souls thought
> For many ages that our body is wrought
> Of air and fire and other elements?
> And now they think of new ingredients;
> And one soul thinks one, and another way
> Another thinks, and 'tis an even lay.

The greatest English poet, indeed, of the century was, or believed
himself to be, a philosophical or theological poet of the same order
as Dante. *Paradise Lost* was written to be a justification of 'the ways
of God to men', resting on a theological system as definite and almost
as carefully articulated in the *De Doctrina Christiana* as that which
Dante had accepted from the *Summa* of Aquinas. And the poet embodied his argument in a dramatic poem as vividly and intensely conceived, as magnificently and harmoniously set forth, as the *Divina
Commedia*. But in truth Milton was no philosopher. The subtleties
of theological definition and inference eluded his rationalistic, practical, though idealistic, mind. He proved nothing. The definitely
stated argument of the poem is an obvious begging of the question.
What he did was to create, or give a new definiteness and sensible

power to, a great myth which, through his poem, continued for a century or more to dominate the mind and imagination of pious protestants without many of them suspecting the heresies which lurked beneath the imposing and dazzling poem in which was retold the Bible story of the fall and redemption of man.

Metaphysical in this large way, Donne and his followers to Cowley are not, yet the word describes better what is the peculiar quality of their poetry than any other, e.g. fantastic, for poetry may be fantastic in so many different ways, witness Skelton and the Elizabethans, and Hood and Browning. It lays stress on the right things—the survival, one might say the reaccentuation, of the metaphysical strain, the *concetti metafisici ed ideali* as Testi calls them in contrast to the simpler imagery of classical poetry, of mediaeval Italian poetry; the more intellectual, less verbal, character of their wit compared with the conceits of the Elizabethans; the finer psychology of which their conceits are often the expression; their learned imagery; the argumentative, subtle evolution of their lyrics; above all the peculiar blend of passion and thought, feeling and ratiocination which is their greatest achievement. Passionate thinking is always apt to become metaphysical, probing and investigating the experience from which it takes its rise. All these qualities are in the poetry of Donne, and Donne is the great master of English poetry in the seventeenth century.

The Italian influence which Wyatt and Surrey brought into English poetry at the Renaissance gave it a more serious, a more thoughtful colour. They caught, especially Wyatt in some of the finest of his sonnets and songs, that spirit of 'high seriousness' which Chaucer with all his admiration of Italian poetry had failed to apprehend. English mediaeval poetry is often gravely pious, haunted by the fear of death and the judgement, melancholy over the 'Falls of Princes'; it is never serious and thoughtful in the introspective, reflective, dignified manner which it became in Wyatt and Sackville, and our 'sage and serious' Spenser, and in the songs of the first group of Elizabethan courtly poets, Sidney and Raleigh and Dyer. One has but to recall 'My lute, awake! perform the last', 'Forget not yet the tried intent', 'My mind to me a kingdom is', and to contrast them in mind with the songs which Henry VIII and Cornish were still composing and singing when Wyatt began to write, in order to realize what Italy and the Renaissance did to deepen the strain of English lyric poetry as that had flowed under French influence from the thirteenth to the sixteenth centuries. But French influence, the influence of Ronsard and his fellows, renewed itself in the seventies, and the great body of Elizabethan song is as gay and careless and impersonal as the earlier lyric had been, though richer in colour and more varied in rhythm. Then came Donne and Jonson (the schoolman and the classical scholar, one might say, emphasizing for the moment single aspects of their work), and new qualities of spirit and form were given to lyrical poetry, and not to lyrical poetry alone.

In dealing with poets who lived and wrote before the eighteenth century we are always confronted with the difficulty of recovering the personal, the biographical element, which, if sometimes disturbing and disconcerting, is yet essential to a complete understanding of their work. Men were not different from what they are now, and if there be hardly a lyric of Goethe's or Shelley's that does not owe something to the accidents of their lives, one may feel sure it was in varying degrees the same with poets three hundred years ago. Poems are not written by influences or movements or sources, but come from the living hearts of men. Fortunately, in the case of Donne, one of the most individual of poets, it is possible to some extent to reproduce the circumstances, the inner experiences from which his intensely personal poetry flowed.

He was in the first place a Catholic. Our history text-books make so little of the English Catholics that one is apt to forget they existed and were, for themselves at any rate, not a political problem, but real and suffering individuals. 'I had my first breeding and conversation', says Donne, 'with men of a suppressed and afflicted religion, accustomed to the despite of death and hungry of an imagined martyrdom.' In these circumstances, we gather, he was carefully and religiously educated, and after some years at Oxford and Cambridge was taken or sent abroad, perhaps with a view to entering foreign service, more probably with a view to the priesthood, and visited Italy and Spain. And then, one conjectures, a reaction took place, the rebellion of a full-blooded, highly intellectual temperament against a superimposed bent. He entered the Inns of Court in 1592, at the age of nineteen, and flung himself into the life of a student and the life of a young man about town, Jack Donne, 'not dissolute but very neat, a great visitor of ladies, a great frequenter of plays, a great writer of conceited verses'. 'Neither was it possible that a vulgar soul should dwell in such promising features.' He joined the band of reckless and raffish young men who sailed with Essex to Cadiz and the Islands. He was taken into the service of Sir Thomas Egerton. Ambition began to vie with the love of pleasure, when a hasty marriage closed a promising career, and left him bound in shallows and in miseries, to spend years in the suitorship of the great, and to find at last, not altogether willingly, a haven in the Anglican priesthood, and reveal himself as the first great orator that Church produced.

The record of these early years is contained in Donne's satires—harsh, witty, lucid, full of a young man's scorn of fools and low callings, and a young thinker's consciousness of the problems of religion in an age of divided faiths, and of justice in a corrupt world—and in his Love Songs and Sonnets and Elegies. The satires were more generally known; the love poems the more influential in courtly and literary circles.

Donne's genius, temperament, and learning gave to his love poems certain qualities which immediately arrested attention and have given them ever since a power at once fascinating and disconcerting despite the faults of phrasing and harmony which, for a century after Dryden, obscured, and to some still outweigh, their poetic worth. The first of these is a depth and range of feeling unknown to the majority of Elizabethan sonneteers and song-writers. Over all the Elizabethan sonnets, in greater or less measure, hangs the suggestion of translation or imitation. Watson, Sidney, Daniel, Spenser, Drayton, Lodge, all of them, with rarer or more frequent touches of individuality, are pipers of Petrarch's woes, sighing in the strain of Ronsard or more often of Desportes. Shakespeare, indeed, in his great sequence, and Drayton in at any rate one sonnet, sounded a deeper note, revealed a fuller sense of the complexities and contradictions of passionate devotion. But Donne's treatment of love is entirely unconventional except when he chooses to dally half ironically with the convention of Petrarchian adoration. His songs are the expression in unconventional, witty language of all the moods of a lover that experience and imagination have taught him to understand—sensuality aerated by a brilliant wit; fascination and scornful anger inextricably blended:

> When by thy scorn, O murdress, I am dead
> And that thou think'st thee free
> From all solicitations from me,
> Then shall my ghost come to thy bed;

the passionate joy of mutual and contented love:

> All other things to their destruction draw,
>   Only our love hath no decay;
> This no to-morrow hath nor yesterday,
>   Running it never runs from us away,
> But truly keeps his first, last, everlasting day;

the sorrow of parting which is the shadow of such joy; the gentler pathos of temporary separation in married life:

> Let not thy divining heart
>   Forethink me any ill,
> Destiny may take thy part,
>   And may thy fears fulfil;
>   But think that we
> Are but turn'd aside to sleep;
> They who one another keep
>   Alive ne'er parted be;

the mystical heights and the mystical depths of love:

> Study me then you who shall lovers be
> At the next world, that is, at the next Spring:
> For I am every dead thing
> In whom love wrought new Alchemy.

If Donne had expressed this wide range of intense feeling as perfectly as he has done at times poignantly and startlingly; if he had given to his poems the same impression of entire artistic sincerity that Shakespeare conveys in the greater of his sonnets and Drayton once achieved; if to his many other gifts had been added a deeper and more controlling sense of beauty, he would have been, as he nearly is, the greatest of love poets. But there is a second quality of his poetry which made it the fashion of an age, but has been inimical to its general acceptance ever since, and that is its metaphysical wit. 'He affects the metaphysics', says Dryden, 'not only in his satires but in his amorous verses where nature only should reign; and perplexes the minds of the fair sex with nice speculations of philosophy when he should engage their hearts and entertain them with the softnesses of love.' 'Amorous verses', 'the fair sex', and 'the softnesses of love' are the vulgarities of a less poetic and passionate age than Donne's, but metaphysics he does affect. But a metaphysical strand, *concetti metafisici ed ideali*, had run through the mediaeval love-poetry of which the Elizabethan sonnets are a descendant. It had attained its fullest development in the poems of Dante and his school, had been subordinated to rhetoric and subtleties of expression rather than thought in Petrarch, and had lost itself in the pseudo-metaphysical extravagances of Tebaldeo, Cariteo, and Serafino. Donne was no conscious reviver of the metaphysics of Dante, but to the game of elaborating fantastic conceits and hyperboles which was the fashion throughout Europe, he brought not only a full-blooded temperament and acute mind, but a vast and growing store of the same scholastic learning, the same Catholic theology, as controlled Dante's thought, jostling already with the new learning of Copernicus and Paracelsus. The result is startling and disconcerting, —the comparison of parted lovers to the legs of a pair of compasses, the deification of his mistress by the discovery that she is only to be defined by negatives or that she can read the thoughts of his heart, a thing 'beyond an angel's art'; and a thousand other subtleties of quintessences and nothingness, the mixture of souls and the significance of numbers, to say nothing of the aerial bodies of angels, the phoenix and the mandrake's *root*, Alchemy and Astrology, legal contracts and *non obstantes*, 'late schoolboys and sour prentices', 'the king's real and his stamped face'. But the effect aimed at and secured is not entirely fantastic and erudite. The motive inspiring Donne's images is in part the same as that which led Shakespeare from the picturesque, natural and mythological, images of A *Midsummer-Night's Dream*

and *The Merchant of Venice* to the homely but startling phrases and
metaphors of *Hamlet* and *Macbeth*, the 'blanket of the dark', the

> fat weed
> That rots itself in ease on Lethe wharf,

'the rank sweat of an enseamed bed'. It is the same desire for vivid and
dramatic expression. The great master at a later period of dramatic
as well as erudite pulpit oratory coins in his poems many a startling,
jarring, arresting phrase:

> For God's sake hold your tongue and let me love:

> Who ever comes to shroud me do not harm
>   Nor question much
> That subtle wreath of hair, which crowns my arm:

> I taught my silks their rustling to forbear,
> Even my opprest shoes dumb and silent were.

> I long to talk with some old lover's ghost
> Who died before the God of love was born;

> Twice or thrice had I loved thee
> Before I knew thy face or name,
> So in a voice, so in a shapeless flame,
> Angels affect us oft and worshipped be;

> And whilst our souls negotiate there
>   We like sepulchral statues lay;
> All day the same our postures were
>   And we said nothing all the day

> My face and brest of haircloth, and my head
> With care's harsh, sudden hoariness o'erspread.

These vivid, simple, realistic touches are too quickly merged in learned
and fantastic elaborations, and the final effect of every poem of
Donne's is a bizarre and blended one; but if the greatest poetry rises
clear of the bizarre, the fantastic, yet very great poetry may be bizarre
if it be the expression of a strangely blended temperament, an intense
emotion, a vivid imagination.

What is true of Donne's imagery is true of the other disconcerting
element in his poetry, its harsh and rugged verse. It is an outcome of
the same double motive, the desire to startle and the desire to approx-
imate poetic to direct, unconventional, colloquial speech. Poetry is
always a balance, sometimes a compromise, between what has to be
said and the prescribed pattern to which the saying of it is adjusted.
In poetry such as Spenser's, the musical flow, the melody and harmony of line and stanza, is dominant, and the meaning is adjusted
to it at the not infrequent cost of diffuseness—if a delightful diffuseness—and even some weakness of phrasing logically and rhetorically

considered. In Shakespeare's tragedies the thought and feeling tend
to break through the prescribed pattern till blank verse becomes almost rhythmical, the rapid overflow of the lines admitting hardly the
semblance of pause. This is the kind of effect Donne is always aiming
at, alike in his satires and lyrics, bending and cracking the metrical
pattern to the rhetoric of direct and vehement utterance. The result
is often, and to eighteenth-century ears attuned to the clear and defined, if limited, harmony of Waller and Dryden and Pope was,
rugged and harsh. But here again, to those who have ears that care
to hear, the effect is not finally inharmonious. Donne's verse has a
powerful and haunting harmony of its own. For Donne is not simply,
no poet could be, willing to force his accent, to strain and crack a prescribed pattern; he is striving to find a rhythm that will express the
passionate fullness of his mind, the fluxes and refluxes of his moods;
and the felicities of verse are as frequent and startling as those of
phrasing. He is one of the first masters, perhaps *the* first, of the elaborate stanza or paragraph in which the discords of individual lines or
phrases are resolved in the complex and rhetorically effective harmony
of the whole group of lines:

> If yet I have not all thy love,
> Deare, I shall never have it all,
> I cannot breathe one other sigh, to move,
> Nor can entreat one other tear to fall,
> And all my treasure, which should purchase thee,
> Sighs, tears, and oaths, and letters I have spent.
> Yet no more can be due to me,
> Than at the bargain made was meant,
> If then thy gift of love was partial,
> That some to me, some should to others fall,
>   Deare, I shall never have thee all.
>
> But I am none; nor will my sunne renew.
> You lovers for whose sake the lesser sunne
>   At this time to the Goat is run
>   To fetch new lust and give it you,
>   Enjoy your summer all;
> Since she enjoys her long night's festival,
> Let me prepare towards her, and let me call
> This hour her Vigil and her Eve, since this
>
> Both the years | and the days | deep mid|night is.

The wrenching of accent which Jonson complained of is not entirely
due to carelessness or indifference. It has often both a rhetorical and
a harmonious justification. Donne plays with rhythmical effects as
with conceits and words and often in much the same way. Mr.
Fletcher Melton's interesting analysis of his verse has not, I think,
established his main thesis, which like so many 'research' scholars he

over-emphasizes, that the whole mystery of Donne's art lies in his use of the same sound now in *arsis*, now in *thesis*; but his examples show that this is one of many devices by which Donne secures two effects, the troubling of the regular fall of the verse stresses by the intrusion of rhetorical stress on syllables which the metrical pattern leaves unstressed, and, secondly, an echoing and re-echoing of similar sounds parallel to his fondness for resemblances in thoughts and things apparently the most remote from one another. There is, that is to say, in his verse the same blend as in his diction of the colloquial and the bizarre. He writes as one who *will* say what he has to say without regard to conventions of poetic diction or smooth verse, but what he has to say is subtle and surprising, and so are the metrical effects with which it is presented. There is nothing of unconscious or merely careless harshness in such an effect as this:

> Poor soul, in this thy flesh what dost thou know?
> Thou know'st thyself so little that thou knowst not
> How thou didst die, nor how thou was begot.
> Thou neither know'st how thou at first camest in,
> Nor how thou took'st the poison of man's sin;
> Nor dost thou though thou know'st that thou art so
> By what way thou art made immortal know.

In Donne's pronunciation, as in southern English to-day, 'thou', 'how', 'soul', 'know', 'though', and 'so' were not far removed from each other in sound and the reiterated notes ring through the lines like a tolling bell. Mr. Melton has collected, and any careful reader may discover for himself, many similar subtleties of poetical rhetoric; for Donne is perhaps our first great master of poetic rhetoric, of poetry, used, as Dryden and Pope were to use it, for effects of oratory rather than of song, and the advance which Dryden achieved was secured by subordinating to oratory the more passionate and imaginative qualities which troubled the balance and movement of Donne's packed but imaginative rhetoric.

It was not indeed in lyrical verse that Dryden followed and developed Donne, but in his eulogistic, elegiac, satirical, and epistolary verse. The progress of Dryden's eulogistic style is traceable from his earliest metaphysical extravagances through lines such as those addressed to the Duchess of York, where Waller is his model, to the verses on the death of Oldham in which a more natural and classical strain has entirely superseded his earlier extravagances and elegancies. In truth Donne's metaphysical eulogies and elegies and epistles are a hard nut to crack for his most sympathetic admirers. And yet they have undeniable qualities. The metaphysics are developed in a more serious, a less paradoxical, strain than in some of the songs and elegies. In his letters he is an excellent, if far from a perfect, talker in verse; and the personality which they reveal is a singularly charming one,

grave, loyal, melancholy, witty. If some of the elegiac pieces are
packed with tasteless and extravagant hyperboles, the *Anniversaries*
(especially the second) remains, despite all its faults, one of the greatest poems on death in the language, the fullest record in our literature
of the disintegrating collision in a sensitive mind of the old tradition
and the new learning. Some of the invocational passages in *Of the
Progresse of the Soule* are among the finest examples of his subtle and
passionate thinking as well as of his most elaborate verse rhetoric.

But the most intense and personal of Donne's poems, after the love
songs and elegies, are his later religious sonnets and songs; and their
influence on subsequent poetry was even more obvious and potent.
They are as personal and as tormented as his earlier 'love-song weeds',
for his spiritual Aeneid was a troubled one. To date his conversion to
Anglicanism is not easy. In his satires there is a veiled Roman tone.
By 1602 he disclaims to Egerton 'all love of a corrupt religion', but
in the autumn of the previous year he had been meditating a satire
on Queen Elizabeth as one of the world's great heretics. His was not
a conversion but a reconciliation, an acquiescence in the faith of his
country, the established religion of his legal sovereign, and the act
cost him some pangs. 'A convert from Popery to Protestantism,' said
Dr. Johnson, 'gives up so much of what he has held as sacred as anything that he retains, there is so much laceration of mind in such a
conversion, that it can hardly be sincere and lasting.' Something of
that laceration of mind is discernible in Donne's religious verse:

Show me dear Christ that spouse so bright and clear.

But the conflict between the old and the reformed faiths was not the
only, nor perhaps the principal trouble for Donne's enlightened mind
ready to recognize in all the Churches 'virtual beams of one sun',
'connatural pieces of one circle'. A harder fight was that between the
secular, the 'man of the world' temper of his mind and the claims of
a pious and ascetic calling. It was not the errors of his youth, as the
good Walton supposed, which constituted the great stumbling block,
though he never ignores these:

O might those sighs and tears return again
Into my breast and eyes, which I have spent,
That I might in this holy discontent
Mourn with some fruit, as I have mourned in vain.

It was rather the temperament of one who, at a time when a public
career was more open to unassisted talent, might have proved an active
and useful, if ambitious, civil servant, or professional man, at war with
the claims of a religious life which his upbringing had taught him was
incompatible with worldly ambition. George Herbert, a much more
contented Anglican than Donne ever became, knew something of the
same struggle before he bent his neck to the collar.

The two notes then of Donne's religious poems are the Catholic and the personal. He is the first of our Anglo-Catholic poets, and he is our first intensely personal religious poet, expressing always not the mind simply of the Christian as such, but the conflicts and longings of one troubled soul, one subtle and fantastic mind. For Donne's technique—his phrasing and conceits, the metaphysics of mediaeval Christianity, his packed verse with its bold, irregular fingering and echoing vowel sounds—remains what it had been from the outset. The echoing sounds in lines such as these cannot be quite casual:

> O might those *sighs* and tears return again
> Into my breast and *eyes,* which *I* have spent,
> That *I* might in this holy discontent
> Mourn with some fruit, as *I* have mourned in vain;
> In mine *Idolat'ry* what showers of rain
> *Mine eyes* did waste? What griefs *my* heart did rent?
> That sufferance was *my* sin; now *I* repent
> Cause *I* did suffer *I* must suffer pain.

In the remaining six lines the same sound never recurs.

A metaphysical, a philosophical poet, to the degree to which even his contemporary Fulke Greville might be called such, Donne was not. The thought in his poetry is not his primary concern but the feeling. No scheme of thought, no interpretation of life became for him a complete and illuminating experience. The central theme of his poetry is ever his own intense personal moods, as a lover, a friend, an analyst of his own experiences worldly and religious. His philosophy cannot unify these experiences. It represents the reaction of his restless and acute mind on the intense experience of the moment, a reading of it in the light now of one, now of another philosophical or theological dogma or thesis caught from his multifarious reading, developed with audacious paradox or more serious intention, as an expression, an illumination of that mood to himself and to his reader. Whether one choose to call him a metaphysical or a fantastic poet, the stress must be laid on the word 'poet'. Whether verse or prose be his medium, Donne is always a poet, a creature of feeling and imagination, seeking expression in vivid phrase and complex harmonies, whose acute and subtle intellect was the servant, if sometimes the unruly servant, of passion and imagination.

T. S. ELIOT
The Metaphysical Poets †

By collecting these poems[1] from the work of a generation more often named than read, and more often read than profitably stuied, Professor Grierson has rendered a service of some importance. Certainly the reader will meet with many poems already preserved in other anthologies, at the same time that he discovers poems such as those of Aurelian Townshend or Lord Herbert of Cherbury here included. But the function of such an anthology as this is neither that of Professor Saintsbury's admirable edition of Caroline poets nor that of the *Oxford Book of English Verse*. Mr. Grierson's book is in itself a piece of criticism, and a provocation of criticism; and we think that he was right in including so many poems of Donne, elsewhere (though not in many editions) accessible, as documents in the case of 'metaphysical poetry'. The phrase has long done duty as a term of abuse, or as the label of a quaint and pleasant taste. The question is to what extent the so-called metaphysicals formed a school (in our own time we should say a 'movement'), and how far this so-called school or movement is a digression from the main current.

Not only is it extremely difficult to define metaphysical poetry, but difficult to decide what poets practice it and in which of their verses. The poetry of Donne (to whom Marvell and Bishop King are sometimes nearer than any of the other authors) is late Elizabethan, its feeling often very close to that of Chapman. The 'courtly' poetry is derivative from Jonson, who borrowed liberally from the Latin; it expires in the next century with the sentiment and witticism of Prior. There is finally the devotional verse of Herbert, Vaughan, and Crashaw (echoed long after by Christina Rossetti and Francis Thompson); Crashaw, sometimes more profound and less sectarian than the others, has a quality which returns through the Elizabethan period to the early Italians. It is difficult to find any precise use of metaphor, simile, or other conceit, which is common to all the poets and at the same time important enough as an element of style to isolate these poets as a group. Donne, and often Cowley, employ a device which is sometimes considered characteristically 'metaphysical'; the elaboration (contrasted with the condensation) of a figure of speech to the furthest stage to which ingenuity can carry it. Thus

† From *Selected Essays*, New Edition, by T. S. Eliot, copyright, 1932, 1936, 1950, by Harcourt, Brace & World, Inc., © 1960, 1964, by T. S. Eliot. Reprinted by permission of Harcourt, Brace & World, Inc., and Faber & Faber Ltd.

1. *Metaphysical Lyrics and Poems of the Seventeenth Century:* Donne to Butler. Selected and edited, with an Essay, by Herbert J. C. Grierson (Oxford: Clarendon Press. London: Milford).

Cowley develops the commonplace comparison of the world to a
chess-board through long stanzas (*To Destiny*), and Donne, with
more grace, in A *Valediction*, the comparison of two lovers to a pair
of compasses. But elsewhere we find, instead of the mere explication
of the content of a comparison, a development by rapid association of
thought which requires considerable agility on the part of the reader.

> On a round ball
> A workeman that hath copies by, can lay
> An Europe, Afrique, and an Asia,
> And quickly make that, which was nothing, *All*,
> So doth each teare,
> Which thee doth weare,
> A globe, yea world by that impression grow,
> Till thy tears mixt with mine doe overflow
> This world, by waters sent from thee, my heaven dissolved so.

Here we find at least two connexions which are not implicit in the
first figure, but are forced upon it by the poet: from the geographer's
globe to the tear, and the tear to the deluge. On the other hand, some
of Donne's most successful and characteristic effects are secured by
brief words and sudden contrasts:

> A bracelet of bright hair about the bone,

where the most powerful effect is produced by the sudden contrast of
associations of 'bright hair' and of 'bone'. This telescoping of images
and multiplied associations is characteristic of the phrase of some of
the dramatists of the period which Donne knew; not to mention
Shakespeare, it is frequent in Middleton, Webster, and Tourneur,
and is one of the sources of the vitality of their language.

Johnson, who employed the term 'metaphysical poets', apparently
having Donne, Cleveland, and Cowley chiefly in mind, remarks of
them that 'the most heterogeneous ideas are yoked by violence together'. The force of this impeachment lies in the failure of the conjunction, the fact that often the ideas are yoked but not united; and
if we are to judge of styles of poetry by their abuse, enough examples
may be found in Cleveland to justify Johnson's condemnation. But
a degree of heterogeneity of material compelled into unity by the
operation of the poet's mind is omnipresent in poetry. We need not
select for illustration such a line as:

> Notre âme est un trois-mâts chercant son Icarie;

we may find it in some of the best lines of Johnson himself (*The
Vanity of Human Wishes*):

> His fate was destined to a barren strand,
> A petty fortress, and a dubious hand;
> He left a name at which the world grew pale,
> To point a moral, or adorn a tale.

where the effect is due to a contrast of ideas, different in degree but the same in principle, as that which Johnson mildly reprehended. And in one of the finest poems of the age (a poem which could not have been written in any other age), the *Exequy* of Bishop King, the extended comparison is used with perfect success: the idea and the simile become one, in the passage in which the Bishop illustrates his impatience to see his dead wife, under the figure of a journey:

> Stay for me there; I will not faile
> To meet thee in that hollow Vale.
> And think not much of my delay;
> I am already on the way,
> And follow thee with all the speed
> Desire can make, or sorrows breed.
> Each minute is a short degree,
> And ev'ry houre a step towards thee.
> At night when I betake to rest,
> Next morn I rise nearer my West
> Of life, almost by eight houres sail,
> Than when sleep breath'd his drowsy gale. . . .
> But heark! My Pulse, like a soft Drum
> Beats my approach, tells *Thee* I come;
> And slow howere my marches be,
> I shall at last sit down by *Thee*.

(In the last few lines there is that effect of terror which is several times attained by one of Bishop King's admirers, Edgar Poe.) Again, we may justly take these quatrains from Lord Herbert's Ode, stanzas which would, we think, be immediately pronounced to be of the metaphysical school:

> So when from hence we shall be gone,
>   And be no more, nor you, nor I,
>   As one another's mystery,
> Each shall be both, yet both but one.

> This said, in her up-lifted face,
>   Her eyes, which did that beauty crown,
>   Were like two starrs, that having faln down,
> Look up again to find their place:

> While such a moveless silent peace
>   Did seize on their becalmed sense,
>   One would have thought some influence
> Their ravished spirits did possess.

There is nothing in these lines (with the possible exception of the stars, a simile not at once grasped, but lovely and justified) which fits Johnson's general observations on the metaphysical poets in his essay on Cowley. A good deal resides in the richness of association which is at the same time borrowed from and given to the word 'becalmed'; but the meaning is clear, the language simple and elegant. It is to be observed that the language of these poets is as a rule simple and pure; in the verse of George Herbert this simplicity is carried as far as it can go—a simplicity emulated without success by numerous modern poets. The *structure* of the sentences, on the other hand, is sometimes far from simple, but this is not a vice; it is a fidelity to thought and feeling. The effect, at its best, is far less artificial than that of an ode by Gray. And as this fidelity induces variety of thought and feeling, so it induces variety of music. We doubt whether, in the eighteenth century, could be found two poems in nominally the same metre, so dissimilar as Marvell's *Coy Mistress* and Crashaw's *Saint Teresa*; the one producing an effect of great speed by the use of short syllables, and the other an ecclesiastical solemnity by the use of long ones:

> Love, thou art absolute sole lord
> Of life and death.

If so shrewd and sensitive (though so limited) a critic as Johnson failed to define metaphysical poetry by its faults, it is worth while to inquire whether we may not have more success by adopting the opposite method: by assuming that the poets of the seventeenth century (up to the Revolution) were the direct and normal development of the precedent age; and, without prejudicing their case by the adjective 'metaphysical', consider whether their virtue was not something permanently valuable, which subsequently disappeared, but ought not to have disappeared. Johnson has hit, perhaps by accident, on one of their peculiarities, when he observes that 'their attempts were always analytic'; he would not agree that, after the dissociation, they put the material together again in a new unity.

It is certain that the dramatic verse of the later Elizabethan and early Jacobean poets expresses a degree of development of sensibility which is not found in any of the prose, good as it often is. If we except Marlowe, a man of prodigious intelligence, these dramatists were directly or indirectly (it is at least a tenable theory) affected by Montaigne. Even if we except also Jonson and Chapman, these two were notably erudite, and were notably men who incorporated their erudition into their sensibility: their mode of feeling was directly and freshly altered by their reading and thought. In Chapman especially there is a direct sensuous apprehension of thought, or a recreation of thought into feeling, which is exactly what we find in Donne:

> in this one thing, all the discipline
> Of manners and of manhood is contained;
> A man to join himself with th' Universe
> In his main sway, and make in all things fit

One with that All, and go on, round as it;
Not plucking from the whole his wretched part,
And into straits, or into nought revert,
Wishing the complete Universe might be
Subject to such a rag of it as he;
But to consider great Necessity.

We compare this with some modern passage:

No, when the fight begins within himself,
A man's worth something. God stoops o'er his head,
Satan looks up between his feet—both tug—
He's left, himself, i' the middle; the soul wakes
And grows. Prolong that battle through his life!

It is perhaps somewhat less fair, though very tempting (as both poets are concerned with the perpetuation of love by offspring), to compare with the stanzas already quoted from Lord Herbert's Ode the following from Tennyson:

One walked between his wife and child,
With measured footfall firm and mild,
And now and then he gravely smiled.
    The prudent partner of his blood
    Leaned on him, faithful, gentle, good,
    Wearing the rose of womanhood.
And in their double love secure,
The little maiden walked demure,
Pacing with downward eyelids pure.
    These three made unity so sweet,
    My frozen heart began to beat,
    Remembering its ancient heat.

The difference is not a simple difference of degree between poets. It is something which had happened to the mind of England between the time of Donne or Lord Herbert of Cherbury and the time of Tennyson and Browning; it is the difference between the intellectual poet and the reflective poet. Tennyson and Browning are poets, and they think; but they do not feel their thought as immediately as the odour of a rose. A thought to Donne was an experience; it modified his sensibility. When a poet's mind is perfectly equipped for its work, it is constantly amalgamating disparate experience; the ordinary man's experience is chaotic, irregular, fragmentary. The latter falls in love, or reads Spinoza, and these two experiences have nothing to do with each other, or with the noise of the typewriter or the smell of cooking; in the mind of the poet these experiences are always forming new wholes.

We may express the difference by the following theory: The poets of the seventeenth century, the successors of the dramatists of the sixteenth, possessed a mechanism of sensibility which could devour any kind of experience. They are simple, artificial, difficult, or fantastic, as their predecessors were; no less nor more than Dante, Guido Cavalcanti, Guinicelli, or Cino. In the seventeenth century a dissociation of sensibility set in, from which we have never recovered; and this dissociation, as is natural, was aggravated by the influence of the two most powerful poets of the century, Milton and Dryden. Each of these men performed certain poetic functions so magnificently well that the magnitude of the effect concealed the absence of others. The language went on and in some respects improved; the best verse of Collins, Gray, Johnson, and even Goldsmith satisfies some of our fastidious demands better than that of Donne or Marvell or King. But while the language became more refined, the feeling became more crude. The feeling, the sensibility, expressed in the *Country Churchyard* (to say nothing of Tennyson and Browning) is cruder than that in the *Coy Mistress*.

The second effect of the influence of Milton and Dryden followed from the first, and was therefore slow in manifestation. The sentimental age began early in the eigtheenth century, and continued. The poets revolted against the ratiocinative, the descriptive; they thought and felt by fits, unbalanced; they reflected. In one or two passages of Shelley's *Triumph of Life*, in the second *Hyperion*, there are traces of a struggle toward unification of sensibility. But Keats and Shelley died, and Tennyson and Browning ruminatéd.

After this brief exposition of a theory—too brief, perhaps, to carry conviction—we may ask, what would have been the fate of the 'metaphysical' had the current of poetry descended in a direct line from them, as it descended in a direct line to them? They would not, certainly, be classified as metaphysical. The possible interests of a poet are unlimited; the more intelligent he is the better; the more intelligent he is the more likely that he will have interests: our only condition is that he turn them into poetry, and not merely mediate on them poetically. A philosophical theory which has entered into poetry is established, for its truth or falsity in one sense ceases to matter, and its truth in another sense is proved. The poets in question have, like other poets, various faults. But they were, at best, engaged in the task of trying to find the verbal equivalent for states of mind and feeling. And this means both that they are more mature, and that they wear better, than later poets of certainly not less literary ability.

It is not a permanent necessity that poets should be interested in philosophy, or in any other subject. We can only say that it appears likely that poets in our civilization, as it exists at present, must be *difficult*. Our civilization comprehends great variety and complexity, and this variety and complexity, playing upon a refined sensibility, must produce various and complex results. The poet must become more and more comprehensive, more allusive, more indirect, in order to force, to dislocate if necessary, language into his meaning. (A brilliant and extreme statement of this view, with which it is not requisite to associate oneself, is that of M. Jean Epstein, *La Poésie d'aujourd'hui*.) Hence we get something which looks very much like the conceit —we get, in fact, a method curiously similar to that of the 'metaphysical poets', similar also in its use of obscure words and of simple phrasing.

O géraniums diaphanes, guerroyeurs sortilèges,
Sacrilèges monomanes!
Emballages, dévergondages, douches! O pressoirs
Des vendanges des grands soirs!
Layettes aux abois,
Thyrses au fond des bois!
Transfusions, représailles,
Relevailles, compresses et l'éternal potion,
Angélus! n'en pouvior plus
De débâcles nuptiales! de débâcles nuptiales![2]

The same poet could write also simply:

Elle est bien loin, elle pleure,
Le grand vent se lamente aussi . . .[3]

Jules Laforgue, and Tristan Corbière in many of his poems, are nearer to the 'school of Donne' than any modern English poet. But poets more classical than they have the same essential quality of transmuting ideas into sensations, of transforming an observation into a state of mind.

Pour l'enfant, amoureux de cartes et d'estampes,
L'univers est égal à son vaste appétit.
Ah, que le monde est grand à la clarté des lampes!
Aux yeux du souvenir que le monde est petit![4]

In French literature the great master of the seventeenth century— Racine—and the great master of the nineteenth—Baudelaire—are in some ways more like each other than they are like anyone else. The greatest two masters of diction are also the greatest two psychologists, the most curious explorers of the soul. It is interesting to speculate whether it is not a misfortune that two of the greatest masters of dic-

---

2. "O transparent geraniums, warrior incantations, / Monomaniac sacrileges! / Packing materials, shamelessnesses, shower baths! O wine presses / Of great evening vintages! / Hard-pressed baby linen, / Thyrsis in the depths of the woods! / Transfusions, reprisals, / Churchings, compresses, and the eternal potion, / Angelus! no longer to be borne (are) / Catastrophic marriages!" This passage is from *Derniers vers X* ("Last Poems," 1890), by Jules La-

forgue (1860-87) [*Editor*].
3. "She is far away, she weeps, / The great wind mourns also." From *Derniers vers XI, Sur une défunte* ("On a Dead Woman") [*Editor*].
4. From Baudelaire's *Le Voyage*: "For the child, in love with maps and prints, / The universe matches his vast appetite. / Ah, how big the world is by lamplight! How small the world is to the eyes of memory!" [*Editor*].

tion in our language, Milton and Dryden, triumph with a dazzling disregard of the soul. If we continued to produce Miltons and Drydens it might not so much matter, but as things are it is a pity that English poetry has remained so incomplete. Those who object to the 'artificiality' of Milton or Dryden sometimes tell us to 'look into our hearts and write'. But that is not looking deep enough; Racine or Donne looked into a good deal more than the heart. One must look into the cerebral cortex, the nervous system, and the digestive tracts.

May we not conclude, then, that Donne, Crashaw, Vaughan, Herbert and Lord Herbert, Marvell, King, Cowley at his best, are in the direct current of English poetry, and that their faults should be reprimanded by this standard rather than coddled by antiquarian affection? They have been enough praised in terms which are implicit limitations because they are 'metaphysical' or 'witty', 'quaint' or 'obscure', though at their best they have not these attributes more than other serious poets. On the other hand, we must not reject the criticism of Johnson (a dangerous person to disagree with) without having mastered it, without having assimilated the Johnsonian canons of taste. In reading the celebrated passage in his essay on Cowley we must remember that by wit he clearly means something more serious than we usually mean to-day; in his criticism of their versification we must remember in what a narrow discipline he was trained, but also how well trained; we must remember that Johnson tortures chiefly the chief offenders, Cowley and Cleveland. It would be a fruitful work, and one requiring a substantial book, to break up the classification of Johnson (for there has been none since) and exhibit these poets in all their difference of kind and of degree, from the massive music of Donne to the faint, pleasing tinkle of Aurelian Townshend—whose *Dialogue between a Pilgrim and Time* is one of the few regrettable omissions from the excellent anthology of Professor Grierson.

J. B. LEISHMAN

["Dissociation of Sensibility"]†

In the seventeenth century a dissociation of sensibility set in, from which we have never recovered; and this dissociation, as is natural, was aggravated by the influence of the two most powerful poets of the century, Milton and Dryden. Each of these men performed certain poetic functions so magnificently well that the magnitude of the effect concealed the absence of others. The language went on and in some respects improved; the best verse of Collins, Gray,

† From J. B. Leishman, *The Monarch of Wit*, copyright 1951, 1959. Pp. 91-94. Reprinted by permission of the publishers, Hutchinson Publishing Group Ltd.

Johnson, and even Goldsmith satisfies some of our fastidious demands better than that of Donne or Marvell or King. But while the
language became more refined, the feeling became more crude.
The feeling, the sensibility, expressed in the *Country Churchyard*
(to say nothing of Tennyson and Browning) is cruder than that in
the *Coy Mistress*.[1]

This famous *pronunciamento* occurs in the essay on *The Metaphysical Poets*; in his essay on Marvell Mr. Eliot returns to this picture and
fills in some of the detail: Dryden, he there declares, isolated the
element of wit and exaggerated it into something like pure fun, while
Milton dispensed with it altogether and contented himself (if I understand Mr. Eliot aright) with mere magniloquence. The phrase 'dissociation of sensibility', which Mr. Eliot coined to describe the process he deplored, and to which he accused Milton and Dryden of contributing, soon led to the coinage (not, I think, by Mr. Eliot himself)
of the phrase 'unified sensibility' to describe that 'mechanism of sensibility' which the earlier seventeenth-century poets possessed, or were
supposed to have possessed; and it is perhaps not going too far to say
that these two phrases alone have enabled several later writers to set
up in business and drive quite a prosperous trade as literary and historical critics.

In these views, these very influential views, on seventeenth-century
poetry, which I have tried to expound and explain as clearly and fairly
as I could, there is, as I said at the outset, much that is true and illuminating together with much that is either very limitedly true or almost
wholly untrue. The question, though, which I chiefly want to raise
is this: *how much* of the work of our so-called metaphysical poets,
and, in particular, to how much of Donne's poetry, does Mr. Eliot's
definition of seventeenth-century wit and his praise of undissociated,
or pre-dissociated, seventeenth-century sensibility really apply? Does
it, for example, apply to any or all of Donne's Elegies, those poems
which we have been reviewing and analysing so carefully? 'Fidelity to
thought and feeling', 'a direct sensuous apprehension of thought, or
a recreation of thought into feeling', 'a recognition, implicit in the
expression of every experience, of other kinds of experience which are
possible': such phrases might well find a place in a description of the
ideal modern poet, the kind of poet Mr. Eliot believes (or once believed) that a modern poet should be—uncommitted, unanchored,
unaccommodated, with, ultimately, only one subject, his own direct
experience of a very puzzling world; an essentially exploring poet,
dealing in hints and guesses rather than in statements; not expound-
ing, illustrating, or building upon some inherited world-picture, philosophy, religion or point of view common to himself and to his readers, but suggesting, glimpsing, various kinds of unity and relationship

1. *Selected Essays*, 274.

in a world which both to himself and to his readers is infinitely complex, puzzling, and questionable. They are indeed the kind of phrases I myself should be inclined to apply to the later work of Rilke. But Donne's Elegies, not only *The Anagram, The Comparison* and the rest, but even the splendidly dramatic ones—for them, with their fundamental unseriousness, is not this rather high language rather out of place? Although it is perhaps not out of place for some of the *Songs and Sonets,* some of the *Divine Poems,* some of Marvell's poems—in a word, for some of the very best seventeenth-century poetry. Is it, though, quite fair, or even quite sensible, to generalize about our so-called metaphysical poetry on the basis of a few anthology pieces, and then to condemn other poets and other poetry for not normally displaying the same virtues? And are even the best pieces, the anthology pieces, quite what Mr. Eliot in these two essays implies? Is he not, to some considerable extent, describing an ideal of poetry which the best work of these poets has suggested to him, and does there not still remain some gap between his praise and even their finest achievements? It is true that he praises them for taking no subject either too lightly or too seriously, but, in his continual insistence on experience and exploration, is he not, perhaps, taking even their more serious poems too seriously, and neglecting, or under-emphasizing, even their very considerable element of play? For although, in comparison with Milton, Donne and Marvell are explorers rather than expounders, they were not explorers in the sense in which Rilke was an explorer: they were never so disinherited, so dependent on their own resources, so naked, so without all hope of receiving any answer from outside themselves as was the poet who exclaimed:

Who, if I cried, from among the angelic orders
would hear me?

Beneath all their disinterested curiosity and play of mind there is a fundamental assurance about ultimate things, and even in their most apparently serious explorations there is nearly always something of light-heartedness, something of play.

But I do not propose to use the example of Rilke in order to depreciate the achievements of Donne and Marvell, as Mr. Eliot used the examples of Donne and Marvell to depreciate the achievement of Milton: all I want to do is to examine the achievement of our so-called metaphysical poets, especially of Donne, rather more disinterestedly, and, in particular, to examine Mr. Eliot's theory and to decide how much of Donne's characteristic wit may be regarded as the expression of what has been called a unified sensibility.

This theory of a dissociation of sensibility which set in during the seventeenth-century is still widely accepted as a proven fact, as a firm foundation upon which to build, but to what extent Mr. Eliot himself still believes in it I do not know; neither, if he does still believe in it, do I know which seventeenth-century poets he still regards as possessing, in contrast to Milton and Dryden, a sensibility that was as yet undissociated. For between 1921 and 1931 Mr. Eliot seems to have lost some of his earlier enthusiasm for Donne. In 1931, in an essay on *Donne in our Time* which he contributed to a volume entitled *A Garland for John Donne*, he declared, as proof that Donne's mind was essentially unmedieval, that, while the encyclopaedic knowledge of the Schoolmen was always directed towards unification, 'in Donne there is a manifest fissure between thought and sensibility' —words which, whatever else they may mean, seem to mean the opposite of that 'direct sensuous apprehension of thought, or recreation of thought into feeling' which in 1921 Mr. Eliot found in Chapman and which, he added, 'is exactly what we find in Donne'.[2] 'One reason,' continues Mr. Eliot, in his 1931 essay,

> one reason why Donne has appealed so powerfully to the recent time is that there is in his poetry hardly any attempt at organization; rather a puzzled and humorous shuffling of the pieces; and we are inclined to read our own more conscious awareness of the apparent irrelevance and unrelatedness of things into the mind of Donne.[3]

I think I am probably right in supposing that this passage contains a kind of oblique confession, or recantation, and that when Mr. Eliot speaks of Donne's having 'appealed so powerfully to the recent time' he means, partly at least, 'appealed so powerfully to me ten years ago and to many of my readers'; also that, as the result of deepened insight, he has found the 'apparent irrelevance and unrelatedness of things' more merely apparent and less real, and is therefore less inclined to read a conscious awareness of such irrelevance and unrelatedness into the mind of Donne. As I say, I do not know whether Mr. Eliot still believes that a dissociation of sensibility set in during the seventeenth-century; neither do I know which, if any, of our seventeenth-century poets he would still regard as exempt from that infection. At any rate, by 1931 he had discovered in Donne 'a manifest fissure between thought and sensibility', which would seem to mean, in the terminology of 1921, that Donne's sensibility was dissociated.***

2. *Selected Essays*, 272.
3. *op. cit.*, 8.

JOSEPH ANTHONY MAZZEO
A Critique of Some Modern Theories of Metaphysical Poetry †

Numerous theories of "metaphysical" poetry have been advanced ever since the appearance of Sir Herbert Grierson's great edition of Donne's poems in 1912 initiated the modern revaluation of the "metaphysical" poets. However, few of these theories seem to have approached the problem from the perspectives offered by sixteenth- and seventeenth-century literary critics themselves. One of the reasons for this oversight is the curious fact that there is no body of critical literature in English on the metaphysical movement written when that movement, under various names, such as "Concettismo," "Marinismo," and "Gongorismo," was flourishing throughout Europe. Another reason is that we seem to have forgotten that the word "conceit," "concetto," or "concepto" also meant metaphor as well as "conceit" in the sense in which Dr. Johnson used the word. This is especially surprising when we consider that many modern critics find the most striking characteristic of the metaphysical poet to be his desire to extend the range and variety of metaphorical expression.

Giordano Bruno, the first critic to attempt a conceptual formulation of "concettismo," as the "metaphysical" style was known in Italy, began his argument to *De gli eroici furori* with an attack on the Petrarchan theory of poetic inspiration. For the older notion of "amore" directed toward personal beauty, Bruno attempted to substitute the idea of "heroic love" directed toward the universe. This second kind of love he interprets as the gift which both the philosopher and the poet have for perceiving the unity of dissimilars or, in other terms, for making heterogeneous analogies. Thus, for Bruno, "metaphysical" poetry was essentially concerned with perceiving and expressing the universal correspondences in his universe.

This conception of the poet as one who discovers and expresses the universal analogies binding the universe together was later developed by the theorists of the conceit in the seventeenth century, the most familiar of whom are Baltasar Gracián in Spain and Emmanuele Tesauro in Italy, and was made the basis for a poetic of "concettismo" or, as I have called it elsewhere, "a poetic of correspondences."[1]

One of the cardinal tenets of the critics of the conceit is that the

† From *Modern Philology*, L (November, 1952), pp. 88-96. Reprinted by permission of the publishers, The University of Chicago Press, and Joseph A. Mazzeo.

1. Giordano Bruno, *Opere italiane*, ed. Giovanni Gentile, Vol. II (Bari, 1927).

I refer the reader to two articles of mine which are in process of publication. One, "A Seventeenth-Century Theory of Metaphysical Poetry," has appeared in *RR* (December, 1951). The other, "Metaphysical Poetry and the Poetic of Correspondences," will appear in *JHI*.

conceit itself is the expression of a correspondence which actually obtains between objects and that, since the universe is a network of universal correspondences or analogies which unite all the apparently heterogeneous elements of experience, the most heterogeneous metaphors are justifiable. Thus the theorists of the conceit justify the predilection of the "school of wit" for recondite and apparently strained analogies by maintaining that even the more violent couplings of dissimilars were simply expressions of the underlying unity of all things.

It is, of course, true that analogical thought is a fundamental property of the human mind in any age and that the notion of universal analogy has a long history which reaches back to Plato. The important point is that Bruno and the theorists of the conceit employed the principle as the basis of a poetic for the first time. The fact that they did so does not "explain" metaphysical poetry any more than Aristotle's *Poetics* "explains" Sophocles. This is not the function of a poetic or a theory of poetry. Rather, it formulates conceptually a concrete body of literature already in existence. As Hegel put it in his preface to *The Philosophy of Right*, "When philosophy paints its gray in gray, a shape of life has grown old . . . it cannot be rejuvenated but only understood. The owl of Minerva spreads its wings at twilight."

What a poetic can do, however, is make explicit the cultural presuppositions which may underlie a particular body of literature, a style, or a genre. That Bruno and the theorists of the conceit should have based their poetic on the principle of universal analogy meant that they wished to justify and formulate philosophically the actual practice of metaphysical poets in making recondite and heterogeneous analogies and in using mundane and "learned" images.

The principle of universal analogy as a poetic, or the poetic of correspondences, offers, in my opinion, a theory of metaphysical poetry which is simpler, in greater harmony with the evidence, and freer from internal contradictions than the major modern theories that have yet been formulated. It is in the light of this theory, contemporary to the metaphysical movement, that I propose to review the various modern theories.

One popular modern theory derives "metaphysical" poetry from the Petrarchan and troubadour traditions and describes it as a decadent and exaggerated version of these earlier traditions.[2] If this is so, we can hardly understand the deliberately "irregular" versification of many of the greatest "metaphysical" poets, such as Donne; the colloquial tone and the homely and technical imagery characteristic of "concettismo"; the fact that Bruno, a "concettista" himself and the probable founder of Neapolitan "concettismo," began his *De gli*

2. Helmut Hatzfeld, "A Clarification of the Baroque Problem in the Romance Literatures," *Comparative Literature*, I (1949), 115-16.

eroici furori with an attack on the Petrarchan and troubadour conventions and offered a clear and determined substitute theory. He, at least, was certain that he was doing something else, and the poetic creations of the "metaphysicals" is sufficient evidence that he was. We can avoid this conclusion only if we insist on regarding the conceit as merely an odd or unusual image, in which case we can find it everywhere (and therefore nowhere) and even take its origin back to Martial. But it is clear that literary history cannot be made from superficial similarities and that the historian of taste must seek and determine the different cultural presuppositions that underlie the creations of minds as diverse as Bruno and Arnaut Daniel, without, at the same time, swallowing up the individual uniqueness and greatness of every great artist and work of art in the general historical categories we construct for them.

Another theory would attribute the "metaphysical" style to the influence of Ramistic logic, but it seems to me that this view raises more questions than it answers. Norman E. Nelson has made an acute criticism of the confusion between poetry, rhetoric, and logic that the defenders of the Ramistic theory are involved in.[3] It is at least questionable whether any system of inference or any empirical construction like rhetoric can have the kind of effect on a culture that Miss Tuve, the originator of this theory, describes. If her almost deterministic view of the influence of logic and rhetoric were true, she would still have to explain away the fact that Milton, who wrote a Ramist logic and defended Ramist theories, was surely no "metaphysical" poet. The connection between "concettismo" and Ramism, if one can be established, is not a causal relationship. Rather, they are both expressive, in different ways, of what we might call the "rhetoricizing" tendency of Renaissance humanism, the belief shared with Ramus by Valla and others that literature or rhetoric, rather than the old scholastic logic, revealed the true path which the mind must take in its quest for truth.[4] It would seem that the confusion of logic and poetry characteristic of our modern "Ramists" is a result of the current use of the term "logical image" to refer to the kind of expanded metaphor characteristic of much "metaphysical" poetry. It is, of course, clear that the "logic" of development of an expanded metaphor has often very little to do with the logic of a syllogism or system of inference and is, indeed, directed toward a different end.

3. This theory is advanced primarily by Rosemond Tuve, *Elizabethan and Metaphysical Imagery* (Chicago, 1946). Nelson's article on *Peter Ramus and the Confusion of Logic, Rhetoric and Poetry* is in the series "University of Michigan Contributions in Modern Philology," No. 2 (April, 1947).
4. This view was characteristic of many humanists who were also nominalists and who therefore banished all previous metaphysical assumptions from logic. The new rhetoric-logic was to teach men how to follow in their voluntary thinking the same "natural" laws that were followed in involuntary thinking. Hence the numerous literary examples to be found in Ramist logics. However, although Ramus abandoned the old metaphysical assumptions, he reintroduced the old categories, arranging them by dichotomies in a purely arbitrary and empirical order.

Another group of scholars relates the "metaphysical" style to the baroque, but variously, sometimes completely identifying it with the baroque and sometimes distinguishing the two. Croce, for example, calls "concettismo" a baroque phenomenon but considers anything baroque a negative aspect of Renaissance history whose only excuse for existence was to purge Western civilization from medievalism. It is otherwise with Hatzfeld, who, distinguishing "concettismo" and baroque, gives the honors to the latter, of which the conceit and its uses are, at most, a degenerate parody.[5] It is difficult to discuss the views of this group, since the term "baroque" itself is, like "Renaissance" and "Romantic," so variable in reference. However, the notion has been applied with greatest success to the study of the visual arts, where it is at least referable to specific techniques. I do not propose to complicate further this already complex problem, but it would seem desirable to keep the characteristics of baroque painting, sculpture, and architecture firmly in mind when we extend this term to other cultural spheres and not allow ourselves to be misled by chronological simultaneity alone. The original fruitful use of the concept of the baroque with reference to the plastic arts suggests that Cassirer's category of "form" and the principle of universal analogy might well be kept separated and that true "concettismo" belongs to the latter, while the baroque, as Croce suggested, is best understood as the transformation of the Renaissance interest in "form" into a preoccupation with "ornament" and in a weakening of the distinctions between the arts.

Perhaps the most widespread theory of the "metaphysical" style is the emblem theory. This view, establishing a causal connection between the emblem movement or "emblem habit" and the conceit which is purportedly its result, is usually expressed in terms of a baroque theory of the "metaphysical" style. Mario Praz, the foremost representative of this group, bases his analysis on Croce's, without assuming the latter's negative attitude toward either the baroque or the "metaphysical" styles. However, his study of the actual creations of this literary movement leads him to a view of the conceit and the emblem which might be called the "game" theory, a position he assumes when he says of the conceit and emblem that they are of the nature of the charade or riddle—the by-products of an amusing, lighthearted (perhaps perverse?) verbal and pictorial game.[6] This is surely an astonishing description of a style in which some of the greatest

5. See René Wellek, "The Concept of Baroque in Literary Scholarship," *Journal of Aesthetics*, V (1946), 77–109, for a discussion of the concept of baroque and for a bibliography on the subject.*** 6. Praz, *John Donne*, p. 7. Other works in support of the emblem theory are Rosemary Freeman, *English Emblem*

Books (London, 1948); Austin Warren, *Richard Crashaw: A Study in Baroque Sensibility* (University, La., 1939); Ruth Wallerstein, *Studies in Seventeenth-Century Poetic* (Madison, 1950). Miss Wallerstein also agrees with Miss Tuve on the influence of Ramist logic.

religious poetry of all time was written, and it is, in effect, denied by the sensitivity of Praz's concrete criticism of John Donne and Richard Crashaw.

I believe that this conclusion is a consequence of Praz's insistence on the intimate relationship between emblem and conceit and between the mass of different styles, some of them quite perverse, which went under the name of "Marinismo," "Gongorismo," "Seicentismo," "Euphuism," etc. However, not only are the resemblances between Donne and Lyly superficial at best, but the easy application of some notion of strangeness or eccentricity in style will find resemblances where none exists and lead to false or useless descriptions of cultural phenomena. Praz seems closer to a working definition of the conceit when he says that it is to poetry what the illusory perspective is to art, although, in the light of both the theory and the practice of the "metaphysical" style, this insight is of somewhat limited utility and best describes a style like Crashaw's.

Praz makes much of the fact that the emblem was usually accompanied by an epigram, and, since he seems to hold that emblem and "metaphysical" poem are related to each other as cause and effect, he concludes that the epigram is the genre most characteristic of "concettismo." This conclusion, in turn, leads to his placing great emphasis on the diffusion of the *Greek Anthology* during the Renaissance as one of the important influences on the growth of the "metaphysical" movement.[7] However, while the *Greek Anthology* stimulated many imitators, it seems to have had little effect on the best of the poets of wit. The long and "conceited" works of Marino, Gongora, Donne, and others preclude accepting this view, at least in the form in which it is stated. Praz's stress on the epigram also leads him to emphasize brevity as the most desirable quality of a good conceit, a quality which presumably helped make it "sharp" or "pointed." Brevity in the conceit was commended by the theorists of the conceit themselves, but they also recognized what we would today call the "expanded metaphor," and they often seem to mean by "brevity" a quality opposed to the Ciceronian notion of *copia*. There is, of course, no reason why an epigram should not have conceits, but there is also no apparent reason to establish a determined relationship between "concettismo" and epigram and, via the epigram, between "concettismo" and the emblem. I shall take up the more fundamental inadequacies of the emblem theory in detail when I discuss the views of Austin Warren below, since he presents this theory in purer form than does Praz. In the latter's version the emblem plays an important role, but mediately, through the epigram, which had to be brief, play-

---

7. Praz, *Richard Crashaw*, pp. 144 ff. This desire to force "influences" leads Praz to find it strange that metaphysical poetry should have flourished in England, although the emblem did not have a very wide vogue there (cf. *Studi dul concettismo*, p. 202).

ful, and puzzling and was analogous to illusory perspective in the arts. However, while this analysis is true of certain individual works, especially of some productions of the school of Marino, it is inadequate to the movement as a whole and gives no real clue to the *forma mentis* of a "concettista."

Indeed, this theory of the conceit was implicitly rejected by the seventeenth-century theorists of the conceit in whose works the emblem and *impresa*, as well as the epigram or "arte lapidaria," are treated as incidental topics involved in the analysis of conceit or metaphor. They were fully aware that any theory of the conceit had to be a theory of metaphor or analogy, not a theory of genres. Emmanuele Tesauro, for example, analyzed all genres, literary and artistic, as forms of "acutezze" or types of metaphorical expression by extending the categories of rhetoric to include all literary and figurative creations.[8] Thus Tesauro himself realized that the roots of "concettismo" lay deeper than any classification of genres and were rooted in the nature of expression itself. Not only the epigram but all genres, including the lyric itself, had become "metaphysical."

Austin Warren, as I observed above, shares some of Praz's conceptions about the emblem to an even greater degree. He says:

> The connection of the emblem with poetry was, from the start, close: indeed the term often transferred itself from the picture to the epigram which ordinarily accompanied it. . . . Thus the arts reinforced one another. The influence on poetry was not only to encourage the metaphorical habit but to import to the metaphors a hardness, a palpability which, merely conceived, they were unlikely to possess. And yet the metaphors ordinarily analogized impalpabilities—states of the soul, concepts, abstractions. . . . Many emblems owe their undeniable grotesqueness to the visualization of metaphors, often scriptural, which were not intended to be visualized.[9]

In this particular passage, I take it that Warren means by "hardness" a kind of precision and by "palpability" a strong visual or sensuous element in the image. In any case the "metaphysical" image purportedly acquired these properties from the "emblem habit," which helped to develop metaphorical habits of mind and, presumably, habits for making recondite metaphors instead of commonplace ones.

However, as I have already explained, the theorists of the conceit either do not deal with the emblem at all or treat it merely as one aspect of the general theory of wit, making no direct connection between emblem and conceit. Taking our cue from them once more, we might observe that the qualities of precision and the strong sen-

8. Emmanuele Tesauro, *Il Cannochiale Aristotelico* (2d ed., 1663), chaps. xiv, xv. In these two chapters Tesauro sketched the outline of his generalized theory of wit. Cf. Croce, *Problemi di estetica*, pp. 313 ff.
9. Warren, pp. 73–74.

suous element to be found in much "metaphysical" poetry can be accounted for, to the degree that any poetic "accounts for" a living and creative poetic tradition, by their theory of wit (*ingegno, ingenio, esprit*) as the faculty which, like Bruno's *genio*, finds and expresses the universal analogies latent in the data of experience. The desire to draw correspondences between heterogeneous things and thereby reveal the unity of what appears fragmentary and the desire to develop these correspondences are bound to give to the resultant imagery some of those qualities Warren discerns in the poets of wit.

From a more general critical point of view, the "palpability" or "hardness" of an image is, after all, a function of what the poet wishes to say and can say. In its own way Dante's imagery is as "hard" and "palpable" as one could wish. What the poet can say and the way he can say it are in part given by his culture, in so far as the culture makes him a man of a particular place, time, and environment, and in large part by his imaginative power, which enables him to "inform" and universalize his cultural and personal experience. No poetic has yet explained the secret of his power, although a poetic which is true to the concrete works of art it attempts to describe theoretically can give us insight into the nature of the imagination by telling us what it did with what it worked with. Universal analogy and its later formulation as a poetic can thus tell us something about the Renaissance imagination and throw light on Donne, Marino, Crashaw, and others, in spite of their differences. In this light, it would seem to be an error to attribute a movement such as "concettismo" to some secondary cultural phenomenon such as the "emblem habit" or Ramist logic and try, by so doing, to obliterate the differences between poets by swallowing them up in an influence.

Warren's version of the emblem theory of "metaphysical" poetry is based on a general theory of imagery involving the nature of the analogues in a metaphor:

> All imagery is double in its reference, a composite of perception and conception. Of the ingredients, the proportions may vary. The metaphorist can collate image with image, or image with concept, or concept with image, or concept with concept.[1]

After discussing the series of combinations according to which the "ingredients" of an image may be arranged, he continues:

> Then too, the metaphorists differ widely in the degree of visualization for which they project their images. The epic simile of Homer and of Spenser is fully pictorial; the intent, relative to the poet's architecture, is decorative. On the other hand, the "sunken" and "radical" types of imagery—the conceits of Donne and the "symbols" of Hart Crane—expect scant visualization by the senses.[2]

1. *Ibid.*, p. 177.
2. *Ibid.*

This passage is especially important because the author is here distinguishing between those poets called "metaphysical" (he also seems to include the modern "neo-metaphysicals") and all others. However, in this passage Warren is not analyzing the school of wit and its imagery in terms of "palpability" or "hardness" purportedly derived from the emblem; indeed, he seems to be saying that the Donnean conceit is capable of "scant visualization." It would therefore lack the properties which the emblem supposedly gave to the conceit. In the passage previously cited, Warren closely connected the emblem to the conceit, while in this passage the conceit is completely severed from those properties which it was supposed to have derived from the emblem.

It is clear that we are involved in a contradiction. Unintentionally, Warren is pointing out one important thing about "metaphysical" poetry and about poetic imagery in general. The qualities of the "metaphysical" image seem to have nothing to do with whether or not it can be visualized or with the sensory content of the image itself, although it may be prominent. The qualities of the "metaphysical" image are a function of the *manner* in which the analogues are related, and it is this very point that the theorists of the conceit make when they insist that the wit is in the "form" of the conceit and not in the "matter."

A further reason for the inevitable inadequacy of the emblem theory is the historical fact that the emblem movement, initiated by the introduction of the *Hieroglyphica* of Horapollo to Renaissance Europe, is a cultural phenomenon distinct from the poetry of wit and has other cultural presuppositions. Although emblem and conceit were later found together, they are found together at a relatively late date and usually in minor authors like Quarles, who gave emblems already in existence a verse commentary.[3] Granted that a poet might find an emblem suggestive of some image or another, the vast bulk of the creations of the school of wit do not seem to be related to the emblem literature in any intrinsic way. The very grotesqueness of many of the emblems is testimony to the fact that the conceit preceded—and was therefore independent of—its graphic expression. If anything, it was the conceit which made the emblem grotesque rather than the emblem making the conceit "harder" and more "palpable." Emblems drawn to many of the conceits of Donne or Crashaw or to much of the so-called "decorative imagery" of Homer would all be equally grotesque.

Perhaps the basic unexamined assumption in this whole theory is that there is a radical distinction in kinds of imagery. The sharp cleavage between what are called "decorative" imagery and "functional"

---

3. Cf. *The Hieroglyphics of Horapollo*, Mr. Boas' introduction is quite valutrans. George Boas (New York, 1950). able.***

imagery needs to be closely examined. We might begin by asking in what sense the imagery of Homer can be said to be decorative. It is clear even from a cursory reading of the *Iliad* that many of Homer's analogues for the events of battle are drawn from the world of peaceful endeavor. One of the obvious functions of these analogues is to heighten the pitch of the battle scenes and to bring the "great" world of peace into relationship with the "little" world of war. In this sense the *Iliad* is as much about peace as about war; metaphor is the link between these two worlds, revealing the nature of war through analogy with the events and experiences of peace. It follows that the poet's "choice" of analogues depends upon what he wants to say, upon what elements in the world of men he wishes to bring into the world of his poem. This is at least one sense in which the microcosm-macrocosm analogy is still profoundly vital.

When Homer compares an attacking army to a huge wave breaking on a beach, he would, in the opinion of some, be making a fully pictorial metaphor. However, all the reader has to do is to try to think of the various ways in which an emblem might be constructed to represent this metaphor to see how grotesque the results could be. Two *separate* pictures could be drawn, and they could be quite photographic. But this would not result in the creation of an emblem, for the emblem would have to embody the whole metaphor at once in one representation. We must bear in mind that the metaphor is part identity and part difference. What Homer wants us to see is the way in which a wave under certain conditions is like an army under certain other conditions. By joining these two particular analogues, he selects those qualities of waves which can be transferred to armies. The pictorial quality is not in the whole metaphor or in the identity but in each analogue separately as a kind of sensuous residue remaining after the identity has been established, and as such it is part of the total effect of the image. Thus the pictorial quality remains precisely that aspect of the image which cannot be transferred from one analogue to the other.

It follows from this analysis that, when we speak of "pictorial imagery," we cannot mean that the metaphor can necessarily be absorbed into a pictorial representation or that, conversely, it was necessarily created by a graphic representation. Both historical evidence and theoretical necessity, therefore, require abandoning the emblem theory of "metaphysical" poetry. The emblem movement is more closely related to the tendency in the baroque plastic arts toward breaking down the barriers between the arts in the effort to create a universal art which would somehow combine all of them. Its great vogue was largely the work of the Jesuits, who found the emblem a useful pedagogic device for propagating the faith.

The failure to see the way in which the emblem is related and the extent to which it is not related to the conceit can lead to some further misinterpretations. Praz, for example, derives the limbeck image as used in the writings of the spiritual alchemists from the emblem tradition and believes that this image is a mere "conceit" or witticism.[4] But it was part of the religious and symbolic vocabulary derived from the symbols of empirical alchemy by application of the principle of universal analogy whereby they were extended to apply to all levels of existence. The limbeck was thus no mere suggestive and fanciful image but the symbol of a process that was recapitulated in every order of a universe seen *sub specie alchemiae*. The failure to realize the nature of this image leads Praz to misunderstand the significance of the work of Michael Maier, the alchemist who published an alchemical work containing both emblems and music to be sung to the various stages of the alchemical process, as a very strange example of baroque sensibility or "concettismo."[5] However, what Maier did was to use the emblems for their pedagogic value, much as a chemistry textbook might have illustrations and equations. Music as a necessary part of the alchemical process was a characteristic result of the conviction that all things are universally related and affect each other through correspondences.

Although, as Warren maintains, "both the emblem and the conceit proceed from wit," they do not proceed from the same kind of wit, or in the same way.[6] The relationship is not, above all, filial but, at most, cousinly. Our own time is less "witty" than the time of Donne, and universal analogy has passed out of existence as a common habit of thought; the difficulty we have in penetrating this view of the world from within and somehow understanding it as "natural" and not "perverse" is, perhaps, the most important reason of all for the confusion about the nature of the poetry of wit. Many students of the movement have been aware that what may impress us as perverse, shocking, or recondite need not have had the same effect on contemporaries. This has sometimes been attributed to habitual usage and "taste." However, the "metaphysical" poets and their contemporaries possessed a view of the world founded on universal analogy and derived habits of thought which prepared them for finding and easily accepting the most heterogeneous analogies.[7]

---

4. Praz, *Studi sul concettismo*, pp. 49–50 n., 199–200.
5. Michael Maier, *Atalanta fugiens* (Oppenheim, 1618). Also John Read, *Prelude to Chemistry* (New York, 1937), chap. vi, which is on Maier. Some samples of his music in modern notation are appended to the work. For spiritual alchemy see H. Bremond, *Histoire littéraire du sentiment religieux en France* (Paris, 1925), Vol. VII, Part II, chap. v; and Evelyn Underhill, *Mysticism* (16th ed.; New York, 1948), pp. 140 ff.
6. Warren, p. 75.
7. *Ibid.*, p. 173.

Donne's Love Poetry

C. S. LEWIS

Donne and Love Poetry in the Seventeenth Century †

Little of Manfred (but not very much of him)
—W. S. GILBERT

I have seen an old history of literature in which the respective claims of Shelley and Mrs. Hemans to be the greatest lyrist of the nineteenth century were seriously weighed; and Donne, who was so inconsiderable fifty years ago, seems at the moment to rank among our greatest poets.

If there were no middle state between absolute certainty and what Mr. Kellett calls the whirligig of taste, these fluctuations would make us throw up criticism in despair. But where it is impossible to go quite straight we may yet resolve to reel as little as we can. Such phenomena as the present popularity of Donne or the growing unpopularity of Milton are not to be deplored; they are rather to be explained. It is not impossible to see why Donne's poetry should be overrated in the twentieth and underrated in the eighteenth century; and in so far as we detect these temporary disturbing factors and explain the varying appearances of the object by the varying positions of the observers, we shall come appreciably nearer to a glimpse of Donne *simpliciter*. I shall concern myself in what follows chiefly with his love poetry.

In style this poetry is primarily a development of one of the two styles which we find in the work of Donne's immediate predecessors. One of these is the mellifluous, luxurious, 'builded rhyme,' as in Spenser's *Amoretti*: the other is the abrupt, familiar, and consciously 'manly' style in which nearly all Wyatt's lyrics are written. Most of the better poets make use of both, and in *Astrophel and Stella* much of Sidney's success depends on deliberate contrast between such poetry as

That golden sea whose waves in curls are broken

† From *Seventeenth-Century Studies Presented to Sir Herbert Grierson*, copyright 1938. Pp. 64-84. Reprinted by permission of the publishers, The Clarendon Press, Oxford.

and such poetry as

He cannot love: no, no, let him alone.

But Wyatt remains, if not the finest, yet much the purest example of
the plainer manner, and in reading his songs, with their conversational
openings, their surly (not to say sulky) defiances, and their lack of
obviously poetic ornament, I find myself again and again reminded
of Donne. But of course he is a Donne with most of the genius left
out. Indeed, the first and most obvious achievement of the younger
poet is to have raised this kind of thing to a much higher power; to
have kept the vividness of conversation where Wyatt too often had
only the flatness; to sting like a lash where Wyatt merely grumbled.
The difference in degree between the two poets thus obscures the
similarity in kind. Donne has so far surpassed not only Wyatt but all
the Elizabethans in what may be called their Wyatt moments, and
has so generally abstained from attempting to rival them in their
other vein, that we hardly think of him as continuing one side of their
complex tradition; he appears rather as the innovator who substituted
a realistic for a decorated kind of love poetry.

Now this error is not in itself important. In an age which was at
all well placed for judging the comparative merits of the two styles, it
would not matter though we thought that Donne had invented what
in fact he only brought to perfection. But our own age is not so placed.
The mellifluous style, which we may agree to call Petrarchan though
no English poet is very like Petrarch, has really no chance of a fair
hearing. It is based on a conception of poetry wholly different from
that of the twentieth century. It descends from old Provençal and
Italian sources and presupposes a poetic like that of Dante. Dante, we
may remember, thinks of poetry as something to be made, to be
'adorned as much as possible', to have its 'true sense' hidden beneath
a rich vesture of 'rhetorical colouring'. The 'Petrarchan' sonneteers
are not trying to make their work sound like the speaking voice. They
are not trying to communicate faithfully the raw, the merely natural,
impact of actual passion. The passion for them is not a specimen of
'nature' to be followed so much as a lump of ore to be refined: they
ask themselves not 'How can I record it with the least sophistication?'
but 'Of its bones what coral can I make?', and to accuse them of in-
sincerity is like calling an oyster insincere because it makes its disease
into a pearl. The aim of the other style is quite different. It wishes to
be convincing, intimate, naturalistic. It would be very foolish to set
up these two kinds of poetry as rivals, for obviously they are different
and both are good. It is a fine thing to hear the living voice, the voice
of a man like ourselves, whispering or shouting to us from the printed
page with all the heat of life; and it is a fine thing, too, to see such
life—so pitiably like our own, I doubt not, in the living—caught up
and transfigured, sung by the voice of a god into an ecstasy no less real

though in another dimension.[1] There is no necessary quarrel between the two. But there are many reasons why one of them should start with overwhelming odds in its favour at the present moment. For many years our poetics have been becoming more and more expressionistic. First came Wordsworth with his theory, and we have never quite worked it out of our system; even in the crude form that 'you should write as you talk', it works at the back of much contemporary criticism. Then came the final break-up of aristocracy and the consequent, and still increasing, distaste for arduous disciplines of sentiment—the wholesale acceptance of the merely and unredeemedly natural. Finally, the psychological school of criticism overthrew what was left of the old conception of a poem as a construction and set up instead the poem as 'document'. In so far as we admire Donne for being our first great practitioner in one of the many possible kinds of lyric, we are on firm ground; but the conception of him as liberator, as one who substituted 'real' or 'live' or 'sincere' for 'artificial' or 'conventional' love lyric, begs all the questions and is simply a prejudice de siècle.

But of course when we have identified the Wyatt element in Donne, we have still a very imperfect notion of his manner. We have described 'Busie old foole' and 'I wonder by my troth' and 'For Godsake hold your tongue, and let me love'; but we have left out the cleaving remora, the triple soul, the stiff twin compasses, and a hundred other things that were not in Wyatt. There were indeed a great many things not in Wyatt, and his manly plainness can easily be overpraised—'pauper videri Cinna vult et est pauper'. If Donne had not reinforced the style with new attractions it would soon have died of very simplicity. An account of these reinforcements will give us a rough notion of the unhappily named 'metaphysical' manner.

The first of them is the multiplication of conceits—not conceits of any special 'metaphysical' type but conceits such as we find in all the Elizabethans. When Donne speaks of the morning coming from his mistress's eyes, or tells how they wake him like the light of a taper, these fanciful hyperboles are not, in themselves, a novelty. But, side by side with these, we find, as his second characteristic, what may be called the difficult conceit. This is clearly a class which no two readers will fill up in quite the same way. An example of what I mean comes at the end of The Sunne Rising where the sun is congratulated on the fact that the two lovers have shortened his task for him. Even the quickest reader will be checked, if only for an infinitesimal time, before he sees how and why the lovers have done this, and will experi-

---

1. Those who object to 'emotive terms' in criticism may prefer to read '. . . used by an accomplished poet to produce an attitude relevant not directly to outer experience but to the central nucleus of the total attitude-and-belief-feeling system'. It must not be supposed, however, that the present writer's theory of either knowledge or value would permit him, in the long run, to accept the restatement.

ence a kind of astonished relief at the unexpected answer. The pleasure of the thing, which can be paralleled in other artistic devices, perhaps in rhyme itself, would seem to depend on recurrent tension and relaxation. In the third place, we have Donne's characteristic choice of imagery. The Petrarchans (I will call them so for convenience) had relied for their images mainly on mythology and on natural objects. Donne uses both of these sparingly—though his sea that 'Leaves embroider'd works upon the sand' is as fine an image from nature as I know—and taps new sources such as law, science, philosophy, and the commonplaces of urban life. It is this that has given the Metaphysicals their name and been much misunderstood. When Johnson said that they were resolved to show their learning he said truth in fact, for there is an element of pedantry, or dandyism, an *odi profanos* air, about Donne—the old printer's address not to the *readers* but to the *understanders* is illuminating. But Johnson was none the less misleading. He encouraged the idea that the abstruse nature of some of Donne's similes was poetically relevant for good or ill. In fact, of course, when we have once found out what Donne is talking about—that is, when Sir Herbert Grierson has told us—the learning of the poet becomes unimportant. The image will stand or fall like any other by its intrinsic merit—its power of conveying a meaning "more luminously and with a sensation of delight." The matter is worth mentioning only because Donne's reputation in this respect repels some humble readers and attracts some prigs. What is important for criticism is his avoidance of the obviously poetical image; whether the intractable which he is determined to poetize is fetched from Thomas Aquinas or from the London underworld, the method is essentially the same. Indeed it would be easy to exaggerate the amount of learned imagery in his poems and even the amount of his learning. He knows much, but he seems to know even more because his knowledge so seldom overlaps with our own; and some scraps of his learning, such as that of angelic consciousness or of the three souls in man, come rather too often—like the soldiers in a stage army, and with the same result. This choice of imagery is closely connected with the surprising and ingenious nature of the connexions which Donne makes between the image and the matter in hand, thus getting a double surprise. No one, in the first place, expects lovers to be compared to compasses; and no one, even granted the comparison, would guess in what respect they are going to be compared.

But all these characteristics, in their mere enumeration, are what Donne would have called a "ruinous anatomie." They might all be used—indeed they all are used by Herbert—to produce a result very unlike Donne's. What gives their peculiar character to most of the *Songs and Sonets* is that they are dramatic in the sense of being addressed to an imagined hearer in the heat of an imagined conversation, and usually addresses of a violently argumentative character. The majority of lyrics, even where nominally addressed to a god, a woman, or a friend, are meditations or introspective narratives. Thus Herbert's "Throw away thy rod" is formally an apostrophe; in fact, it is a picture of Herbert's own state of mind. But the majority of the *Songs and Sonets*, including some that are addressed to abstractions like Love, present the poet's state of mind only indirectly and are ostensibly concerned with badgering, wheedling, convincing, or upbraiding an imagined hearer. No poet, not even Browning, buttonholes us or, as we say, "goes for" us like Donne. There are, of course, exceptions. *Goe and catche a falling starre*, though it is in the form of an address, has not this effect; and *Twicknam Garden* or the *Nocturnall* are in fact, as well as in pretension, soliloquies. These exceptions include some of Donne's best work; and indeed, one of the errors of contemporary criticism, to my mind, is an insufficient distinction between Donne's best and Donne's most characteristic. But I do not at present wish to emphasize this. For the moment it is enough to notice that the majority of his love lyrics, and of the *Elegies*, are of the type I have described. And since they are, nearly always, in the form of arguments, since they attempt to extort something from us, they are poetry of an extremely exacting kind. This exacting quality, this urgency and pressure of the poet upon the reader in every line, seems to me to be the root both of Donne's weakness and his strength. When the thing fails it exercises the same dreadful fascination that we feel in the grip of the worst kind of bore—the hot-eyed, unescapable kind. When it succeeds it produces a rare intensity in our enjoyment—which is what a modern critic meant (I fancy) when he claimed that Donne made all other poetry sound less "serious." The point is worth investigation.

For, of course, in one sense these poems are not serious at all. Poem after poem consists of extravagant conceits woven into the preposterous semblance of an argument. The preposterousness is the point. Donne intends to take your breath away by the combined subtlety and impudence of the steps that lead to his conclusion. Any attempt to overlook Donne's "wit" in this sense, or to pretend that his rare excursions into the direct expression of passion are typical, is false criticism. The paradox, the surprise, are essential; if you are not enjoying these you are not enjoying what Donne intended. Thus *Womans Constancy* is of no interest as a document of Donne's "cynicism"— any fool can be promiscuously unchaste and any fool can say so. The merit of the poem consists in the skill with which it leads us to expect a certain conclusion and then gives us precisely the opposite conclusion, and that, too, with an appearance of reasonableness. Thus, again, the art of *The Will* consists in keeping us guessing through each stanza what universal in the concluding triplet will bind together the odd particulars in the preceding six lines. The test case is

The Flea. If you think this very different from Donne's other poems you may be sure that you have no taste for the real Donne. But for the accident that modern cleanliness by rendering this insect disgusting has also rendered it comic, the conceit is exactly on the same level as that of the tears in A *Valediction: of weeping.*

And yet the modern critic was right. The effect of all these poems is somehow serious. 'Serious' indeed is the only word. Seldom profound in thought, not always passionate in feeling, they are none the less the very opposite of gay. It is as though Donne performed in deepest depression those gymnastics which are usually a sign of intellectual high spirits. He himself speaks of his '*concupiscence* of wit'. The hot, dark word is well chosen. We are all familiar—at least if we have lived in Ireland—with the type of mind which combines furious anger with a revelling delight in eloquence, nay grows more rhetorical as anger increases. In the same way, wit and the delight in wit are, for Donne, not only compatible with, but actually provoked by, the most uneasy passions—by contempt and self-contempt and unconvinced sensuality. His wit is not so much the play as the irritability of intellect. But none the less, like the angry Irishman's *clausulae*, it is still enjoyed and still intends to produce admiration; and if we do not hold our breaths as we read, wondering in the middle of each complication how he will resolve it, and exclaiming at the end 'How ever did you think of *that?*" (Carew speaks of his 'fresh invention'), we are not enjoying Donne.

Now this kind of thing can produce a very strong and a very peculiar pleasure. Our age has nothing to repent of in having learned to relish it. If the Augustans, in their love for the obviously poetical and harmonious, were blind to its merits, so much the worse for them. At the same time it is desirable not to overlook the special congeniality of such poetry to the twentieth century, and to beware of giving to this highly specialized and, in truth, very limited kind of excellence, a place in our scheme of literary values which it does not deserve. Donne's rejection of the obviously poetical image was a good method —for Donne; but if we think that there is some intrinsic superiority in this method, so that all poetry about pylons and *non obstantes* must needs be of a higher order than poetry about lawns and lips and breasts and orient skies, we are deceived—deceived by the fact that we, like Donne, happen to live at the end of a great period of rich and nobly obvious poetry. It is natural to want your savoury after your sweets; but you must not base a philosophy of cookery on that momentary preference. Again, Donne's obscurity and occasional abstruseness have sometimes (not always) produced magnificent results, and we do well to praise them. But, as I have hinted, an element of dandyism was present in Donne himself—he 'would have no such readers as he could teach'—and we must be very cautious here lest

shallow call to shallow. There is a great deal of dandyism (largely of
Franco-American importation) in the modern literary world. And
finally, what shall we say of Donne's 'seriousness', of that persistency,
that nimiety, that astringent quality (as Boehme would have said)
which makes him, if not the saddest, at least the most uncomfortable,
of our poets? Here, surely, we find the clearest and most disturbing
congeniality of all. It would be foolish not to recognize the growth in
our criticism of something that I can only describe as literary Mani-
chaeism—a dislike of peace and pleasure and heartsease simply as
such. To be bilious is, in some circles, almost the first qualification
for a place in the Temple of Fame.[2] We distrust the pleasures of
imagination, however hotly and unmerrily we preach the pleasures of
the body. This seriousness must not be confused with profundity. We
do not like poetry that essays to be wise, and Chaucer would think
we had rejected 'doctryne' and 'solas' about equally. We want, in fact,
just what Donne can give us—something stern and tough, though not
necessarily virtuous, something that does not conciliate. Born under
Saturn, we do well to confess the liking complexionally forced upon
us; but not to attempt that wisdom which dominates the stars is pusil-
lanimous, and to set up our limitation as a norm—to believe, against
all experience, in a Saturnocentric universe—is folly.

Before leaving the discussion of Donne's manner I must touch,
however reluctantly, on a charge that has been brought against him
from the time of Ben Jonson till now. Should he, or should he not,
be hanged for not keeping the accent? There is more than one reason
why I do not wish to treat this subject. In the first place, the whole
nature of Donne's stanza, and of what he does within the stanza, cannot be profitably discussed except by one who knows much more than
I do about the musical history of the time. *Confined Love*, for example, is metrically meaningless without the tune. But I could make
shift with that difficulty: my real trouble is of quite a different kind.
In discussing Donne's present popularity, the question of metre forces
me to a statement which I do not make without embarrassment. Some
one must say it, but I do not care for the office, for what I have to say
will hardly be believed among scholars and hardly listened to by any
one else. It is simply this—that the opinions of the modern world on
the metre of any poet are, in general, of no value at all, because most
modern readers of poetry do not know how to scan. My evidence for
this amazing charge is twofold. In the first place I find that very many
of my own pupils—some of them from excellent schools, most of
them great readers of poetry, not a few of them talented and (for their
years) well-informed persons—are quite unable, when they first come
to me, to find out from the verse how Marlowe pronounced Barabas

---

2. In this we have been anticipated. See
Emma, ch. 25: 'I know what worthy
people they are. Perry tells me that Mr.
Cole never touches malt liquor. You
would not think it to look at him, but he
is bilious—Mr. Cole is very bilious.'

or Mahomet. To be sure, if challenged, they will say that they do not believe in syllable-counting or that the old methods of scansion have been exploded, but this is only a smoke screen. It is easy to find out that they have not got beyond the traditional legal fiction of longs and shorts and have never even got so far: they are in virgin ignorance. And my experience as an examiner shows me that this is not peculiar to my own pupils. My second piece of evidence is more remarkable. I have heard a celebrated belle-lettrist—a printed critic and poet— repeatedly, in the same lecture, so mispronounce the name of a familiar English poem as to show that he did not know a decasyllabic line when he met it. The conclusion is unavoidable. Donne may be metrically good or bad, in fact; but it is obvious that he might be bad to any degree without offending the great body of his modern admirers. On that side, his present vogue is worth precisely nothing. No doubt this widespread metrical ignorance is itself a symptom of some deeper change; and I am far from suggesting that the appearance of *vers libre* is simply a result of the ignorance. More probably the ignorance, and the deliberate abandonment, of accentual metres are correlative phenomena, and both the results of some revolution in our whole sense of rhythm—a revolution of great importance reaching deep down into the unconscious and even perhaps into the blood. But that is not our business at the moment.

The sentiment of Donne's love poems is easier to describe than their manner, and its charm for modern readers easier to explain. No one will deny that the twentieth century, so far, has shown an extraordinary interest in the sexual appetite and has been generally marked by a reaction from the romantic idealization of that appetite. We have agreed with the romantics in regarding sexual love as a subject of overwhelming importance, but hardly in anything else. On the purely literary side we are wearied with the floods of uxorious bathos which the romantic conception undoubtedly liberated. As psychologists we are interested in the new discovery of the secreter and less reputable operations of the instinct. As practical philosophers we are living in an age of sexual experiment. The whole subject offers us an admirable field for the kind of seriousness I have just described. It seems odd, at first sight, that a sixteenth-century poet should give us so exactly what we want; but it can be explained.

The great central movement of love poetry, and of fiction about love, in Donne's time is that represented by Shakespeare and Spenser. This movement consisted in the final transmutation of the medieval courtly love or romance of adultery into an equally romantic love that looked to marriage as its natural conclusion. The process, of course, had begun far earlier—as early, indeed, as the *Kingis Quhair*—but its triumph belongs to the sixteenth century. It is most powerfully expressed by Spenser, but more clearly, and philosophically by

Chapman in that under-estimated poem, his *Hero and Leander*. These poets were engaged, as Professor Vinaver would say, in reconciling Carbonek and Camelot, virtue and courtesy, divine and human love; and incidentally in laying down the lines which love poetry was to follow till the nineteenth century. We who live at the end of the dispensation which they inaugurated and in reaction against it are not well placed for evaluating their work. Precisely what is revolutionary and creative in it seems to us platitudinous, orthodox, and stale. If there were a poet, and a strong poet, alive in their time who was failing to move with them, he would inevitably appear to us more 'modern' than they.

But was Donne such a poet? A great critic has assigned him an almost opposite role, and it behoves us to proceed with caution. It may be admitted at once that Donne's work is not, in this respect, all of a piece; no poet fits perfectly into such a scheme as I have outlined —it can be true only by round and by large. There are poems in which Donne atttempts to sing a love perfectly in harmony with the moral law, but they are not very numerous and I do not think they are usually his best pieces. Donne never for long gets rid of a medieval sense of the sinfulness of sexuality; indeed, just because the old conventional division between Carbonek and Camelot is breaking up, he feels this more continuously and restively than any poet of the Middle Ages.

Donne was bred a Roman Catholic. The significance of this in relation to his learned and scholastic imagery can be exaggerated; scraps of Calvin, or, for that matter, of Euclid or Bacon, might have much the same poetical effect as his scraps of Aquinas. But it is all-important for his treatment of love. This is not easily understood by the modern reader, for later-day conceptions of the Puritan and the Roman Catholic stand in the way. We have come to use the word 'Puritan' to mean what should rather be called 'rigorist' or 'ascetic', and we tend to assume that the sixteenth-century Puritans were 'puritanical' in this sense. Calvin's rigorist theocracy at Geneva lends colour to the error. But there is no understanding the period of the Reformation in England until we have grasped the fact that the quarrel between the Puritans and the Papists was not primarily a quarrel between rigorism and indulgence, and that, in so far as it was, the rigorism was on the Roman side. On many questions, and specially in their view of the marriage bed, the Puritans were the indulgent party; if we may without disrespect so use the name of a great Roman Catholic, a great writer, and a great man, they were much more Chestertonian than their adversaries. The idea that a Puritan was a repressed and repressive person would have astonished Sir Thomas More and Luther about equally. On the contrary, More thought of a Puritan as one who 'loved no lenten fast nor lightly no fast else, saving breakfast and eat fast and drink fast and luske fast in their lechery'—a person only too likely to end up in the 'abominable heresies' of the Anabaptists about communism of goods and wives. And Puritan theology, so far from being grim and gloomy, seemed to More to err in the direction of fantastic optimism. 'I could for my part', he writes, 'be very well content that sin and pain and all were as shortly gone as Tindall telleth us: but I were loth that he deceved us if it be not so.' More would not have understood the idea, sometimes found in the modern writers, that he and his friends were defending a 'merry' Catholic England against sour precisions; they were rather defending necessary severity and sternly realistic theology against wanton labefaction— penance and 'works' and vows of celibacy and mortification and Purgatory against the easy doctrine, the mere wish-fulfillment dream, of salvation by faith. Hence when we turn from the religious works of More to Luther's *Table-talk* we are at once struck by the geniality of the latter. If Luther is right, we have waked from nightmare into sunshine: if he is wrong, we have entered a fools' paradise. The burden of his charge against the Catholics is that they have needlessly tormented us with scruples; and, in particular, that 'Antichrist will regard neither God nor the love of women'. 'On what pretence have they forbidden us marriage? 'Tis as though we were forbidden to eat, to drink, to sleep.' 'Where women are not honoured, temporal and domestic government are despised.' He praises women repeatedly: More, it will be remembered, though apparently an excellent husband and father, hardly ever mentions a woman save to ridicule her. It is easy to see why Luther's marriage (as he called it) or Luther's 'abominable bichery' (if you prefer) became almost a symbol. More can never keep off the subject for more than a few pages.

This antithesis, if once understood, explains many things in the history of sentiment, and many differences, noticeable to the present day, between the Protestant and the Catholic parts of Europe. It explains why the conversion of courtly love into romantic monogamous love was so largely the work of English, and even of Puritan, poets; and it goes far to explain why Donne contributes so little to that movement.

I trace in his poetry three levels of sentiment. On the lowest level (lowest, that is, in order of complexity), we have the celebration of simple appetite, as in *Elegy XIX*. If I call this a pornographic poem, I must be understood to use that ugly word as a descriptive, not a dyslogistic, term. I mean by it that this poem, in my opinion, is intended to arouse the appetite it describes, to affect not only the imagination but the nervous system of the reader.[3] And I may as well say at once

3. The restatement of this in terms acceptable to the Richardian school (for whom all poetry equally is addressed to the nervous system) should present no difficulty. For them it will be a distinction between parts, or functions, of the system.

—but who would willingly claim to be a judge in such matters?—that it seems to me to be very nearly perfect in its kind. Nor would I call it an immortal poem. Under what conditions the reading of it could be an innocent act is a real moral question; but the poem itself contains nothing intrinsically evil.

On the highest, or what Donne supposed to be the highest, level we have the poems of ostentatiously virtuous love, *The Undertaking*, *A Valediction: forbidding mourning*, and *The Extasie*. It is here that the contrast between Donne and his happier contemporaries is most marked. He is trying to follow them into the new age, to be at once passionate and innocent; and if any reader will make the experiment of imagining Beatrice or Juliet or Perdita, or again, Amoret or Britomart, or even Philoclea or Pamela, as the auditress throughout these poems, he will quickly feel that something is wrong. You may deny, as perhaps some do, that the romantic conception of 'pure' passion has any meaning; but certainly, if there is such a thing, it is not like this. It does not prove itself pure by talking about purity. It does not keep on drawing distinctions between spirit and flesh to the detriment of the latter and then explaining why the flesh is, after all, to be used. This is what Donne does, and the result is singularly unpleasant. The more he labours the deeper 'Dun is in the mire', and it is quite arguable that *The Extasie* is a much nastier poem than the nineteenth *Elegy*. What any sensible woman would make of such a wooing it is difficult to imagine—or would be difficult if we forgot the amazing protective faculty which each sex possesses of not listening to the other.

Between these two extremes falls the great body of Donne's love poetry. In certain obvious, but superficial, respects, it continues the medieval tradition. Love is still a god and lovers his 'clergie'; oaths may be made in 'reverentiall feare'' of his 'wrath'; and the man who resists him is 'rebell and atheist'. Donne can even doubt, like Soredamors, whether those who admit Love after a struggle have not forfeited his grace by their resistance, like

> Small townes which stand stiffe, till great shot
> Enforce them.

He can personify the attributes of his mistress, the 'enormous gyant' her Disdain and the 'enchantress *Honor*', quite in the manner of *The Romance of the Rose*. He writes *Albas* for both sexes, and in the *Holy Sonnets* repents of his love poetry, writing his palinode, in true medieval fashion. A reader may wonder, at first, why the total effect is so foreign to the Middle Ages: but Donne himself has explained this when he says, speaking of the god of Love,

> If he wroung from mee a teare, I brin'd it so
> With scorne or shame, that him it nourish'd not.

This admirable couplet not only tells us, in brief, what Donne has effected but shows us that he knew what he was doing. It does not, of course, cover every single poem. A few pieces admittedly express delighted love and they are among Donne's most popular works; such are *The Good-morrow* and *The Anniversarie*—poems that again remind us of the difference between his best and his typical. But the majority of the poems ring the changes on five themes, all of them grim ones—on the sorrow of parting (including death), the miseries of secrecy, the falseness of the mistress, the fickleness of Donne, and finally on contempt for love itself. The poems of parting stand next to the poems of happy love in general popularity and are often extremely affecting. We may hear little of the delights of Donne's loves, and dislike what we hear of their 'purity'; the pains ring true. The song *Sweetest love, I do not goe* is remarkable for its broken, but haunting, melody, and nowhere else has Donne fused argument, conceit, and classical imitation into a more perfect unity. *The Feaver* is equally remarkable, and that for a merit very rare in Donne—its inevitability. It is a single jet of music and feeling, a straight flight without appearance of effort. The remaining four of our five themes are all various articulations of the 'scorne or shame' with which Donne 'brines' his reluctantly extorted tributes to the god of Love; monuments, unparalleled outside Catallus, to the close kinship between certain kinds of love and certain kinds of hate. The faithlessness of women is sometimes treated, in a sense, playfully; but there is always something—the clever surprise in *Womans Constancy* or the grotesque in *Goe and catche a fallinge starre*—which stops these poems short of a true anacreontic gaiety. The theme of faithlessness rouses Donne to a more characteristic, and also a better, poetry in such a hymn of hate as *The Apparition*, or in the sad mingling of fear, contempt, and self-contempt in *A Lecture upon the Shadow*. The pains of secrecy give opportunity for equally fierce and turbulent writing. I may be deceived when I find in the sixteenth *Elegy*, along with many other nauseas and indignations, a sickened male contempt for the whole female world of nurses and 'midnight startings' and hysterics; but *The Curse* is unambiguous. The ending here is particularly delicious just because the main theme—an attack on *Jalosie* or the 'lozengiers'—is so medieval and so associated with the 'honour of love'. Of the poet's own fickleness one might expect, at last, a merry treatment; and perhaps in *The Indifferent* we get it. But I am not sure. Even this seems to have a sting in it. And of *Loves Usury* what shall I say? The struggle between lust and reason, the struggle between love and reason, these we know; but Donne is perhaps the first poet who has ever painted lust holding love at arm's length, in the hope 'that there's no need to trouble himself with any such thoughts yet'—and all this only as an introduction to the crown-

ing paradox that in old age even a reciprocated love must be endured.
The poem is, in its way, a masterpiece, and a powerful indirect expression of Donne's habitual 'shame and scorne'. For, in the long run,
it must be admitted that 'the love of hatred and the hate of love' is
the main, though not the only, theme of the *Songs and Sonets*. A
man is a fool for loving and a double fool for saying so in 'whining
poetry'; the only excuse is that the sheer difficulty of drawing one's
pains through rhyme's vexation 'allays' them. A woman's love at best
will be only the 'sphear' of a man's—inferior to it as the heavenly
spheres are to their intelligences or air to angels. Love is a spider that
can transubstantiate all sweets into bitter: a devil who differs from
his fellow devils at court by taking the soul and giving nothing in exchange. The mystery which the Petrarchans or their medieval predecessors made of it is 'imposture all', like the claims of alchemists. It is
a very simple matter (*foeda et brevis voluptas*), and all it comes to
in the end is

> that my man
> Can be as happy as I can.

Unsuccessful love is a plague and tyranny; but there is a plague even
worse—Love might try

> A deeper plague, to make her love mee too!

Love enjoyed is like gingerbread with the gilt off. What pleased the
whole man now pleases one sense only—

> And that so lamely, as it leaves behinde
> A kinde of sorrowing dulnesse to the minde.

The doctors say it shortens life.

It may be urged that this is an unfair selection of quotations, or
even that I have arrived at my picture of Donne by leaving out all his
best poems, for one reason or another, as 'exceptions', and then describing what remains. There is one sense in which I admit this. Any
account of Donne which concentrates on his love poetry must be unfair to the poet, for it leaves out much of his best work. By hypothesis,
it must neglect the dazzling sublimity of his best religious poems, the
grotesque charm of *The Progresse of the Soule*, and those scattered,
but exquisite, patches of poetry that appear from time to time amidst
the insanity of *The First and Second Anniversaries*. Even in the *Epistles* there are good passages. But as far as concerns his love poetry, I
believe I am just. I have no wish to rule out the exceptions, provided
that they are admitted to be exceptions. I am atempting to describe
the prevailing tone of his work, and in my description no judgement
is yet implied.

To judgement let us now proceed. Here is a collection of verse describing with unusual and disturbing energy the torments of a mind

which has been baffled in its relation to sexual love by certain temporary and highly special conditions. What is its value? To admit the 'unusual and disturbing energy' is, of course, to admit that Donne is a poet; he has, in the modern phrase, 'put his stuff across'. Those who believe that criticism can separate inquiry into the success of communication from that into the value of the thing communicated will demand that we should now proceed to evaluate the 'stuff'; and if we do so, it would not be hard to point out how transitory and limited and, as it were, accidental the appeal of such 'stuff' must be. But something of the real problem escapes under this treatment. It would not be impossible to imagine a poet dealing with this same stuff, marginal and precarious as it is, in a way that would permanently engage our attention. Donne's real limitation is not that he writes *about*, but that he writes *in*, a chaos of violent and transitory passions. He is perpetually excited and therefore perpetually cut off from the deeper and more permanent springs of his own excitement. But how is this to be separated from his technique—the nagging, nudging, quibbling stridency of his manner? It a man writes thus, what can he communicate but excitement? Or again, if he finds nothing but excitement to communicate, how else should he write? It is impossible here to distinguish cause from effect. Our concern, in the long run, must be with the actual poetry (the 'stuff' *thus* communicated, this communication of *such* 'stuff') and with the question how far that total phenomenon is calculated to interest human imagination. And to this question I can see only one answer: that its interest, save for a mind specially predisposed in its favour, must be short-lived and superficial, though intense. Paradoxical as it may seem, Donne's poetry is too simple to satisfy. Its complexity is all on the surface—an intellectual and fully conscious complexity that we soon come to the end of. Beneath this we find nothing but a limited series of 'passions'—explicit, mutually exclusive passions which can be instantly and adequately labelled as such—things which can be readily talked about, and indeed, must be talked about because, in silence, they begin to lose their hard outlines and overlap, to betray themselves as partly fictitious. That is why Donne is always arguing. There are puzzles in his work, but we can solve them all if we are clever enough; there is none of the depth and ambiguity of real experience in him, such as underlies the apparent simplicity of *How sleep the brave* or *Songs of Innocence*, or even Αἰαῖ Λευψύδριον.[4] The same is true, for the most part, of the specifically 'metaphysical' comparisons. One idea has been put into each and nothing more can come out of it. Hence they tend to die on our hands, where some seemingly banal comparison of a woman to a flower or God's anger to flame can touch us at innumerable levels and

---

4. The superficial simplicity here is obvious; the deeper ambiguity becomes evident if we ask whether Lipsydrion is an object of detestation or of nostalgic affection.

renew its virginity at every reading. Of all literary virtues 'originality', in the vulgar sense, has, for this reason, the shortest life. When we have once mastered a poem by Donne there is nothing more to do with it. To use his own simile, he deals in earthquakes, not in that 'trepidation of the spheres' which is so much less violent but 'greater far'.

Some, of course, will contend that his love poems should interest me permanently because of their 'truth'. They will say that he has shown me passion with the mask off, and catch at my word 'uncomfortable' to prove that I am running away from him because he tells me more truth than I can bear. But this is the mere frenzy of anti-romanticism. Of course, Donne is true in the sense that passions such as he presents do occur in human experience. So do a great many other things. He makes his own selection, like Dickens, or Gower, or Herrick, and his world is neither more nor less 'real' than theirs; while it is obviously less real than the world of Homer, or Virgil, or Tolstoy. In one way, indeed, Donne's love poetry is less true than that of the Petrarchans, in so far as it largely omits the very thing that all the pother is about. Donne shows us a variety of sorrows, scorns, angers, disgusts, and the like which arise out of love. But if any one asked 'What is all this *about*? What is the attraction which makes these partings so sorrowful? What is the peculiarity about this physical pleasure which he speaks of so contemptuously, and how has it got tangled up with such a storm of emotions?', I do not know how we could reply except by pointing to some ordinary love poetry. The feeblest sonnet, almost, of the other school would give us an answer with coral lips and Cupid's golden wings and the opening rose, with perfumes and instruments of music, with some attempt, however trite, to paint that iridescence which explains why people write poems about love at all. In this sense Donne's love poetry is parasitic. I do not use this word as a term of reproach; there are so many good poets, by now, in the world that one particular poet is entitled to take for granted the depth of a passion and deal with its froth. But as a purely descriptive term, 'parasitic' seems to me true. Donne's love poems could not exist unless love poems of a more genial character existed first. He shows us amazing shadows cast by love upon the intellect, the passions, and the appetite; to learn of the substance which casts them we must go to other poets, more balanced, more magnanimous, and more humane. There are, I well remember, poems (some two or three) in which Donne himself presents the substance; and the fact that he does so without much luxury of language and symbol endears them to our temporarily austere taste. But in the main, his love poetry is *Hamlet* without the prince.

Donne's influence on the poets of the seventeenth century is a commonplace of criticism. Of that influence at its best, as it is seen in the great devotional poetry of the period, I have not now to speak. In love poetry he was not, perhaps, so dominant. His *nequitiae* probably encouraged the cynical and licentious songs of his successors, but, if so, the imitation is very different from the model. Suckling's impudence, at its best, is light-hearted and very unlike the ferocity of Donne; and Suckling's chief fault in this vein—a stolid fleshliness which sometimes leads him to speak of his mistress's body more like a butcher than a lecher—is entirely his own. The more strictly metaphysical elements in Donne are, of course, lavishly reproduced; but I doubt if the reproduction succeeds best when it is most faithful. Thus Carew's stanzas *When thou, poor Excommunicate* or Lovelace's *To Lucasta, going beyond the Seas* are built up on Donne's favourite plan, but both, as it seems to me, fail in that startling and energetic quality which this kind of thing demands. They have no edge. When these poets succeed it is by adding something else to what they have learned from Donne—in fact by reuniting Donne's manner with something much more like ordinary poetry. Beauty (like cheerfulness) is always breaking in. Thus the conceit of asking where various evanescent, beautiful phenomena go when they vanish and replying that they are all to be found in one's mistress is the sort of conceit that Donne might have used; and, starting from that end, we could easily work it up into something tolerably like bad Donne. As thus:

> Oh fooles that aske whether of odours burn'd
> The seminall forme live, and from that death
> Conjure the same with chymique arte—'tis turn'd
> To that quintessence call'd her Breath!

But if we use the same idea as Carew uses it we get a wholly different effect:

> Ask me no more where Jove bestows
> When June is past, the fading rose:
> For in your beauty's orient deep
> These flowers, as in their causes, sleep.

The idea is the same. But the choice of the obvious and obviously beautiful rose, instead of the recondite seminal form of vegetables, the great regal name of Jove, the alliteration, the stately voluptuousness of a quatrain where all the accented syllables are also long in quantity (a secret little known)—all this smothers the sharpness of thought in sweetness. Compared with Donne, it is almost soporific; compared with it, Donne is shrill. But the conceit is there; and 'as in their causes, sleep' which looks at first like a blunder, is in fact a paradox that Donne might have envied. So again, the conceit that the lady's hair outshines the sun, though not much more than an Elizabethan conceit, might well have appeared in the *Songs and Sonets*; but Donne would neither have wished, nor been able, to attain the radiance of Lovelace's

But shake your head and scatter day!

This process of enchanting, or, in Shakespeare's sense, 'translating' Donne was carried to its furthest point by Marvell. Almost every element of Donne—except his metrical roughness—appears in the *Coy Mistress*. Nothing could be more like Donne, both in the grimness of its content and in its impudently argumentative function, than the conceit that

> worms shall try
> That long preserved virginity.

All the more admirable is the art by which this, and everything else in that poem, however abstruse, dismaying, or sophistical, is subordinated to a sort of golden tranquility. What was death to Donne is mere play to Marvell. 'Out of the strong', we are tempted to say, 'has come sweetness', but in reality the strength is all on Marvell's side. He is an Olympian, ruling at ease for his own good purposes, all that intellectual and passionate mobility of which Donne was the slave, and leading Donne himself, bound, behind his chariot.

From all this we may conclude that Donne was a 'good influence'— a better influence than many greater poets. It would hardly be too much to say that the final cause of Donne's poetry is the poetry of Herbert, Crashaw, and Marvell; for the very qualities which make Donne's kind of poetry unsatisfying poetic food make it a valuable ingredient.

JOAN BENNETT

The Love Poetry of John Donne †

A Reply to Mr. C. S. Lewis

In that brilliant and learned book *The Allegory of Love* Mr. Lewis writes, 'cynicism and idealism about women are twin fruits on the same branch—are the positive and negative poles of a single thing'. Few poets provide a better illustration of this than John Donne. These *Songs and Sonets* and *Elegies* which, Mr. Lewis would have us believe, never explain 'why people write poems about love at all', are the work of one who has tasted every fruit in love's orchard, from that which pleased only while he ate it—

> And when hee hath the kernell eate
> Who doth not fling away the shell?—

† From *Seventeenth-Century Studies Presented to Sir Herbert Grierson*, copyright 1938. Pp. 85-104. Reprinted by permission of the publishers, The Clarendon Press, Oxford.

to that which raised a thirst for even fuller spiritual satisfaction, so
that he wrote:

> Here the admyring her my mind did whett
> To seeke thee God.

How is it then that distinguished critics wonder what it is all about;
that Dryden declares 'Donne perplexes the minds of the fair sex with
nice speculations of philosophy, when he should engage their hearts
and entertain them with the softness of love'; and that Mr. Lewis
wonders 'what any sensible woman can make of such love-making'? A
part of the trouble is, I believe, that they are accustomed to, or that
they prefer, another kind of love poetry, in which the poet endeavours
to paint the charms of his mistress:

> Some asked me where Rubies grew
>   And nothing I did say:
> But with my finger pointed to
>   The lips of Julia.
> Some asked how Pearls did grow and where?
>   Then spoke I to my Girle,
> To part her lips and show them there
>   the Quarelets of Pearl.

Donne tells us very little about that beauty of 'colour and skin'
which he describes in *The Undertaking* as 'but their oldest clothes'.
He writes almost exclusively about the emotion, and not about its
cause; he describes and analyses the experience of being in love, if I
may use that word for the moment to cover his many kinds of experience which range from the mere sensual delight presupposed in *Elegy
XIX* to the 'marriage of true minds' celebrated in *The Good-morrow*,
or in *The Valediction: forbidding mourning*. In *Elegy XIX*, for instance, Donne is writing of the same kind of experience as that of
which Carew writes in *The Rapture*. But Carew expends his poetic
gifts in description of the exquisite body of the woman, so that the
reader can vicariously share his joys. Donne, on the other hand, gives
two lines to description, and even so they are not really about what
he sees; he is content to suggest by analogy the delight of the eye
when the woman undresses:

> Your gown going off, such beauteous state reveals,
> As when from flowry meads th' hills shadow steales.

The poem is not about her exquisite body, but about what he feels
like when he stands there waiting for her to undress. Now it may be
that 'any sensible woman' would rather be told of

> Thy bared snow and thy unbraided gold,

but I am not sure. She can see that in her looking-glass, or she may
believe she sees these things reflected in the work of some painter, for

the painter's art can show such things better than any words. It may
interest her more to know what it feels like to be a man in love. In
any case, it is of that that Donne chooses to write. He is not incapable
of describing physical charms; his description of a blush in *The Second Anniversary*:

> her pure, and eloquent blood
> Spoke in her cheekes, and so distinctly wrought,
> That one might almost say, her body thought;

is better, in my judgement, than Spenser's

> And troubled bloud through his pale face was seene
> To come and goe with tydings from the hart.[1]

Or again, Mr. Lewis speaks of the radiance of Lovelace's line,

> But shake your head and scatter day,

which was anticipated, and perhaps suggested, by Donne's

> Ev'ry thy haire for love to worke upon
> Is much too much, some fitter must be sought;
> For, nor in nothing, nor in things
> Extreme, and scatt'ring bright, can love inhere.

But the fact remains that such touches of description are very rare in
Donne's poetry. His interest lay elsewhere, namely in dramatizing,
and analysing, and illustrating by a wealth of analogy the state, or
rather states, of being in love.

But what does he mean by love? We have the whole mass of
Donne's poems before us, thrown together higgledy-piggledy with no
external evidence as to when or to whom any one of them was written.
And in some of them love is 'imposture all', or 'a winter-seeming summers night'; in others physical union is all in all so that two lovers in
bed are a whole world; and elsewhere we are told that

> Difference of sex no more wee knew
> Than our Guardian Angells doe.

And elsewhere again:

> Our bodies why doe wee forbeare?
> They are ours, though they are not wee, Wee are
> The intelligences, they the spheare.
> We owe them thankes because they thus
> Did us, to us, at first convay,
> Yeelded their forces, sense, to us,
> Nor are drosse to us, but allay.

The temptation to assign each poem to a particular period and to
associate each with a particular woman is very strong. It has been

---

1. *The Faerie Queene*, I. ix, 51.

yielded to again and again, not only in Sir Edmund Gosse's biography, but much more recently. Yet it must be resisted for two reasons: first because we have no evidence as to when any one of the *Songs and Sonets* was written, and secondly because we cannot know how far the experience of which any one of them treats was real or imaginary. Mr. Lewis is very well aware of these things. But it is no less misleading to go to the other extreme and read them as though they were all written at one time, or all with equal seriousness and sincerity. We have some important facts to guide us. Between the years 1597 and 1601 Donne fell in love with Anne More. He married her in 1601, as Walton puts it, 'without the allowance of those friends whose approbation always was, and ever will be necessary, to make even a virtuous love become lawful'. He had nine children by her, and watched over them with her when they were sick, and suffered with her when some of them died. He had been married seven years when he wrote a letter headed 'From mine hospital at Mitcham', in which he says:

> I write from the fire-side in my parlour, and in the noise of three gamesome children, and by the side of her whom, because I have transplanted to such a wretched fortune, I must labour to disguise that from her by all such honest devices, as giving her my company and discourse.

Three years later, in 1611, Donne is reluctant to leave home and travel with his patron Sir Robert Drury, because his wife, who was then with child, 'professed an unwillingness to allow him any absence from her saying her divining soul boded her some ill in his absence'. The wording of that sentence, quoted by Walton, is heard again in one of Donne's loveliest songs, but the sense is reversed. Experience tells us that when we are afraid to let a loved one go it is not, as a rule, because *we* may come to harm in his absence. It is much more probable that Anne Donne was afraid for her husband on those dangerous seas to which his poetry so often refers, and that he then wrote the lyric for her, which pleads:

> Let not thy divining heart
>   Forethinke me any ill,
> Destiny may take thy part,
>   And may thy feares fulfill;
>   But thinke that wee
> Are but turn'd aside to sleepe;
> They who one another keepe
>   Alive n'er parted bee.

This is of course conjecture, and I claim no more than a strong probability. It was on this journey with Sir Robert, which Donne finally and reluctantly undertook, that he saw that 'vision of his wife a dead child in her arms' that Walton so convincingly describes. I am not concerned with the authenticity or otherwise of the vision, but with the direction of Donne's thoughts. In 1614, thirteen years after his marriage, we have further evidence of the constancy and of the quality of Donne's love for his wife. In a letter to Sir Robert More, on 10 August of that year, he again explains why he cannot and will not leave Anne in solitude:

> When I begin to apprehend that, even to myself, who can relieve myself upon books, solitariness was a little burdensome, I believe it would be much more so to my wife if she were left alone. So much company therefore, as I am, she shall not want; and we had not one another at so cheap a rate as that we should ever be weary of one another.

Such words need no comment. But if any more evidence is required as to the nature and endurance of Donne's love for his wife, we have *Holy Sonnet XVII*, written after her death in 1617:

> Since she whom I lov'd hath payd her last debt
> To Nature, and to hers, and my good is dead,
> And her Soule early into heaven ravished,
> Wholly on heavenly things my mind is sett.
> Here the admyring her my mind did whett
> To seeke thee God; so streames do shew their head.

Without claiming any knowledge as to the dates of particular poems, we are bound to recognize that seventeen years of married love will have taught Donne something he did not know when he wrote, for instance, *Elegy VII*. And we do, in fact, find that the poems express views of love which could scarcely all have been held at the same time.

Mr. Lewis, of course, recognizes that Donne's love poetry is 'not all of a piece'. 'There are poems', he admits, 'in which Donne attempts to sing of a love perfectly in harmony with the moral law, but they are not very numerous and I do not think they are usually among his best pieces'. That judgement seems to me very odd, but it is impossible to discuss it without first deciding of what 'moral law' we are thinking. The moral law governing sexual relations has veen very differently conceived of in different periods of the world's history. No one has expounded the medieval view more clearly than Mr. Lewis himself in *The Allegory of Love* where he explains[2] that, for the medieval Church,

> love itself was wicked and did not cease to be wicked if the object of it were your own wife. . . . The views of the medieval churchman on the sexual act within marriage are limited by two complementary agreements. On the one hand nobody ever asserted that the act was intrinsically sinful. On the other hand all were agreed that some evil element was present in every concrete instance of it since the Fall.

2. On page 14.

Mr. Lewis believes that Donne never for long freed himself from this 'medieval sense of the sinfulness of sexuality'. Born a Roman Catholic, and deeply read in the Fathers of the Church, he must of course have considered it. But does his poetry support the belief that he continued to accept it? The value of Donne's love poetry largely depends upon the answer. 'The great central movement of love poetry in Donne's time', Mr. Lewis reminds us, was at variance with the medieval view. It was now believed that marriage sanctified sexual love; and for Spenser, once the marriage ceremony is over, the sexual act is its proper consummation and the chaste moon bears witness to it in the *Epithalamion*:

> Who is the same, which at my window peepes?
> Or whose is that faire face that shines so bright?
> Is it not Cinthia, she that never sleepes,
> But walkes about high heaven al the night?
> O fayrest goddesse, do thou not envy
> My love with me to spy:
> For thou likewise didst love, though now unthought,
> And for a fleece of wooll, which privily
> The Latmian shepherd once unto thee brought,
> His pleasure with thee wrought.
> Therefore to us be favorable now;
> And sith of womens labours thou hast charge,
> And generation goodly dost enlarge,
> Encline thy will t'effect our wishful vow,
> And the chaste wombe informe with timely seed,
> That may our comfort breed:
> Till which we cease our hopeful hap to sing,
> Ne let the woods us answere, nor our Eccho ring.

On the other hand, in Chapman's *Hero and Leander*, to which Mr. Lewis especially invites our attention, we have the reverse aspect of this view of the morality of love. The sexual act before marriage, albeit the expression of true love, is not in harmony with the moral law:

> By this the Sovereign of Heavens golden fires,
> And young *Leander*, Lord of his desires,
> Together from their lovers armes arose:
> Leander into Hellespontus throwes
> His Hero-handled bodie, whose delight
> Made him disdaine each other Epithete,
> And as amidst the enamoured waves he swims,
> The God of gold of purpose guilt his lims,
> That this word guilt, including double sence,
> The double guilt of his *Incontinence*,
> Might be exprest, that had no stay t'employ
> The treasure which the Love-God let him joy
> In his deare Hero, with such sacred thrift,
> As had beseemed so sanctified a gift:

But like a greedie vulgar Prodigall
Would on the stock dispend, and rudely fall
Before his time, to that unblessed blessing,
Which for lusts plague doth perish with possessing.

Where does Donne stand in relation either to this belief that marriage, and marriage alone, sanctifies the sexual act, or to the medieval view that it is alike sinful within or without the marriage bond? If I read the poetry aright, he accepts neither view, or rather he totally rejects the second and does not consider the first. The purity or otherwise of the act depends for him on the quality of the relation between the lovers. We have in *The Sunne Rising* a celebration of the same event as in the stanza quoted from *Epithalamion*; but the difference in treatment is noteworthy. Donne is joyously impudent to the sun, whereas Spenser is ceremoniously respectful to the moon, and (which is the point here relevant), in Donne's poem we neither know nor care whether the marriage ceremony has taken place. For Donne, if delight in one another is mutual, physical union is its proper consummation; but, if the lovers are not 'inter-assuréd of the mind', then 'the sport' is 'but a winter-seeming summers night', and

at their best
Sweetnesse and wit they are but *mummy* possest.

There are a number of poems in which Donne is writing about love which has not reached physical consummation, but there is only one, *The Undertaking*, in which he writes as though this state of affairs were satisfactory. Elsewhere he makes it plain that he has merely acquiesced, not without protest, in the human laws that forbade what he holds to be the natural expression of human loves. This reluctant obedience to the rules is most clearly stated in *The Relique*, where he explains precisely how he and the woman behaved, and makes known in a parenthesis what he thinks of the law that inhibited them:

Comming and going, wee
Perchance might kisse, but not between those meales
Our hands ne'er toucht the seales,
Which nature, injur'd by late law, sets free.

Donne's poetry is not about the difference between marriage and adultery, but about the difference between love and lust. He does not establish the contrast between them in any one poem, but we arrive at his views by submitting ourselves to the cumulative evidence of all his poetry and, in so far as they are relevant, of his prose and his life as well. The most important part of this evidence is the violent contrast between his cynical poems and those in which he celebrates

our waking souls
Which watch not one another out of feare.

In order to establish that contrast I must, unfortunately, refer to the vexed question of Donne's rhythm. Mr. Lewis assures us that 'most modern readers do not know how to scan'. However that may be, unless they can hear the difference between quick and slow movements, or between smooth and staccato, and unless they can submit to the rhythm sufficiently to throw the emphasis precisely where Donne has arranged for it to fall, they cannot understand his poetry. If they can hear these things they will be aware of the difference between the bored, flippant tone of

> Will no other vice content you?
> Will it not serve your turn to do, as did your mothers?
> Or have you all old vices spent, and now would finde out others?
> Or doth a feare, that men are true, torment you?
> Oh we are not, be not you so,
> Let mee, and doe you, twenty know;

and the tone of angry scorn in

> Must I alas
> Frame and enamell Plate, and drinke in Glasse?
> Chase waxe for others seales? breake a colts force
> And leave him then, beeing made a ready horse;

and, so utterly remote from either, the controlled emotion in

> I scarce believe my love to be so pure
>   As I had thought it was,
>   Because it doth endure
> Vicissitude, and season, as the grasse;
> Methinks I lyed all winter when I swore,
> My love was infinite, if spring make' it more.

The greatness of Donne's love poetry is largely due to the fact that his experience of the passion ranged from its lowest depths to its highest reaches. No one, not even Shakespeare, knew better than he that

> The expense of spirit in a waste of shame
> Is lust in action; and till action, lust
> Is perjured, murderous, bloody, full of blame,
> Savage, extreme, rude, cruel, not to trust;
> Enjoy'd no sooner but despised straight;
> Past reason hunted; and no sooner had,
> Past reason hated.

Many of the *Songs and Sonets* and the *Elegies* dramatize the experience which Shakespeare here describes. But Donne came to know also the 'marriage of true minds', and many of his poems are about that experience. Nor does he repent of this love poetry in the *Holy Sonnets*; on the contrary, he expressly states that love for his wife led directly to the love of God. He does not even overlook his grosser experiences, but is prepared to use 'prophane love' to illustrate his faith in Christ's pity:

> No, no, but as in my idolatrie
> I said to all my profane mistresses
> Beauty, of pitty, foulnesse only is
> A signe of rigour: so I say to thee,
> To wicked spirits are horrid shapes assign'd
> This beauteous forme assures a piteous minde.

There is no note of shame here, neither wallowing self-abasement nor a hiding or forgetting of the past. He is simply using, characteristi-cally, just what is relevant for his present purpose. Physical beauty, which his poetry so seldom describes, he nevertheless accepts as a type of the soul's beauty:

> For though mind be the heaven where love doth sit
> Beauty a convenient type may be to figure it.

Donne never despised the flesh. Even in a Lenten sermon he asks his hearers 'what Christian is denied a care of his health and a good habitude of body, or the use of those things which may give a cheerfulness to his heart and a cheerfulness to his countenance', and in his *Litany* he prays

> From thinking us all soule, neglecting thus
> Our mutuall duties, Lord deliver us.

Mr. Lewis's objections to *The Extasie* depend upon Donne's treatment of the relation between soul and body, and it is therefore important to discover what in fact Donne thought about this. 'Love does not', writes Mr. Lewis, 'prove itself pure by talking about purity. It does not keep on drawing distinctions between spirit and flesh to the detriment of the latter and then explaining that the flesh is after all to be used.' I must admit that I find this rather perplexing. Perhaps nothing can be proved by talking about it, neither the purity of love nor the purity of Donne's poetry. But language is the poet's only means of communication, and if Chapman is allowed to express his conception of the immorality of premarital relations by talking about it, why may not Donne, by the same means, express his belief that

> As our blood labours to beget
>   Spirits as like soules as it can,
> Because such fingers need to knit
>   That subtile knot that makes us man:
> So must pure lovers soules descend
>   T'affections, and to faculties,
> Which sense may reach and apprehend,
>   Else a great Prince in prison lies.

On what grounds does Mr. Lewis object to Donne 'drawing distinctions between spirit and flesh to the detriment of the latter'? What else could he do? Could a man of his time and of his religion have thought of the flesh either as equal to or as indistinguishable from the spirit? Donne, like any man of his time, and, I suppose, any Christian of any time, thinks of the body as inferior to the soul, although it can be the 'temple of the Holy Ghost'. He is not singular in supposing that, in this life, the soul can and must express itself through the body. Milton goes so far as to assert that even the Angels need some equivalent for this means of expression:

> Whatever pure thou in the body enjoy'st
> (And pure thou wert created,) we enjoy
> In eminence; and obstacle find none
> Of membrane, joint, or limb, exclusive bars;
> Easier than air with air, if Spirits embrace,
> Total they mix, union of pure with pure
> Desiring, nor restrain'd conveyance need,
> As flesh to mix with flesh, or soul with soul.[3]

Donne, in *The Extasie*, is attempting (by his usual means of employing a series of analogies) to explain that the union of spirit with spirit expresses itself in the flesh, just as the soul lives in the body and, in this world, cannot exist without it. The passage quoted above includes one of these analogies, an obscure one for modern readers because it depends on contemporary physiology. Sir Herbert Grierson supplies a quotation from Burton's *Anatomy of Melancholy* which gives the explanation:

> The spirits in a man which are the thin and active part of the blood, and so are of a kind of middle nature, between soul and body, those spirits are able to doe, and they doe the office, to unite and apply the faculties of the soul to the organs of the body, and so there is a man.

Sir Herbert also refers us to Donne's twenty-sixth sermon which throws yet more light on the notion to which the poem refers:

> As the body is not the man [writes Donne], nor the soul is not the man, but the union of the soul and the body, by those spirits through which the soul exercises her faculties in the organs of the body, makes up the man; so the union of the Father and the Son to one another, and of both to us, by the Holy Ghost, makes up the body of the Christian religion.

There are, I suppose, three possible views of the relation between soul and body: the Manichaean view that the body is the work of the Devil; the materialist view that 'explains all psychical processes by physical and chemical changes in the nervous system', and so makes

3. *Paradise Lost*, Bk. viii, 622-9.

the soul non-existent; and the orthodox Christian view that the body and the soul are both from God and therefore both good. We seem to have wandered far from Donne's *Extasie*, and if Mr. Lewis is right in thinking it a 'nasty' poem, these philosophical considerations are irrelevant, and these theological considerations even worse. But is he right? The point Donne wishes to make in *The Extasie*, as in so many of his serious love poems, is that a man and a woman united by love may approach perfection more nearly than either could do alone:

> A single violet transplant
>   The strength, the colour, and the size,
> (All which before was poore, and scant,)
>   Redoubles still, and multiplies.
> When love, with one another so
>   Interinanimates two soules,
> That abler soule, which thence doth flow,
>   Defects of loneliness controules.

I have tried to show that Donne was very far from retaining 'the medieval view of the sinfulness of sex'; but Mr. Lewis has yet another accusation to bring, equally incompatible with my own belief that Donne is one of the greatest love poets in the English language. Contempt for women seems to him to permeate the poetry. Once again I shall be forced to assume that readers are more sensitive to rhythm than Mr. Lewis supposes, for I am going to quarrel with Mr. Lewis's interpretation of *Elegy XVI* largely by appealing to the reader's ear. He admits that he 'may be deceived' when he finds here 'a sickened male contempt for the whole female world of nurses and "midnight startings"'. Most certainly he is deceived, and the varied rhythms of that poem are an important index of the extent of that deception. One of the most remarkable things about the poem is the contrast between the solemn, tender music of the verse whenever Donne addresses the woman, and the boisterous staccato in which he describes the foreign lands to whose dangers she will be exposed if she insists upon following him abroad. I must beg leave to quote the poem at sufficient length to illustrate the nature and extent of this difference.

> By our first strange and fatall interview,
> By all desires which thereof did ensue,
> By our long starving hopes, by that remorse
> Which my words masculine perswasive force
> Begot in thee, and by the memory
> Of hurts, which spies and rivals threatned me,
> I calmly beg: But by thy fathers wrath,
> By all paines, which want and divorcement hath
> I conjure thee, and all the oathes which I
> And thou have sworne to seale joynt constancy,
> Here I unsweare, and overswear them thus,

Thou shalt not love by wayes so dangerous.
Temper, O faire love, loves impetuous rage,
Be my true Mistris still, not my faign'd Page.

It is tempting to quote even more of his melodious pleading, but this
is enough to illustrate the liturgical music of his address to this beloved of whom Mr. Lewis can think Donne is contemptuous. When,
in the same poem, he wants to express contempt, his music is very
different:

Men of France, changeable Camelions,
Spittles of diseases, shops of fashions,
Loves fuellers, and the rightest company
Of Players, which upon the worlds stage be,
Will quickly know thee, and no lesse, alas!
Th'indifferent Italian, as we passe
His warme land, well content to thinke thee Page,
Will hunt thee with such lust, and hideous rage,
As *Lots* faire guests were vext.

And now, in case the point is not yet proven, let us hear how he speaks
of her 'midnight startings', and how the rhythm changes once again
as she comes back into the picture:

When I am gone, dreame me some hapinesse,
Nor let thy lookes our long hid love confesse,
Nor praise, nor dispraise me, nor blesse, nor curse
Openly loves force, nor in bed fright thy Nurse
With midnight startings, crying out oh, oh
Nurse, O my love is slaine, I saw him goe
O'r the white Alpes alone; I saw him I,
Assail'd, fight, taken, stabb'd, bleed, fall, and die.
Augure me better chance, except dread *Jove*
Thinke it enough for me to'have had thy love.

I said I would argue my case 'almost' solely on the grounds of rhythm,
but in case Mr. Lewis is right in thinking modern readers are for the
most part impervious to the music of verse, they will, I trust, be convinced that the mere prose sense of the last line is incompatible with
contempt for the woman.

No one will deny that at one period of his life Donne wrote of
women with contempt. At this time he despised them equally for
yielding to his lust or for denying themselves to him. There is nothing
to choose between his contempt for the woman whom he addresses
as 'Nature's lay Idiot' in *Elegy* VII and his contempt for the woman
who has refused him, and to whom he addresses that brilliant piece
of vituperation *The Apparition*. (Whether either situation had its
exact counterpart in real life is beside the point, the contempt in the
poems is real enough.) At this time he treats with equal scorn the
whore, both

Her whom abundance melts and her whom want betraies,

and the 'fain'd vestall', and the woman who

> will bee
> False e'er I come, to two or three.

But the measure of his contempt for easy virtue, coyness, and faith-lessness is the measure of his admiration when he finds a woman to whom he can say

> So thy love may be my love's sphere.

But to Mr. Lewis that, too, sounds contemptuous; and as *Aire and Angels* has been variously understood, it is worth while to pause and examine the sentence in its context. The poem is an account of Donne's search for, and final discovery of, the true object of love. It begins with much the same idea as he expresses in the first stanza of *The Good-morrow*:

> If ever any beauty I did see,
> Which I desired, and got, 'twas but a dream of thee.

In *Aire and Angels*:

> Twice or thrice had I loved thee,
> Before I knew thy face or name;
> So in a voice, so in a shapelesse flame,
> *Angells* affect us oft, and worship'd bee;
> Still when, to where thou wert, I came
> Some lovely glorious nothing I did see.

And here, as so often elsewhere in the *Songs and Sonets*, Donne asserts his belief that 'pure lovers soules' must 'descend t'affections, and to faculties':

> But since my soule, whose child love is,
> Takes limmes of flesh, and else could nothing doe,
> More subtile than the parent is,
> Love must not be, but take a body too.

And at first he imagines that the physical beauty of the loved woman is the object of his search:

> And therefore what thou wert, and who,
> I bid love aske, and now
> That it assume thy body, I allow,
> And fix it selfe in thy lip, eye, and brow.

So far the progress is one to which we are accustomed, both in the literature of love and in experience; from a general reaching out after beauty to a particular worship of one person who sums up and over-reaches all that had seemed fair in others. So Romeo catches sight of Juliet and forgets Rosalind:

Did my heart love till now? forswear it, sight!
For I ne'er saw true beauty till this night.

But Donne is not satisfied. There is no rest for his love in the bewildering beauty of his mistress:

Whilst thus to ballast love, I thought,
And so more steddily to have gone,
With wares that would sinke admiration,
I saw, I had loves pinnace overfraught,
　Ev'ry thy haire for love to worke upon
Is much too much, some fitter must be sought;
　For, nor in nothing, nor in things
Extreme, and scatt'ring bright, can love inhere.

The search is not yet over. But it is to end in a discovery surely more pleasing to any woman in love than would be the mere worship of her beauty. Beauty is transient, but love can last if it be for something which, though expressed in the body, is yet not the body:

Then as an Angell, face and wings
Of aire, not pure as it, yet pure doth weare,
　So thy love may be my loves spheare.

The doctrine of St. Thomas Aquinas, about the Angels assuming a body of air, provided Donne with the analogy he wanted:

Et sic Angeli assumunt corpora ex aere, condensando ipsum virtute divina, quantam necesse est ad corporis assumendi formationem.

So much is necessary; the point of the image for Donne is that the air-body of the Angels is neither nothing, nor too much, but just sufficient to confine a spirit on earth. So the woman's love for him is a resting-place for his spirit. It is, of course, the final couplet of the poem that has led to mis-understanding. Dr. Leavis, in *Revaluations*,[4] speaks of 'the blandly insolent matter-of-factness of the close' of *Aire and Angels*; and, isolated from its context, that is how it sounds:

　Just such disparitie
As is twixt Aire and Angells puritie,
'Twixt womens love, and mens will ever bee.

There are two possible ways of reading this. The way which I am combating supposes that Donne, reversing the sentiment of the rest of the poem, throws out a contemptuous generalization about the impurity of woman's love in comparison with man's. My own view is that Donne, satisfied with the logical aptness of his image, is, characteristically, indifferent to the associations of the word 'purity', whose meaning is, to his mind, made sufficiently clear by the context. The

4. p. 12.

air-body is only less pure than the angel in so far as it can exist on earth and so enable a spirit to appear to men. A woman's love is only less pure than a man's in so far as it is focused upon a single object and does not continually reach out towards 'some lovely glorious nothing'. I would support this view by referring the reader to other instances in which Donne shows a similar indifference to the irrelevant associations his words may suggest. The use of the word 'pure' in *Loves Growth* is similarly circumscribed by its context:

> I scarce believe my love to be so pure
> As I had thought it was,
> Because it doth endure
> Vicissitude, and season as the grasse.

The sense in which it is not so pure is explained in the next stanza:

> Love's not so pure, and abstract, as they use
> To say, which have no Mistresse but their Muse,
> But as all else, being elemented too,
> Love sometimes would contemplate, sometimes do.

Donne is not saying that love is unclean, or less clean than he had supposed; we have already seen that he does not think of the flesh as impure in that sense, but that, like everything else on earth, it is composed of diverse elements. He is arguing that the quickening of love in the springtime is not an increase, since his love was complete before,

> And yet no greater, but more eminent
> Love by the spring is growne;
> As, in the firmament,
> Starres by the sunne are not inlarg'd, but showne;

and, to make his meaning clear, Donne adds three more images or illustrations:

> Gentle love deeds, as blossomes on a bough,
> From loves awakened root do bud out now.
> If, as in water stir'd more circles bee
> Produc'd by one, love such additions take,
> Those like so many spheares, but one heaven make,
> For, they are all concentrique unto thee.

And finally, the 'blandly matter-of-fact' image:

> As princes doe in times of action get
> New taxes, but remit them not in peace.

Here, however, the last line of the poem,

> No winter shall abate this spring's increase,

prevents the reader from supposing that the prosaic image implies a reversal of the emotional tone of the poem. The point relevant to my argument about *Aire and Angels* is that Donne always trusts the reader to ignore irrelevant associations. The political image here is logically apt, and that is a sufficient reason for him to use it. In a sermon on *The Nativity* he develops at some length an image in which the Saviour is likened to a good coin with which man's debt to God is paid:

> First he must pay it in such money as was lent; in the nature and flesh of man; for man had sinned and man must pay. And then it was lent in such money as was coined even with the image of God; man was made according to his image: that image being defaced, in a new mint, in the womb of the blessed Virgin, there was new money coined; the image of the invisible God, the second person in the Trinity, was imprinted into the human nature. And then, that there might be all fulness, as God, for the payment of this debt, sent down in bullion, and the stamp, that is, God to be conceived in man, and as he provided the mint, the womb of the blessed Virgin, so hath he provided an exchequer, where this money is issued; that is his church, where his merits should be applied to the discharge of particular consciences.

No one, I suppose, will imagine that because Donne uses this mundane imagery he is speaking irreverently of God, of the Virgin Mary, of Christ, and of the Church. He chooses the image, here as elsewhere, because it provides him with an apt analogy.

I hope I may have persuaded some readers that Donne did not think sex sinful, and that contempt for women is not a general characteristic of his love poetry. But Mr. Lewis brings yet one more accusation against him: 'He is perpetually excited and therefore perpetually cut off from the deeper and more permanent springs of his own excitement'. Now one way of answering this would be to say that love is an exciting experience, and that great love poetry is therefore bound to communicate excitement. But with this I am not quite content. Love is exciting, but it is also restful. Unreciprocated love is a torment of the spirit, but reciprocated love is peace and happiness. In the astonishment and uncertainty of the early stages of love there is excitement and there is also fear, but there comes a time when there is confidence and a sense of profound security. Donne is a great love poet because his poetry records and communicates these diverse experiences. He would be less great if it were true that he is 'perpetually excited'. The truth is that, just as his early contempt for women is the measure of his later reverence for one woman, so his vivid experience of the torment of insecure love has made him the more keenly relish the peace of a love

> inter-assured of the mind.

He tells in *The Good-morrow* of lovers who

> Watch not one another out of feare;

and in *The Anniversarie* the final glory of a well-spent year is the sense of safety with which it has endowed the lovers:

> Who is so safe as wee? Where none can doe
> Treason to us except one of us two.

In *The Canonization* he tells us that future lovers will address him and his mistress as

> You to whom love was peace, that now is rage.

And in *The Dissolution* we read of a love so secure that the 'elements' of love, 'fire of Passion, sighs of ayre, water of teares and earthly sad despaire' were 'ne'ere worne out by loves securitie'. There are two alternative readings of this line; it may be 'ne'ere worne out' (never) or 'neere worne out' (nearly). The former seems to me the more probable reading, since Donne is arguing that he is now overburdened with elements, which he is more likely to be if they had not been spent. Moreover, in 'loves securitie', 'fire of Passion, sighs of ayre, water of teares and earthly sad despaire' are not 'worne out' (such love does not call for the expense of spirit); 'never' fits the sense better than 'nearly', but, for my present argument, it is not of vital importance which reading we choose, the significant word is 'securitie'. Nor does Donne merely tell us of the fearlessness, safety, peace, and security that love may give; the serenity of which he speaks is reflected in the movement of his verse, the quiet speaking voice is heard in the rhythm of *The Good-morrow*, and in *A Valediction: forbidding mourning*, and quiet pleading in the last stanza of *A Valediction: of weeping*:

> O more then Moone,
> Draw not up seas to drowne me in thy spheare,
> Weepe me not dead, in thine armes but forbeare
> To teach the sea, what it may do too soone;
> Let not the winde
> Example finde,
> To doe me more harme, than it purposeth;
> Since thou and I sigh one another's breath,
> Who e'r sighs most, is cruellest, and hasts the others death;

and in that gracious lyric, 'Sweetest love I do not goe'.

Since writing the above I have read Professor Crofts's article on John Donne in *Essays and Studies*, vol. xxii, in which he presents much the same case against the love poetry as Mr. Lewis. Their hostility to Donne springs from the same causes. Both are unable to believe that a poet so brilliantly cynical is to be taken seriously when he is reverent or tender. Yet this very diversity of experience and feeling is among Donne's singular merits. Professor Crofts complains (p. 131) that for Donne 'Love when it comes is not an experience which . . . wipes away the trivial, fond records of youthful apostasy'. And that is true;

the memory of trivial and bitter moments was clear enough for him to draw upon them for analogies even in the *Holy Sonnets*; whether this is regrettable or no is a matter of taste. There is no doubt, however, that Donne's habit of drawing upon all and any of his past experience bewilders some readers; it is not customary. Equally unusual is the absence of description which vexes both Mr. Lewis and Professor Crofts. 'He cannot see her—does not apparently want to see her; for it is not of her that he writes but of his relation to her'. That also is perfectly true; the only question is whether good love poetry need be descriptive.

But, in addition to these matters of taste and opinion, Professor Crofts adduces two matters of fact in opposition to the view that Donne's conception of love was altered by his relations with Anne More. The first is Ben Jonson's remark in the *Conversations with Drummond* that 'all his best pieces were written ere he was twenty five years of age'. But we neither know which poems Jonson had read when he made his remark, nor which he thought were the best. The second fact is that the *Metempsychosis* was dated by Donne himself Aug. 1601, four months before his marriage, and it contains cynical generalizations about women. As it is a fragment of a bitter satire against Queen Elizabeth, prompted by the sacrifice of Essex, that is not surprising. Moreover, is it so strange to be contemptuous of many, or even of most women and to love and reverence a few? The love and friendships which Donne enjoyed did not expunge his former experiences, but they enlarged his understanding so that the body of his poetry has a completeness which it could not otherwise have had. He had felt almost everything a man can feel about a woman, scorn, self-contempt, anguish, sensual delight, and the peace and security of mutual love. And he shapes such poems out of all this that we are, as Professor Crofts says, 'aware of the man speaking in a manner and to a degree hardly to be paralleled in our reading of lyric poetry. Every word is resonant with his voice, every line seems to bear the stamp of his peculiar personality'. Is this not enough to set him among the great love poets?

CLEANTH BROOKS

The Language of Paradox †

Few of us are prepared to accept the statement that the language of poetry is the language of paradox. Paradox is the language of sophistry, hard, bright, witty; it is hardly the language of the soul. We are

† Abridged from "The Language of Paradox" in *The Well-Wrought Urn*, copyright 1942, 1947, by Cleanth Brooks. Pp. 3, 9-21. Reprinted by permission of Harcourt, Brace & World, Inc.

willing to allow that paradox is a permissible weapon which a Chesterton may on occasion exploit. We may permit it in epigram, a special subvariety of poetry; and in satire, which though useful, we are hardly willing to allow to be poetry at all. Our prejudices force us to regard paradox as intellectual rather than emotional, clever rather than profound, rational rather than divinely irrational.

Yet there is a sense in which paradox is the language appropriate and inevitable to poetry. It is the scientist whose truth requires a language purged of every trace of paradox; apparently the truth which the poet utters can be approached only in terms of paradox. I overstate the case, to be sure; it is possible that the title of this chapter is itself to be treated as merely a paradox. But there are reasons for thinking that the overstatement which I propose may light up some elements in the nature of poetry which tend to be overlooked.

* * *

T. S. Eliot has commented upon "that perpetual slight alteration of language, words perpetually juxtaposed in new and sudden combinations," which occurs in poetry. It *is* perpetual; it cannot be kept out of the poem; it can only be directed and controlled. The tendency of science is necessarily to stabilize terms, to freeze them into strict denotations; the poet's tendency is by contrast disruptive. The terms are continually modifying each other, and thus violating their dictionary meanings. To take a very simple example, consider the adjectives in the first lines of Wordsworth's evening sonnet: *beauteous, calm, free, holy, quiet, breathless.* The juxtapositions are hardly startling; and yet notice this: the evening is like a nun breathless with adoration. The adjective "breathless" suggests tremendous excitement; and yet the evening is not only quiet but *calm.* There is no final contradiction, to be sure: it is *that* kind of calm and *that* kind of excitement, and the two states may well occur together. But the poet has no one term. Even if he had a polysyllabic technical term, the term would not provide the solution for his problem. He must work by contradiction and qualification.

We may approach the problem in this way: the poet has to work by analogies. All of the subtler states of emotion, as I. A. Richards has pointed out, necessarily demand metaphor for their expression. The poet must work by analogies, but the metaphors do not lie in the same plane or fit neatly edge to edge. There is a continual tilting of the planes; necessary overlappings, discrepancies, contradictions. Even the most direct and simple poet is forced into paradoxes far more often than we think, if we are sufficiently alive to what he is doing.

But in dilating on the difficulties of the poet's task, I do not want to leave the impression that it is a task which necessarily defeats him, or even that with his method he may not win to a fine precision. To use Shakespeare's figure, he can

                                    with assays of bias
By indirections find directions out.

Shakespeare had in mind the game of lawnbowls in which the bowl is
distorted, a distortion which allows the skillful player to bowl a curve.
To elaborate the figure, science makes use of the perfect sphere and
its attack can be direct. The method of art can, I believe, never be
direct—is always indirect. But that does not mean that the master of
the game cannot place the bowl where he wants it. The serious difficulties will only occur when he confuses his game with that of science
and mistakes the nature of his appropriate instrument. Mr. Stuart
Chase a few years ago, with a touching naïveté, urged us to take the
distortion out of the bowl—to treat language like notation.

I have said that even the apparently simple and straightforward
poet is forced into paradoxes by the nature of his instrument. Seeing
this, we should not be surprised to find poets who consciously employ
it to gain a compression and precision otherwise unobtainable. Such
a method, like any other, carries with it its own perils. But the dangers
are not overpowering; the poem is not predetermined to a shallow and
glittering sophistry. The method is an extension of the normal language of poetry, not a perversion of it.

I should like to refer the reader to a concrete case. Donne's "Canonization" ought to provide a sufficiently extreme instance. The basic
metaphor which underlies the poem (and which is reflected in the
title) involves a sort of paradox. For the poet daringly treats profane
love as if it were divine love. The canonization is not that of a pair of
holy anchorites who have renounced the world and the flesh. The
hermitage of each is the other's body; but they do renounce the world,
and so their title to sainthood is cunningly argued. The poem then is
a parody of Christian sainthood; but it is an intensely serious parody
of a sort that modern man, habituated as he is to an easy yes or no, can
hardly understand. He refuses to accept the paradox as a serious rhetorical device; and since he is able to accept it only as a cheap trick,
he is forced into this dilemma. Either: Donne does not take love seriously; here he is merely sharpening his wit as a sort of mechanical exercise. Or: Donne does not take sainthood seriously; here he is merely
indulging in a cynical and bawdy parody.

Neither account is true; a reading of the poem will show that
Donne takes both love and religion seriously; it will show, further,
that the paradox is here his inevitable instrument. But to see this
plainly will require a closer reading than most of us give to poetry.

The poem opens dramatically on a note of exasperation. The "you"
whom the speaker addresses is not identified. We can imagine that it
is a person, perhaps a friend, who is objecting to the speaker's love
affair. At any rate, the person represents the practical world which
regards love as a silly affectation. To use the metaphor on which the

poem is built, the friend represents the secular world which the lovers have renounced.

Donne begins to suggest this metaphor in the first stanza by the contemptuous alternatives which he suggests to the friend:

> . . . chide my palsie, or my gout,
> My five gray haires, or ruin'd fortune flout. . . .

The implications are: (1) All right, consider my love as an infirmity, as a disease, if you will, but confine yourself to my other infirmities, my palsy, my approaching old age, my ruined fortune. You stand a better chance of curing those; in chiding me for this one, you are simply wasting your time as well as mine. (2) Why don't you pay attention to your own welfare—go on and get wealth and honor for yourself. What should you care if I do give these up in pursuing my love.

The two main categories of secular success are neatly, and contemptuously epitomized in the line

> Or the Kings reall, or his stamped face . . .

Cultivate the court and gaze at the king's face there, or, if you prefer, get into business and look at his face stamped on coins. But let me alone.

This conflict between the "real" world and the lover absorbed in the world of love runs through the poem; it dominates the second stanza in which the torments of love, so vivid to the lover, affect the real world not at all—

> What merchants ships have my sighs drown'd?

It is touched on in the fourth stanza in the contrast between the word "Chronicle" which suggests secular history with its pomp and magnificence, the history of kings and princes, and the word "sonnets" with its suggestions of trivial and precious intricacy. The conflict appears again in the last stanza, only to be resolved when the unworldly lovers, love's saints who have given up the world, paradoxically achieve a more intense world. But here the paradox is still contained in, and supported by, the dominant metaphor: so does the holy anchorite win a better world by giving up this one.

But before going on to discuss this development of the theme, it is important to see what else the second stanza does. For it is in this second stanza and the third, that the poet shifts the tone of the poem, modulating from the note of irritation with which the poem opens into the quite different tone with which it closes.

Donne accomplishes the modulation of tone by what may be called an analysis of love-metaphor. Here, as in many of his poems, he shows that he is thoroughly self-conscious about what he is doing. This second stanza, he fills with the conventionalized figures of the Petrarchan

tradition: the wind of lovers' sighs, the floods of lovers' tears, etc.—
extravagant figures with which the contemptuous secular friend might
be expected to tease the lover. The implication is that the poet himself recognizes the absurdity of the Petrarchan love metaphors. But
what of it? The very absurdity of the jargon which lovers are expected
to talk makes for his argument: their love, however absurd it may appear to the world, does no harm to the world. The practical friend
need have no fears: there will still be wars to fight and lawsuits to
argue.

The opening of the third stanza suggests that this vein of irony is
to be maintained. The poet points out to his friend the infinite fund
of such absurdities which can be applied to lovers:

> Call her one, mee another flye,
> We'are Tapers too, and at our owne cost die. . . .

For that matter, the lovers can conjure up for themselves plenty of
such fantastic comparisons: *they* know what the world thinks of
them. But these figures of the third stanza are no longer the threadbare Petrarchan conventionalities; they have sharpness and bite. The
last one, the likening of the lovers to the phoenix, is fully serious, and
with it, the tone has shifted from ironic banter into a defiant but controlled tenderness.

The effect of the poet's implied awareness of the lovers' apparent
madness is to cleanse and revivify metaphor; to indicate the sense in
which the poet accepts it, and thus to prepare us for accepting seriously the fine and seriously intended metaphors which dominate the last
two stanzas of the poem.

The opening line of the fourth stanza,

> Wee can dye by it, if not live by love,

achieves an effect of tenderness and deliberate resolution. The lovers
are ready to die to the world; they are committed; they are not callow
but confident. (The basic metaphor of the saint, one notices, is being
carried on; the lovers in their renunciation of the world, have something of the confident resolution of the saint. By the bye, the word
"legend"—

> . . . if unfit for tombes and hearse
> Our legend bee—

in Donne's time meant "the life of a saint.") The lovers are willing to
forego the ponderous and stately chronicle and to accept the trifling
and insubstantial "sonnet" instead; but then if the urn be well
wrought, it provides a finer memorial for one's ashes than does the
pompous and grotesque monument. With the finely contemptuous,
yet quiet phrase, "halfe-acre tombes," the world which the lovers reject expands into something gross and vulgar. But the figure works

further; the pretty sonnets will not merely hold their ashes as a decent earthly memorial. Their legend, their story, will gain them canonization; and approved as love's saints, other lovers will invoke them.

In this last stanza, the theme receives a final complication. The lovers in rejecting life actually win to the most intense life. This paradox has been hinted at earlier in the phoenix metaphor. Here it receives a powerful dramatization. The lovers in becoming hermits, find that they have not lost the world, but have gained the world in each other, now a more intense, more meaningful world. Donne is not content to treat the lovers' discovery as something which comes to them passively, but rather as something which they actively achieve. They are like the saint, God's athlete:

> Who did the whole worlds soule *contract*, and *drove*
> Into the glasses of your eyes. . . .

The image is that of a violent squeezing as of a powerful hand. And what do the lovers "drive" into each other's eyes? The "Countries, Townes," and "Courtes," which they renounced in the first stanza of the poem. The unworldly lovers thus become the most "worldly" of all.

The tone with which the poem closes is one of triumphant achievement, but the tone is a development contributed to by various earlier elements. One of the more important elements which works toward our acceptance of the final paradox is the figure of the phoenix, which will bear a little further analysis.

The comparison of the lovers to the phoenix is very skillfully related to the two earlier comparisons, that in which the lovers are like burning tapers, and that in which they are like the eagle and the dove. The phoenix comparison gathers up both: the phoenix is a bird, and like the tapers, it burns. We have a selected series of items: the phoenix figure seems to come in a natural stream of association. "Call us what you will," the lover says, and rattles off in his desperation the first comparisons that occur to him. The comparison to the phoenix seems thus merely another outlandish one, the most outrageous of all. But it is this most fantastic one, stumbled over apparently in his haste, that the poet goes on to develop. It really describes the lovers best and justifies their renunciation. For the phoenix is not two but one, "we two being one, are it"; and it burns, not like the taper at its own cost, but to live again. Its death is life: "Wee dye and rise the same . . ." The poet literally justifies the fantastic assertion. In the sixteenth and seventeenth centuries to "die" means to experience the consummation of the act of love. The lovers after the act are the same. Their love is not exhausted in mere lust. This is their title to canonization. Their love is like the phoenix.

I hope that I do not seem to juggle the meaning of *die*. The meaning that I have cited can be abundantly justified in the literature of the period; Shakespeare uses "die" in this sense; so does Dryden. Moreover, I do not think that I give it undue emphasis. The word is in a crucial position. On it is pivoted the transition to the next stanza,

> Wee can dye by it, if not live by love,
> And if unfit for tombes . . .

Most important of all, the sexual submeaning of "die" does not contradict the other meanings: the poet is saying: "Our death is really a more intense life"; "We can afford to trade life (the world) for death (love), for that death is the consummation of life"; "After all, one does not expect to live *by* love, one expects, and wants, to die *by* it." But in the total passage he is also saying: "Because our love is not mundane, we can give up the world"; "Because our love is not merely lust, we can give up the other lusts, the lust for wealth and power"; "because," and this is said with an inflection of irony as by one who knows the world too well, "because our love can outlast its consummation, we are a minor miracle, we are love's saints." This passage with its ironical tenderness and its realism feeds and supports the brilliant paradox with which the poem closes.

There is one more factor in developing and sustaining the final effect. The poem is an instance of the doctrine which it asserts; it is both the assertion and the realization of the assertion. The poet has actually before our eyes built within the song the "pretty room" with which he says the lovers can be content. The poem itself is the well-wrought urn which can hold the lovers' ashes and which will not suffer in comparison with the prince's "halfe-acre tomb."

And how necessary are the paradoxes? Donne might have said directly, "Love in a cottage is enough." "The Canonization" contains this admirable thesis, but it contains a great deal more. He might have been as forthright as a later lyricist who wrote, "We'll build a sweet little nest,/ Somewhere out in the West,/ And let the rest of the world go by." He might even have imitated that more metaphysical lyric, which maintains, "You're the cream in my coffee." "The Canonization" touches on all these observations, but it goes beyond them, not merely in dignity, but in precision.

I submit that the only way by which the poet could say what "The Canonization" says is by paradox. More direct methods may be tempting, but all of them enfeeble and distort what is to be said. This statement may seem the less surprising when we reflect on how many of the important things which the poet has to say have to be said by means of paradox: most of the language of lovers is such—"The Canonization" is a good example; so is most of the language of religion—"He who would save his life, must lose it"; "The last shall be first." Indeed, almost any insight important enough to warrant a great poem apparently has to be stated in such terms. Deprived of the character of paradox with its twin concomitants of irony and wonder, the matter of Donne's poem unravels into "facts," biological, sociological, and economic. What happens to Donne's lovers if we consider them "scientifically," without benefit of the supernaturalism which the poet confers upon them? Well, what happens to Shakespeare's lovers, for Shakespeare uses the basic metaphor of "The Canonization" in his *Romeo and Juliet?* In their first conversation, the lovers play with the analogy between the lover and the pilgrim to the Holy Land. Juliet says:

> For saints have hands that pilgrims' hands do touch
> And palm to palm is holy palmers' kiss.

Considered scientifically, the lovers become Mr. Aldous Huxley's animals, "quietly sweating, palm to palm."

For us today, Donne's imagination seems obsessed with the problem of unity; the sense in which the lovers become one—the sense in which the soul is united with God. Frequently, as we have seen, one type of union becomes a metaphor for the other. It may not be too far-fetched to see both as instances of, and metaphors for, the union which the creative imagination itself effects. For that fusion is not logical; it apparently violates science and common sense; it welds together the discordant and the contradictory. Coleridge has of course given us the classic description of its nature and power. It "reveals itself in the balance or reconcilement of opposite or discordant qualities: of sameness, with difference; of the general, with the concrete; the idea, with the image; the individual, with the representative; the sense of novelty and freshness, with old and familiar objects; a more than usual state of emotion, with more than usual order. . . ." It is a great and illuminating statement, but is a series of paradoxes. Apparently Coleridge could describe the effect of the imagination in no other way.

Shakespeare, in one of his poems, has given a description that oddly parallels that of Coleridge.

> Reason in it selfe confounded,
> Saw Division grow together,
> To themselves yet either neither,
> Simple were so well compounded.

I do not know what his "The Phoenix and the Turtle" celebrates. Perhaps it *was* written to honor the marriage of Sir John Salisbury and Ursula Stanley; or perhaps the Phoenix is Lucy, Countess of Bedford; or perhaps the poem is merely an essay on Platonic love. But the scholars themselves are so uncertain, that I think we will do little violence to established habits of thinking, if we boldly pre-empt the poem for our own purposes. Certainly the poem is an instance of that magic power which Coleridge sought to describe. I propose that we take it for a moment as a poem about that power;

> So they loved as love in twaine,
> Had the essence but in one,
> Two distincts, Division none,
> Number there in love was slaine.

> Hearts remote, yet not asunder,
> Distance and no space was seene
> Twixt this *Turtle* and his Queene;
> But in them it were a wonder. . . .

> Propertie was thus appalled,
> That the selfe was not the same;
> Single Natures double name,
> Neither two nor one was called.

Precisely! The nature is single, one, unified. But the name is double, and today with our multiplication of sciences, it is multiple. If the poet is to be true to his poetry, he must call it neither two nor one: the paradox is his only solution. The difficulty has intensified since Shakespeare's day: the timid poet, when confronted with the problem of "Single Natures double name," has too often funked it. A history of poetry from Dryden's time to our own might bear as its subtitle "The Half-Hearted Phoenix."

In Shakespeare's poem, Reason is "in it selfe confounded" at the union of the Phoenix and the Turtle; but it recovers to admit its own bankruptcy:

> Love hath Reason, Reason none,
> If what parts, can so remaine. . . .

and it is Reason which goes on to utter the beautiful threnos with which the poem concludes:

> Beautie, Truth, and Raritie,
> Grace in all simplicitie,
> Here enclosde, in cinders lie.

> Death is now the *Phoenix* nest,
> And the *Turtles* loyall brest,
> To eternitie doth rest. . . .

> Truth may seeme, but cannot be,
> Beautie bragge, but tis not she,
> Truth and Beautie buried be.

> To this urne let those repaire,
> That are either true or faire,
> For these dead Birds, sigh a prayer.

Having pre-empted the poem for our own purposes, it may not be too outrageous to go on to make one further observation. The urn to

which we are summoned, the urn which holds the ashes of the phoenix, is like the well-wrought urn of Donne's "Canonization" which
holds the phoenix-lovers' ashes: it is the poem itself. One is reminded
of still another urn, Keats's Grecian urn, which contained for Keats,
Truth and Beauty, as Shakespeare's urn encloses "Beautie, Truth, and
Raritie." But there is a sense in which all such well-wrought urns contain the ashes of a Phoenix. The urns are not meant for memorial purposes only, though that often seems to be their chief significance to
the professors of literature. The phoenix rises from its ashes; or ought
to rise; but it will not arise for all our mere sifting and measuring the
ashes, or testing them for their chemical content. We must be prepared to accept the paradox of the imagination itself; else "Beautie,
Truth, and Raritie" remain enclosed in their cinders and we shall end
with essential cinders, for all our pains.

CLAY HUNT

Elegy 19: "To His Mistress Going to Bed" †

The nineteenth Elegy is the most astonishing performance of
Donne's early phase as a brilliant young practitioner in the verse of
wit and impudence. It is an easy poem to enjoy and to understand in
general, and much of it needs no explanation to anyone past the age
of twelve. But after a loosely written and relatively conventional beginning, the poem suddenly rises to verse of passion and power, and it
concludes with a closely contrived passage of perverse philosophic ingenuity which is one of Donne's most intricate and exciting pieces of
intellectual virtuosity. It is this latter half of the poem, especially the
concluding section, which is worth our attention. These are the passages which make the Elegy something more than a piece of mere
clever indecency.

The Elegy belongs almost certainly to the early or middle 1590's, to
the period when Donne was writing poems like "The Indifferent,"
and it was clearly written against the particular social and literary
background which I have described in discussing that poem. Donne
expects his reader to be familiar with some of the stock imagery of
Petrarchan love poetry and to be struck by the novelty in his treatment of the standard poetic propositions that a love affair is a war and
the mistress the "loved foe," that the mistress is an angel, that love is
religious devotion, and that the mistress's beauties are the treasures of
the Indies. He is writing also against the background of the general

† From *Donne's Poetry: Essays in Literary Analysis*, by Clay Hunt, copyright
1954 by Yale University Press. Pp. 18-
31, 207-14. Reprinted by permission of
Yale University Press.

Debate between the Body and the Soul which was the dominant intellectual issue in the literary treatment of love in the 1590's. The two most sharply opposed points of view in this debate can be roughly identified, in their literary manifestations, with the Ovidian and the Platonic traditions in Elizabethan love poetry. Those theorists on love who espoused the doctrines of Renaissance Platonism looked on the body as inessential temporal clothing for the eternal reality of soul; and they believed, if they carried their doctrine to its ultimate conclusion, that the rational lover not only should aspire to rise above sensuality but might hope to advance beyond even a purely spiritual union with the soul of a woman, progressing up the steps of the Stair of Love until his love was finally consummated by the union of his soul with God in the Mystic Experience. Standing against the Platonists was a group of philosophic opponents who thought this conception of the essential nature of love absurd. To this school, who found their chief literary ancestor in Ovid, love was bodily passion unhampered by reason—where both deliberated, the love was slight.[1] True love, in their view, was the irrational and satisfying experience of mere lust.

An Elizabethan reader would have had some hint of what to expect of Elegy 19 from the verse form itself. As a poem about love, written in heroic couplets and entitled an "elegy," it is cast in the currently fashionable literary form derived from Ovid's *Amores*. It was to be expected that a poem in this form would adhere to the Ovidian tradition, that the author would align himself with the proponents of the Body and celebrate the techniques of seduction from the sophisticated point of view of a man about town, and that his literary style would display his ingenuity and wit in elaborate conceits. Donne does not disappoint these expectations.

The Elegy seems to present an actual dramatic situation. The poem is apparently spoken by a lover who is lying in bed waiting for his mistress to join him. It is cast in the form of an argument urging her to undress and get into bed, and it maintains a certain argumentative character throughout. But the latter part of the poem evolves into what is less a direct address to the mistress than a transcript of the private workings of the lover's excited imagination as he anticipates the successive stages of his love-making. At the end of the poem the mistress is still undressing and her lover is still waiting for her. When we have finished the poem, the dramatic situation which it presents appears to be less an actuality than a vividly imagined fiction. The Elegy

1. I am using terms like "school" and "opponents" purposely. Donne himself sometimes dramatized the contemporary analysis of love as a theological dispute between rival philosophic factions. In a letter to Sir Henry Wotton he wrote: "You (I think) and I am much of one sect in the philosophy of love; which, though it be directed upon the mind, doth inhere in the body, and find piety entertainment there." (*The Works of John Donne*, ed. Alford [London, 1839], 6, 352.)

is a dramatized love letter, an Ovidian verse epistle to an only moderately coy mistress.

Donne starts the poem powerfully, with one of the explosive, theatrical openings which are among the distinctive effects of his love poetry. The first four lines derive from one of the most common of the Petrarchan conventions, the comparison of love to warfare, but Donne freshens this stale conceit by exploiting its latent dramatic possibilities. He makes the beginning of the poem a call to battle, a vigorous challenge delivered in a tone of swagger and arrogance. And the sexual puns which he scatters through these lines produce a tough, anti-romantic quality that accentuates the brusque tone suggested by the call-to-battle image.

After this promising beginning, the rest of the opening section (lines 5-24) offers little more than an exercise in the mannerisms of the genre. This passage is jaunty and conventionally indelicate, but it has very little dramatic continuity and no central artistic structure. It presents merely a string of disconnected, flashy, and far-fetched conceits, enlivened by sexual innuendoes.[2] Donne is straining to be novel and clever, but what he writes in these lines is simply a routine performance in the conventional manner of Ovidian erotic verse.

But the poem comes to life again, after the slackness of these lines, in the dramatic power of the following section. The exuberant exploration conceit of this passage has become a *locus classicus* to illustrate the passion and imaginative excitement which the Elizabethans found in geographic exploration and in the discovery of the New World, but the emotional power of Donne's image is the counterpart of a lively intellectual elaboration which explores the analogy in precise detail. The basic metaphor—a comparison of the physical beauties of the mistress to be material riches which the Indies offered to the Renaissance voyagers—is one of the commonplaces of Elizabethan love poetry,[3] but Donne's dramatizing imagination works this routine ma-

2. The following words in the opening section either are sexual puns or carry sexual ambiguities: "powers" (1), "labour" (2), "standing," "fight" (4), "world" (6), "stand" (12), "tread" (17), "received" (20). Donne gets some minor shock effects by playing these suggestions against the theological ambiguities of certain words in these lines. "Safely" in line 17 carres the ambiguity of "in a state of salvation," and "receive" (line 20) is a technical theological term for a mortal's apprehension of supernatural influences or revelations. (Cf. Donne's use of this word in "The First Anniversary," 416. For its sexual meaning, see Webster, *The White Devil*, III, ii, 102.)
3. Cf. Sidney, *Astrophel and Stella*, Sonnet 32; Spenser, *Amoretti*, Sonnet 15; and Romeo's speech in the balcony scene (II, ii, 82):

    wert thou as far
As that vast shore wash'd with the farthest sea,
I would adventure for such merchandise.

The image recurs throughout Donne's poetry, usually in the form of the conventional antithesis between the two Indies—the "India of Spice" (the East Indies) and the "India of Mine" (the West Indies). The phrase "Mine of precious stones" in line 29 stands as a concrete, factual detail of the general image of America, since Donne normally thinks of the New World as the land which offers the voyager gold and precious stones. Cf. Sermon 14: "This sets up upon the two hemispheres of the world; the western hemisphere, the land of gold, and treasure, and the eastern hemisphere, the land of spices and perfumes." (*Works*, ed. Alford, *1*, 281-2.)

terial to sharp concreteness in the treatment of both the metaphor itself and the sexual experience that it describes, which is presented
with an almost anatomical precision. The lover addresses the mistress
in the specific role of an explorer who is requesting a royal patent ("license") which will permit him to discover a new land, explore its unknown riches, conquer it, and, having established himself as its autocratic monarch, bring it under the firm mastery of his civil authority.
The political implications of the conceit are sharpened by allusions to
some of the commonplaces of Renaissance political thought, to the
view that an autocratic monarchy is the most stable form of government (line 28), and to the doctrine that the ruler's freedom in exer-
cising his power is offset by the responsibilities ("bonds") which that
power entails (line 31).[4] This development of the conceit comes to a
dramatic climax in the final line of the passage, which presents the
lover's assumption of full command over his mistress in terms of the
authoritative conclusion to a legal document or proclamation: "To
this I have set my hand and seal." The pun on "seal" in this line, like
the other sexual ambiguities throughout the passage, parallels the particularity of the metaphor with an equally concrete realism in present-
ing the experience to which the metaphor refers.[5]

These lines present, then, a splurge of virtuoso wit in Donne's elaboration of a detailed parallel between the lover's sexual advances and
the discovery and political subjugation of a new land. The exploration
image dramatizes vividly not only the lover's passionate excitement
but also his exultant sense of power in his sexual mastery of his mistress. And the cadences of the verse—the slow, powerful surge of
rhythms through "Before, behind, between, above, below" to the
outburst of "O my America! my new-found-land"—underscore the
metaphoric suggestion of rapt physical passion. The effect of the emotional climax of the passage in line 32, like that of the opening of the
poem, is one of bold, swaggering theatricality.

This effect of cumulative intensity carries over into the exclamatory
opening of the following section and is sustained throughout the passage as the lover excitedly imagines the "whole joys" of sexual con-

4. The detail of the general conceit which
equates the woman's body with a "kingdom" also reflects the political cast of
Donne's imagination in these lines. It
derives from a conventional associative
pattern in the Renaissance mind which
was a part of the system of "correspondences" in the Ordered Universe—the
analogy between the human body and
the Body Politic, which the Renaissance
mind usually thought of as naturally and
properly a kingdom, an autocratic monarchy.
5. For Donne's use of "seal" as a sexual pun see Elegy 7, line 29, and "The
Relic," 29. "License" (25) and "free"
(31) both carry ambiguities of licen-

tiousness in Renaissance usage. (Cf. *As
You Like It*, II, vii, 68, where Shakespeare plays on the sexual suggestion of
both of these words.) And I think Donne
intends also a sexual reference in the
word "mine" in line 29. (See the discussion below of the opening lines of "Love's
Alchemy.") In "A Rapture," which is
based in part on this Elegy, Carew makes
a similar use of "mine" as a sexual metaphor (lines 33–4). The pun on "discovering" (= undressing) is, of course, the
logical basis for the entire conceit, since
it analogizes the situation which the
poem deals with to geographical exploration.

summation. And the intellectual ingenuity which has been operating in the preceding section drives to a climax of virtuosity in lines 33–45 as Donne launches into an intricate and detailed analogy between the ecstatic physical consummation of this *affairé de corps* and the consummation of a purely spiritual love in the religious ecstasy of the Beatific Vision. The link which relates this piece of breezy blasphemy to the general subject of the mistress's undressing is the conventional clothing metaphor suggested in lines 34–5, an image which Donne often used in his later serious treatments of spiritual love and of the Mystic Experience.[6] Since those who regarded love as essentially an impulse of the soul thought of the body as mere evanescent "clothing" for the eternal reality of spirit, the Mystic Ecstasy might be thought of as an experience in which the soul divested itself of its temporal clothes and went naked to immediate contact with God.[7] The basic intellectual maneuver which Donne performs at this point in the poem is simply to turn this stock metaphor upside down. The fanciful argument which this section of the poem develops reduces, then, to the following logical proposition, which is implied in lines 34–5: since the Beatific Vision is like taking off your clothes to experience full joy, then taking off your clothes to experience full joy is like the Beatific Vision. This argument is expanded in the passage as a pseudo-theological validation for nakedness and lust.

Before examining the details with which Donne develops the conceit, we might pause to reflect on how a Renaissance reader would react to this analogy. It is certainly the most startling of all Donne's paradoxes. The basic conceit not only equates the sinful pleasures of the flesh with the pure bliss of heaven, but in effect it also equates the soul with the body, since it identifies the full intellectual "joys" of the naked soul with the full sensual joys of the naked body. Donne thus obliterates, by a single stroke of wit, that sharp dichotomy between Sense and Reason, body and soul, temporal matter and eternal spirit, "things visible" and "things invisible," which was not only the central organizing concept in his own thought but also one of the fundamental conceptual antitheses in the thought of the whole Renaissance. The bright young man who set himself up, at the start of his literary career, as a special practitioner in the shock effect of witty paradox never devised a more shocking paradox than this.

6. This metaphor evidently made a particular appeal to Donne's imagination. He uses it as the basic image for a love directed toward the soul in his most explictly Platonic love poem, "The Undertaking," 13–20. See also the parallel use of the image in the verse letters "To Mrs. M. H." ("Mad paper stay"), 29–32, and "To the Countess of Bedford" ("Honour is so sublime perfection"), 26; and in "A Funeral Elegy," 61. In "Obsequies to the Lord Harrington," 12–13, Donne refers to an "ecstasy" as an "unapparelling" of the mind. The image appears in a sexual context in the "Epithalamion" for the Earl of Somerset, 208–11, and it recurs throughout his other poetry in connection with treatments of the doctrines of philosophic idealism.

7. Cf. Satire 1, lines 43–4:
And till our souls be unapparelled
Of bodies, they from bliss are
banished.

But the perverse wit of this passage would have had a further and more spcific point for the Elizabethan reader. When one reads the poem in the context of the love debate which runs through Elizabethan love poetry, it seems certain that Donne's irreverent allusions to spiritual love and to the Beatific Vision in the climactic section of a poem celebrating the pleasures of purely physical sex could be intended only as ridicule of the school of Platonic Love. The clothing metaphor on which the conceit is based was a conventional analogy not only in Christian mysticism but also in Renaissance Platonism. Though the details of Donne's phrasing and some of the analogies which he uses suggest that his actual source for the doctrines on which the conceit is based was Christian mystical literature rather than the writings of the Renaissance Platonists, the logical progression which is suggested by the analogies in these lines is nevertheless that of the Platonic progression up the Stair of Love. In fact, the details of the conceit in this passage take on logical continuity only when one supplies the theory of Platonic Love as an implied philosophic context. The poetic proposition of this section of the Elegy asserts, in effect, that loving a woman's naked body is philosophically equivalent to loving her soul, and that consummation in sexual intercourse and consummation in the Mystic Experience add up to pretty much the same thing. And that, one might think, would dispose of the Platonists once and for all.

But this passage of the poem needs closer scrutiny, because the powerful shock of Donne's conceit derives chiefly from the rich philosophic and theological implications of the precise details with which he elaborates the basic analogy.[8] The technique of the passage is extremely compressed: Donne throws out, in quick succession, a series of literary or philosophic commonplaces which are intended to call up to the reader's mind a whole systematic body of thought. In order to make clear the logical pattern which gives continuity to the suggestions of each of these details, I will confine my commentary at this point purely to the imaginative implications of the passage, without pausing to point out what each of the details of Donne's conceit actually refers to, in terms of the facts of the situation which the poem presents. It may be useful, therefore, to set out at the start the basic imaginative equations on which Donne builds the entire structure of metaphor in these lines:

(a) As the fundamental equations:
   the body = clothes.
   the soul (or spiritual essence) = the naked body.

8. Compare the different effect which Donne gets from the same analogy in stanza 6 of the "Epithalamion" for the marriage of the Princess Elizabeth. His gingerly treatment of the comparison there makes it a casual conceit, a piece of mere cleverness with little shock value.

(b) Therefore:
> ordinary, sensual lovers = lovers who are content with women who keep their clothes on.
>
> enlightened, Platonic lovers = enlightened lovers like the speaker, who want women naked.

(c) Finally (lines 42-5):
> God = the mistress's naked body.
>
> The Beatific Vision = the sexual orgasm.

The pseudo-logical premise for this fanciful argument is laid down at the start in lines 34–5:

> As souls unbodied, bodies unclothed must be,
> To taste whole joys.

These lines refer to the intellectual joys which the soul can experience fully only by direct contact with God in heaven. The joys of mortal life, by contrast, are partial, since the soul, while it is imprisoned in the earthly body, can know God only mediately, through the distorting veil of sense experience. The soul's yearning for the "whole joys" of immediate, intellectual apprehension of God's Essence can therefore be satisfied only when it strips off the fleshly clothing of the body, when the soul is "unbodied." For most men the soul can be unbodied only after death, but a few chosen spirits are privileged to know this bliss at certain moments during mortal life, when their souls are temporarily withdrawn from their bodies in the Mystic Experience—or, to use Donne's normal terminology, in an "ecstasy."

These are the full doctrinal implications of the first two lines of the conceit. My rather specific expansion of their philosophic suggestion is based on Donne's development of these ideas in the lines which follow, and particularly on the implicit reference to the soul's apprehension of God's Essence in lines 43–5, but the doctrines are so much a commonplace in the formal thought of the Renaissance that an alert and philosophically sophisticated contemporary reader might have guessed what Donne was doing from these lines alone.[9]

In the following lines the imagery defines more fully the implications of lines 34–5 and outlines the process by which a mortal may attain "whole joys." If one responds only to the suggestions of Donne's structure of metaphor and neglects the factual reference of these lines, the following ordered philosophic argument plays above this section of the poem like a continuous, discordant obbligato, clashing violently at every note with what Donne is actually saying. The process of at-

9. These doctrines recur throughout Donne's work. (Cf., e.g., the distinction between mediate and immediate knowledge in "The Second Anniversary," 290–314, and the contrast between the "accidental" joys of earthly life and the "essential" joys of heaven in the conclusion to that poem, lines 471 ff.) The casual, glancing reference which Milton makes to these ideas in a passage in *Areopagitica* suggests how widely current they were in the Renaissance: "but he who thinks we . . . have attained the utmost prospect of reformation that the mortal glass wherein we contemplate can show us till we come to beatific vision . . ." (*Works* [Columbia edition], *4*, 337).

taining "whole joys" will start (lines 35–8) with the love of earthly women. But this love must not be sensual. Women's bodies ("gems" in line 35 = clothes[1]) appeal, to be sure, to men's physical senses ("views" = the sense of sight), but this sexual appeal is superficial and will attract only the unenlightened lovers ("fools"). These lovers misdirect their love into sensuality because that is all which their minds can comprehend: they have "earthly souls," which give them the faculties of physical sensation, but they lack the higher faculty of reason, which should distinguish man from the beasts.[2] Therefore their love is distracted (the Atalanta analogy[3]) from its proper object: it is spent in physical desire for the inessential temporal bodies of women ("theirs") instead of being rationally directed toward women's metaphysical essences, their eternal souls ("them").[4] But (lines 39–40) these sensual lovers misunderstand God's purpose in creating physical beauty if they believe that beautiful women are intended to serve no further end than physical satisfaction. God created the beautiful bodies of women for a purpose analogous to the church's use of religious "pictures" to instill faith in the layman. The church does not intend these pictures to be enjoyed simply in themselves and to provide mere pleasure for the senses. They are intended, rather, to give to ordinary men, who acquire knowledge solely through their senses, a visual experience of beauty which should lead them to the higher, suprasensory understanding which comes from reason and faith.[5]

---

1. Donne substitutes "gems" for "clothes" to permit the Atalanta conceit. He is thinking of the elaborately bejewelled dress of an Elizabethan lady.

2. The phrase "earthly soul" alludes to the scholastic doctrine of the tripartite soul. According to this doctrine, man's soul was divided into three parts: a soul of growth, which he shared with the plants; a soul of sense, which he shared with the animals; and a soul of reason, which was man's distinctive possession and which was the only part of his soul that was immortal. Or Donne may be thinking of a variant of this doctrine in Renaissance Platonic literature which divided man's soul into two parts, a soul of appetite and a soul of reason. (See the passage on Platonic Love in Castiglione's *Book of the Courtier* [Everyman edition], pp. 282–3.) The phrase "earthly soul" refers, then, to the soul of appetite, or the soul of sense. Compare "A Valediction: Forbidding Mourning," 13–20, where Donne draws a distinction between rational lovers, whose love is based on the soul, and common lovers, whose love is mere animal sensuality: "Dull sublunary lovers' / (Whose soul is sense) . . ."

3. The inaccuracy of Donne's reference to the Atalanta myth is interesting as an indication of the casualness of his interest in classical mythology. He evidently thinks that the golden apples were thrown by Atalanta herself to distract the lovers who were pursuing her. Donne's references to mythology are infrequent and occur mostly in the "Elegies"—probably because he had read Ovid before he wrote some of them, or because mythological allusions were part of the machinery of the genre of the love elegy.

4. Donne frequently uses this distinction between the genitive case and the other cases of personal pronouns to suggest the metaphysical difference between the body and the soul. This grammatical trick reflects the philosophic distinction between a man's "substance," his metaphysical identity (the soul—"he," "him") and the "accidents" of his substance (the body —"his"). Cf. Elegy 18, line 26; "The Ecstasy," 51; "The Cross," 36.

5. Donne is referring here to a traditional justification for religious iconography. Cf. Sermon 27: "They had wont to call pictures in the church, the layman's book, because in them, he that could not read at all might read much." (*Works, 1,* 542.) Donne cites Calvin as his source for this analogy in Sermon 122, where he presents an expanded discussion of the idea and distinguishes between the "right use" and the "abuse" of religious pictures. (*Works, 5,* 177.)

And, on the same grounds, those men who are intellectually incapable of a direct, rational response to the content of a sacred book may be drawn indirectly to the knowledge which it offers through their sensory responses to its beautiful binding.[6] For the same reason, God has "arrayed" a woman's soul, her essence, in a physically beautiful body. He has done this in order that ordinary men ("laymen"), after responding to the initial sensory attraction, may be led beyond this physical experience to a rational response to the beauty of her soul and thus to an awareness of the eternal reality of spirit, of which the beautiful body is merely a transitory physical manifestation.

The superior lovers ("we"), on the other hand, neither desire nor need this intermediate sensory step to attain the intellectual enlightenment which is the proper end of love. Having renounced sensuality, they feel only a rational attraction to the intellectual beauty of women's souls ("themselves," "them," as distinguished from "theirs").[7] They desire to apprehend their souls directly by seeing the souls divested of their fleshly clothing ("themselves . . . we . . . must see revealed").

At this point in the poem (lines 42–3) Donne's language takes on a specifically theological reference. This shift in the connotative suggestions of his diction produces a quick imaginative transition. It suggests that, in the metaphoric structure of his conceit, Donne is no longer thinking merely of women's souls as an example of the kind of metaphysical essence which may be apprehended by the enlightened lover, but has turned his thoughts instead to the Essence of God. What actually happens here, as Donne elaborates the logic of his conceit, is that his imagination suddenly takes a quick skip up several steps of the Platonic Stair. According to the doctrine of the Platonists, the lover who has learned to love the beauty of his mistress's soul and to rise above the attraction of her bodily beauty has reached only the first step in the Stair of Love. As he progresses up the logical steps of the stair he proceeds, next, to a love of the beauty of all women; then to the formulation of a universal concept of beauty "that is generally spread over all the nature of man"; and finally to an awareness of God as "the fountain of the sovereign and right beauty." He sees then that the consummation which his amorous soul desires is that of being

---

6. The contrast between the binding and the book as an image for the distinction between the body and the soul is a common metaphor in Elizabethan literature. Cf. *Romeo and Juliet*, III, ii, 83–4 ("Was ever book containing such vile matter / So fairly bound?"), and Lady Capulet's extended development of the conceit in I, iii, 81 ff.

7. For Donne's use of "self" to mean "soul" see Satire 3, line 37, and Sermon 38: "Remember that thy soul is thyself" (*Works*, 2, 80). This usage seems to have been common in the Renaissance. Cf. Sidney, *Astrophel and Stella*, Sonnet 52, line 13.

"haled from the body" and "coupled" with God in the Mystic Experience.[8]

Donne's imagination jumps to this final stage of the Platonic progression in lines 42–3 as he elaborates the hint contained in the word "mystic." "See revealed" carries strong theological overtones. It suggests a desire for a supernatural "revelation" of God rather than for a mere apprehension of a woman's soul.[9] That this transition has been accomplished—that, in the imaginative structure of the conceit, the concept of the spiritual essence of a woman ("themselves") has shaded over into the logically analogous concept of the Essence of God, and that the Platonic lover is now desiring to see God "revealed" in the Beatific Vision—is made clear by line 42, which implies that the revelation will come through the lover's receiving "imputed grace." Donne here uses a technical term from theology[1] to imply a specific theological doctrine—a doctrine which would not need to be introduced into the poem if the erotic experience to which the conceit alludes at this point were nothing beyond the Platonic lover's rational apprehension of the intellectual beauty of a woman's soul. For this kind of intellectual apprehension, the imputation of Grace would not be required. But God's Grace would have to be imputed before a mortal could enjoy the Mystic Ecstasy. The Mystic Experience was not regarded by Christian theologians as in any way an automatic reward for the Platonic lover, or for the Christian mystic, who mortified the flesh and followed a prescribed regimen of devotion. It was a privilege granted to few men in this life, and they did not receive it by virtue of any inherent right or any righteousness to which they could attain as mortals. Moreover, from the standpoint of Christian theology, the apprehension of God's Essence which resulted from the experience did not come through any natural powers that their souls possessed. The Beatific Vision was granted to the soul, and the soul was enabled to

8. I am quoting here from Hoby's translation of Peter Bembo's speech in *The Book of the Courtier* (pp. 317–22). Bembo sums up this progression in his charge to true lovers: "Let us climb up the stairs which at the lowermost step have the shadow of sensual beauty, to the high mansion place where the heavenly, amiable, and right beauty dwelleth, which lieth hid in the innermost secrets of God, lest unhallowed eyes should come to the sight of it; and there shall we find a most happy end for our desires." (Pp. 320-1.) I am citing this passage not as Donne's direct source but rather as one of the chief sources for the doctrines of Platonic Love in Elizabethan England. As I have suggested, not only this section of the Elegy but also those of Donne's other poems in which he treats Platonic Love seriously indicate that Donne was influenced only in general by the literature of Renaissance Platonism: the details of his poetic treatments of Platonic Love are usually drawn from its collateral relative, Christian mysticism, and from scholastic theology. The theological reference of a number of the details in this passage of the Elegy (lines 39–40, 42, 43–5) suggests that Donne's primary sources here are sacred rather than secular. And it is worth noting that the use of sexual imagery in treating the Mystic Experience is frequent in Christian mystical literature. The central conceit in lines 33–45 of this poem derives from a simple inversion of this kind of imagery.

9. "Revelation" is one of the terms which Donne applies specifically to the Mystic Experience. Cf. "A Letter to the Lady Carey and Mrs. Essex Riche," 53–4: "This my Ecstasy and revelation of you both." Line 42 plays, of course, with an ambiguity on "revealed" = undressed.

1. See *N.E.D.*: "impute", 2; and Holy Sonnet 6, line 13: "impute me righteous."

experience it, only through God's special "imputation" of Grace to a being who was inherently neither worthy nor capable of the experience.[2] Donne's reference to this doctrine, then, in lines 42–3, in conjunction with the word "mystic" in the preceding line, implies that the lover seeks this special dispensation which will enable him to pass beyond a union of soul with an earthly woman to the consummation of his love through the union of his naked soul with God.[3]

The following lines (43–5) climax Donne's development of the basic conceit and finally define specifically the philosophic implications of the reference to the "whole joys" of "souls unbodied" at the beginning of the passage. If one responds merely to their imaginative implication and neglects their factual reference, these lines suggest the lover's prayer to God to impute to him the Grace which will permit him to experience the Mystic Ecstasy.[4] They are a plea to God to manifest His Essence so fully ("liberally . . . show thy self") that the desires of the lover's soul may be completely satisfied.[5] This satisfaction is the experiencing of the "whole joys" referred to in line 35: it will consist in "knowing" (line 43)—and at this point Donne alludes

2. Cf. Aquinas, *Summa Theologica*, Q. 12, Art. 4: "It follows, therefore, that to know self-subsistent being . . . is beyond the natural power of any created intellect. . . . Therefore a created intellect cannot see the essence of God unless God by His grace unites Himself to the created intellect." This line of the poem plays on the phrase "imputed grace" to suggest also a woman's gracious granting of sexual favors to a lover who is all unworthy —the conventional Petrarchan love situation.

3. The connotations of "mystic" (= pertaining to the direct communion of the soul with God) in line 41 help accomplish the imaginative transition from the subject of the spiritual love of woman to that of the Mystic Experience. But the primary function of "mystic books" is to complete the layman image of lines 39–40. The phrase develops the implied contrast between the ordinary, sensual lover (the layman who must be attracted to sacred books by their bindings) and the enlightened lover (the clergyman who is permitted to read the book and who thus learns religious mysteries directly). But it is clear from "*see* revealed," and from the rest of lines 43 and 44, which certainly refer to the Beatific Vision, that Donne discards at this point the analogy to the clergyman's understanding of a sacred book. The "revelation" of a woman's body is analogized, not just to an understanding of the religious mysteries which are "revealed" to men in a "mystic book," but rather to a kind of revelation which is seen, to the Sight of God in the Beatific Vision. The woman's body is thus equated, at this point, with God's Essence as "known" directly by the soul of the mystic, and not merely with the kind of knowledge of God which the clergyman gains through a sacred book. The ultimate reference of the book analogy to the undressing situation which the poem deals with indicates also that Donne is punning on "mystic" in its Renaissance sense of "hidden" (= dressed).

4. Compare the prayer which concludes Bembo's exposition of Platonic Love in Book 4 of *The Book of the Courtier*.

5. "Self" is used here, as in line 41, to refer to soul, or metaphysical essence. The questions of whether all souls who experienced the Beatific Vision received an equally full comprehension of God, and whether God granted, through this experience, a partial or a complete manifestation of His Essence—and thus a partial or full knowledge of Himself— had been subjects of scholastic controversy. (See *Summa Theologica*, Q. 12, Arts. 6 and 8.) Cf. Sermon 21, where Donne describes the Beatific Vision and reviews some of the controversy:

And then [in heaven] our way to see him is *patefactio sui*, God's laying himself open, his manifestation, his revelation, his evisceration, and embowelling of himself to us there. Doth God never afford this patefaction, this manifestation of himself in his essence, to any in this life? We cannot answer yea, nor no, without offending a great part in the School, so many affirm, so many deny that God hath been seen in his essence in this life. (*Works, 1*, 423.)

to one of the key biblical texts which provide authority for the concept of the Beatific Vision in Christian theology.[6] The soul's joy in the Mystic Ecstasy will consist in the satisfaction of its thirst for knowledge through a complete comprehension of metaphysical reality, which, since the soul is "unbodied," will be revealed without the distortions of the veil of sense and can thus be apprehended by the soul directly and intellectually.

It may be necessary at this point to issue a reminder that this elaborate structure of philosophic idealism, in the specialized forms of the doctrines of Platonic Love and Christian mysticism, exists in the poem merely as an imaginative analogue to the factual implications of Donne's conceit in these lines. Considered in terms of its denotation, the passage is actually a pseudo-logical presentation of the metaphysic of lust, and Donne's real subject is the sheer physical pleasure of sexual intercourse. Donne brings his reader down to earth, and drives home the shock of his general conceit, by sprinkling the prayer in lines 43–5 with sexual puns. He puns, first, on the sexual meaning of "know," then on "liberally," which carries its Renaissance ambiguity of "lewdly,"[7] and on "show," which is an indecent Renaissance colloquialism for sexual exposure.[8] These ambiguities give the lines a tonal quality which is far from delicate, but Donne's final thrust is reserved for the word "self" in line 45. In line 41 "selves" refers—on the poem's factual level—to a woman's naked body; but the ambiguity on "show" and the precise anatomical suggestions of the phrase "as liberally, as to a midwife" limit the reference of the word in line 45 and make clear that "self" in that line refers not to the woman's body as a whole but rather to her genitals. This twist in the reference of the word is enforced also by the suggestion of the imagery of these lines: this imagery equates the mystic's passionate desire to see the innermost depths of God's Essence with the lustful lover's desire to see the

---

6. The source for Donne's phrasing in "since that I may know" is 1 Corinthians. xiii. 12: "For now we see through a glass darkly; but then face to face: now I know in part; but then shall I know even as also I am known." This biblical allusion operates to enforce the suggestion of the Beatific Vision in the other details of these lines. The same text lies behind the image of the "mortal glass" in Milton's reference to the Beatific Vision in the passage cited above in n. 9. And compare Donne's Sermon 154: *Erimus sicut angeli,* says Christ, "There we shall be as angels." The knowledge which I have by nature shall have no clouds; here it hath. That which I have by grace shall have no reluctation, no resistance; here it

hath. That which I have by revelation shall have no suspicion, no jealousy; here it hath.... There our curiosity shall have this noble satisfaction, we shall know how the angels know by knowing as they know. (*Works, 6,* 184.)

7. Donne makes the same pun in "An Epithalamion ... on the Lady Elizabeth and Count Palatine," 96. Cf. *Hamlet,* IV, vii, 171: "That liberal shepherds give a grosser name."

8. Cf. *Hamlet,* III, ii, 155–9:
   Hamlet: Ay, or any show that you'll show him: be not you ashamed to show, he'll not shame to tell you what it means.
   Ophelia: You are naught, you are naught.

sexually essential part of the mistress' naked body.[9] The modern, secularized reader might pause, at this point, to consider the effect of these lines for the reader of a theologically religious age: they do nothing less than identify a woman's genitals with the Essence of God.

The lover's imagination has now returned from metaphysical acrobatics to concrete fact, and he thinks of the moment when the mistress, in the sequence of events that he anticipates, will have removed all her clothes except her shift. The theological preoccupation of the preceding lines carries over into his final command to her, as he ironically compares her white linen to the ecclesiastical garb of virgins and religious penitents:

> Cast all, yea, this white linen hence,
> Here is no penance, much less innocence.[1]

And the poem's argument for the desirability of undressing concludes, in a summary point of wit, as the lover puns on the sexual meaning of "covering."

The Elegy shows Donne as a brilliant apprentice who is still short of technical mastery. It is an uneven performance, ordinary in some passages and dazzling in others. Though it shows more sense of form than most of Donne's Elegies, the poem as a whole lacks the clear imaginative organization and precise formal definition of his mature work. And the closing section (lines 33 ff.) certainly makes extraordinary demands on the reader. Donne's conception in these lines is brilliant, but it is only partly realized in the execution. In this passage he certainly pays heavily in loss of clarity for what he gains through compression, and I wonder how many of his contemporaries could

9. I think one can trace the steps of Donne's imagination here quite closely. He seems to visualize an essence, or "form," spatially, as something located in the center of a body. See his reference, in the passage cited in note 5, to God's manifestation of His Essence as "his evisceration, and embowelling of himself." Donne's use of the word "centric" to mean "essential" carries a spatial ambiguity in "Love's Alchemy," 2, and in Elegy 18, line 36. Both of these passages show a process of imaginative association similar to that in lines 41–5 of Elegy 19. The various ambiguities which they imply for "centric" set up the following analogical progression: spiritual essence = a woman's soul = a geometric center of a body = a woman's genitals.

1. I think this was the original form of the line. Bennett used this version in his edition of Donne's poems, but Grierson and Hayward prefer the variant reading: "There is no penance due to innocence." Each version has the support of several manuscripts. Probably both are by Donne, and one is a later revision of his original text. The version I use seems to me almost certainly what Donne originally wrote. Its tough, man-of-the-world tone is perfectly consistent with the tone of the whole poem and with the kind of love affair which the poem deals with. Also, it gives the conclusion of this section a dramatic punch which is similar to the effect that Donne builds to at the end of each of the preceding sections of the poem. The other reading of the line makes the poem go startlingly pure and sweet at this point, and for no intrinsic reason that I can see. Grierson agrees that the version which I give was probably the original form of the line and suggests a plausible explanation for Donne's having softened it up later: a marginal note in one of the manuscripts (which gives the sweeter version of the line) indicates that Donne may have revised the poem to use it as an epithalamion, possibly as his own. (*The Poems of John Donne* [Oxford, 1912], 2, 90.)

have followed the skittering of his speculative imagination through these lines. In fact, I wonder how many of them would have noticed at all the high-powered intellectual activity which goes on, at this point, beneath the bright, slick surface of the poem.[2] On the other hand, in its dramatic power, in the adventurousness of its imaginative conjunctions, and in the vividness of its shock effects, the Elegy belongs with Donne's finest work.

The final tone of the poem, and the precise state of mind behind it, are a little hard to define. In many ways the Elegy seems simply a poem of juice and high spirits. It is verse of flash and glitter, the display of a young virtuoso who is showing what he can do with the themes of Ovidian poetry by playing them on his own instrument. But, though I think this was probably Donne's initial intention in the poem, there is a good deal left over when one tries to define the temper of the poem in this way. For one thing, the formal rhetoric of the Elegy gives it qualities of weight and dignity which are lacking in most of the Renaissance erotic verse in the Ovidian tradition.[3] And certain parts of the poem carry a voltage which is far beyond the potential of the conventional Ovidian verse of witty and sophisticated indecency. The evocative power of the exploration metaphor in lines 25–32, and the climactic effect in lines 33–45, as Donne drives the logical implications of his conceit with utter ruthlessness to a culminating intellectual shock, are of the order of intensity of serious poetry. This final section of the poem seems, in the last analysis, much more than a piece of outrageous intellectual impudence on Donne's part. When one turns back to this poem after having read "The Ecstasy," "The Canonization," "A Valediction: Forbidding Mourning," and "The Good-Morrow," the concluding section takes on a different character. One of the peculiar characteristics of those later love poems is Donne's use of extravagant intellectual ingenuity as a mode of expres-

2. The marginal comment on a manuscript referred to in n. 1 suggests that a good deal of the poem went over the head of at least one of Donne's contemporary admirers. It reads: "Why may not a man write his own epithalamium if he can do it so modestly?" "Modestly" here may refer primarily to the poet's modesty about his sexual prowess, but even in this sense the word is hardly accurate for the sexual braggadocio of the speaker in the poem. And the word certainly carries connotations of a social attitude as well. When one makes every allowance for the wide difference between modern and seventeenth-century standards of sexual propriety—a difference which is suggested by the writer's feeling that this poem was perfectly proper for use as both a marriage gift to one's wife and a public document about the marriage—"modestly" is still pretty astonishing. I can conclude only that the unknown admirer who wrote this comment missed a good deal of what goes on in lines 33–45 of the poem.

3. The distinctive quality in Donne's handling of the materials of Ovidian love poetry can be seen if one compares this poem with Carew's "A Rapture." Carew's poem shows not only the general influence of the tradition of Ovidian verse but also the particular influence of Donne's work. The central theological conceit which the title suggests is a variation of the central conceit of "The Ecstasy," and the poem shows both general and specific debts to Donne's eighteenth and nineteenth Elegies. But the sustained lightness of tone and the effect of prettily decorated indecency in "A Rapture" place it in the main stream of the Ovidian tradition and give a tonal quality quite different from that of Elegy 19.

sion for strong feeling. In these poems the florid virtuosity of wit is not, as the eighteenth century and Romantic critics thought, a force in artistic conflict with emotion—it is simply Donne's poetic vehicle for emotion. When read in the context of Donne's later work, these lines in Elegy 19 appear as some of his most passionate love poetry; and the tonal pattern of the last half of the poem seems not that of an impassioned climax in lines 25–32, followed by a passage of virtuoso cleverness, but rather that of a continuous crescendo of emotion to a point of incandescent intensity.

Moreover, when one looks back at the Elegy with an awareness of Donne's lifelong effort to find a philosophic reconciliation for the conflicting claims of the soul and of the body in his personal experience, this section has the effect of suddenly adding a new dimension to Donne's treatment of sexual experience in the poem, a dimension which is entirely lacking in Donne's assumption of the poetic role of sexual libertine in "The Indifferent." Up to this point the Elegy has presented unreflecting passion unreflectingly. The play of Donne's intellect over this material has been directed into elaborating conceits which have little or no philosophic import. But the sustained philosophic overtones of the concluding section finally place the sexual act in a metaphysical context. Here Donne's mind seems suddenly to pierce through the flesh to see what this act means. The shock of these lines is the intellectual shock of what he sees. In effect, they present the wholehearted acceptance of sensual satisfaction as an act which entails taking up a philosophic option, which forces one to embrace a philosophic materialism and to reject completely the doctrines of philosophic idealism—to reject, in fact, the fundamental doctrines of Christianity. In these lines Donne's celebration of lust becomes literally and substantially metaphysical.

Furthermore, the rough treatment which Donne gives to the Mystic Experience in this passage shows a remarkable conceptual accuracy and reflects an interest in the subject which is clearly more than casual. And this poem's identification of sexual experience with religious mysticism echoes throughout the serious love poetry and religious poetry of Donne's maturity, as well as in some of the great prose passages in his sermons. It reappears most strikingly in "The Ecstasy," where the same comparison is presented in a different key—this time with essential seriousness, as an analogy which has a genuine psychological and metaphysical validity.

I think it would be forcing a point to insist that these portentous emotional and intellectual implications are of primary importance in the effect of the last section of this Elegy. They are present in the passage only as over- and undertones. But they give to the lines a fullness of resonance which is not the tonal quality of verse that is just wittily indecent. What seems to have happened in the writing of Elegy 19 is like what evidently happened in "The Apparition," that piece of mordant realism which takes off from one of the most artificial conventions of Petrarchan *vers de société*. I think when Donne started to write the Elegy he probably planned to write a piece of clever erotic verse in the Ovidian manner. But some of what came out, after this material was processed by a powerful literary imagination, was, for all its high-spirited gaiety, not light verse at all.

I think, then, that the artistic paradox of the Elegy—its mixture of bumptious, perverse wit with excited philosophic speculation and strong emotion—is never fully resolved in the poem. Probably the poem as a whole was never brought to complete definition in Donne's mind; it grew on him as he wrote. And I think that, for all its brilliance, the poem never quite assumes shape as an artistic whole. But for the student of Donne's poetry the Elegy provides one of the earliest glimpses of the major poet latent in the bright young man who was "a great visitor of ladies, a great frequenter of plays, a great writer of conceited verses." And the poem reveals also the identity of mind and temperament which lies beneath the surface contrast between Donne's secular verse in the "Elegies" and the "Songs and Sonnets," and his religious verse in the "Divine Poems." In his later years, when he was Dean of St. Paul's and the most powerful and sensational preacher of his day, Donne sometimes dramatized his assumption of a new role in life by thinking of his career as divided between two lives: "Jack Donne," who had written the witty and paradoxical work of his early career, and "Doctor Donne," who was writing the sermons. But that sharp dichotomy was a theatricality of Donne's imagination. It is not surprising that in trying to elucidate the difficulties of Jack Donne's poem I have found some of the most helpful commentary in Doctor Donne's sermons.

THEODORE REDPATH

[The *Songs and Sonnets*] †

Donne's *Songs and Sonets* are among the three or four finest collections of love-lyrics in the English language. Such a high valuation still requires emphasis, despite the fact that these poems are read and appreciated far more than they were, say, fifty years ago. Too many readers of poetry, even in England, would still omit Donne's name from a list of the supreme love-lyrists of England, while readily including the names of Herrick, Shelley, Tennyson, Browning, and Swin-

† From Theodore Redpath, *The Songs and Sonnets of John Donne*, copyright 1956. Pp. xv-xvi and xxvii-xxxix. Reprinted by permission of Methuen & Co., Ltd., and Barnes & Noble.

burne. This is probably partly because the *Songs and Sonets* still remain comparatively little known:[1] but there are other reasons. One reason is the lingering prejudice that love-lyrics should be expressions of feeling unalloyed with any marked degree of cerebration. Donne's love-lyrics spring partly from a strong and ingenious head. They are therefore liable to give the impression of being merely brain-spun. In fact, that is very seldom the case, since they also come from a passionate heart. Another reason is that many people are put off by the sheer difficulty of the sense of many passages. Ben Jonson prophesied that the poetry of Donne would perish for lack of being understood. It has not yet perished, but though it is read now perhaps much more than at any time since the seventeenth century, it offers much difficulty, and it is doubtful how far even the bare sense of some of the poems is really understood. In the case of the *Songs and Sonets*, however, trouble taken in trying to understand the sense is almost always amply rewarded. A further obstacle to the just evaluation of the poems is the fairly widespread conception of Donne as a merely flippant, cynical love poet. Among the causes of the spread of this idea are probably the choice of cynical poems for anthologies, e.g. the *Song*, 'Go and catch a falling star'; the cumulative impression of the *Songs and Sonets* and the mostly cynical *Elegies*, when taken together; and the influence of certain outstanding critical studies. In actual fact, the *Songs and Sonets* cover a very wide range of feeling from flippant cynicism to the most tender and even idealistic love. Finally, many people fail to find in Donne's love-lyrics the music which they demand from such poems. That is a pity, for there is really great variety and subtlety of music in the *Songs and Sonets*, and once it is properly sensed, it can be felt to have attractions at least equal to and sometimes transcending those of music of a more obvious character.

The *Songs and Sonets* are, in fact, superior as a body of love-lyrics to any equivalent number of poems by Herrick, Shelley, Tennyson, Browning, or Swinburne. Indeed, if we survey English poetry from end to end I doubt if we shall find any serious rivals to the *Songs and Sonets*, except the sonnets of Sidney and Shakespeare, and the love-lyrics of Yeats, and, possibly, of Hardy.

* * *

One of the most striking features of the *Songs and Sonets* is undoubtedly the way in which the most diverse thoughts, images and allusions are pressed into the service of love poetry. References are made to such varied fields as astronomy, law, religion, war and mili-

---

1. In a widely circulated anthology (*The Oxford Book of English Verse*) only 7 pages are allotted to Donne (as compared with 21 to Herrick, 19 to Shelley, 23 to Tennyson, 20 to Browning, and 12 to Swinburne). Moreover, of the seven poems ascribed to Donne, one is probably not by him at all; and only four of the *Songs and Sonets* are given. Again, in the last edition of Palgrave's *Golden Treasury* (1941, reprinted 1954), not a single poem by Donne is included.

tary affairs, medicine, eating and drinking, the human body, time, marriage and divorce, the weather, scholastic philosophy, politics, alchemy, death, fire and heat, astrology, business, learning, and everyday life. Very often there is an astonishing difference between the field to which reference is made and the context in which the reference appears in the poem. A celebrated instance is Donne's comparison of himself and his wife to a pair of compasses. Another particularly striking instance occurs in A *Fever*, a poem which deals with the illness of some woman to whom the poet seems greatly attached. The Stoics had disputed among themselves as to what sort of fire would consume the world at the end of each cycle of existence; and a similar controversy about the origin and nature of a world-consuming fire had occurred in the theology of the Early Christian era. Donne deliberately makes a preposterous use of that old dispute:

> O wrangling schools, that search what fire
>   Shall burn this world, had none the wit
> Unto this knowledge to aspire,
>   That this her fever might be it?
>   (A *Fever*, ll. 13–16)

The turn of wit adds a special strengthening savour to the poignancy of the poem. Even the most far-fetched references generally seem compellingly apt within their context in the poems. The combination of surprise and aptness is certainly one of the chief merits of the imagery and allusion in the *Songs and Sonets*.

It was possibly more especially Donne's references to scholastic philosophy that led Dryden to censure him for affecting metaphysics even 'in his amorous verses, where nature only should reign'. It was probably this censure that brought into currency the application of the term 'metaphysical' to the poetry of Donne and his followers. But the term 'metaphysical'' soon acquired a more general sense than Dryden probably intended, and came to connote the employment of learning as the stuff of poetry. Later still, the term, owing to its traditional association with the work of particular poets such as Donne, Crashaw and Cowley, acquired a still broader connotation, namely the body of characteristics common and peculiar to the work of those English poets whom tradition has called 'metaphysical'. Thus the term 'metaphysical imagery', for instance, would now be quite commonly understood to refer to imagery which was *inter alia* both far-fetched and apt, like much of that of such poets as Donne, Crashaw and Cowley.

The effect of the diversity of reference in the *Songs and Sonets* is often described by the rapidity with which reference to one field succeeds reference to another sometimes very different field. Noteworthy examples occur in the last stanzas of *The Relic* and *The Broken Heart*.

Equally characteristic of the *Songs and Sonets* is the marked absence of mythological and pastoral imagery and allusion. This was early recognized as a general characteristic of Donne's poetry. It was, no doubt, partly to this feature that Carew was referring in the following lines from his admirable Elegy on Donne's death:

> The Muses' garden with pedantic weeds
> O'erspread, was purg'd by thee; the lazy seeds
> Of servile imitation thrown away,
> And fresh invention planted.
> (Carew's *Elegy* on Donne's death, ll. 25–8)

This absence of mythological and pastoral allusion entails the absence of conventional remoteness and gallantry from the *Songs and Sonets*. In their place a firm and even a stern realism is often imparted to the poems by the references to war and military affairs, death, law, politics, medicine, fire and heat, business, the human body, and many of the features of home life: while, on the other hand, a certain lofty, *recherché* strain is often provided by the references to Scholastic doctrine, astronomy, religion, and learning: and a less lofty strangeness is injected by the references to alchemy, astrology and superstition.

The *Songs and Sonets* are also remarkable for the strength and range of the feelings they express. There is the incandescent but controlled fury of *The Apparition*; there is the violent allergy to love expressed in *Love's Usury*; there is the uprush of poignant longing in the opening lines of *A Fever*; there is the turbulent sadness of parting in *A Valediction: of weeping*; there is the protective tenderness of the *Song*, 'Sweetest love, I do not go'; there is the firm confidence in mutual love which pervades *A Valediction: forbidding mourning*; there is the desolate grief of *A Nocturnal upon St Lucy's Day*.

Besides the overall variety of the feeling expressed in the *Songs and Sonets* as a whole, there is also often (though not always) considerable variety of feeling within individual poems. One especially interesting type of case is where negative feelings like petulance, bitterness, cynicism, irritation or contempt arise in the course of poems which are predominantly positive. *The Sun Rising* is a happy poem of consummated love: but it is strewn with insults and scornful references. *The Canonization* is a vigorous glorification of love, but it begins with a voluminous outpouring of exasperation and contempt. Even in *Lovers' Infiniteness*, where the wooing is conducted on the whole in a tone of gentle reasonableness, there are overtones of petulance in places, e.g. in the use of such words as 'bargain' (l. 8), 'stocks' (l. 16) and 'outbid' (l. 17), which introduce the bitter suggestion of a love-market. If the matter is looked into it will be found that there is scarcely a single positive poem into which some such feeling as cynicism, bitterness or contempt does not to some degree intrude. This strengthens the poems: for just as when a hard man weeps it is impressive, so it is when a sceptical or cynical man loves.

It should be added that the feeling in the *Songs and Sonets* as a whole gives a strong impression of masculinity. Lovers may die in these poems, but they do not faint, as they do in Keats and Shelley. The language is generally manly and vigorous, and sometimes sudden, or even harsh. The detailed reference to such masculine activities as war and politics also contributes to the total impression of masculine feeling.

On the other hand, contrary to a fairly widespread idea about them, the *Songs and Sonets*, though they often express or imply the view that physical passion is a good thing, yet (in contrast with the *Elegies*) rather seldom express actual feelings of physical lust. This is one of the ways in which the *Songs and Sonets* are distinguishable from much of the work of those other great love poets, Ovid, Propertius and Ronsard.

Another leading feature of the *Songs and Sonets* is their rather peculiar sensory atmosphere. They contain very little colour: though there are, from time to time, remarkably sharp, colourless visual impressions. Even these, however, are exceptional, and the focus of attention is very rarely the visual aspect of experience. The rarity of auditory sensations is even more marked. There is nothing in the whole of the *Songs and Sonets* like Wordsworth's 'casual shout that broke the silent air', or Vigny's

J'aime le son du cor, le soir, au fond des bois.

There is, indeed, scarcely any reference to sounds at all. Again, sense-impressions of smell as distinct from taste do not seem to occur in the *Songs and Sonets*. There are, on the other hand, a few references to sensations of taste, and a fair number to the motor sensations involved in sucking, feeding, drinking, and swallowing. This strain of often rather coarse physicality gives its definite tang to the poems in which it occurs, and sometimes contrasts strangely with the intellectual and spiritual interests which lie beside it. Other motor sensations are frequently referred to, e.g. the sensations involved in running, walking, snatching, winking, leaning. So also are organic sensations, such as the sense of inflammation of the veins which love may cause, or the sensation of 'sorrowing dulness' after sexuality. In point of fact, in the *Songs and Sonets* motor and organic sensations definitely predominate over sensations of sight, sound, smell, taste, and even touch, and that is so even if we include in 'touch' cutaneous sensations of temperature as well as those of pressure. This probably helps to account for a feeling of *inwardness* that one quite frequently senses in the poems, despite all their references to the outside world.

With regard to what psychologists would call the 'feeling-tone' of the poems, painful sense-impressions are quite often stimulated in the course of poems which are predominantly pleasurable. This is a parallel feature to that already noted in the case of feelings.

The use of language in the *Songs and Sonets* has also some special features. The diction (as contrasted with the thought) is generally simple: though Donne often combines the simple words in unexpected ways, forming strange compounds or odd phrases or sentences:

And makes one little room, an *everywhere*.
(*The Good-morrow*, l. 11)

Thou are so *truth*, . . .
(*The Dream*, l. 7)

A *she-sigh* from my mistress' heart, . . .
(*Love's Diet*, l. 10)

And if some lover, such as we,
    Have heard this *dialogue of one*, . . .
(*The Ecstasy*, ll. 73–4)

No *tear-floods*, nor *sigh-tempests* move; . . .
(*A Valediction: forbidding mourning*, l. 6)

But since this god produc'd a destiny,
And that *vice-nature*, custom, lets it be; . . .
(*Love's Deity*, ll. 5–6)

Sometimes he puns, though punning does not appear to be frequent. Sometimes he repeats words or types of phrase, throwing them up like a juggler. He is particularly fond of playing with pronouns and demonstrative adjectives:

Coming and staying show'd thee, thee,
But rising makes me doubt, that now
    Thou art not thou.
(*The Dream*, ll. 21–3)

To me thou, falsely, thine,
And I to thee mine actions shall disguise.
(*A Lecture upon the Shadows*, ll. 20–1)

This sort of passage gives a combined impression of virtuosity and intimacy.

From time to time, though rather seldom, Donne deviates from the normal simplicity of the diction, by employing learned language: and on such occasions the work takes on a certain sophistication. On the other hand, he more frequently interpolates coarse diction, which imparts to the poetry a rasping force. On other occasions special effects are obtained by the use of words with associations that are homely rather than coarse:

> Because such fingers need to *knit*
> That subtle *knot*, which makes us man: . . .
> (*The Ecstasy*, ll. 63–4)

> If he wrung from me a tear, I *brin'd* it so
> With scorn or shame, that him it nourish'd not; . . .
> (*Love's Diet*, ll. 13–14)

Donne occasionally achieves a peculiar effect of some subtlety by veiling the full meaning of a word or phrase which is really charged with intense implications. One example occurs in the first stanza of *Love's Usury*. Donne is there bargaining with Love, and begging Love not to ensnare him till middle-age, but meanwhile to allow him to give full rope to the caprices of lust:

> Till then, Love, let my body reign, and let
> Me travel, sojourn, snatch, plot, have, forget,
> Resume my last year's relict: think that yet
> We'd never met. (ll. 5–8)

The true import of the intensely contemptuous word 'relict', viz. cast-off-mistress, is veiled under its apparent generality. Other instances are the phrase 'think Thou call'st for more' (meaning more sexual play) in ll. 8–9 of *The Apparition*, and the word 'mistake' (meaning mistake and sleep with) in l. 11 of *Love's Usury*: both of which have an uncanny pregnancy. It is also possible that there is a very bold instance of this technique in stanza 2 of *The Relic*: for it is not out of the question that the vague phrase 'a something else thereby' (l. 18) may really mean a bone of Christ's.

The general tone of the language of the *Songs and Sonets* is colloquial. The poems have the flexibility and liveliness of spoken language. The openings are often particularly colloquial in tone. This has the effect of making the poems seem to grow naturally out of definite situations in individual lives. Sentences, on the other hand, are generally somewhat longer than one would expect to find in ordinary speech. Yet Donne manages to keep the vital and passionate phrases he writes, in continuity with one another, so as to form wholes which have both firmness and shape.

Donne is acutely alive to the sound-values of words: and the sound is sometimes almost magically interwoven with the sense. Particularly striking instances of this are to be found in *The Expiration, The Apparition, Twickenham Garden, Mummy* or *Love's Alchemy*, and *A Nocturnal upon St Lucy's Day*.

Everywhere in the poems are to be found instances of rapid and ingenious thinking. The Protean changes of imagery and allusion have already been mentioned. There is also a strong tendency to the violence of paradox, and to the sort of convolution of thought exemplified in the following lines from *Love's Exchange*:

> Love, let me never know that this
> Is love, or, that love childish is;
> Let me not know that others know
> That she knows my pains, lest that so
> A tender shame make me mine own new woe.
>
> (ll. 17–21)

Typical, too, is the kind of intellectual juggling we find in the clever play on personal identity in stanza 2 of *The Legacy*:

> I heard me say: 'Tell her anon,
>   That my self' (that is, you, not I)
>   'Did kill me'; and when I felt me die,
> I bid me send my heart, when I was gone;
> But I alas could there find none,
>   When I had ripp'd me, and search'd where hearts did lie; . . .
>
> (ll. 9–14)

What is remarkable is that such intellectual acrobatics seldom detract from the overall strength of the poems in which they occur. Indeed they often add to it, and sometimes even (as e.g. in *The Primrose*) form a central part of the total effect.

The intellectual agility and ingenuity of the poems are special manifestations of an intellectual strength also shown in other ways, and especially in the relevance and tight concatenation of the thought throughout almost all the poems. Each poem has its specific conception, its focal centre, and there is very rarely any drifting away from the point, however diverse the objects which are referred to, or the images and ideas which occur. This is true both in the simplest sort of case, such as *The Apparition*, where the whole poem of seventeen lines consists of one sentence of concentrated ironic loathing; and in the most complex sort of case, such as that of *A Nocturnal upon St Lucy's Day*, where allusions of considerable diversity and subtlety are strewn thickly through the poem, affording intellectual satisfaction in themselves, but no less certainly contributing to the emotional and intellectual totality of the poem. Where there is apparent irrelevance it is almost certain to serve some deliberate purpose, as in the brilliant effect of the last two lines of *The Curse*. As to the concatenation of the thought within the poems, this is almost everywhere controlled and sure. It has sometimes even been said that the texture of the *Songs and Sonets* is argumentative. This is too sweeping a generalization. The thought arises at the start from the situation out of which the poem itself grows, and it then develops, sometimes indeed by way of argument, but at other times by way of narrative, or analogy, or extended metaphor, or through the play of fancy, or at the prompting of some fresh feeling which has come into play, or in some other way; though almost always so that the connections of the thought are close, whether this is obvious or appears only after scrutiny.

With regard to the attitudes towards love expressed or implied in the poems, their variety has already been indicated. It is, however, worth noticing certain other important features of these attitudes. For one thing, there runs through the *Songs and Sonets*, taken as a whole, the belief that physical passion is a good thing. Sometimes, especially in the apparently earlier poems, it is seen as good in itself, even, at times, as preferable to the perils of love. Sometimes it is seen as a necessary and valuable element in a full and satisfying mutual attachment. For another thing, love is generally considered in these poems either as a danger or as a wonder. It is not thought of coolly as something that can be handled or trifled with, and seldom thought of simply as one of the pleasures of life. We are most often in the realm of *amour passion*, comparatively rarely in the realm of *amour physique*, and never in that of *amour goût*, to make use of Stendhal's illuminating distinctions.[2] Passionate feeling is paramount; even *passionate* sensuality is secondary; mere elegant gallantry (so frequent in Restoration love-lyrics) is completely absent.

Again, there are one or two special thoughts about love, which recur in a number of the poems. One is that love is a mystery in which Donne and his lady are adepts. The most extensive expression of this thought occurs in *The Ecstasy*. Clearly linked with it is Donne's practice of crediting his beloved with religious significance, as in *The Relic*, *A Nocturnal upon St Lucy's Day* and *Air and Angels*. In *The Dream* he even goes so far as to maintain that his lady has some of the divine attributes. This practice seems to associate some of the poems with the tradition of the *amour courtois*. Another typical thought is that two lovers are self-sufficient. Donne sometimes hyperbolically extends this idea, and asserts that together they are the whole world. In this way some of the poems become more than love poems: they become glorifications of love. On the other hand, Donne tends to be temperate in his forecast of the future of a love already in existence. We do not find him saying that it will last for ever, or even for a long time. He does express hope that a love will continue, but when he expresses a faith that it will, the faith is only a hypothetical one. 'If you and I love equally, and take care, our love will continue.' This is what Donne says in several places. Statements of this sort are indeed almost tautologous: but these near-tautologies seem much more satisfyingly near the truth than rash categorical faith in eternal constancy. Another, rather subtle, way in which Donne's thought about love distin-

2. See Stendhal, *De l'Amour, where the distinctions are fully discussed.*

guishes itself from more commonplace views, is in hs uncertainty as to how far lovers are really united by their love (see *A Valediction: forbidding mourning, The Ecstasy* (ll. 41–56) and *The Good-morrow* (ll. 20–1). This uncertainty should, I believe, be regarded as the sign of an honest attempt not to exaggerate about the relationship of love, while at the same time recognizing its unifving force.

Finally, something must be said as to the forms and metres of the poems. The forms are almost all stanzaic. They are exceedingly various, and many of them are very complex. There is only one stanza form that Donne uses more than once: the simple octosyllabic quatrain with alternate rhymes, which he uses in three poems. It seems that over forty of the stanza forms were probably invented by him. The vast majority of the poems are in stanzas of from six to eleven lines. Eight- and nine-line stanzas occur most frequently. Occasionally two or three poems have the same rhyme scheme; but where that is so, they differ in line-length. It is as if Donne proudly scorned to repeat the same stanza form.

Donne is fond of reiterated rhymes. Eighteen of the poems, for instance, end in triplets or quadruplets. This gives an effect of insistence. Again, over twenty of the poems begin with a couplet; and the opening rhyme-scheme *aabb* is very common. The use of reiterated rhymes, whether in the openings or endings or in the body of the poems, acts as a counterforce to the strong tendency in many of the poems for the metric form to be distorted by the speech-rhythms which cut across it. The verse might so easily break into utter disorder. Reiterated rhymes help to prevent this. The triplets in ll. 5–7 of each stanza of *A Nocturnal upon St Lucy's Day* afford an instance of their steadying effect.

Some of the stanza forms are very attractive in themselves. Much play is made with variations of line length. Stanzas of more than six lines seem to give Donne the scope he so often needs to develop the complex interplay of thought and feeling which is so typical of him. With exceptions, the poems in shorter stanzas tend to be thin or slight.

In some cases the stanza forms seem especially appropriate to their respective poems. This is so, for instance, with the *Song*, 'Go and catch a falling star', where the piquant slightness of the short lines prepares by contrast the elongated sting in the tail of each stanza. A similar effect is achieved in *The Blossom*, where the short sixth line of each stanza sets off the epigrammatic couplet which follows. Again, the sharp changes of line length in *A Valediction: of weeping* accord magnificently with the turbulent passion underlying the poem: while the steady fixity of the lines of *A Valediction: forbidding mourning* is at one with the firm and substantial love in which the poem shows such settled confidence. The stanza forms do not always seem so peculiarly appropriate as in these cases: but they frequently delight by their intricacy; and the fact that the rich texture of passion, thought and imagery, and the odd quirks and ironies, could be made to take on shapes of such fairly strict complexity, is often a subject for wonder.

The overall forms of the poems are sometimes very clearly patterned, as in the ternary forms of *The Message*, the *Song*, 'Go and catch a falling star', *Lover's Infiniteness* and *The Prohibition*. At other times there is no apparent relation between the number of stanzas and the substance of the poem. In most cases, however, the poems give one a definite impression of firm shape. Sometimes, as in the device of the 'dialogue of one' in *The Ecstasy*, and the wonderful thematic modification of the opening line of *A Nocturnal* at the close of the poem, we come across especially satisfying examples of formal beauty.

The metres are normally iambic: but the actual rhythms which play over the basic metrical structure are very various. Drummond tells us that Ben Jonson said that 'for not keeping of accent' Donne 'deserved hanging'. In saying this, however, Jonson only revealed one of his own limitations. Remarkable literary man though Jonson was, the validity of Donne's use of true speaking language springing straight from passion and vigorous and subtle thinking, and not to be strait-laced by the demands of external metres, was beyond him. In point of fact, Donne's verse is generally more regular than Jonson's statement would suggest: provided we construe regularity more liberally than Jonson did. Let us consider, for instance, the fine bitter opening of *Twickenham Garden*. Syllabically, the first two lines are quite regular. The first has ten syllables: the second eight. Pedally, on the other hand, they are admittedly far from being examples of the basic lines, the iambic pentameter and the iambic tetrameter.

Blásted with síghs, | and surr | óunded with téars,

is best scanned as shown, i.e. as two choriambic feet separated by a pyrrhic.[3]

Hither I cóme | to séek | the spring.

is best scanned as a choriambus followed by two iambic feet. Only cramping pedantry, however, could find these lines anything but excellent. If the whole poem had been written in lines of the same types as these (which would have been one way of 'regularizing' them!), then it would have been hopelessly monotonous; and the pedal character of these particular lines, which is in complete keeping with their meaning and feeling, would have lost its point. In actual fact, the lines, though pedally irregular, are made to seem regular enough:

3. This was apparently in part pointed out by a contemporary of Donne's, Giles Oldisworth, in his notes on Donne. (See John Sampson, 'Contemporary Light upon John Donne' (Essays and Studies of the English Association, vii, 87)).

partly because, syllabically, they *are* regular; partly because the first line has a regularity of its own, since it is perfectly symmetrical, and the second line repeats the choriambic rhythm which has been set up; and partly because the lines merge at once into the general iambic pattern, since the last two feet of the second line are both iambic, and the third line is a regular iambic line. What is more, they satisfy us, in any case, by their force and naturalness, so that we are not inclined to think cantankerously about rules. This is a particularly striking example of Donne's regular irregularity; but it would be possible to cite countless instances from the poems. The *Songs and Sonets* are little short of miraculous in their blend of the freedom and vitality of the spoken language with the reasonable exigencies of metrical form.

* * *

R. A. DURR

Donne's "The Primrose" †

"The Primrose", though seldom noticed by students of Donne, seems to me to delineate, in ordered sequence, a fundamental action of the *Songs and Sonets* as a whole. This is the action that originates in the desire to find a true—a fixed and perfect—love and the security and rest inherent in it, that in its passage through Donne's astute and honest intellect, tutored by corrosive experience, passes into a cynical disintegration of the hope of realizing that ideal, and concludes in "gay" abandonment to the sensual flux of casual delights. "The Primrose," once recognized as microcosmic of this pattern, may thus afford a point of reference for the reading of Donne's secular verse.

The first stanza breathes the air of faith and innocence, as the poet walks upon a lovely primrose hill seeking to find a true love.[1] We understand the ideality involved. For to Donne a true love meant the perfect union of harmonious souls, a union wherein, as in "The Extasie," their oneness seems a substance externally real between them, a third element, an "abler soule," transcending all the tensions inevi-

† From *Journal of English and Germanic Philology*, LIX (April, 1960), 218-22. Reprinted by permission of The University of Illinois Press and R. A. Durr.
1. It has been suggested to me that "true Love" might be an allusion to the Herb Paris, or Herb True-love, whose four leaves and berry form a true-love knot, according to the herbals. The allusion would be highly appropriate to Donne's theme and consonant with its imagery: in a field of primroses, in a world of ordinary—i.e., false—woman, he seeks

Herb True-love, a constant woman. Yet the possibility of Donne's having used the association, except as a passing connotation, is not supported by the rest of the poem. For Herb Paris has four leaves, which is the number assigned that creature who is *less* than "mere woman," not the ideal of woman. The four, five, and six refer to different primroses—typical woman (five) and two aberrations; the choice is among these, not between Herb Paris and primrose.

table to sex. In "The Canonization," for example, this "one neutrall thing" to which both sexes fit" is likened to the Phoenix, an androgynous creature.[2] True love had power, moreover, to translate the lovers from the incoherent sphere of mutability into a region, a condition, free of all mundane dimension. Space, the world—expanding disconcertingly before Elizabethan eyes—contracts into the closed and numinous circle of love's involvement:

> For love, all love of other sights controules,
> And makes one little roome, an every where.
>
> > ("The good-morrow")[3]

> She'is all States, and all Princes, I,
> Nothing else is.
>
> > ("The Sunne Rising")

Even time cannot disturb this union:

> What ever dyes, was not mixt equally;
> If our two loves be one, or, thou and I
> Love so alike, that none doe slacken, none can die.
>
> > ("The good-morrow")

> Love, all alike, no season knowes, nor clyme,
> Nor houres, dayes, moneths, which are the rags of time.
>
> > ("The Sunne Rising")

> All other things, to their destruction draw,
> Only our love hath no decay . . .
>
> > ("The Anniversarie")

The disparate and decaying world, the All, becomes distilled in love's crucible into the One of the lovers' interfused souls, and this One, in turn, becomes the All, but now transformed by love's alchemy from base to perfect metal:

> so wee shall
> Be one, and one another's All.
>
> > ("Lovers infinitenesse")

But it is not necessary to go to Donne's other poems, except for confirmation, to realize what true love meant to him, for the imagery of the first stanza of "The Primrose" contains its own definition of that ideal. The primrose, being of the primula family and somewhat resem-

---

2. Donne might have had in mind the alchemical use of the phoenix, along with the eagle, or the Rebis (two-headed hermaphrodite), for example, as a symbol of the *Coniunctio oppositorum*, the union of opposites, in the *hieros gamos*, or "chymical marriage," wherein, according to C. G. Jung, "the supreme opposites, male and female . . . , are melted into a unity purified of all opposition and therefore incorruptible" (*Psychology and Alchemy*, trans. R. F. C. Hull [London, 1953],

p. 37). There is perhaps a left-handed allusion in stanza one of "The Primrose" to the alchemical process of distillation (*per descensum*, in this case)—the shower is no ordinary one—for what is distilled in alchemy is the Elixir, the water of life, that can transmute base to perfect metal, imperfect to perfect—true—love.
3. Quotations are from *The Poems of John Donne*, ed. H. J. Grierson, 2 vols. (London, 1912).

bling a star, was sometimes called the "star-primula" in the herbals; and such star-flowers were commonly used as emblems and water marks in association with the various symbols of Eden, or the Orchard of the Rose, or the Garden of Grace—all conventionally situated upon a mountain or hill. The field of primroses is not a casual patch of simple flowers; it is a "terrestriall Galaxie," a circular swathe of star flowers (since the Milky Way was circular to seventeenth-century eyes), a symbol of heaven, perfection, on earth. These flowers thus, watered by heaven as they are nourished by earth, "grow Manna": true love is both spiritual and physical, and it is man's sustenance in his wanderings through the waste lands of a faithless and disjointed world. This primrose hill is only superficially related to Montgomery Castle. It is essentially a landmark in the country of the soul.

If stanza one, in its imagery suggestive of a fusion of earth and heaven, flesh and spirit, defines the ideal of a true love, the second stanza dialectically destroys belief in the possibility of its attainment. We witness Donne converting "Manna to gall" ("Twicknam garden") by the action of his sceptical mind. In reality, the images of perfection of the first stanza had contained the germs of their own dissolution, not only in the hesitancy of the subjunctive mood but also in the circumstance that, while the primrose in a context of stars and circles may legitimately be associated with the connotations of the star-flower and the Garden, it was most commonly the emblem of fugacity. The "prim-rose" is the first rose and the best, the time of youth's freshness and love's first flushed exuberance, which every poet knows fast decays but which Donne would bid stay. Moreover, as with Shakespeare's primrose path of dalliance and Milton's yellow-skirted fayes who wore primroses, the flower conveyed the additional odor of wantonness; and this is prognostic of the poem's conclusion.

Reason has made it obvious that a true love, a constant woman, must be different from, either less or more than, average woman, and the poet thus finds himself faced with a disconcerting choice: either a lump of animated clay, "scarce any thing," if less than woman, or a Petrarchan abstraction, if more than woman, who would transfer relations from the properly sexual to the pallidly Platonic level of intercourse. "Both these were monsters." His decision is unavoidable; he must accept the normal woman, who is false by nature, because either alternative leads only to another and worse kind of falsity: the "four" and the "six" are monstrous, unnatural. He could better endure to deal with ordinary woman, who, in being false, is at least true to her nature—since she "can have no way but falsehood to be true" ("Womans constancy"); she at least is natural and not monstrous. By now the poet is a long way from where he started, and the progress has been all down hill; the glow of the flowery Galaxie of stanza one has been quite put out.

Ratiocination having brought him from faith in the possibility of finding a true love to the reverse conviction that "no where/lives a woman true, and faire" ("Song: Goe, and catche a falling starre"), Donne will not bemoan his loss; he will acknowledge the truth, and more than that he will cynically pursue the truth to its farthest implications. He will in the destructive element immerse and assure himself and us that the water is fine. Woman's "mysterious number" is five, which is half of ten, the "farthest number," since it includes the elements of all possible numbers and therefore, in the Pythagorean and medieval systems which the numerology assumes,[4] of all things. Hence each woman is entitled to half of all men, a generous allowance. But Donne will not pause there; if there can be no *One*, there shall be no in-between either. The resignation of a Jack Donne understands no middle way; it is defiantly and desperately abandoned. Thus he reasons, since five contains the first even and the first odd number,[5] and since all numbers are either even or odd, woman is entitled not just to half but to *all* men; she is entitled by nature, by her innate falseness, to unqualified promiscuity.

But it would be to misrepresent the final shape and course of this action in Donne's work simply to conclude where "The Primrose" concludes. His scepticism and abandonment, which appear decisive and abiding in the *Songs and Sonets*, are in reality defensive and transitional. He laid claim to wantonness, insisted upon it, because he despaired of constancy; he assumed the posture of the easy cynic because he could determine upon no way that led to Truth. His going around and around is not the motion of a mind in simple engagement with itself but the action of a soul climbing the winding stair of the watchtower of Truth, that it might find rest.

What Jack Donne wanted all along was what we would like to believe Dean Donne found—at least in that measure commensurate with a fallen world and a sinful, passionate man: the repose and fixity of a constant love. He had known something of it in this world through his wife, perhaps, but here nothing finally endures. "In this world we enjoy nothing; enjoying presumes perpetuity; and here, all things are fluid, transitory: There I shall enjoy, and possess for ever, God himself" (*L Sermons*, 48). It is God alone, he came to understand, Who is "th'Eternall root / of true Love" ("A Hymne to

---

4. Grierson runs into difficulties, it seems to me, in trying to interpret the last stanza outside this orientation. Charles Monroe Coffin (*John Donne and the New Philosophy* [New York, 1937], pp. 157–58) incorporates and elaborates Grierson's reading. But see E. D. Cleveland, *The Explicator*, VIII (October, 1949), 4.
5. In *Essays in Divinity* (ed. E. M. Simpson [Oxford, 1952], p. 10), Donne writes: "The Author of these first five books is *Moses*. In which number, com-

pos'd of the first even, and first odd . . ." Miss Simpson in her note refers to "The Primrose"; but the symbolical value of the number five she cites from M. P. Ramsay—who quotes Chaignet's summary of Nicomachus of Gerasa's conception of the number—is only partially relevant to the poem; for while five may function in "The Primrose" as "le plus naturel des nombres," it does not, except perhaps by ironic inversion, function as "le plus parfait."

Christ, at the Authors last going into Germany"); for, as the contemplatives always knew, in the words of Thomas à Kempis, "love is born of God, and cannot rest but in God, above all created things" (*The Imitation of Christ*, 111, 5). The author of the famous *Quia amore langueo* has expressed this Christian fundamental in terms peculiarly like those of Donne:

> In a valey of this restles minde
> > I soughte in mounteine and in mede,
> Trustinge a trewe love for to finde.
> > Upon an hill than I took hede . . .

He finds Christ, Who tells him, "I am true love that fals was nevere."[6]

In Holy Sonnet XVII she whom Donne had truly loved is dead, but the experience of that earthly joy has served to point him toward its sublime analogue:

> Here the admyring her my mind did whett
> To seeke thee God; so streames do shew their head . . .

We are reminded perhaps of Dante and Petrarch, or yet of Augustine, passionate lovers, and consider the voice to have spoken truth that inspired Yeats to record in *A Vision* that "the love the Saint brings to God at his twenty-seventh phase was found in some past life upon a woman's breast."

6. *Early English Lyrics,* ed. E. K. Chambers and F. Sidgwick (London, 1926) p. 151.

Donne's Divine Poems
and the Anniversaries

HELEN GARDNER
The Religious Poetry of John Donne †

* * *

Most critics have agreed in regarding 'La Corona' and 'A Litany' as inferior to the 'Holy Sonnets', which give an immediate impression of spontaneity. Their superiority has been ascribed to their having been written ten years later, and their vehemence and anguished intensity have been connected with a deepening of Donne's religious experience after the death of his wife. There can be no question of their poetic greatness, nor of their difference from 'La Corona' and 'A Litany'; but I do not believe that greatness or that difference to be due to the reasons which are usually given. The accepted date rests on an assumption which the textual history of the sonnets does not support: the assumption that the three 'Holy Sonnets' which the Westmoreland manuscript alone preserves were written at the same time as the other sixteen. These three sonnets are, as Sir Herbert Grierson called all the 'Holy Sonnets', 'separate ejaculations'; but the other sixteen fall into clearly recognizable sets of sonnets on familiar themes for meditation. They are as traditional in their way as 'La Corona' and 'A Litany' are, and as the three Hymns are not. The Hymns are truly occasional; each arises out of a particular situation and a personal mood. But in theme and treatment the 'Holy Sonnets', if we ignore the three Westmoreland sonnets, depend on a long-established form of religious exercise: not oral prayer, but the simplest method of mental prayer, meditation. To say this is not to impugn their originality or their power. Donne has used the tradition of meditation in his own way; and it suits his genius as a poet far better than do the more formal ways of prayer he drew upon in 'La Corona' and 'A Litany'. Yet although, with the possible exception of the Hymns, the 'Holy Sonnets' are his greatest divine poems, I do not myself feel that they spring

† From Helen Gardner, *John Donne: The Divine Poems*. Pp. xxix-xxxv, l-lv, copyright 1952. Reprinted by permission of the publishers, the Clarendon Press, Oxford.

from a deeper religious experience than that which lies behind 'A Litany'. The evidence which points to a date in 1609 does not seem to me to conflict with their character as religious poems; on the contrary it accords rather better with it than does the hitherto accepted date.

Many readers have felt a discrepancy between the 'Holy Sonnets' and the picture which Walton gives of Donne's later years, and between the 'Holy Sonnets' and the sermons and Hymns. There is a note of exaggeration in them. This is apparent, not only in the violence of such a colloquy as 'Batter my heart', but also in the strained note of such lines as these:

> But who am I, that dare dispute with thee?
> O God, Oh! of thine onely worthy blood,
> And my teares, make a heavenly Lethean flood,
> And drowne in it my sinnes blacke memorie.
> That thou remember them, some claime as debt,
> I thinke it mercy, if thou wilt forget.

At first sight the closing couplet seems the expression of a deep humility; but it cannot be compared for depth of religious feeling with the 'Hymn to God the Father', where, however great the sin is, the mercy of God is implied to be the greater, or with such passages as the following on the phrase *virga irae*:

> But truely, beloved, there is a blessed comfort ministred unto us, even in that word; for that word *Gnabar*, which we translate *Anger*, *wrath*, hath another ordinary signification in Scripture, which, though that may seem to be an easier, would prove a heavier sense for us to beare, than this of *wrath* and *anger*; this is, *preteritio*, *conniventia*, Gods forbearing to take knowledge of our transgressions; when God shall say of us, as he does of *Israel*, *Why should ye be smitten any more?* when God leaves us to our selves, and studies our recovery no farther, by any more corrections; for, in this case, there is the lesse comfort, because there is the lesse *anger* show'd. And therefore, S. *Bernard*, who was heartily afraid of this sense of our word, heartily afraid of this preterition, that God should forget him, leave him out, affectionately, passionately embraces this sense of the word in our Text, *Anger*; and he sayes, *Irascaris mihi Domine*, *Domine mihi irascaris*, *Be angry with me O Lord*, *O Lord be angry with me, lest I perish!*[1]

This is the tone of the last lines of 'Good Friday':

> O thinke mee worth thine anger, punish me,
> Burne off my rusts, and my deformity,
> Restore thine Image, so much, by thy grace,
> That thou may'st know mee; and I'll turne my face.

1. *Fifty Sermons*, xlviii. 455.

Both make the close of the sonnet seem facile.

The almost histrionic note of the 'Holy Sonnets' may be attributed partly to the meditation's deliberate stimulation of emotion; it is the special danger of this exercise that, in stimulating feeling, it may falsify it, and overdramatize the spiritual life. But Donne's choice of subjects and his whole-hearted use of the method are symptoms of a condition of mind very different from the mood of '*La Corona*' or even from the conflicts which can be felt behind 'A Litany'. The meditation on sin and on judgement is strong medicine; the mere fact that his mind turned to it suggests some sickness in the soul. The 'low devout melancholie' of '*La Corona*', the 'dejection' of 'A Litany' are replaced by something darker. In both his preparatory prayers Donne uses a more terrible word, despair. The note of anguish is unmistakable. The image of a soul in meditation which the 'Holy Sonnets' present is an image of a soul working out its salvation in fear and trembling. The two poles between which it oscillates are faith in the mercy of God in Christ, and a sense of personal unworthiness that is very near to despair. The flaws in their spiritual temper are a part of their peculiar power. No other religious poems make us feel so acutely the predicament of the natural man called to be the spiritual man. None present more vividly man's recognition of the gulf that divides him from God and the effort of faith to lay hold on the miracle by which Christianity declares that the gulf has been bridged.

Donne's art in writing them was to seem 'to use no art at all'. His language has the ring of a living voice, admonishing his own soul, expostulating with his Maker, defying Death, or pouring itself out in supplication. He creates, as much as in some of the *Songs and Sonnets*, the illusion of a present experience, throwing his stress on such words as 'now' and 'here' and 'this'. And, as often there, he gives an extreme emphasis to the personal pronouns:

> Take mee to you, imprison mee, for I
> Except you'enthrall mee, never shall be free,
> Nor ever chast, except you ravish mee.

The plain unadorned speech, with its idiomatic turns, its rapid questions, its exclamatory Oh's and Ah's, wrests the movement of the sonnet to its own movement. The line is weighted with heavy monosyllables, or lengthened by heavy secondary stresses, which demand the same emphasis as the main stress takes. It may be stretched out to

> All of whom warre, dearth, age, agues, tyrannies,

after it has been contracted to

> From death, you numberlesse infinities.

Many lines can be reduced to ten syllables only by a more drastic use of elision than Donne allowed himself elsewhere, except in the *Satires*; and others, if we are to trust the best manuscripts, are a syllable short and fill out the line by a pause. This dramatic language has a magic that is unanalysable: words, movement, and feeling have a unity in which no element outweighs the other.

The effect of completely natural speech is achieved by exploiting to the full the potentialities of the sonnet.[2] The formal distinction of octave and sestet becomes a dramatic contrast. The openings of Donne's sestets are as dramatic as the openings of the sonnets themselves: impatient as in

> Why doth the devill then usurpe in mee?

or gentle as in

> Yet grace, if thou repent, thou canst not lacke;

or imploring as in

> But let them sleepe, Lord, and mee mourne a space.

Though the *turn* in each of these is different, in all three there is that sudden difference in tension that makes a change dramatic. Donne avoids also the main danger of the couplet ending: that it may seem an afterthought, or an addition, or a mere summary. His final couplets, whether separate or running on from the preceding line, are true rhetorical climaxes, with the weight of the poem behind them. Except for Hopkins, no poet has crammed more into the sonnet than Donne. In spite of all the liberties he takes with his line, he succeeds in the one essential of the sonnet: he appears to need exactly fourteen lines to say exactly what he has to say. Donne possibly chose the sonnet form as appropriate for a set of formal meditations, but both in meditation and in the writing of his sonnets he converts traditional material to his own use. He was not, I believe, aiming at originality, and therefore the originality of the 'Holy Sonnets' is the more profound.

With the exception of 'The Lamentations of Jeremy', in which Donne, like so many of his contemporaries, but with more success than most, attempted the unrewarding task of paraphrasing the Scriptures, the remainder of the *Divine Poems* are occasional. The poem 'Upon the Annunciation and Passion' is very near in mood and style to '*La Corona*'. As there, Donne writes with strict objectivity. He contemplates two mysteries which are facets of one supreme mystery, and tries to express what any Christian might feel. On the other hand,

---

2. As in '*La Corona*', Donne keeps to two rhymes in the octave, and varies his sestet, using either *cddcee* or *cdcdee*. No general plan governs his choice here of which type of sestet he uses.

'Good Friday, Riding Westward' is a highly personal poem: a free, discursive meditation arising out of a particular situation. The elaborate preliminary conceit of the contrary motions of the heavenly bodies extends itself into astronomical images, until the recollection of the Passion sweeps away all thoughts but penitence. As in some of the finest of the *Songs and Sonnets,* Donne draws out an initial conceit to its limit in order, as it seems, to throw it away when "to brave clearnesse all things are reduc'd'. What he first sees as an incongruity —his turning his back on his crucified Saviour—he comes to see as perhaps the better posture, and finally as congruous for a sinner. The poem hinges on the sudden apostrophe:

> and thou look'st towards mee,
> O Saviour, as thou hang'st upon the tree.

After this, discursive meditation contracts itself to penitent prayer. The mounting tension of the poem—from leisurely speculation, through the imagination kindled by 'that spectacle of too much weight for mee', to passionate humility—makes it a dramatic monologue. So also does the sense it gives us of a second person present— the silent figure whose eyes the poet feels watching him as he rides away to the west.

'Good Friday' is the last divine poem Donne wrote before his ordination and it points forward to the Hymns. They also arise from particular situations, are free, not formal meditations, and have the same unforced feeling. They are the only lyrics among the *Divine Poems,* and it is not only in their use of the pun and conceit that they remind us of the *Songs and Sonnets.* They have the spontaneity which 'La Corona' and 'A Litany' lack, without the overemphasis of the 'Holy Sonnets'. In them Donne's imagination has room for play. Each sprang from a moment of crisis. The 'Hymn to Christ' was written on the eve of his journey overseas with Doncaster, a journey from which, as his Valediction Sermon shows, he felt he might not return. It is a finer treatment of the subject of the sonnet written after his wife's death in the Westmoreland manuscript. While the sonnet is general and reflective, in the Hymn his imagination is fired by his immediate circumstances and he translates his thoughts into striking and moving symbols. The 'Hymn to God the Father' was written, according to Walton, during Donne's grave illness of 1623, and the 'Hymn to God my God, in my sickness', whether it should be dated during the same illness or in 1631, was written when he thought himself at the point of death. In both the conclusion is the same: 'So, in his purple wrapp'd receive mee Lord', and 'Sweare by thy selfe'. Donne's earliest poem on religion, the third Satire, ended with the words 'God himselfe to trust', and it is fitting that what is possibly his last divine poem, and certainly one of his best known, should end with the memory of the

promise to Abraham, the type of the faithful.[3] For the *Divine Poems*
are poems of faith, not of vision. Donne goes by a road which is not lit
by any flashes of ecstasy, and in the words he had carved on his tomb
'aspicit Eum cujus nomen est Oriens'. The absence of ecstasy makes
his divine poems so different from his love poems. There is an ecstasy
of joy and an ecstasy of grief in his love poetry; in his divine poetry we
are conscious almost always of an effort of will. In the 'Holy Sonnets'
there is passion and longing, and in the Hymns some of the 'modest
assurance' which Walton attributed to Donne's last hours, but there
is no rapture.

* * *

The meditation is a very old religious exercise. Its essence is an
attempt to stimulate devotion by the use of the imagination. The
method of meditation was systematized in the sixteenth century by
St. Ignatius Loyola, whose *Exercitia Spiritualia* was printed with Papal
approval in 1548. A meditation on the Ignatian pattern, employing
the 'three powers of the soul', consists of a brief preparatory prayer,
two 'preludes,' a varying number of points, and a colloquy. The preparatory prayer is 'to ask God our Lord for grace that all my intentions,
actions and operations may be ordered purely to the service and praise
of His divine Majesty'.[4] The first prelude is what is called the *compositio loci*: the seeing 'with the eyes of the imagination' either a place
'such as the Temple or the mountain where Jesus Christ is found', or,
if the meditation is of an invisible thing such as sin, a situation: 'that
my soul is imprisoned in this corruptible body, and my whole com-
pound self in this vale [of misery] as in exile amongst brute beasts.'
The second prelude is a petition 'according to the subject matter';
thus, if the meditation is of the Passion, the petition will be for 'sorrow, tears, and fellowship with Christ in his sufferings'; if the meditation is of sin, the petition will be for 'shame'. The meditation proper
follows, divided into points, usually three or five. Lastly, the memory,
the storehouse of images, having been engaged in the preludes, and
the reason in the points, the third power of the soul, the will, is employed in the colloquy, which is a free outpouring of the devotion
aroused.

The Ignatian method can be applied to any topic and was widely
popular. Donne, with his Jesuit uncles, his pious mother, and his tu-
tors who were of her faith, must have been familiar as a boy and young

3. Cf. Gen. xxii. 16: 'By myself have I
sworn, saith the Lord'; and Heb. vi. 13–
18: 'For when God made promise to
Abraham, because he could swear by no
greater, he sware by himself. . . . For
men verily swear by the greater: and an
oath for confirmation is to them an end
of all strife. Wherein God, willing more
abundantly to shew unto the heirs of
promise the immutability of his counsel,
confirmed it by an oath: that by two
immutable things, in which it was impossible for God to lie, we might have a
strong consolation, who have fled for
refuge to lay hold upon the hope set before us.'
4. Quotations are taken from *The Spiritual Exercises*, translated from the
Spanish with a Commentary, by W. H.
Longridge, S.S.J.E. (1930).

man with systematic meditation. His teachers probably took the advice of St. Peter of Alcantara, who taught that beginners should specially practice two kinds of meditation: on the Last Things, 'which like sharpe prickes doe spurre us on to the love and feare of God', and on the life and Passion of our Lord, 'which is the springe and fountaine of all our good'.[5] Donne begins his set of sonnets on the Last Things in the proper manner with a preparatory prayer. In the octave of the first sonnet he recollects himself, remembers his creation and redemption and that he has received the gift of the Holy Spirit; in the sestet he laments the power of the devil upon him and asks for grace. The next three sonnets show very clearly the two preludes of a meditation, which correspond neatly to the two parts of a sonnet: the *compositio loci* occupying the octave, and the 'petition according to the subject' the sestet. In his second sonnet, where he imagines himself dangerously ill. Donne uses a pair of vivid images to make himself realize the situation. He is here doing what St. Ignatius advised in the 'Additions for the purpose of helping the exercitant to make the Exercises better':

> setting before myself examples, e.g. as if a knight were to find himself in the presence of his king and all his court, covered with shame and confusion because he has grievously offended him from whom he has first received many gifts and favours. Likewise in the second Exercise, considering myself a great sinner, bound with chains, and about to appear before the supreme eternal Judge, taking as an example how prisoners in chains, and worthy of death, appear before their temporal judge.

These examples, or 'congruous thoughts' as they are sometimes called, were regarded as an important element in meditation. Donne's pilgrim, who has done treason abroad, and his thief, who on the way to execution longs for the prison from which he had wished to be delivered, are excellent examples of 'congruous thoughts'. These brief, vivid, realistic images from human life are very characteristic of the 'Holy Sonnets', which show none of that elaboration of a simile or an analogy into a conceit which is characteristic of the *Songs and Sonnets*. After imagining the sick man's predicament, Donne in the sestet draws out the moral: that grace will follow repentance, and that grace is needed to repent. This is hardly a petition, though it comes near to one; but in the third and fourth sonnets a true 'petition according to the subject' follows a brilliant first prelude. In the third sonnet, the actual moment of death is imagined and the prayer is for a 'safe issue'

5. See *A Golden Treatise of Mental Prayer*, translated by G. W. (Brussels, 1632), pp. 6–8. The original was written about 1558. St. Peter provides two sets of seven meditations to be used either on the mornings and evenings of one week, or in successive weeks. The first set are on Sin, the Miseries of Life, Death, the Judgement, Hell, Heaven, the Blessings of God; the second on the events of the Passion, the Resurrection, and Ascension. Similar sets can be found in another popular book of devotion: *The Exercise of a Christian Life*, by the Italian Jesuit, Gaspar Loarte, written in 1569 and translated into English in 1584.

from death. In the fourth, the *compositio loci* is a picture of the Last Judgement, when those who have met death in such diverse ways and distant ages rise together at the Trump; this is followed by the petition to the Lord to delay the summons and teach a present repentance. The fifth sonnet, on the other hand, has no *compositio loci*—its octave is more like a 'point' drawn out from a meditation on hell—though its sestet contains a striking petition; while the sixth, the sonnet to Death, is only linked to the others by its subject; in manner and temper it is quite undevotional. This is what we should expect with Donne, who always as he writes develops his material in his own way. He is a poet using for his own purposes various elements from a familiar tradition; not a pious versifier, turning common material into rhyme.

The last six sonnets of the twelve printed in 1633 depend less on the preludes of the Ignatian meditation than on the colloquy. They serve the purpose of the second set of meditations suggested by St. Peter of Alcantara and others, in that they fix the mind on the saving love of God in Christ; but they handle the subject with the discursive freedom of a colloquy. The eleventh sonnet, the 'wholsome meditation', which along with the twelfth appears to have been Donne's original pendant to his set on the Last Things, recalls the colloquy with which St. Ignatius concludes the first exercise, on sins:

> Imagining Christ our Lord present before me on the Cross, to make a colloquy with Him, asking Him how it is that being the Creator, He has come to make Himself man, and from eternal life has come to temporal death, and in this manner to die for my sins. Again, reflecting on myself, to ask what have I done for Christ, what am I doing for Christ, what ought I to do for Christ. Then beholding Him in such a condition, and thus hanging upon the Cross, to make the reflections which may present themselves.

In these last sonnets, the influence of the meditation is felt, not in the structure of the sonnets, but in such things as the vivid sense of the actualities of the Passion in 'Spit in my face', the imagining of the face of Christ on the Cross in 'What if this present were the worlds last night', and the use of 'congruous thoughts' in this last sonnet and in the one that follows it, 'Batter my heart'.

The four penitential sonnets are less obviously meditations, because their subject is an invisible thing, sin. There is, therefore, less scope for a recognizable *compositio loci*. In the order in which they are printed here they form a brief sequence, beginning with the regular preparatory prayer. The sonnet which I have placed second, 'I am a little world', is a general meditation, with a very short *compositio loci*, in which Donne reminds himself, as St. Ignatius advised in meditating on sin, that both body and soul are given over to sin. This is followed by a long second prelude asking for repentance. The sonnet which I have placed third, 'O might those sighes and teares', specifies a particular sin, 'sufferance', in the sense of indulgence, particularly indulgence in excessive and misdirected grief. Its particularity makes it more suitably follow than precede the sonnet on sin in general. It also leads on to the last, 'If faithful soules be alike glorifi'd', which develops a subsidiary point, arising out of the likeness and contrast between the tears he shed as a lover and the tears he sheds as a penitent: tears may be the signs of many kinds of grief, and only God, the giver of true grief, can know if grief is true. The four sonnets are closely linked together. It is the sin in his 'feebled flesh' that weighs him down in the opening prayer, 'lust and envie' that have burned his little world in the second sonnet: indulgence which has caused him mourning that he mourns in the third. The meditation on sin is the opening exercise of the *Spiritual Exercises* and Donne develops the subject on the lines suggested there. But here again he writes with the freedom of a poet whose imagination is not tied to an initial plan. The second sonnet has only a very short *compositio loci*; the third expands the *compositio* to fill the whole sonnet, which is wholly given up to the imagining of his predicament and contains no petition; while the fourth has no relation to the form of a meditation, but is an individual moralization, containing neither *compositio* nor petition.

The influence of the formal meditation lies behind the 'Holy Sonnets', not as a literary source, but as a way of thinking, a method of prayer. Mr. Louis Martz has recently shown that the Ignatian method of meditating by points and the use of parallel sets of meditations for mornings and evenings of a week provided Donne with the structure of the two *Anniversaries*.[6] That such different works as the 'Holy Sonnets' and the *Anniversaries* can be shown to depend on the same exercise points to real familiarity with the method. When we are genuinely familiar with something we can use it with freedom for our own purposes. There is no need to feel surprise that Donne, at a time when he was engaged in bitter controversy with the Jesuits, should be drawing on Jesuit spirituality in his poetry, and presumably had continued to use a Jesuit method of prayer. He would be making a distinction here which Protestants made without difficulty—taking the corn and leaving the chaff. At the close of the sixteenth century perfectly orthodox Protestant works of devotion made use of contemporary Catholic devotional works, inspired by the Jesuit revival. Many Protestants felt that, in the bitter theological controversies of the time, the Christian life of prayer and devotion was in danger of perishing. They could not recommend the great medieval works of devotion, for these were al-

6. See Louis L. Martz, 'John Donne in Meditation: the *Anniversaries*' (*E. L. H.*, December 1947). It was after I had come to my own conclusions on the date and origins of the 'Holy Sonnets' that I read Mr. Martz's article. It was encouraging to find that we had independently arrived at similar conclusions with such different poems.

most all written for members of religious communities, and Protestants rejected the life of the cloister. But books such as Loarte's *The Exercise of a Christian Life*, which in its Protestant English dress converted Robert Greene, were, with judicious pruning, easily made suitable for devout Protestants.[7]

As in '*La Corona*' and 'A Litany', so in the 'Holy Sonnets', Donne is using as the material of his poetry ways of devotion he had learnt as a child. We have not accounted for the 'Holy Sonnets' if we say that he wanted to write sets of meditations in sonnet form, any more than we have accounted for *Paradise Lost* if we say that Milton wished to write a classical epic on a Christian subject. But recognition of a poet's conscious intentions takes us some way towards appreciation of his achievement, and can save us from too simple a correlation between the experience of the poet and his translation of it into poetry.

LOUIS L. MARTZ

[Donne's "Holy Sonnets" and "Good Friday, 1613"]†

What I should like to stress at this point is the way in which the total movement of these poems [of Southwell] resembles, in its rudiments, the "intellectual, argumentative evolution" of Donne's or Herbert's poetry: the "strain of passionate, paradoxical reasoning which knits the first line to the last," and performs this knitting through close analysis and elaboration of concrete imagery. Southwell seems to be struggling toward the qualities that Hutchinson has thus accurately described as the dominant characteristic of Herbert: "Almost any poem of his has its object well defined; its leading idea is followed through with economy and brought to an effective conclusion, the imagery which runs through it commonly helping to knit it together." Southwell's poems give that impression of a "predetermined plan" which Palmer has noted as a characteristic of many of Herbert's poems,[1] and which is also, I think, a strong characteristic of Donne's. May it not be that all three poets are working, to some extent, under the influence of methods of meditation that led toward the deliberate evolution of a threefold structure of composition (memory), analysis (understanding), and colloquy (affections, will)?

7. See Helen C. White, 'Some Continuing Traditions in English Devotional Literature' (*P.M.L.A.* lxvii, 1942, pp. 966–80). The one medieval work which never lost its hold was the *Imitation of Christ*, which as Miss White rightly points out is the most deeply Scriptural of devotional works. This, for Protestants, outweighed the fact that it is impregnated with the spirit of the cloister.

† From Louis L. Martz, *The Poetry of Meditation*, copyright 1954. Pp. 43-56. Reprinted by permission of the publishers, The Yale University Press.
1. *The Works of George Herbert*, ed. F. E. Hutchinson (2nd ed., Oxford, Clarendon Press, 1945), p. xlix; *The English Works of George Herbert*, ed. George Herbert Palmer (3 vols., Boston and New York, Houghton Mifflin, 1905), I, 142.

The "Holy Sonnets" seem to bear out this conjecture. Holy Sonnet 12 bears a very close resemblance to the conclusion of St. Ignatius Loyola's second exercise for the First Week, a "meditation upon sins," where the fifth and last point is:

> an exclamation of wonder, with intense affection, running through all creatures in my mind, how they have suffered me to live, and have preserved me in life; how the angels, who are the sword of the Divine Justice, have borne with me, and have guarded and prayed for me; how the saints have been interceding and praying for me; and the heavens, the sun, the moon, the stars, and the elements, the fruits of the earth, the birds, the fishes, and the animals; and the earth, how it is it has not opened to swallow me up . . . .
>
> The whole to conclude with a colloquy of mercy, reasoning and giving thanks to God our Lord, for having given me life till now, and proposing through His grace to amend henceforward. (pp. 24–5)[2]

In Sonnet 12 this problem, simply and firmly proposed in the opening line, is elaborated with a single, scientific instance in the first quatrain:

> Why are wee by all creatures waited on?
> Why doe the prodigall elements supply
> Life and food to mee, being more pure then I,
> Simple, and further from corruption?

The problem is then examined in greater detail through a shift to direct questioning of the animals, which runs through the next six lines:

> Why brook'st thou, ignorant horse, subjection?
> Why dost thou bull, and bore so seelily
> Dissemble weaknesse, and by'one mans stroke die,
> Whose whole kinde, you might swallow and feed upon?
> Weaker I am, woe is mee, and worse then you,
> You have not sinn'd, nor need be timorous.

The "colloquy of mercy" then appears to follow, as the speaker addresses himself, the representative of all mankind, "reasoning," developing the sense of "wonder," and implicity "giving thanks":

> But wonder at a greater wonder, for to us
> Created nature doth these things subdue,
> But their Creator, whom sin, nor nature tyed,
> For us, his Creatures, and his foes, hath dyed.

Puente's development of this Ignatian topic will provide, perhaps, a more convincing proof of our argument for Jesuit influence here:

> The fourth pointe, shall bee, to breake out with these considerations into an exclamation, with an affection vehement, and full of

2. *The Text of the Spiritual Exercises of St. Ignatius, Translated from the Original Spanish*, with preface by John Morris (4th ed., Westminster, Md., 1943).

amazement; As, that the creatures have suffered me, I having so grievously offended their Creator, and benefactor . . . . That the elements, the birdes of the aire, the fishes of the sea, the beastes, and plantes of the earthe have helped to sustaine mee. I confesse that I deserve not the breade I eate, nor the water I drinke, nor the aire I breathe in: neither am I worthy to lift up myne eyes to heaven . . . . (1, 70–1)[3]

At the same time, it seems that Holy Sonnet 15 bears some general relation to St. Ignatius' "Contemplation for obtaining love," a special meditation, annexed to the Fourth Week, which aims at achieving "an interior knowledge of the many and great benefits I have received, that, thoroughly grateful, I may in all things love and serve His Divine Majesty." The meditation opens by calling to mind

the benefits received, of my creation, redemption, and particular gifts, dwelling with great affection on how much God our Lord has done for me, and how much He has given me of that which He has; and consequently, how much He desires to give me Himself in so far as He can according to His Divine ordinance; and then to reflect in myself what I, on my side, with great reason and justice, ought to offer and give to His Divine Majesty. (pp. 74–5)

This seems to be exactly what the speaker is so deliberately telling himself to do in Sonnet 15:

Wilt thou love God, as he thee! then digest,
My Soule, this wholsome meditation,
How God the Spirit, by Angels waited on
In heaven, doth make his Temple in thy brest.
The Father having begot a Sonne most blest,
And still begetting, (for he ne'r begonne)
Hath deign'd to chuse thee by adoption,
Coheire to'his glory, 'and Sabbaths endlesse rest.
And as a robb'd man, which by search doth finde
His stolne stuffe sold, must lose or buy'it againe:
The Sonne of glory came downe, and was slaine,
Us whom he'had made, and Satan stolne, to unbinde.
'Twas much, that man was made like God before,
But, that God should be made like man, much more.

In lines 3 and 4 there may be a reminiscence of a part of the "second point" of this exercise, where one is advised to "consider how God dwells in creatures . . . and so in me, giving me being, life, feeling, and causing me to understand: making likewise of me a temple . . . ." But the resemblances are only general, and of course the sonnet does not trace the progress of a complete exercise: it is analysis only, understanding; part of a complete exercise.

3. Luis de la Puente, *Meditations upon the Mysteries of our Holie Faith, with the Practice of Mental Prayer touching the same,* [trans. John Heigham], (2 vols., St. Omer, 1619). The original work appeared in 1605.

This, I believe, is what we should expect to find in most of the "Holy Sonnets" (and in most of the other religious poems of the time related to the art of meditation): a portion of an exercise which has been set down in explicit poetry; especially the colloquy, in which the "three powers" fuse, become incandescent, as Fray Luis de Granada says: "When we talke unto almightie God, then the understanding mounteth up on highe, and after it followeth also the will, and then hath a man commonly on his parte greater devotion, and attention, and greater feare, and reverence of the majestie of almightie God, with whom he speaketh . . . ." (p. 309)[4] The complete exercise was long—an hour or more in duration—and its deliberate, predominantly intellectual method would not, for most of its course, provide material for poetry. Now and then a poet might recapitulate an exercise in miniature, or compose a poem that developed under the impulse of his frequent practice of the stages in a full sequence; but more often we should expect the poetry to reflect chiefly the final stages of the sequence. Furthermore, the formal procedure for a full exercise was not by any means necessarily followed on every occasion. All the meditative treatises explain that this full framework is provided as an aid for beginners or as a method to fall back upon in times of spiritual dryness. Even the Jesuit exercises, which might appear to prescribe the most rigorous of all plans, are actually very flexible, for St. Ignatius expects them to be performed under the direction of a priest who will adapt them to the needs and capacities of each individual. Adepts in meditation are encouraged, both by the Jesuits and by other writers, to follow the lead of their affections. Thus we find Tomás de Villa-castín warning that "the infinite goodness and liberality of God is not tyed to these rules" (p. 55)[5]; Fray Luis de Granada explaining that he has set down "diverse and sundrie poyntes, to the intent, that emonge so great varietie of considerations, everie one might make his choice of such thinges, as might best serve his devotion" (p. 49); and St. François de Sales urging the reader to "take this for a generall rule, never to restraine, or with-hold thy affections once inflamed with any devout motion, but let them have their free course." (p. 138)[6]

In accordance with this freedom of procedure we find that colloquies may be made not only at the end of the set sequence but at any time during an exercise: indeed, the Jesuit Gibbons says "it will be best, and almost needfull so to do" (§2, ¶ 25)[7]; and Puente proves the point by scattering colloquies frequently throughout the course of his

4. *Of Prayer and Meditation*, [trans. Richard Hopkins], (Douay, 1612).
5. *A Manual of Devout Meditations and Exercises* . . . [trans. H. More], (St. Omer, 1618). The original appeared c. 1610.
6. *An Introduction to a Devoute Life*, [trans. John Yakesley], (3rd ed., Rouen, 1614).
7. Richard Gibbons, "The Practical Methode of Meditation," prefixed to Gibbons' translation: *An Abridgment of Meditations of the Life, Passion, Death and Resurrection of our Lord and Saviour Jesus Christ*. . . [St. Omer], 1614.

meditations. In these colloquies of Puente we find something very close to the tone and manner of Donne's religious poetry: subtle theological analysis, punctuated with passionate questions and exclamations:

> O my soule, heare what this our Lord saieth: Which of you can dwell with devouring fier? O who shallbee able to dwell in these perpetuall ardours? If thou darest not touche the light fier of this life, why doest thou not tremble at the terrible fier of the other? Contemplate this fier with attention, that the feare thereof may consume the fier of thy insatiable desire, if thorough thy want of fervent zeale, the fier of God's love bee not sufficient to consume them. (1, 144)

> O God of vengeance, how is it that thou hast not revenged thy selfe on a man so wicked as I? How hast thou suffred mee so long a time? Who hath withhelde the rigour of thy justice, that it should not punish him, that hath deserve[d] so terrible punishment? O my Soule, how is it, that thou doest not feare, and tremble, considering the dreadefull judgement of God against his Angells? If with so great severitye hee punished creatures so noble, why should not so vile, and miserable a creature as thou, feare the like punishment? O most powerful creator, seeing thou hast shewed thy selfe to mee not a God of vengeance, but a father of mercye, continue towardes mee this thy mercye, pardonning my sinnes, and delivering mee from hell, which most justly for them I have deserved. (1, 55)

More specific similarities are found in the passage where Puente urges that in addressing colloquies to God, or Christ, or the Trinity we should offer "titles and reasons, that may move them to graunt us what wee demand." In Christ, he says, we may claim such titles as his sufferings and his love,

> Sometimes speaking to the eternall Father, beseeching him to heare mee for the Love of his Sonne; for the Services hee did him; and the Paines that for his love hee endured. Other times speaking to the Sonne of God: alledging unto him the love that hee bare us, the Office that hee holdeth of our Redeemer, and Advocate; and the greate Price that wee cost him . . . .
> Other Titles there are on the part of our Necessitye, and Miserye, alledging before our Lord; like *David*, that wee were conceived in Sinne, that wee have disordered passions, strong enemies . . . and that without him wee are able to doe nothing. That we are his Creatures made according to his owne Image, and Likenesse, and that for this cause the devill persecuteth us to destroye us, and that therefore it appertayneth to him to protect us. (1, 4–5)

Donne's Sonnet 2 certainly looks like a colloquy stemming from such advice as this:

> As due by many titles I resigne
> My selfe to thee, O God, first I was made

By thee, and for thee, and when I was decay'd
Thy blood bought that, the which before was thine;
I am thy sonne, made with thy selfe to shine,
Thy servant, whose paines thou hast still repaid,
Thy sheepe, thine Image, and, till I betray'd
My selfe, a temple of thy Spirit divine;
Why doth the devill then usurpe on mee?
Why doth he steale, nay ravish that's thy right?
Except thou rise and for thine owne worke fight,
Oh I shall soone despaire, when I doe see
That thou lov'st mankind well, yet wilt'not chuse me,
And Satan hates mee, yet is loth to lose mee.

Such general or fragmentary parallels between Donne's poetry and Jesuit methods of meditation are strongly supported by the fact that at least four of the "Holy Sonnets" appear to display, in their total movement, the method of a total exercise: they suggest the "premeditation" or the recapitulation, in miniature, of such an exercise; or, at least, a poetical structure modeled on the stages of a complete exercise. Such a threefold structure, of course, easily accords with the traditional 4–4–6 division of the Petrarchan sonnet, and thus provides a particularly interesting illustration of the way in which poetical tradition may be fertilized and developed by the meditative tradition. Perhaps the clearest example is found in Holy Sonnet 11, which suggests the traditional meditative procedure briefly described by Antonio de Molina: "Thus when we see our Saviour taken prisoner, and used so ill, whipped and nayled on the Crosse; we must consider that we be there present amongst those villaines, and that our sinnes be they who so abuse him, and take away his life";[8] and developed with dramatic detail by Puente:

Then I am to set before mine eyes Christ Jesus crucified, beholding his heade crowned with thornes; his face spit upon; his eyes obscured; his armes disioincted; his tongue distasted with gall, and vineger; his handes, and feete peerced with nailes; his backe, and shoulders torne with whippes; and his side opened with a launce: and then pondering that hee suffereth all this for my sinnes, I will drawe sundrye affections from the inwardest parte of my heart, sometimes trembling at the rigour of God's iustice . . . sometimes bewailing my sinnes which were the cause of these dolours: and sometimes animating myselfe to suffer somewhat in satisfaction of myne offences, seeing Christ our Lord suffered so much to redeeme them. And finally I will beg pardon of him for them, alledging to him for a reason, all his troubles, and afflictions, saying unto him in amorous colloquie.

O my most sweete Redeemer, which descendest from heaven, and ascendest this Crosse to redeeme men, paying their sinnes with

8. Antonio de Molina, *A Treatise of Mental Prayer*, [trans. J. Sweetman], ([St. Omer], 1617), pp. 60–1. The original appeared in 1615.

thy dolours, I present myselfe before thy Majestie, grieved that my grievous sinnes have been the cause of thy terrible paines. Upon mee, O Lord, these chastizements had been iustlie imployed, for I am hee that sinned, and not upon thee that never sinnedst. Let that love that moved thee to put thyselfe upon the Crosse for mee, move thee to pardon mee what I have committed against thee. (1, 59–60)

Similarly, in Donne's sonnet, the speaker has made himself vividly present at the scene, so dramatically conscious of his sins that he cries out to Christ's persecutors in lines that throw a colloquial emphasis on the words "my," "mee," and "I":

Spit in my face, you Jewes, and pierce my side,
Buffet, and scoffe, scourge, and crucifie mee,
For I have sinn'd, and sinn'd, and onely hee,
Who could do no iniquitie hath dyed:

but after this passionate outcry the tone of the next quatrain shifts to one of tense, muted, intellectual brooding, as the understanding explores the theological significance of the scene:

But by my death can not be satisfied
My sinnes, which passe the Jewes impiety:
They kill'd once an inglorious man, but I
Crucifie him daily, being now glorified.

And then, with another marked shift in tone, the speaker turns to draw forth in himself the appropriate "affections," suffusing intellectual analysis with the emotions of love and wonder:

Oh let me then, his strange love still admire:
Kings pardon, but he bore our punishment.
And *Iacob* came cloth'd in vile harsh attire
But to supplant, and with gainfull intent:
God cloth'd himselfe in vile mans flesh, that so
Hee might be weake enough to suffer woe.

Likewise, in the first quatrain of Sonnet 7 we may see the dramatic operations of both imagination and memory, for here the speaker remembers the description of Doomsday in the book of Revelation, especially the opening of the seventh chapter: "I saw four angels standing on the four corners of the earth"; and he cries out, seeing them there in a vivid composition of place:

At the round eaths imagin'd corners, blow
Your trumpets, Angells, and arise, arise
From death, you numberlesse infinities
Of soules, and to your scattred bodies goe . . . .

With the "matter" of the meditation thus "composed" and defined, the understanding then performs its analysis in the second quatrain, "discoursing" upon the causes of death throughout human history: a summary of sin and a reminder of its consequences:

> All whom the flood did, and fire shall o'erthrow,
> All whom warre, dearth, age, agues, tyrannies,
> Despaire, law, chance, hath slaine, and you whose eyes,
> Shall behold God, and never tast deaths woe.

Finally, in the sestet, the will expresses its "affections" and "petitions" in colloquy with God, "as one friend speaks to another, or as a servant to his master":

> But let them sleepe, Lord, and mee mourne a space,
> For, if above all these, my sinnes abound,
> 'Tis late to aske abundance of thy grace,
> When wee are there; here on this lowly ground,
> Teach mee how to repent; for that's as good
> As if thou'hadst seal'd my pardon, with thy blood.

"When wee are there"—those words which so puzzled I. A. Richards' students[9] may be explained if we realize that this is part of a traditional colloquy with God after a visualization of the Day of Doom. "Wee," though no doubt including all sinners, suggests primarily God and the individual speaker's soul; "there" refers to the throne of Judgment in the heavens, as presented in the book of Revelation; "there" is thus in sharp contrast with the "lowly ground" where the soul now prays for grace, with theological overtones relating to the Catholic sacrament of Penance.

Somewhat the same procedure appears also to be operating in Holy Sonnet 9, where an example of Donne's besetting sin of intellectual pride is "proposed" in an audacious, blasphemous evasion of responsibility:

> If poysonous mineralls, and if that tree,
> Whose fruit threw death on else immortall us,
> If lecherous goats, if serpents envious
> Cannot be damn'd; Alas; why should I bee?

The problem thus set forth concretely is then pursued abstractly in the second quatrain, which reveals the speaker's knowledge of the proper theological answer to his question, but he continues the evasion and increases the blasphemy by first an implied ("borne in mee"), and then a direct, attack on God's justice:

9. I. A. Richards, *Practical Criticism* (New York, Harcourt, Brace, 1935), pp. 44–5. Miss Gardner would interpret this sonnet as developing in accordance with the two preludes of the Ignatian method, the octave giving the "composition" and the sestet the petition "according to the subject-matter." This seems to me a valid interpretation: since the whole progress of the exercise would have been "premeditated" and foreseen, the action of the "three powers" would be anticipated in the preludes. See her excellent analysis of this and other "Holy Sonnets" in John Donne, *The Divine Poems*, ed. Helen Gardner (Oxford, Clarendon Press, 1952), pp. l–liv.

Why should intent or reason, borne in mee,
Make sinnes, else equall, in mee more heinous?
And mercy being easie, and glorious
To God; in his sterne wrath, why threatens hee?

But at last, and very suddenly, the thin wall of this uneasy argument collapses and the poem concludes with one of Donne's most vehement colloquies, giving the answer that has been implicit and premeditated throughout:

But who am I, that dare dispute with thee
O God? Oh! of thine onely worthy blood,
And my teares, make a heavenly Lethean flood,
And drowne in it my sinnes blacke memorie;
That thou remember them, some claime as debt,
I thinke it mercy, if thou wilt forget.

And fourthly, with a slightly different division of lines, I believe that we can follow the same movement in Sonnet 5, which presents in its first four lines a "composition by similitude" defining precisely the "invisible" problem to be considered:

I am a little world made cunningly
Of Elements, and an Angelike spright,
But black sinne hath betraid to endlesse night
My worlds both parts, and (oh) both parts must die.

The next five lines form a unit overflowing the usual Petrarchan division; and appropriately, since the intellect is here using a mode of violent hyperbole:

You which beyond that heaven which was most high
Have found new sphears, and of new lands can write,
Powre new seas in mine eyes, that so I might
Drowne my world with my weeping earnestly,
Or wash it, if it must be drown'd no more:

and then, inevitably, the last five lines, another firm unit, show the passionate outburst of the affections thus aroused, ending with a petition in colloquy with God:

But oh it must be burnt! alas the fire
Of lust and envie have burnt it heretofore,
And made it fouler; Let their flames retire,
And burne me ô Lord, with a fiery zeale
Of thee and thy house, which doth in eating heale.[1]

---

1. Cf. Puente, *1*, 88: "O most just judge, and most mercifull Father, I confesse that I am thorough my sinnes a blacke, and filthy cole, and halfe burnt with the fier of my passions, washe mee, o Lord, and whiten mee with the living water of thy grace, and therwith quenche this fier that burneth mee . . . ." Also Puente, *1*, 274: "in steede of drowning the worlde againe with another deluge; or burning it with fier like Sodom; hee [God] would drowne it with abundance of mercies, and burne it with the fier of his love . . . ."

We can see then why, as Grierson records, three manuscripts of the "Holy Sonnets" entitle them "Devine Meditations."[2] They are, in the most specific sense of the term, meditations, Ignatian meditations: providing strong evidence for the profound impact of early Jesuit training upon the later career of John Donne.

Finally, let us turn to examine the adumbrations of this method of meditation in one of Donne's longest, greatest religious poems, one for which, unlike the "Holy Sonnets," we can give the precise date and occasion: "Goodfriday, 1613. Riding Westward." The manuscript headings recorded by Grierson fill out our information: "Riding to Sr Edward Harbert in Wales"; "Mr J. Dun goeing from Sir H. G. on good friday sent him back this meditation on the way."[3] The first ten lines of this meditation form an elaborate, deliberately evolved "composition by similitude":

> Let mans Soule be a Spheare, and then, in this,
> The intelligence that moves, devotion is,
> And as the other Spheares, by being growne
> Subject to forraigne motions, lose their owne,
> And being by others hurried every day,
> Scarce in a yeare their naturall forme obey:
> Pleasure or businesse, so, our Soules admit
> For their first mover, and are whirld by it.
> Hence is't, that I am carryed towards the West
> This day, when my Soules forme bends toward the East.

The composition has thus precisely set the problem: profane motives carry the soul away from God, while the soul's essence ("forme"), *devotion*, longs for another, greater object. The speaker then proceeds, by intellectual analysis, to develop (lines 11–32) this paradox of human perversity, by playing upon the idea that the speaker, in going West on human "pleasure or businesse," is turning his back upon the Cross. He is thus refusing to perform the devotion proper to the day; he is refusing, that is, to *see* the place and participate in its agony as if he were "really present":

> There I should see a Sunne, by rising set,
> And by that setting endlesse day beget;
> But that Christ on this Crosse, did rise and fall,
> Sinne had eternally benighted all.
> Yet dare I'almost be glad, I do not see
> That spectacle of too much weight for mee.
> Who sees Gods face, that is selfe life, must dye;
> What a death were it then to see God dye?

2. *The Poems of John Donne*, ed. Herbert J. C. Grierson (2 vols., Oxford, Clarendon Press, 1912), *1*, 322.
3. *Idem*, *1*, 336.

Nevertheless, in the very act of saying that he does not see these things, he develops the traditional paradoxes of the scene in lines that echo the meditative treatises:

> Could I behold those hands which span the Poles,
> And turne all spheares at once, peirc'd with those holes?
> Could I behold that endlesse height which is
> Zenith to us, and our Antipodes,
> Humbled below us? or that blood which is
> The seat of all our Soules, if not of his,
> Made durt of dust, or that flesh which was worne
> By God, for his apparell, rag'd, and torne?[4]

And next, as we should expect of one reared in the Catholic meditative tradition, he considers the sorrows of the Virgin:

> If on these things I durst not looke, durst I
> Upon his miserable mother cast mine eye,
> Who was Gods partner here, and furnish'd thus
> Halfe of that Sacrifice, which ransom'd us?

And now, with the analysis completed, the speaker ends his meditation, with perfect symmetry, in a ten-line colloquy which accords with the directions of St. Ignatius Loyola:

> Imagining Christ our Lord before us and placed on the Cross, to make a colloquy with Him . . . Again, to look at myself, asking what I have done for Christ, what I am doing for Christ, what I ought to do for Christ; and then seeing Him that which He is, and thus fixed to the Cross, to give expression to what shall present itself to my mind. (p. 23)

> Though these things, as I ride, be from mine eye,
> They'are present yet unto my memory,
> For that looks towards them; and thou look'st towards mee,
> O Saviour, as thou hang'st upon the tree;
> I turne my backe to thee, but to receive
> Corrections, till thy mercies bid thee leave.
> O thinke mee worth thine anger, punish mee,
> Burne off my rusts, and my deformity,
> Restore thine Image, so much, by thy grace,
> That thou may'st know mee, and I'll turne my face.

---

4. Cf. Luis de Granada, pp. 288–9: "Lift up thyne eies unto that holie roode, and consider all the woundes, and paines, that the Lorde of maiestie suffereth there for thy sake . . . Beholde that divine face (which the Angels are desirous to beholde) how disfigured it is, and overflowed with streames of bloude . . . .
"That goodly cleare forhead, and those eies more bewtifull than the Sunne, are now dimmed and darkened with the bloude and presence of deathe. Those eares that are wonte to heare the songes of heaven, doe now heare the horrible blasphemies of synners. Those armes so well fashioned and so large that they embrace all the power of the worlde, are now disjoynted, and stretched out upon the crosse. Those handes that created the heavens, and were never injurious to anie man, are now nayled and clenched fast with harde and sharpe nayles."

Thus similitude, visualization, theological analysis and the eloquent motions of the will have all fused into one perfectly executed design —a meditation expressing the state of devotion which results from the integration of the threefold Image of God: memory, understanding, will. And thus once again the process of meditation appears to have made possible a poem which displays this "articulated structure," this "peculiar blend of passion and thought":[5] the perfect equipoise of carefully regulated, arduously cultivated skill.

STANLEY ARCHER

Meditation and the Structure of Donne's "Holy Sonnets" †

In recent years two important works dealing with Donne's "Holy Sonnets" have appeared. I am referring of course to Miss Gardner's edition of *The Divine Poems* and to *The Poetry of Meditation* by Professor Louis L. Martz. Mr. Martz moves far beyond the scope of Miss Gardner's critical work, tracing the meditative tradition in poetry throughout the seventeenth century. The chief accomplishments of Miss Gardner's work are a regrouping of the poems and a thorough annotation. It is interesting to note that both Miss Gardner and Professor Martz reached independently several conclusions in regard to the structure of the "Holy Sonnets":

1. Their structure was influenced by meditative literature or by the meditative tradition as it was expressed during the Counter Reformation, probably from the *Spiritual Exercises* of St. Ignatius Loyola.

2. Donne more than likely received such influence during his childhood from his family environment.

3. Such structure cannot be accounted for in the poetic tradition, but it is a result of a fusion of both the poetic and meditative traditions.

The evidence provided by these two important scholars of Donne in support of these conclusions is indeed impressive. And indeed one would ordinarily accept it without critical examination, thinking it naïve of him to imagine any longer that in the "Holy Sonnets" Donne is attempting to write poetry by anything other than the "predeter-

5. *Works of Herbert*, ed. Palmer, *1*, 140; *Metaphysical Lyrics and Poems*, ed. Herbert J. C. Grierson (Oxford, Clarendon Press, 1921), p. xvi.
† From *English Literary History*, XXVIII (June, 1961), 137-47. Reprinted by permission of the publishers, The Johns Hopkins Press, and Stanley Archer.

mined plan" of the spiritual exercises.[1] However, in this instance, there is an interesting discrepancy in the way each writer demonstrates his hypothesis.

Professor Martz tells the reader that one need not expect to find an entire meditation according to the threefold Ignatian plan in many of the "Holy Sonnets," the reason for this being that the sonnets are short whereas the exercise covered a long period of time. Such poems correspond to merely a fragment of the meditation, usually the colloquy, or conclusion.[2] But as his chief internal evidence for relating the sonnets to the *Spiritual Exercises* he examines four sonnets which capture an entire exercise—Sonnets 11, 7, 9, and 5.[3] These and Sonnet 12 he separates into three parts to show their threefold structure corresponding to the three parts of the meditation.

Now let us examine what Miss Gardner says about these particular sonnets. Of Sonnet seven she writes:

> in the fourth [i.e., according to her grouping] the *composito loci* is a picture of the Last Judgment; . . . this is followed by the petition to the Lord to delay the summons and teach a present repentance.[4]

It is clear that she does not stress the threefold structure emphasized by Professor Martz, but rather sees the meditation as twofold. But she does agree that this is a meditative sonnet. Of Sonnet nine she writes:

> The fifth sonnet, on the other hand, has no *composito loci*—its octave is more like a 'point' drawn out from a meditation on hell.[5]

She adds that in this sonnet Donne has taken great liberty with the material of meditation. But of Sonnets eleven and twelve she writes:

> The last six sonnets of the twelve printed in 1633 depend less on the preludes of the Ignatian meditation than on the colloquy. They serve the purpose of the second set of meditations of St. Peter of Alcantra and others, in that they fix the mind on the saving love of God in Christ; but they handle the subject with the discursive freedom of the colloquy.

> In these last sonnets, the influence of the meditation is felt, not in the structure of the sonnets, but in such things as the vivid sense of the actualities of the Passion in "Spit in my face." . . .[6]

It will be remembered that Professor Martz demonstrates the threefold structure of the meditation in two of these very sonnets. The last sonnet used by Professor Martz Miss Gardner styles a "general meditation, with a very short *compositio loci*."[7]

1. See Louis L. Martz, *The Poetry of Meditation* (New Haven, 1955), p. 43.
2. *Ibid.*, p. 46.
3. Since Professor Martz uses Sir Herbert Grierson's grouping, and since I shall deal in more detail with his discussion, I have retained his numbering rather than Miss Gardner's.
4. Helen Gardner, ed., *John Donne: The Divine Poems* (Oxford, 1952), p. lii.
5. *Ibid.*
6. *Ibid.*, p. liii.
7. *Ibid.*

Thus we note that two scholars, in applying the same hypothesis, have arrived at dissimilar conclusions. The difference seems to lie in the concept of the meditative process as held by each. From this one gathers that varied conclusions may be reached, according to which meditative writer influences the critic. When ideas about a work of art bear such diverse results, there is some warrant for a re-examination of the evidence which led to the idea.

Since Professor Martz examines the question at greater length than does Miss Gardner, it is necessary to examine his discussion in some detail. He conjectures that Donne was influenced by the structure of the meditation and notes, "The 'Holy Sonnets' seem to bear out this conjecture."[8] Before the examination is complete this statement takes on enormous proportions:

> They [the "Holy Sonnets"] are, in the most specific sense of the term, meditations. Ignatian meditations: providing strong evidence for the profound impact of early Jesuit training upon the later career of John Donne.[9]

The reader is not unprepared for such a conclusion. Professor Martz has reminded us, as did Miss Gardner, of Donne's Jesuit uncles, his Catholic upbringing, and his own statement about the influence of his early training. Meditative literature was popular during Donne's day, and there can be little doubt that in his delving into theology Donne read a good deal of it. It will be necessary to return to this evidence later on. Now I shall consider another matter concerning Professor Martz's argument.

From his analogy between Donne and Joyce,[1] Mr. Martz apparently does not believe that Donne was consciously copying the structure of a meditation in many of the sonnets, since only a few of the sonnets follow this structure. In others there is matter unsuitable for formal meditation,[2] as in the second quatrain of "If Poysonious Mineralls" in which Donne with the intellect imagines that God's decrees are unjust. But Mr. Martz points out that the threefold structure of certain ones of the sonnets is analogous to that of the Ignatian meditation, as found in the *Meditation upon the Mysteries of our Holie Faith, with the Practise of Mental Prayer touching the same* by the Spanish Jesuit, Luis de la Puente, which appeared in 1605 (English translation, 1619). Furthermore, according to St. François de Sales, the beginning of a meditation should be a dramatic one, wherein one imagines himself in intimacy with the matter of meditation, and such dramatic beginnings are common in the "Holy Sonnets": "Oh my blacke Soule!," "Spit in my face, you Jewes," "At the round earth's

8. Martz, p. 43.
9. *Ibid.*, p. 53.
1. *Ibid.*, p. 146.
2. Professor Martz criticizes Donne for his departure in this. Of Sonnet 13 he writes (p. 84): "Unfortunately, the sestet of this sonnet is unworthy of this opening: the reference to 'all my profane mistresses' is in the worst of taste: there is almost a tone of bragging here."

imagin'd corners."[3] One wonders why it is necessary to attribute the dramatic openings of these specific poems to the meditative tradition, for they abound in the earlier poems of Donne as well.

From the opening, corresponding to the memory, "the meditation" develops by means of the other two "powers of the soul," reason or understanding and will, as described by Puente.[4] One gets a subject, a mystery of faith, or other such appropriate subject. This the memory sets forth imaginatively; the reason or understanding studies the implications; and the will draws forth religious affection, or is turned to praise of God. In short, the will poses some application or conclusion for the matter.

It will be seen that the structure of Sonnet seven, analyzed in the manner of Mr. Martz, corresponds to the structure of the meditation.

> At the round earths imagin'd corners, blow
> Your trumpets, Angells, and arise, arise
> From death, you numberlesse infinities
> Of soules, and to your scattred bodies goe,
>
> All whom the flood did, and fire shall o'erthrow,
> All whom warre, dearth, age, agues, tyrannies,
> Despaire, law, chance, hath slaine, and you whose eyes,
> Shall behold God, and never tast deaths woe.
>
> But let them sleepe, Lord, and mee mourne a space,
> For, if above all these, my sinnes abound,
> 'Tis late to aske abundance of thy grace,
> When wee are there; here on this lowly ground,
> Teach mee how to repent; for that's as good
> As if thou hadst seal'd my pardon, with thy blood.

The first section sets forth dramatically the matter of meditation, the day of judgment, though in this sonnet, as in others, the imagination rather than the memory presents the subject. The subject is also set forth in the form of a petition. In the second, the understanding reasons about death. Actually, this quatrain seems more an afterglow of the imagination in the first, though in other sonnets the break between memory and reason is more pronounced. And in the sestet there is a prayer or petition to God dealing with the implications drawn from the preceding meditation. Professor Martz shows this basic structure in four other sonnets.

But is there perhaps another source or other sources for such structure other than the meditative literature of the Counter Reformation? Must one conclude with Professor Martz that it demonstrates a fusion of the poetic and meditative traditions?

In reading Donne's *Songs and Sonnets* one is struck by the number

3. *Ibid.*, p. 51.
4. *Ibid.*, pp. 34–35.

of poems written in three stanzas. There are eighteen to be exact. Let us examine one of them. "A Valediction: Of Weeping" will do:

> Let me powre forth
> My teares before thy face, whil'st I stay here,
> For thy face coines them, and thy stampe they beare,
> And by this Mintage they are something worth,
> For thus they bee
> Pregnant of thee;
> Fruits of much griefe they are, emblemes of more,
> When a teare falls, that thou falls which it bore,
> So thou and I are nothing then, when on a divers shore.
>
> On a round ball
> A workeman that hath copies by, can lay
> An Europe, Afrique, and an Asia,
> And quickly make that, which was nothing, *All*:
> So doth each teare,
> Which thee doth weare,
> A globe, yea world by that impression grow,
> Till thy teares mixt with mine doe overflow
> This world, by waters sent from thee, my heaven dissolved so.
>
> O more than Moone,
> Draw not up seas to drowne me in thy spheare,
> Weepe me not dead, in thine armes, but forbeare
> To teache the sea, what it may doe too soone;
> Let not the winde
> Example finde,
> To doe me more harme, than it purposeth;
> Since thou and I sigh one anothers breath,
> Who e'r sighes most, is cruellest, and hastes the others death.

In the first stanza, the situation is dramatically set forth, reconstructed, of course, from the memory. The scene is the parting of the two lovers, and the poet is particularly concerned with the tears they are shedding at parting. The reader gets a picture of these tears in the first stanza. In the second stanza the reasoning is about the significance of these tears. The reasoning in this stanza is hyperbolic, much the same as that of Sonnet 5.[5] In the last stanza the will presents a petition, to the love of the poet rather than to God, but none the less a petition.

The "Sunne Rising" is another example of a similar structure. In the first stanza, the subject of the poem, love, is dramatically set forth by means of a petition to the sun. In the second stanza the poet reasons about the nature, and, particularly, the power of this love. The last stanza represents "affections" drawn from the subject. In the conclusion of the poem the poet affirms the value of love.

5. *Ibid.,* p. 53.

Such is the structure of others of the *Songs and Sonnets*, indicating that the structure of the "Holy Sonnets" derives from Donne the poet rather than Donne the religious. It is highly doubtful that Donne was influenced in these early and profane poems by the meditative literature of the day, though he was reading a great deal of the Fathers and of polemic literature.

Yet one may object to the above conclusions on the grounds that the *Songs and Sonnets* conceivably may have been written later than or contemporary with the "Holy Sonnets" and therefore cannot have influenced their structure. Although it seems unlikely that the same environment could have given rise to the two groups, it is necessary to deal with the argument. Fortunately, certain of Donne's poems can be dated with some exactness, particularly the satires, the earlier of which were written in the years 1593–1594.[6] Let us then examine "Satyre I" to see whether it has the same threefold structure and the dramatic portrayal of the subject.

The beginning presents the dramatic conflict. The poet is being enticed from his study, and he blurts out:

> Away thou fondling motley humorist,
> Leave me, and in this standing wooden chest,
> Consorted with these few bookes, let me lye
> In prison, and here be confin'd, when I dye.

The situation and subject matter for the poems are here set forth by the imagination.

> Here are Gods conduits, grave Divines; and here
> Natures Secretary, the Philosopher;
> And jolly Statesmen, which teach how to tie
> The sinewes of a cities mistique bodie;
> Here gathering Chroniclers, and by them stand
> Giddie fantastique Poëts of each land.

In these lines the reason explores the benefits of the library, just as the poet explores death and its causes in the second quatrain of "At the round earths imagin'd corners." The conclusion which follows affects the will:

> Shall I leave all this constant company,
> And follow headlong, wild uncertaine thee?

At the next line another threefold structure begins, and they are repeated in the poem. The one beginning at line forty-two is interesting. In the preceding group the poet has reproached the humorist for his lack of virtue and his rich attire.

6. Sir Edmund Gosse, *Life and Letters of John Donne* (New York, 1899), Vol. I, pp. 36–40.

At birth, and death, our bodies naked are;
And till our Soules be unapparrelled
Of bodies, they from bliss are banished.

The subject as set forth is the state of man's soul. The reason then examines the cause:

Mans first blest state was naked, when by sinne
Hee lost that, yet hee was cloath'd but in beasts skin,
And in this course attire, which I now weare,
With God, and with the Muses I conferre.

The poet's instruction, by the time of the last division, has taken effect. The humorist repents, and the poet's will is swayed:

But since thou like a contrite penitent,
Charitably warn'd of thy sinnes, dost repent
These vanities, and giddinesse, loe
I shut my chamber doore, and come, lets goe.

This threefold structure may be found in many others of the poems—the *Songs and Sonnets*, and *Elegies*, the *Satyres*.

The picture is now clear in regard to the structure of the "Holy Sonnets." Similar structure is found in Donne's poetry from the first poems to the last. Therefore, the explanation that the structure of the "Holy Sonnets" was patterned upon the formal exercises of "meditation" found in the literature of their day is not the better explanation. They are poems which in their structure fit neatly into the entire pattern of Donne's poetry. As he grew older, his environment and interests changed, but his poems kept their same fundamental structure and dramatic tone.

There is however one major objection to this argument. Perhaps Donne was introduced to meditation in his childhood. Such training might have served as an unconscious influence upon his poetic style throughout his life and culminated in the "Holy Sonnets." It is a considerable argument, not easily refuted. Let us examine the facts, such as they are. Gosse expresses them this way:

An exciting event in the family must have been the appearance of the boy's uncle, Father Jasper Heywood, on a mission to England from Rome. He arrived in the summer of 1581, when Donne was eight years old, in company with Father William Holt. The severity with which the Heywoods had been used had always been somewhat relaxed in the case of Jasper, who was understood not to belong to the extreme party. He was allowed to leave Dillingen, and become Superior of the English Jesuits in succession to Parsons. He must have been a quaint, fantastic person. He appeared to have no sense of the delicacy of his position in England. He assumed the perilous airs of a Papal Legate, and was positively accused of a parade of wealth and pomp in his private life in London. He had lax views of discipline, and quarrelled with the austerer section of his co-religionists to such an extent that he was recalled by Rome in 1583, after having outraged the commonest prudence by summoning a Council under the style of Provincial of the Jesuits in England.[7]

Gosse goes on to say that Father Heywood was permanently exiled in January 1585, at which time Donne had been in Hart Hall, Oxford, for three months. This picture of Father Heywood is not that of a man who would suffer the little children. He might be expected to insist with some severity that they know their catechism.[8] But to suppose that he spent time teaching them the meditations designed especially for the Society of Jesus is to hazard an unlikely guess. Further, to suppose that such meditation, had it been taught, could have had such a lasting influence that it shaped the poet's later thought to a great extent is difficult indeed.

A fascinating account of Jesuit activity in England during this period is the autobiography of the Jesuit Father John Gerard. Father Gerard was sent to England by the Society of Jesus to minister to the Catholics there and to recruit young Englishmen for the order. In reading through this book one is struck by the number of times the author refers to the *Spiritual Exercises*. As far as he himself is concerned, it seems that his practice of these meditations was not consistent in degree. For when he is in prison, they become much more important in his life than when he is out.[9] But there are many to whom he teaches these exercises. He teaches them to mature prospective seminarians, and older, staunch Catholics who wish to progress toward spiritual perfection. These people are well-educated and usually of high birth. An example is Robert Lee:

> He was a gentleman of good family and a very fine character and his charming manners made him a favorite with everyone. . . . Everything he did, he did well, and he was a Catholic too; in fact he was such a good man that he was thinking of withdrawing from the world to follow Christ more closely. When I was in the Clink, he came to visit me frequently, and it was easy to see that he was called to higher things than catching birds. . . . I had, therefore, fixed a date to give this good friend of mine a retreat, for I wanted him to discover by means of the Exercises the straight road that leads to life. . . .[1]

The conditions which Father Gerard lists preceding his decision to instruct Lee in the *Exercises* indicate that he used some degree of

7. *Ibid.*, p. 13.
8. "*En tête de son programme pédogogique il (le jésuite) plaça la religion, et dans ce programme la première étude fut celle du catéchisme.*" Rochemontieux, *Un Collège au XVIIe et XVIIIe Siècles* (1889), quoted in M. P. Ramsay, *Les Doctrines Médiévales Chez Donne* (Paris, 1924), pp. 35–36.
9. John Gerard, *The Autobiography of a Hunted Priest*, trans. by Philip Caraman (New York, 1952), pp. 72, 116.
1. *Ibid.*, p. 151.

reticence in teaching them. Such instruction required time which could be devoted to more practical teaching; moreover, it was not necessary for salvation.

While he instructed many in the *Spiritual Exercises*, he gave instruction of a different nature to others. It is clear that he distinguishes between these exercises and the art of meditation by this quotation concerning Lee's friend, Hart, who was to become a Jesuit:

> ... in place of the Exercises, I taught him the method of daily meditation.[2]

This art of meditation Father Gerard taught to many—among them women. Yet he never mentions having taught a woman the *Spiritual Exercises*. The method of meditation itself was not taught to all his acquaintances. It too was for people with more than a practical interest in religion. He mentions teaching it to Lady Vaux:

> Then I taught her how to meditate, for she was capable of it—in fact she had intelligence and talents of a high order.[3]

Again, the reader is assured that this is not instruction for everyone.

Among the thirty or more candidates for the priesthood whom Father Gerard sends to the Continent some are "boys." We do not know how old they were, but they must have been old enough to travel alone for a great distance. Now while many of the candidates had received instruction from the *Spiritual Exercises*, apparently these "boys" did not. Father Gerard mentions giving them letters and instruction, but nowhere does he mention having taught them the *Spiritual Exercises* or the meditations. Nor is there any record in the entire book of his having taught either of these to a boy or a girl. Thus it seems apparent that Father Gerard's attitude toward these disciplines was that they were for people who had reached a spiritual plateau and were ready to advance to one much higher.

It cannot of course be proved that Donne did not receive such instructions in meditation at the age of eleven, or before. However, in view of Father Gerard's attitude toward instruction in them, it seems highly improbable that he did.

If the meditative influence is discounted in the structure of the "Holy Sonnets," one is faced with the problem of determining another source for their structure. Long ago Gosse suggested that Donne in his satires imitated Persius, and certainly the dramatic tone in the first lines of some of the Persius poems is similar to that of Donne, indicating a possible influence of the Latin poet. I have shown that the threefold structure of the sonnets is found in the earlier poems of

2. *Ibid.*, p. 173.
3. *Ibid.*, p. 147.

Donne as well. The ultimate source of the threefold structure in the work of Donne is not easily determined. I believe that it is highly probable that this structure can be traced in poems of Donne's time and in forms other than the Petrarchan structure of the sonnet. This threefold structure recalls the strophe, antistrophe, and epode of the Greek chorus, a form almost as old as poetry itself. But such a study would extend far beyond the scope of this paper. Even if it is not made, it would not be too surprising to find that Donne, who is novel in his use of imagery and diction, makes some contribution to structure as well. Such a conclusion would be more reasonable than trying to account for the structure of the "Holy Sonnets" through the impressions received by a child of eleven or younger. The evidence presented here has shown that this structure, continuing throughout the poems of Donne, should not surprise when it appears in the "Holy Sonnets." One need not explore the mass of "meditative" literature to explain its presence there.

READINGS OF *HOLY SONNET XIV*: A CRITICAL DISCUSSION

J. C. LEVENSON: [The First Quatrain] †

Dramatic immediacy often short-circuits one's literary perception. The first quatrain of Donne's *Holy Sonnet*, xiv exemplifies this for me, since the words reverberated in my mind for a number of years without creating any discomfort at insufficient comprehension. Donne's strong, intimate tone, "agonized and clear," and his explosive shifting from one verb to another, as though no single metaphor could be adequate,—these are the most important characteristics of the first four lines. The switching of verbs conveys the intensity of the poet's emotion, but beneath the changes there is the fundamental consistency of a fully realized conceit. The various metaphors coherently suggest a single situation: God is a tinker, Donne a pewter vessel in the hands of God the artisan. A modern version of the Biblical potter-and-clay image holds together the centrifugal fragments of Donne's expostulation. As in the best dramatic poetry, the major esthetic effect can occur long before one's anatomical curiosity asserts itself and can be reinforced by that same analytic process which leaves merely melodramatic lines in shards.

† From J. C. Levenson, "Donne's *Holy Sonnets*, XIV," in *Explicator*, XI (March, 1953), Item 31. Reprinted by permission of *Explicator* and J. C. Levenson.

GEORGE HERMAN: [The Extended Metaphor] †

Mr. J. C. Levenson's interpretation of the first quatrain of Donne's *Holy Sonnets*, xiv (EXP., Mar., 1953, xi, 31) seems to me quite unsatisfactory. It isn't likely that any good poet, much less Donne, limited to fourteen lines, would start by addressing a "three-personed God," shift to "a fully realized conceit" involving God the tinker and Donne the pewter vessel, and then get on to the usurped and besieged town. Donne's extended metaphor seems to me reasonably clear and consistent *throughout* the poem, and it has nothing to do with a tinker or a pewter vessel—though I cannot say that I fully realize it. God the Father as yet but knocks at the gate (or the heart). God the Holy Ghost as yet but breathes upon the heart, which is also the town and a woman; it *may* be that Donne is playing with "breathe" and the phrase "breathe upon," meaning "to taint, corrupt," for which the *NED* gives the following subsidiary quotation: "1591 Shaks. *Two Gent*. v, iv, 131. Take but possession of her, with a Touch: I dare thee, but to breath vpon my Loue." God the Son (Sun) as yet but shines upon the heart-town-woman. The three-fold, three-personed effort as yet but seeks to mend the defect. But a greater violence is required: God the Father needs to break instead of merely knock. God the Holy Ghost needs to blow instead of merely breathe; it *may* be that Donne is playing with "blow" and the phrase "blow upon," meaning to "bring into discredit, defame," for which the *NED* gives the following quotation: "1470–85 (ed. 1634) Malory, *Arthur* (1816) 11.438. Then Sir Gawaine made many men to blow upon Sir Launcelot, and all at once they called him "False recreant Knight!" God the Son (Sun) needs to burn rather than merely to shine upon. This greater three-fold, three-personed effort would seek to remake her entirely. Clearly, "make" had the appropriate popular meaning in Donne's day that it has today, and it seems to me likely that Donne here consciously employed the pun. (Cf. *Merry Wives of Windsor*, iii, iii, 43–47. Also, the phrase "to meddle or make" of MWW,i,iv, 115; *Troilus and Cressida*, i,i,14, also 87; *Much Ado About Nothing*, iii, iii, 55. NED gives an obsolete meaning of "meddle" as "To have sexual intercourse (*with*). Also refl [exive]." Cf. *Coriolanus*, iv,v,50.) Eric Partridge calls "make my play," of *Henry VIII*, i, iv, 46–50, "an erotic pun" (*Shakespeare's Bawdy*; cf. entries *thing* and *make one's play*). The besieged and occupied woman-town, despite her better Reason, has acquiesced to her possession by God's enemy and is betrothed to him. She asks God to break that bond ("Divorce me, etc."),

† From George Herman, "Donne's *Holy Sonnets*, XIV," in *Explicator*, XII (December, 1953), Item 18. Reprinted by permission of *Explicator* and George Herman.

to take her, to ravish her, and thereby, paradoxically, to make her chaste.

Incidentally, wouldn't it be rather futile to attempt to shine pewter?

J. C. LEVENSON: [Three Conceits]†

The interpretation of figurative language, when we are prepared to find a great variety of practice, can help us towards an understanding of poetry. Mr. George Herman's comment on Donne's *Holy Sonnets*, XIV (EXP., Dec., 1953, XII, 18) seems to me to err in stating *a priori* that no good poet, "much less Donne," would develop a conceit of metal-working in his first quatrain, a military conceit in his second quatrain, and a sexual conceit in his sestet, given the contracted space of fourteen lines in which to work. This is, of course, precisely what Donne did, apparently satisfied that the unified theme, the common denominator of violence, and the specific verbal linkages established a sufficient connection among his three conceits. The word "o'erthrow" in line 3 makes it seem to have been less of a jump when we have shifted from the artisan's workshop to the beleaguered town; the words "weak and untrue" in line 8 offer an easy transition from thoughts of siege to thoughts of sex; and the word "enemy" in line 10 reaches back in association, even though the enemy is now singular rather than collective.

The complexity of Donne's poetic practice is different from that of Mr. Herman's interpretation, and considerably less difficult. The monistic assumption that the three systems of imagery in this sonnet are congruent provides a specious simplification. It is not only not simple, but just about impossible to conceive as an entity one literal and two metaphorical images as disparate as "the heart, which is also a town and a woman." The trouble with this hypothesis is (1) it makes us go through the cycle of changed reference several times instead of only once, (2) it opens a field for scatological interpretation of which Mr. Herman has barely ploughed a corner, and (3) it leads, as Mr. Herman sees, to a notion of God as "corrupting" man, an idea which it is unlikely any good poet, much less Donne, would seriously entertain. On the other hand, Donne's habit of shifting metaphors, common enough in his secular poetry, extends to the *Holy Sonnets*, as in IV, "Oh my black Soule!" where the soul is successively pilgrim, prisoner, and penitent, and even changes color from black to red; IX, "If poysonous minerals," where the mineral, vegetable, and animal kingdoms are traversed in just three lines; or X, "Death be not proud," in which death is treated as "mighty and dreadfull," as pleasant anodyne,

† From J. C. Levenson, "Donne's *Holy Sonnets*, XIV," in *Explicator* XII (April, 1954), Item 36. Reprinted by permission of *Explicator* and J. C. Levenson.

and, in the sestet alone, as slave, criminal, and soporific. As Johnson remarked, "who would imagine it possible that in a very few lines so many remote ideas could be brought together?"

My initial comment on *Sonnet* XIV (EXP., Mar., 1953, XI, 31) dealt with the stylistic obstacles to seeing any conceit at all in the first quatrain, and overcome by the discovery of a single implied metaphor, I rushed into oversimplifications of my own which should be corrected. The argument that Donne's neologism for the potter-and-clay metaphor makes God here a worker in metals seems to me to hold. But even though pewter *can* be shined, there is obviously no authority in the text for saying that Donne the vessel in God's hands is specifically of one metal rather than another. My calling God a "tinker" with reference to this metal vessel was a decidedly poor use of words, since the argument of the first four lines is that God should cease to tinker ("seek to mend") the damaged object, but demolish it, melt it down, and make it new. This conceit fits with Mr. Herman's observation that lines 2 and 4 show a threefold effort that follows from the apostrophe to "three-personed God." (The triple series recurs in line 11 and again in lines 12–14.) In each case the three particular verbs are summed up in the abstract unity of the final phrase, and although Mr. Herman's argument that the verbs in triple series refer to Father, Holy Ghost, and Son (in that order!) rests on untenable theological premises and uses tenuous lexicographical methods, his basic observation stands if we see the one-in-threeness as determined here by the vehicle of the metal-working metaphor. The most marked relation which this conceit bears to the next is one of contrast; the novel image drawn from common life is followed in the second quatrain by a conventional, heroic image. Donne brought together in his poetry not only remote ideas, but both "plain" and "elevating" figures.

GEORGE KNOX: [Contemplation of the Trinity] †

I disagree with two recent readings of this sonnet (*Exp.*, Mar., 1953, XI, 31; *Exp.*, Dec., 1953, XII, 18) and offer the following interpretation as more complete. Mr. Levenson's and Mr. Herman's explications seem somewhat oblivious of the obvious. It seems very clear to me that the very first line invites contemplation of the Trinity and that this concept determines the structure of the whole sonnet. Mr. Levenson's God-the-tinker idea does not take us beyond the first quatrain, and Mr. Herman's mention of the Trinity is spoiled by his woman-town ratio. We begin with: "three-personed God," for in the tripartite division the Father is power, the Son the bringer of light

† From George Knox, "Donne's *Holy Sonnets*, XIV," in *Explicator* XV (October, 1956), Item 2. Reprinted by permission of *Explicator* and George Knox.

(allowing Mr. Herman his "Sun" pun), and the Holy Ghost the in-fusion of love or Grace. Hence, in the second line, "knock, breathe, shine," reflect these forces as they are contemplated in the poetic in-vocation. Knocking represents first God's courting, and second the power employed to "break" the hardened human heart and the ob-durate walls of the will; the breathing with or through is the inter-change or interflowing of infinite and finite substance, a common image in Christian symbology; and shining is the casting and reflect-ing of the light of divine intelligence. Carried into the violent, imme-diate secular execution, or rather as interpreted on the material plane of consciousness, and employed against the unregenerate ego, these forces must be translated: "break, blow, burn." The paradox develops thus: in order that the poet (his inner self, his heart first) may be regenerated ("That I may rise, and stand,") the "three-personed God" must "seek to mend" man's being. God must "make me anew" (i.e., remake me).

In the second quatrain the forces are embodied in a military action in the image of a besieged town. God's trinitarian powers labor to enter into possession of His rightful grounds but the poet's Reason ("Your viceroy") which should defend him against his unjust captor (sinful living) is weakened and "untrue." The word "untrue" carries us on from "heart" and further anticipates the love-courtship theme so intensely finalized in the third quatrain. The degenerate will and spirit, though weakened, still love and want to be loved by God; but the poet's being ("usurped town"), although "due" to God ("an-other") is "betrothed" to Satanic forces ("Your enemy"). Now, since the poem opened with a wish that God batter the heart, it is right that it should be rounded out structurally by a consummation through love.

The necessity of forceful overpowering and violent reshaping (con-version paradox) means that one dies so that he may live, loses that he may gain. This is made clear in the first quatrain as an invocational demand. The necessity for regeneration through redeemed Reason is indirectly requested in the second. In the third quatrain the sonnet has progressed to the point where a resolution must be achieved in terms equally as violent as those of the first quatrain. The poet's pres-ent imprisonment in sinful living must be replaced by a new imprison-ment in the triune personality of God. The word "enthrall" carries the meaning of being captivated by love, of being enamored in love, and of being subjugated to love: bent and mended in accordance with God's will, which is complete love. Paradoxically, we have here freedom in enthrallment. Although man is bound anew he is in es-sence or in substance free.

The triadic division of the sonnet into quatrains follows the exten-sion of the "knock, breathe, shine," and the "break, blow, burn," alignments. The first quatrain calls on God the Father's omnipotence to batter the heart. The second envisions the admission of God through the medium or agency of Rectified Reason, Reason rectified through love. The third exemplifies the reborn understanding (en-*light*ened through the Son) conceiving the consubstantiality of man and God through imagery of interpenetration. Man is to be imprisoned in God by being totally inspired (breathed in and into) completely (the town image) and opening and receiving God. That is, the fallen one must be ravished before he become spiritually chaste. I would save Mr. Herman the strain of trying to imagine the poet in the role of woman. The sexual ravishment involves no bisexuality on the part of the poet nor does it require our imagining literally the relation between man and God in heterosexual terms. The traditions of Christian mysticism allow such symbolism of ravishment as a kind of "as if."

A. L. CLEMENTS: [The Paradox of Three-in-One] †

Several critics have commented that the three persons of the "three-person'd God" in Donnes *Holy Sonnet XIV*, "Batter my heart," are to operate separately: God the Father is to break instead of merely knocking; God the Holy Ghost is to blow instead of merely breathing; and God the Son (Sun) is to burn instead of merely shining.[1] Certainly *three-person'd God* of the first line occasions such an expectation, and it seems both natural and inevitable that Donne should draw upon the traditional emphasis of the symbolism of the Three Persons—the Father as Power, the Son as Light, and the Holy Ghost as Breath. Correct in so far as it goes, this view of the poem tends, however, to overlook certain rich biblical values and associations of *knocke, breathe, shine*, associations of which Donne would not have been ignorant. (The very order of *knocke, breathe, shine* and of Donne's translation of these to the violent *breake, blowe, burn* suggests the inaccuracy of exclusively assigning each word respectively to the Father, the Holy Ghost, and the Son: to reflect the traditional order of Father, Son, and Holy Ghost, Donne could instead have written "knocke, shine, breathe" and "breake, burn, blowe.") A brief examination of several biblical uses of *knocke, breathe, shine* should indicate, at least for the purposes of the poem, that each of the other

† From A. L. Clements, "Donne's 'Holy Sonnet XIV,'" in *Modern Language Notes*, LXXVI (June, 1961), 484-89. Reprinted by permission of the publishers, The Johns Hopkins Press, and A. L. Clements.

1. Doniphan Louthan, *The Poetry of John Donne* (New York, 1951), p. 124; George Herman, "Donne's Holy Sonnets, XIV," *Explicator*, xii (December 1953), Item 18; George Knox, "Donne's Holy Sonnets, XIV," *Explicator*, xv (October 1956), Item 2.

Persons is "involved" in the activity of any one; in other words, the paradox of three-in-one is truly and profoundly a paradox and is operative as such in the poem.

Traditionally the courting of man by God, the knocking at his heart, is associated with Christ, not the Father. The bridegroom of the Song of Solomon is usually taken to symbolize Christ; the heart of man is the Bridegroom's, the Saviour's Chamber, but the heart is hardened with sin, and the Bridegroom, standing outside, must knock to gain entrance. "I sleep, but my heart waketh: it is the voice of my beloved that knocketh, saying, Open to me ..." (Song of Solomon 5:2). In the New Testament, Revelation 3:20 follows this tradition: "Behold, I stand at the door and knocke: if any man hear my voice, and open the door, I will come in to him, and will sup with him, and he with me."[2] Christ's knocking is, I think, definitely germane to the poem's theme of love and courtship, even though this theme has been characteristically transformed by Donne to a violent love and courtship. With his translation of *knocke* to *breake*, Donne is not only calling on the power of the Father but he is also imploring Christ to court him not in Christ's usual role and manner of mild Lamb but rather as battering, overpowering Ram.[3] Moreover, since Donne is seeking God's courtship and love—"Yet dearely I love you, and would be loved faine"—and since, traditionally, the Holy Ghost infuses love into the hearts of men—"... the love of God is shed abroad in our hearts by the Holy Ghost" (Romans 5:5)—there seems to be no necessity for reading the poem as excluding the Comforter from the activity of courting or knocking.

Breathe is traditionally associated with the Holy Ghost's infusion of grace into the heart of man, yet is also linked, biblically, inevitably, with activities of both the Father and the Son. From Genesis on, the Father is referred to as the giver of life to man by breathing into his nostrils the breath of life.[4] This is at least relevant to the sonnet since Donne is asking for new, innocent life, as was given Adam before the Fall: "make me new." After His resurrection Christ appeared to his disciples, and "he breathed on them, and saith unto them, Receive ye the Holy Ghost" (John 20:22). Grace may be infused into man's heart not by the activity of the Third Person alone but by the activity of the Son as well. The possible objection that New Testament theology took the breath of life to be the Spirit of God, that is, the Holy Spirit or Ghost, and that *breathed* in the verse just quoted is a signal of the Third Person merely emphasizes, in effect, the ultimate identity of the Three Persons and thus their actually united trinitarian actions in the poem; for, as St. John of the Cross says, "the Holy Spirit, Who

2. See also Luke 12:36 and John 14:23.
3. The Lamb-Ram contrast is of course only implicit in this sonnet; but cf. the seventh of the *La Corona* sonnets, lines 9–10: "O strong Ramme, which hast

batter'd heaven for mee,/Mild Lambe, which with thy blood, hast mark'd the path."
4. Genesis 2:7; see also, e.g., Job 33:4, Isaiah 30:33, 42:5, Acts 17:24–25.

is love, is also compared to air in the Divine Scripture, since he is the breath of the Father and the Son." [5]

There can be no disputing about the relation between the Son and *shine*. In "A Hymne to God the Father," Donne writes "Sweare by thy selfe, that at my death thy Sunne Shall shine as it shines now . . ."; the Son-sun pun is familiar enough. And the many biblical references to Christ as the Light or the bringer of light, most notably in John, need no quoting. But, in some ways, the First and Third Persons are also associated with light and shining. The Father is, to begin with, the creator of light, and many verses link light and the word *shine* with God the Father or with just God without distinction made as to person: 2 Corinthians 4:6, for example, reads, "God, who commanded the light to shine out of darkness [this is clearly God the Father] hath shined in our hearts."[6] Especially because the poem refers to "Reason your viceroy in mee," the activity and efficacy of the Third Person, who shines upon and rectifies the weak and unfaithful reason or understanding, may also be designated, though perhaps less obviously than the Father and Son, by the word *shine*. The Holy Ghost, who is truth, descended in "tongues like as of fire" upon the apostles, enabling them to shed the light, the word of God, abroad in many tongues; as Christ promised, "the Comforter, which is the Holy Ghost . . . shall teach you all things . . . will guide you into all truth." [7] When Christ absents himself to go to the Father, the Holy Ghost will bring the truth or light to men, that is, will shine in their hearts. There seems, then, to be no justification in the sonnet, and no need, for ignoring the association of the First and Third Persons with light and *shine*.

May we not grant that Donne is exploiting both the traditional distinctions among the Three Persons (Father-Power, Son-Light, Holy Ghost-Breath) and also the traditional biblical values and associations of *knocke, breathe, shine*? His undoubted familiarity with all these biblical passages would not, I think, have permitted the oversimplifying division of powers along the lines suggested by the critics, a division which tends to rationalize and diminish the paradox of the Trinity. Profound paradox and the consequent greater complexity of the poem are characteristic of Donne, who in this sonnet is asking *three person'd God* to break (not just the Father alone), to blow (not just the Holy Ghost alone), to burn (not just the Son alone) and make him new. It is as if all the triple strength of the Three Persons acting as one, with truly trinitarian force, is required to raise Donne from his deeply sinful life and hence to effect his salvation.

5. *Complete Works*, trans. and ed. E. A. Peers (London, 1953), II, 70; for this quotation I am indebted to R. A. Durr.
6. See also 2 Samuel 22: 29, Numbers 6: 25, Job 41: 32, Psalms 18: 28, 31: 16, 36: 9, 67: 1, 80: 3, 80: 19, 84: 11, 119: 135, James 1: 17.
7. John 14: 26, 16: 13. See also John 14: 16–17, 15: 26, 16: 7–12, Acts 2: 2–11, 19: 2–6, 1 John 5: 6.

A consequence of recognizing the full implications of *knocke*, *breathe*, *shine* is that the sonnet's structure cannot then be viewed as the development of three quatrains each separately assigned to each of the Three Persons.[8] Rather, I believe the organizing principle of the poem is, with Donne's qualification of it, the paradox of death and rebirth, the central paradox of Christianity: "Except a corn of wheat fall into the ground and die, it abideth alone: but if it die, it bringeth forth much fruit. He that loveth his life shall lose it; and he that hateth his life in this world shall keep it unto life eternal" (John 12:24–25). To enter the kingdom of God man must die and be born again. Donne knows he must give up his unregenerate sinful life, but he feels his heart and will are so black and obdurate, his sense of sin so great, that (the thought is almost blasphemous) the "ordinary" means of God's mercy and grace, His knocking, breathing, shining, will not suffice. God must forcefully overpower and overwhelm him, must batter and overthrow him in order that he may rise reborn.[9] To the familiar biblical paradox Donne has added his own peculiar meaning; it is in his characteristic manner that Donne insists on the necessity of God's forceful overpowering.

This paradox of dividing in order to unite, destroying in order to revive, throwing down in order to raise, determines the choice of and finds expression in the poem's figurative language, which is of two kinds: one kind is warlike, military, destructive, dividing; the other is marital, sexual, or uniting. Each kind of figurative language operates *throughout* the sonnet, in the first two quatrains and in the sestet. Looking at words and phrases, we can recognize the military and destructive kind in *Batter, o'erthrow, bend your force, breake, blowe, burn* of the first quatrain; most obviously in the beseiged, usurped town imagery of the second quatrain; and in *enemie, divorce, untie, breake, imprison, enthrall*, and *ravish* of the sestet. The marital, regenerating or uniting kind can be observed in *heart, knocke, breathe, shine, rise, stand, make me new* of the first quatrain; *untrue* in the second quatrain; all of line 9, *betroth'd, divorce, Take mee to you, enthrall, chast, ravish* in the sestet. The first quatrain, as we have seen, using traditional biblical terms and Donne's translation of these into new and violent metaphors, calls on the triune God to destroy the sinful old man and remake, regenerate him.[1] The terms *Batter, o'er-*

8. See esp. Knox: "The triadic division of the sonnet into quatrains follows the extension of the 'knock, breathe, shine,' and the 'break, blow, burn,' alignments. The first quatrain calls on God the Father's omnipotence to batter the heart. The second envisions the admission of God through the medium or agency of Rectified Reason, Reason rectified through love. The third exemplifies the reborn understanding (en*light*ened through the Son) . . ."

9. Cf. line 3 of this sonnet, "That I may rise, and stand, o'erthrow mee . . ." with the last line of "Hymne to God, my

God, in my Sicknesse": "Therefore that he may raise, the Lord throws down."

1. Perhaps also in the first quatrain, on a secondary level, the heart is being compared metaphorically to an alchemical object; note esp. line 4 and cf. "Good-friday, 1613. Riding Westward," lines 40–41: "Burne off my rusts, and my deformity, Restore thine Image . . ." Or Holy Sonnets, XIV," *Explicator*, XI perhaps (see J. C. Levenson, "Donne's [March 1953], Item 31 and XII [April 1954], Item 36) the conceit is that of the heart as a metal object in God's, the metal-worker's hands.

throw, bend your force and *breake, blowe, burn* prepare for and serve as a transition to the besieged, usurped town imagery of the second quatrain, if they do not actually participate in that metaphor. Through the development of military metaphors, the heart is compared to a town wrongfully appropriated and helplessly possessed by God's "enemie." Briefly, in the second quatrain, Donne *implies* what the first quatrain states, that God must act for him, must batter down and overthrow his sinful heart in order to raise it purified since his reason is captive and he cannot help himself.

The word *untrue* (in the sense of "unfaithful" it is a marital kind of metaphor) serves as a transition to the sestet, which develops overtly on the level of violence and rape the theme of love and courtship implicit in lines 1 and 2, particularly in *heart* and *knocke*. The heart is now metaphorically construed as a woman. In lines 9 and 10, Donne says explicitly that his sinful heart still loves and would be loved by God but is willfully bound to satanic powers. *Enemie*, at the end of line 10, is a return to military metaphor and provides the transition to the rough and irresistible love of lines 11 and 12, exceptionally heavy-stressed lines, and of lines 13 and 14, the paradoxical explanatory couplet. Again, Donne implies, so great is his sense of sin and helplessness, that God must forcefully sever his sinful bonds, must release him from the prison of sin to bind and imprison him in the triune God and thereby, paradoxically, free him. He will never be essentially free unless God enthralls him and never chaste, that is pure, innocent, whole, holy, unless God ravishes him.

Throughout the sonnet there has been this paradox of destroying in order to make whole, of throwing down in order to raise, expressed by the two basic kinds of figurative language. Significantly, the words *divorce, enthrall, ravish* in lines 11, 13, 14 partake of both kinds of metaphor: a divorce is a dividing, yet the word is associated with marriage; to enthrall is both to subjugate and to captivate or enamor; ravishing is both sexual and violent. In lines 11 to 14, then, the organizing paradox, having been argued throughout the poem in Donne's characteristic intellectual mode, even though the poem is highly emotional and personal, is enhanced and compounded in force not just by a juxtaposition but now by a fusing or uniting of the two kinds of metaphor; it is as if the metaphors are made to achieve between themselves what Donne wishes to achieve with God.

JOHN E. PARISH: [The Sonnet's Unity] †

Within the last ten years four critics have published articles about No. 14 of Donne's *Holy Sonnets*. In the first (*Explicator*, March

† From John E. Parish, "No. 14 of Donne's *Holy Sonnets*", in *College English*, January, 1963. Reprinted with the permission of the National Council of Teachers of English and John E. Parish.

1953), J. C. Levenson suggested that in the opening quatrain God is compared to a tinker and sinful man to a damaged pewter vessel. Later in the same year (*Explicator*, December 1953) George Herman expressed doubt that the image of a tinker is implied. More likely, he felt, the sonnet is unified by a single extended metaphor which (if it could be realized) would demonstrate the part each Person of the Trinity plays in saving the penitent, since (according to Herman) in the first quatrain God the Father is implored to *breake* rather than merely *knocke*, the Holy Ghost to *blowe* rather than simply *breathe*, and God the Son (Sun) to *burn* rather than gently *shine* on the sinner's heart, "which is also the town and a woman." In the words *make me new* Herman believed that all three Persons are beseeched to act on the heart-town-woman and that, as applied to the woman, *make me* is a plea (like that in the sestet) to be violated. "Clearly, *make* had the appropriate popular meaning in Donne's day that it has today, and it seems to me likely that Donne here consciously employed the pun."

After three years George Knox replied to Herman (*Explicator*, October 1956), whom he wished to spare "the strain of trying to imagine the poet in the role of woman." According to Knox, "the traditions of Christian mysticism allow such symbolism of ravishment as a kind of 'as if.'" (One must infer that in Knox's opinion such symbolism shares nothing with metaphor in its effect on the imagination). Describing the interpretations of both Levenson and Herman as "somewhat oblivious of the obvious," Knox claimed to see the unifying conceit that had eluded Herman: "It seems very clear to me that the very first line invites contemplation of the Trinity and that this concept determines the structure of the whole sonnet. . . . The first quatrain calls on God the Father's omnipotence to batter the heart. The second envisions the admission of God through the medium or agency of Rectified Reason, Reason rectified through love [the Son]. The third exemplifies the reborn understanding (en*light*ened through the Son) conceiving the consubstantiality of man and God through imagery of interpenetration [the Holy Ghost]."

Then in 1961 Arthur L. Clements (*Modern Language Notes*, June 1961)—by citing biblical passages associating each of the verbs *knocke*, *breathe* and *shine* with all three Persons of the Trinity—proved beyond doubt (in my opinion) that "the sonnet's structure cannot then be viewed as the development of three quatrains each separately assigned to each of the Three Persons." Contending that "the organizing principle of the poem . . . is the paradox of death and rebirth, the central paradox of Christianity," Clements pointed out further that to illustrate this paradox of destroying in order to revive or throwing down in order to raise Donne employs throughout the sonnet two kinds of figurative language: "one kind is warlike, military, destructive; the other is marital, sexual, or uniting." The two kinds of metaphor are fused in lines 11–14 and are "made to achieve between themselves what Donne wishes to achieve with God."

Like Clements, I must join those whom Knox considered "oblivious of the obvious," those who cannot perceive three divisions of the sonnet devoted respectively to the Father, the Son, and the Holy Ghost. I believe that the sinner's only reason for addressing God as "three person'd" is that he is imploring him to exert all his power, his triple power, to rescue him from Satan. I hope that my interpretation will show, even more clearly than Clements has shown, how the interlocking of the various metaphors and of the stanzaic divisions gives the sonnet its unity.

In the first quatrain, I believe, the repentant sinner compares his heart to a walled town, one of many over which God is the rightful King. Upon approaching, the King has found this particular town closed to him, a Usurper (Satan) having captured it. Now the King with his army is encamped outside the walls, knocking at the gates and asking to be re-admitted so that he can restore (*mend*) whatever has been demolished in the capture and whatever has deteriorated during the occupation. But, declares the sinner, such gentle overtures will not suffice. The King must burst open the gates with *a battering ram*. (On another level, God *is* the battering ram). Beyond all mending, the town must be completely destroyed, after which a new one will *rise* in its place, built by the King to *stand* forever.

The verbs *batter*, *breake*, and *burn* all suggest storming a citadel; and even *blowe* may be intended to suggest the use of gunpowder to blow up the fortress or blow it into smithereens. One is reminded of the violent scenes described by Aeneas in telling Dido about the fall of Troy and (faintly) of the fact that a new Troy is fated to rise. Even richer and more apt, however, are the allusions to the destruction of Jerusalem by Nebuchadnezzar (God's unwitting agent) and to the many predictions by the Prophets of the New Jerusalem to rise when a chastened people come to deserve it. There are also echoes of "the name of the city of my God, which is new Jerusalem" and of "Behold, I stand at the door and knock: if any man hear my voice and open the door, I will come in to him" (Revelation iii:12, 20).

The sonnet as a whole is unified by a shifting viewpoint which produces the effect of God's boring from the outside into the very center of the human heart. In the first quatrain the perspective is mainly that of the King outside the walls, seeking admission. In the second, the reader is carried inside the usurped town and sees the lamentable state of affairs through the eyes of the populace, rightfully the subjects of the King and of the Princess whom he has appointed as his Viceroy (these subjects being all the forces of man that should be governed by reason, here identified with the soul). In the sestet the point of view is that of the captive Princess herself (Reason, or the Soul), who has entered into a shameful marriage with the Usurper and is held in solitary confinement deep within the citadel.

Still further to invigorate and unify the prayer, Donne personifies the fortified town of the first quatrain as a woman, a woman urging her suitor to take her by force rather than by courtship. (In the Psalms, fallen Jerusalem or Zion is often personified as a mourning woman). This plea of the personified city for violent attack anticipates the similar plea which the dishonored Princess makes in the sestet.[1]

The phrase *usurpt towne* is deliberately ambiguous and transitional, connecting the first and second quatrains. It refers back to the walled town, of course; but simultaneously is designates the wretched people within the town, just as one might have said in 1944 "Paris awaits her deliverers," meaning that the *people* of Paris were hoping soon to be liberated. The complaint of the populace in the second quatrain is that though they acknowledge their duty to the King and labor to admit him, without the guidance of the Princess their efforts are futile. (It is not clear to me how the nonspiritual forces in man, unaided by the reason-soul, can labor at all to admit God). Since the capture of the town, the Usurper has held the Princess incommunicado; and her unhappy people, while aware of her shameful marriage, are unable to pass fair judgment on it, not knowing whether it was forced on her or whether she has voluntarily shifted allegiances to the Usurper and is therefore guilty of treason (*untrue*).

After the prayers of the personified city and of the leaderless people, finally in the sestet the captive Princess is heard from her solitary confinement. In language of almost unendurable anguish, which gives the sonnet much of its tone of passionate sincerity, she beseeches the King to deliver her from shame, declaring paradoxically that she can never be free unless he enthralls her and can never be chaste again unless he ravishes her. Appropriately, since the subject of the sonnet is remorse,[2] Donne is alluding again to the third chapter of Revelation—this time to the nineteenth verse: "As many as I love, I rebuke and *chasten*: be zealous therefore, and repent," and he has in mind two meanings of the verb *chasten*: to castigate and to purify.

Readers like Knox, who find it a strain "to imagine the poet in the role of woman," should remember that with Donne (as with Shake-

1. This begging for violation is less shocking when the woman is a personified city than when she is the soul of the repentant sinner. Few readers will detect this imagery in the first quatrain until *after* discovering it in the sestet; but in a re-reading, awareness of its first employment will mollify the shock of the second.

2. Here I disagree with Helen Gardner, who regards this sonnet (No. 10 in her

arrangement) as one of three "on the love man owes to God and to his neighbour." (*The Divine Poems* [Oxford, 1952], p. xli). Donne's sonnet seems to me to be a sinner's plea that remorse enough be put into his heart to start him on the way to repentance. As such, it would serve admirably as the first of a sequence; but perhaps all the sonnets are what Grierson called them—"separate ejaculations."

speare, Spenser and others) the soul is always feminine. For example, in No. 2 of the *Holy Sonnets*, in the first nine lines the penitent describes himself as (among other things) one of God's sons and then as a temple of God's spirit presently usurped by Satan; but in the last five lines the feminine soul urges God to rescue her from Satan, who has kidnaped and ravished her.

To represent man's body as a temple or a castle and his soul as the priestess or governess was conventional.[3] Alma within her beleaguered castle, in Book Two of *The Faerie Queene*, is the most celebrated example; but since Alma has managed to remain chaste, a passage from *The Rape of Lucrece* more closely resembles Donne's sonnet. Shakespeare attributes to Tarquin, after he has committed the crime, something indistinguishable from Christian remorse. He is "a heavy convertite"; both his body (a temple) and his soul (a princess now as dishonored as Lucrece herself) have been polluted by his lustful will. Shakespeare's choice of words is remarkably like Donne's:

Besides his soules faire temple is defaced,
  To whose weake ruines muster troopes of cares,
  To aske the spotted Princesse how she fares.
Shee sayes her subiects with fowle insurrection,
Haue batterd downe her consecrated wall,
And by their mortall fault brought in subiection
Her immortalitie, and made her thrall,
To liuing death and payne perpetuall.
  Which in her prescience shee controlled still,
  But her foresight could not forestall their will. (719–728)

But if the exhausted metaphor of the castle-body and the princess-soul was anemic by the 1590's, until Donne wrote his *Holy Sonnets* no poet had thought of wedding it to the equally weary and thin-blooded convention of comparing a cold mistress to a castle and her lover to the general of an army besieging it. Miraculously, this marriage of two ancient weaklings produced an abnormally vigorous offspring, a sonnet in which Donne, with his accustomed daring, requires the reader to see God wearing (with a difference) the rue of a Petrarchan lover.

FRANK MANLEY
John Donne: The Anniversaries †

The *Anniversaries* were never very popular. As early as April, 1612, Donne received letters from England criticizing them in the same way

3. During Elizabeth's long reign, English poets must have found new value in the old conceit, since a flesh-and-blood Princess was God's viceroy over them and sole head (under God) of their church.

† From Frank Manley, *John Donne: The Anniversaries*, copyright 1963. Pp. 6-10, 16-20, 40-50. Reprinted by permission of the publishers, The Johns Hopkins Press.

they have been criticized ever since: that they say too much, that the praise is too fulsome, the imagery too extravagant. Ben Jonson summed it up in his classic remark to William Drummond of Hawthornden: "that Dones Anniversarie was profane and full of Blasphemies/that he told Mr Donne, if it had been written of ye Virgin Marie it had been something. . . ." Yet Donne always defended the poems. He replied to the criticism in his letters:

> I hear from England of many censures of my book of Mistress Drury; if any of those censures do but pardon me my descent in printing anything in verse (which if they do they are more charitable than myself . . .), I doubt not but they will soon give over that other part of that indictment, which is that I have said so much; for nobody can imagine that I who never saw her, could have any other purpose in that, than that when I had received so very good testimony of her worthiness, and was gone down to print verses, it became me to say, not what I was sure was just truth, but the best that I could conceive; for that had been a new weakness in me, to have praised anybody in printed verses, that had not been capable of the best praise that I could give.[1]

And he told Jonson, in what is undoubtedly the most acute defense of the poems ever made, "that he described the Idea of a Woman and not as she was." The purpose of this introduction will be in great part to expand the implications of that statement.

Later in the century the *Anniversaries* were imitated a number of times, though none of the imitations implies a very profound criticism of the poems. Almost immediately after they were written, they were used by Webster in his *Duchess of Malfi* (1613), to help build up the context of allusion, the air of mystery and sanctity surrounding his central character.[2] William Drummond of Hawthornden imitated a number of passages of *The First Anniversary*, particularly the new philosophy section, in his prose meditation on death, *The Cypresse Grove* (1623). And some years later, in 1692, John Dryden celebrated the death of the Countess of Abdingdon in a "panegyrical" elegy entitled *Eleonora*, written directly in imitation of Donne's "admirable Anniversaries." Dryden never saw the Countess of Abdingdon and therefore took the *Anniversaries* as the solution to the problem of how to write an elegy about someone of whom he knew nothing. In his hands, however, Donne's "Idea of a Woman" lost all its numen and became reduced to a flat, abstract pattern of virtue. As Dryden explained in the Preface to the poem:

> I have followed his [Donne's] footsteps in the design of his panegyric, which was to raise an emulation in the living, to copy out the example of the dead. And therefore it was that I once intended to

1. Edmund Gosse, *The Life and Letters of John Donne* (London, 1899), I, 305–6.

2. Most of the allusions are pointed out by Charles Crawford, *Collectanea* (Stratford-on-Avon, 1907), I, 50–65.

have called this poem 'The Pattern;' and though, on a second con-
sideration, I changed the title to the name of that illustrious person,
yet the design continues, and Eleonora is still the pattern of charity,
devotion, and humility; of the best wife, the best mother, and the
best of friends.[3]

In the eighteenth century the *Anniversaries* were largely forgotten,
along with the rest of Donne. They were remembered, if at all, primarily through an allusion in *Spectator Paper, No. 41*, which quoted
a few lines and remarked that they referred to one of Donne's mistresses. The error echoed through the century. Fielding, for example,
picked it up in *Tom Jones* (IV, ii), where he has the same lines refer
to Tom's mistress, Sophia. By the nineteenth century even the mistake in the *Spectator Papers* was forgotten.

In the twentieth century, however, the *Anniversaries* shared in the
general rehabilitation of Donne, though they were not read as enthu-
siastically or as carefully as the *Songs and Sonets* or the *Divine Poems*.
The general feeling was that despite a number of passages as brilliant
and complex as Donne ever wrote, the poems as a whole left one curiously unsatisfied and confused. Fifteen years ago, however, Louis L.
Martz discovered that "the full meaning of each [of the *Anniversaries*]
grows out of a deliberately articulated structure" and that the structure is not essentially elegiac, but meditative, based on the strict principles of meditation established by Ignatius Loyola.[4] The discovery
was extremely important. It established the process by which Donne
transforms the death of Elizabeth Drury into an image of his own
heart's loss of wisdom. But Martz failed to do anything with it. He
regarded the poems as only partially successful. In *The Second Anniversary*, according to Martz, the meditative structure is organic; in
The First, it is mechanical. One poem therefore is a success, the other
a qualified failure.

The second major contribution to the study of the *Anniversaries* in
this century was made by Marjorie Nicolson, who discovered that the
poems are not two, but one: the antithetical poles of the same logical
unit:

> The *Anniversaries* are . . . as artfully though not so obviously artic-
> ulated as 'L'Allegro' and 'Il Penseroso.' The first is a lament over
> the body—the body of man and the body of the world—a medita-
> tion upon death and mortality. The second is a vision of the release
> of the soul from its prison. The whole, with antitheses of doubt and
> faith, despair and hope, death and the triumph of immortality, is a
> great symphony in which the harmony is more profound because of
> cacophony.[5]

3. *Works*, ed. Sir Walter Scott, rev.
George Saintsbury (Edinburgh, 1885),
XI, 124.
4. "John Donne in Meditation: *The
Anniversaries*," *ELH*, XIV (1947),
247–73, reprinted in *The Poetry of
Meditation* (New Haven, 1954), pp.
219–48.
5. *The Breaking of the Circle* (Evans-
ton, Ill., 1950), pp. 65–66.

The discovery was vitiated somewhat by Miss Nicolson's fantastic theory of the "Double Shee," but even there she was correct in recognizing some obscure symbolic process at work in the poems.

As a result of the work of Martz and Nicolson the *Anniversaries* have come to be regarded with something like respect, though no one purports to know precisely what they are about. Everyone agrees that they are meditations, that they have something to do with religion, and that they are in some way a bridge between Donne's early and late verse, his love poetry and the *Divine Poems*. But other than that the criticism remains the same as it was in the seventeenth century: that the *Anniversaries* are "profane and full of Blasphemies." And the answer remains the same too, if we could once discover what it means: that they are about "the Idea of a Woman and not as she was."

* * *

But the problem then becomes, what is she a symbol of? And the answer is not easy, any easier than it is with Beatrice. The general area seems clear enough. She has to do with the state of our own souls. As Donne explains in the very first lines of the poem:

> When that rich soule which to her Heauen is gone,
> Whom all they celebrate, who know they haue one,
> (For who is sure he hath a soule, vnlesse
> It see, and Iudge, and follow worthinesse,
> And by Deedes praise it? He who doth not this,
> May lodge an In-mate soule, but tis not his.)   [1–6]

She is not only directly identified as a "rich soule" herself, but she is celebrated only by those who know they have a soul; and *celebrated* in this sense means not only *memorialized* but also *reinacted, reperformed*, as in the celebration of the mass. As Donne explains a little later on (lines 67–78), "the matter and the stuffe" of the new world created in her memory is her virtue, but "the forme our practise is." She has to do with the *possibilitatem boni* Augustine thought was lost in the fall, the innate uprightness of the soul which is restored only by grace.[6] She is the soul's likeness to God, the "intrinsique balme" that preserves it from the putrefaction of spiritual death:

> Physitians say, That man hath in his Constitution, in his Complexion, a natural vertue, which they call *Balsamum suum*, his owne Balsamum, by which, any wound which a man could receive in his body, would cure it selfe, if it could be kept cleane from the anoiances of the aire, and all extrinsique encumbrances. Something that hath some proportion and analogy to this Balsamum of the

6. Cf. Donne, *Sermons*, ed. George R. Potter and Evelyn M. Simpson (Berkeley and Los Angeles, 1953–62), II, 55: "in that wound, as wee were all shot in *Adam*, we bled out *Impassibilitatem*, and we sucked in *Impossibilitatem;* There we lost our *Immortality*, our *Impassibility*, our assurance of Paradise, and then we lost *Possibilitatem boni*, says S. *Augustine:* all possibility of recovering any of this by our selves." Hereafter cited as *Sermons*.

body, there is in the soule of man too. The soule hath *Nardum suam*, her Spikenard . . . , a naturall disposition to Morall goodnesse, as the body hath to health. But therein lyes the souls disadvantage, that whereas the causes that hinder the cure of a bodily wound, are extrinsique offences of the Ayre, and putrefaction from thence, the causes in the wounds of the soule, are intrinsique, so as no other man can apply physick to them; Nay, they are hereditary, and there was no time early inough for our selves to apply any thing by way of prevention, for the wounds were as soone as we were, and sooner.[7]

But all that remains metaphoric and vague. There is no clear, explicit identification of the symbolism in the poem, and for that reason it has run off in the minds of critics to Jesus Christ or the Catholic Church, Queen Elizabeth, the Virgin Mary, the Logos, Astraea. There is nothing to bring it into sharp focus, and we are left with a feeling of incompleteness.

I am not certain that any sharp focus is possible. The symbol is too complex for all its parts to be held in the mind at once discursively. Moreover, it is the nature of symbols to suggest more than they seem to contain. They resist all efforts at precise, intellectual definition. But in present-day terms perhaps a vague idea of what Donne was getting at is available in C. G. Jung's concept of the *anima*, which is in itself vague, but which in general represents the "Idea of a Woman" in man, the image of his own soul, his own deepest reality. It is a universal symbol of otherness in man, either of desire, the completion of one's own androgynous self, as in the Platonic myth, or of strange intuitive knowledge otherwise unavailable to him, " a source of information about things for which a man has no eyes."[8] In Donne's own time, however, the clearest formulation was in terms of the traditional concept of Wisdom, which, like the *anima*, was almost always symbolized by woman, who represented the subconscious, intuitive, feminine intelligence of the heart as opposed to the active, conscious, masculine intelligence of the mind. "What is Wisdome?" Donne asks, modifying the ancient Stoic definition:

we may content our selves, with that old definition of Wisdome, that it is *Rerum humanarum, & divinarum scientia;* The Wisdome that accomplishes this cleannesse, is the knowledge, the right valuation of this world, and of the next; To be able to compare the joyes of heaven, and the pleasures of this world, and the gaine of the one, with the losse of the other, this is the way to this cleanenesse of the heart; because that heart that considers, and examines, what it takes in, will take in no foule, no infectious thing [*Sermons*, VII, 336].

7. *Sermons*, V, 347–49.
8. *The Collected Works of C. G. Jung,* ed. H. Read, M. Fordham, and G. Adler (New York, 1953), VII, 186.

It is that Wisdom that the total experience of the *Anniversaries* presents. Donne says in effect:

> Looke then upon the greatnes of God and the smalnesse of man; the goodnes of God, and the vilenesse of man; the wisdome of God, and the folly of man; the love of God, and the hate of man; the grace of God, and the disgrace of man; the mercy of God, and tyranny of man; and the glory of God, and the infamy of man: and fixing the eye of the heart upon the one and the other, how canst thou but to the glory of God, and shame of thy selfe . . . cry with the Prophet David, *Oh Lord what is man that thou doest visit him?*[9]

It forms the essential structure of each poem—the alternation of contempt for the world (meditation) and praise of virtue (eulogy)—as well as the total structure of both poems taken together as a unit. In the first Donne realizes imagistically, through the death of a girl he never saw, the grace and the indwelling wisdom of God, *sapientia creata*, that was lost in the fall; and the entire movement is downward to decay. In the second, however, he has found his direction; through the realization of his soul's loss he has regained the wisdom that orients him toward God, and the entire poem surges upward toward eternal life. It is as a concrete image of that Wisdom, its direct emotional apprehension, that the mysterious figure of woman at the center of the poem is best understood. She is in herself both the object and the wit: the realization as well as the means to realize it, for the only way to understand the *Anniversaries* is intuitively, through symbolic understanding. The poems make sense only to those who realize, with Donne, that

> no thing
> Is worth our trauaile, griefe, or perishing,
> But those rich ioyes, which did possesse her hart,
> Of which shee's now partaker, and a part.
> [*The First Anniversary*, 431–434]

According to Augustine, in a phrase echoed by Donne in the opening lines of the poem, they only know they have a soul who see (*meminit*), judge (*intelligit*) and follow (*diligit*) God; and "that is true wisdom": *quod est sapientia.*[1]

* * *

Considered in terms of the tradition of Wisdom, certain things about the *Anniversaries* become immediately clear. I have already mentioned the fundamental structure of the poems, the alternation of contempt and glorification based on the definition of wisdom as "the right valuation of this world, and of the next." As Donne ex-

9. Nicholas Breton, *Divine Considerations of the Soule* (1608), cited in Martz, *op. cit.*, pp. 227–28.
1. *De Trinitate, PL* 42, 1047.

plained in *The First Anniversary*, the purpose of the poem was to demonstrate to the "new world"

> The dangers and diseases of the old:
> For with due temper men do then forgoe,
> Or couet things, when they their true worth know.
>
> [88–90]

The tradition also explains why the poems were written in the form of traditional Ignatian meditations. As Louis L. Martz has pointed out, each of the *Anniversaries* is divided into various large structural units, or meditations, each of which in turn is divided into three main parts. In *The First Anniversary* they are: (1) a meditation on the decay of the world and the effects of original sin on man and the entire frame of the universe; (2) a eulogy of Elizabeth Drury as a lost pattern of virtue; and (3) a refrain and moral, urging us to forget this crippled, dying world. Martz's divisions, I think, are entirely correct, but what he has failed to notice, though he mentions it in other parts of his book,[2] is that these three recurrent parts of the poem correspond to the three traditional parts of the rational soul—memory, understanding, and will. In what Martz terms the *meditations*, Donne sends his mind back in time toward Eden. Through the tradition of the decay of the world, which, as a tradition, represents the collective memory of man, he "remembers" imaginatively the perfection of the first days of the earth and searches out the cause for the present decay. He then turns to the intellect. In the so-called *eulogies*, he probes the significance of a young girl's recent death and discovers in it an answer to what caused the decay. She is a way of comprehending the lost perfection of man's soul, the grace of God in Paradise—not logically, but emotionally, in symbolic terms. And finally, from this combination of memory and understanding, Donne arrives at an act of will: to forget this rotten world now that she is dead.

The most important of these three recurrent parts of the poem is the last, the ultimate act of will; for the will, as Donne pointed out in his sermons, has a certain *Virtus transformativa*: "by it we change our selves into that we love most" (*Sermons*, IX, 373):

> *Primus actus voluntatis est Amor:* Philosophers and Divines agree in that, That the will of man cannot be idle, and the first act that the will of man produces, is Love; for till it love something, prefer and chuse something, till it would have something, it is not a Will; neither can it turn upon any object, before God. So that this first, and general, and natural love of God, is not begotten in my soul, nor produced by my soul, but created and infus'd with my soul, and as my soul; there is no soul that knows she is a soul, without such a general sense of the love of God [*Sermons*, VI, 361].

2. Martz, *op. cit.*, pp. 34–36.

It echoes in the very first lines of the poem:

> For who is sure he hath a soule, vnlesse
> It see, and Iudge, and follow worthinesse,
> And by Deedes praise it? [3–5]

And ultimately that is what the *Anniversaries* perform. They detach our love from this world and direct it toward the next, toward the luminous "Idea of a Woman," who represents the image of God in man.

But the will is not capable of acting alone. "All sin is from the perverseness of the will," Donne noted, but "all disorder in the will [is] from errour in the understanding" (*Sermons*, VIII, 364–365). All three faculties of the soul must flow together to form one total act of love, for all three were thought to be analogous to the Trinity, though three, yet one. In traditional Augustinian psychology the memory, understanding, and will constitute potentially the Image of God in man. When directed toward their proper goal, they enter into what they love and restore the lost likeness of the soul to God. They become in themselves Wisdom, *sapientia creata*, the image of the increate Wisdom of God:

> The Trinity in the mind itself is the Image of God, by which it remembers, understands, and loves God—which is true wisdom (*sapientia*). This Trinity of the mind therefore is the Image of God not because the mind remembers, understands, and loves itself, but because it remembers, understands, and loves the one by whom it was made. When it does that, it is wise (*sapiens*). If it does not, . . . it is stupid (*stulta*). . . . In brief, it should worship the uncreated God, who made it capable of himself (*cujus ab eo capax est facta*) and capable of being a partaker of himself (*et cujus particeps esse potest*); according to which it is written, 'Behold, the love of God (*Dei cultus*), that is wisdom' (*Job*, 28:28). And not by its own light, but by participation in the highest light will it become wise, and where eternal, there will it reign blessed.[3]

* * *

It is impossible to express in discursive language, but at this point it becomes apparent that the tripartite structure of the *Anniversaries* is identical with the central symbol that rises from it. Put into Aristotelian terms, it is the same as the relationship between efficient and final cause. The symbol is the principle because of which the poem moves toward the production of its effect. It is the form. But at the same time, seen from a slightly different perspective, the symbol is also the process itself that produces the effect. It is both the object and the wit. More concretely, if through the process of the poem— the threefold act of memory, understanding, and will—we arrive at the right valuation of this world and the next, we will have achieved

3. Augustine, *De Trinitate, PL* 42, 1047.

within ourselves the Image of God that was lost. Our souls will have become transformed into the mysterious symbol at the center of the poem:

> Love is a Possessory Affection, it delivers over him that loves into the possession of that that he loves; it is a transmutatory Affection, it changes him that loves, into the very nature of that that he loves, and he is nothing else [*Sermons*, I, 184–185].

In the second place, the tradition of Wisdom helps put into proper perspective the celebrated "new philosophy" section of *The First Anniversary*:

> And new Philosophy calls all in doubt,
> The Element of fire is quite put out;
> The Sunne is lost, and th'earth, and no mans wit
> Can well direct him, where to looke for it.
> And freely men confesse, that this world's spent,
> When in the Planets, and the Firmament
> They seeke so many new; they see that this
> Is crumbled out againe to his Atomis.
> 'Tis all in pieces, all cohaerence gone;
> All iust supply, and all Relation. [205–214]

The passage is usually taken out of context to illustrate the impact of scientific rationalism on the Medieval world picture and the consequent unsettling of the Renaissance mind. "Donne," according to Douglas Bush, echoing Coffin, Nicolson, and others, "is wandering between two worlds, that of cosmic unity and that of meaningless disorder and decay, and he cannot resolve the conflict."[4] Such a conflict undoubtedly stands somewhere behind the *Anniversaries*—as it does behind every other poem in the Renaissance—and helps explain why they were written. But it is not the statement that the poems themselves make. The *Anniversaries* are not simply a symbolic action, an elaborate gesture of intellectual despair.

Nor, on the other hand, are they Menippian satires, as Northrop Frye recently claimed: "where the death of a girl expands into a general satire or 'anatomy'."[5] In Frye's elaborate and suggestive system of genres the anatomy, or Menippian satire, is directed not against people themselves, but against mental attitudes or types—"Pedants, bigots, cranks, parvenus, virtuosi, enthusiasts, rapacious and incompetent professional men of all kinds." Evil and absurdity are regarded not as moral or social phenomena, but intellectual, "a kind of maddened pedantry which the *philosophus gloriosus* at once symbolizes and defines." According to this view, Donne overwhelms "his pedantic targets with an avalanche of their own jargon."[6] He hoists them

4. *English Literature in the Earlier Seventeenth Century*, 1600–1660 (Oxford, 1945), p. 132.

5. *Anatomy of Criticism: Four Essays* (Princeton, 1957), p. 298.

6. *Ibid.*, pp. 309; 311.

on their own petard by using the most famous discoveries of the day only to prove the decay of the world. The new medicine of Paracelsus, for example, is equated with the new disease of syphilis:

> With new diseases on our selues we warre,
> And with new phisicke, a worse Engin farre.   [159–160]

And of course Frye is correct. *The First Anniversary* is shot through with satire of that sort. But again the danger is in reading the part for the whole: a complexity of tone for formal satire. The *Anniversaries* contain satire, but they are not themselves contained by it. In terms of Renaissance poetic theory they are formal *epitaphia*, one *recens*, the other, *anniversarium*, written in the mode of Ignatian meditations.

There is, however, a third alternative, which subsumes the previous two. For if the *Anniversaries* are a lament for the loss of Wisdom, *sapientia creata*, then the learning of the new philosophy as well as Donne's own hypothetical disillusion are simply forms of false wisdom that stand in contrast to it. Instead of proving the glory of man, they reveal only further the hideous deformity and decay of the world:

> Those therefore who are wise in and concerning visible things (as are all those outside the Faith and those who are ignorant of God and a future life) understand nothing and are wise in nothing, that is, they are neither intelligent (*intelligentes*) nor wise (*sapientes*), but foolish and blind. And though they may think themselves wise men, yet they have become fools. For they are wise, not in the wisdom of secret, hidden things, but of that which can be found in a human way.[7]

The distinction was traditional and ultimately goes back to Augustine:

> It is written concerning our Lord Jesus Christ that in him 'are hid all the treasures of wisdom and knowledge' (*Coloss.*, 2:3). The eloquence of Scripture also indicates, however, that these two—that is, wisdom (*sapientiam*) and knowledge (*scientiam*)— are different from one another, and in particular the holy words of Job, where each is defined to a certain extent. For he says, 'Behold, the love of God (*pietas*), *that* is wisdom; to refrain from evil, however, is knowledge' (*Job*, 28:28). Not incorrectly we perceive (*intelligimus*) wisdom in understanding (*cognitione*) and in love (*dilectione*) of the one who always is and who remains immutable, that is God. *To refrain from evil*, however, which he says is knowledge, what is that but to be cautious and prudent in the midst of a crooked and perverse nation, as in the night of this century. . . .[8]

Scientia is the knowledge of this world only.[9] It is limited to what is perceived by the senses and represents the extent of man's wisdom in a state of nature.[1] *Sapientia*, on the other hand, is the knowledge of

---

7. Luther, cited in Rice, *The Renaissance Idea of Wisdom*, p. 139; see also the entire chapter, pp. 124–48.

8. Augustine, *PL* 37, 1760.
9. *PL* 42, 1037.
1. *PL* 40, 139.

this world and of the next. It is a supernatural gift of God, *de sursum descendens:* the direct intellectual comprehension of eternal things.[2] In *The Second Anniversary*, for example, the satire and the agonized anatomy of the world gives way to a harmonious *docta ignorantia*, which forms the prelude to true wisdom:

> In this low forme, poore soule what wilt thou doe?
> When wilt thou shake off this Pedantery,
> Of being taught by sense, and Fantasy?
> Thou look'st through spectacles; small things seeme great,
> Below; But vp vnto the watch-towre get,
> And see all things despoyld of fallacies:
> Thou shalt not peepe through lattices of eies,
> Nor heare through Laberinths of eares, not learne
> By circuit, or collections to discerne.
> In Heauen thou straight know'st all, concerning it,
> And what concerns it not, shall straight forget.   [290–300]

It suffuses the entire poem:

> Forget this world, and scarse thinke of it so,
> As of old cloaths, cast of a yeare agoe.
> To be thus stupid is Alacrity;
> Men thus lethargique haue best Memory.
> Looke vpward; that's towards her, whose happy state
> We now lament not, but congratulate.   [61–66]

Finally, the tradition of Wisdom helps explain the fundamental difference between the two poems: they stand in the same relation to one another as *scientia* to *sapientia*. As Donne explained in one of his sermons,

> a regenerate Christian, being now a *new Creature*, hath also *a new facultie of Reason.* . . . Divers men may walke by the Sea side, and the same beames of the Sunne giving light to them all, one gathereth by the benefit of that light pebels, or speckled shells, for curious vanitie, and another gathers precious Pearle, or medicinall Ambar, by the same light. So the common light of reason illuminates us all; but one imployes this light upon the searching of impertinent vanities, another by a better use of the same light, finds out the Mysteries of Religion; and when he hath found them, loves them. . . . Some men by the benefit of this light of Reason, have found out things profitable and usefull to the whole world; As in particular, *Printing* . . . [and] *Artillery*, by which warres come to quicker ends then heretofore, and the great expence of bloud is avoyded. . . . But . . . their light seems to be great out of the same reason, that a Torch in a misty night, seemeth greater then in a clear, because it hath kindled and inflamed much thicke and grosse Ayre round about it. . . .

2. *PL* 42 1012.

But, if thou canst take this light of reason that is in thee, this poore snuffe, that is almost out in thee, thy faint and dimme knowledge of God, that riseth out of this light of nature, if thou canst in those embers, those cold ashes, finde out one small coale, and wilt take the paines to kneell downe, and blow that coale with thy devout *Prayers*, . . . if . . . thou canst turne this little light inward, and canst thereby discerne where thy diseases, and thy wounds, and thy corruptions are, and canst apply those teares, and blood and balme to them, . . . thou shalt never envy the lustre and glory of the great lights of worldly men. . . . Their light shall set at noone; even in their heighth, . . . and thy light shall grow up, from a *faire hope*, to a modest assurance and *infallibility*, that that light shall never go out . . . ; as thy light of *reason* is exalted by *faith* here, so thy light of *faith* shall be exalted into the light of *glory*, and fruition in the Kingdome of heaven . . . ; in a man regenerate by faith, that light does all that reason did, *and more* [*Sermons*, III, 359–362].

The First Anniversary is concerned only with the light of reason, unaided by faith. Its tone, therefore, is analytic and satirical; through the use of reason it explores the limits of reason. It proceeds "punctually" from part to part in rigid logical sequence, but its overall movement is downward to decay. Its ultimate discovery is a universe of death. At the same time, however, proceeding from the operation of reason in the poem is the silent process of transformation by which the soul is changed into the very nature of that which it loves. As Donne explains toward the end of the poem, he has rewritten the Song of Moses for his own times, traditionally regarded as the complete summary of the Law, teaching the fear of the Lord and the severity of judgment. It marked the furthest extent to which man could proceed by human reason alone; beyond lay the dispensation of Grace. Therefore, after delivering the Song to his people, Moses ascended Mount Nebo with the Lord and from the top of Pisgah looked over into the Promised Land. But he was not able to enter.

In *The Second Anniversary*, however, Donne crossed over, and the entire poem surges upward toward eternal life:

> Looke vpward; that's towards her, whose happy state
> We now lament not, but congratulate. [65–66]

The meditations begin with death ("Thinke then, My soule, that death is but a Groome"), the point at which *The First Anniversary* and natural man end, and proceed beyond:

> But thinke that Death hath now enfranchis'd thee,
> Thou hast thy'expansion now and libertee;
> Thinke that a rusty Peece, discharg'd, is flowen
> In peeces, and the bullet is his owne,
> And freely flies: This to thy soule allow,
> Thinke thy sheell broke, thinke thy Soule hatch'd but now.
> [179–184]

The symbolism diminishes. Elizabeth Drury becomes more and more recognizable as an idealized pattern of virtue. For the soul itself has now attained the Wisdom that was lost. It has become internalized, and the emotions that were once concentrated within the symbol have now become diffused throughout the entire poem. The total movement of *The Second Anniversary* is harmonious and organic not, as is usually believed, because it is a success and *The First Anniversary* a failure, but because through the purgative process of *The First Anniversary* the soul has at last arrived at a right valuation of this world, and of the next, and rests secure in the love of God. As Dante remarked, commenting on the phrase, "When Israel went out of Egypt":

> If we regard the *literal* sense alone it signifies the departure of the sons of Israel from Egypt in the time of Moses; *allegorically*, it signifies our redemption through Christ; *morally*, it signifies the conversion of the soul from the grief and misery of sin to the state of grace; *anagogically*, it signifies the departure of the blessed soul from the slavery of this corruption to the freedom of everlasting glory.[3]

3. *Opere*, ed. Moore, p. 415.

A Selected Bibliography

The standard edition of Donne's complete poetry is still Sir Herbert Grierson's *The Poems of John Donne*, 2 volumes, Oxford, 1912. For The *Anniversaries*, the student should consult Frank Manley's *John Donne: The Anniversaries*, Baltimore, 1963; for Donne's religious poetry, see Helen Gardner's *John Donne: The Divine Poems*, Oxford, 1952. Editions by Miss Gardner of the rest of the poems are in progress and undoubtedly will, as they are published, supersede Grierson. (Miss Gardner's edition of *The Elegies and the Songs and Sonnets*, Oxford, 1965, appeared as this book was going to press; however, close examination of both texts has revealed substantial agreement.)

For additional bibliographical information the student may consult Geoffrey Keynes, *A Bibliography of Dr. John Donne*, Cambridge, England, 1958; Theodore Spencer and Mark Van Doren, *Studies in Metaphysical Poetry: Two Essays and a Bibliography*, New York, 1939; Spencer and Van Doren's work is continued by Lloyd E. Berry, *A Bibliography of Studies in Metaphysical Poetry, 1939-1960*, Madison, 1964; also see William White, *John Donne Since 1900: A Bibliography of Periodicals*, Boston, 1942.

H. C. Combs and Z. R. Sullens have published *A Concordance to the English Poems of John Donne*, Chicago, 1940.

Selections reprinted in this edition and referred to in the glosses are not included below.

BIOGRAPHY

Bald, Robert Cecil. *Donne and the Drurys*. Cambridge, England, 1959.
Fausset, Hugh I'Anson. *John Donne: A Study in Discord*. London, 1924.
Gosse, Sir Edmund. *The Life and Letters of John Donne*, 2 vols. London, 1899.
Hardy, Evelyn. *John Donne: A Spirit in Conflict*. London, 1942.
Le Comte, Edward. *Grace to a Witty Sinner: A Life of Donne*. New York, 1965.
Simpson, Evelyn M. *A Study of the Prose Works of John Donne*, 2nd ed. Oxford, 1948. Chapter II contains biographical material.
Walton, Izaak. *The Lives . . .* London, 1670. *Life of Donne* was first published with *LXXX Sermons*, 1640; it was enlarged and issued separately in 1658.

GENERAL STUDIES

Alvarez, A. *The School of Donne*. London, 1962.
Bennett, Joan. *Five Metaphysical Poets*, rev. ed. Cambridge, England, 1963.
Bredvold, L. I. "The Naturalism of Donne in Relation to Some Renaissance Traditions," *Journal of English and Germanic Philology*, XXII (1923), 471-502.
Bush, Douglas. *English Literature in the Earlier Seventeenth Century, 1600-1660*, 2nd ed. rev. Oxford, 1962.
Coffin, Charles M. *John Donne and the New Philosophy*. New York, 1958. First published 1937.
Leishman, J. B. *The Metaphysical Poets: Donne, Herbert, Vaughan, Traherne*. Oxford, 1934.
Nicolson, Marjorie H. *The Breaking of the Circle: Studies in the Effect of the "New Science" Upon Seventeenth Century Poetry*, rev. ed. New York, 1960.
Sharp, Robert L. *From Donne to Dryden: The Revolt Against Metaphysical Poetry*. Chapel Hill, N. C., 1940.
Spencer, Theodore, ed. *A Garland for John Donne*. Gloucester, Mass., 1958. First published 1931.
Tillyard, E. M. W. *The Elizabethan World Picture*. London, 1960. First published 1943.
Tuve, Rosemond. *Elizabethan and Metaphysical Imagery*. Chicago, 1947.
White, Helen. *The Metaphysical Poets*. New York, 1936.
Williamson, George. *The Donne Tradition*. Cambridge, Mass., 1930.

CRITICISM

Biographical and background material also appears in some of the works listed below. Since it is neither possible nor desirable to list here all of the criticism published on Donne, this section is arbitrarily limited to some of the criticism published in the last twenty-five years.

Chambers, A. B. " 'Goodfriday, 1613. Riding Westward': The Poem and the Tradition," *ELH* XXVIII (1961), 31-53.

Colie, R. L. "John Donne's Anniversary Poems and the Paradoxes of Epistomology," Part II of "The Rhetoric of Transcendence," *Philological Quarterly*, XLIII (April 1964), 159-170.

Duncan, E. H. "Donne's Alchemical Figures," *ELH* IX (1942), 257-285.

Freccero, John. "Donne's 'Valediction Forbidding Mourning,' " *ELH* XXX (1963), 335-376.

Gardner, Helen. "The Argument about 'The Ecstasy,' " in *Elizabethan and Jacobean Studies*, pp. 279-306. Oxford, 1959.

———, ed. *John Donne: A Collection of Critical Essays*. Englewood Cliffs, N. J., 1962.

Gransden, K. W. *John Donne*. London, 1954.

Harding, D. W. "Coherence of Theme in Donne's Poetry," *Kenyon Review*, XIII (1951), 427-444.

Kermode, Frank, ed. *Discussions of John Donne*. Boston, 1962.

Louthan, Doniphan. *The Poetry of John Donne*. New York, 1951.

Martz, Louis L. "John Donne: The Meditative Voice," *Massachusetts Review*, I (1960), 326-342.

Mazzeo, Joseph A. "Notes on John Donne's Alchemical Imagery," *Isis* XLVIII (1957), 103-123.

Mueller, William R. "Donne's Adulterous Female Town," [*Holy Sonnet XIV*], *Modern Language Notes*, LXXVI (1961), 312-314.

Newton, Willoughby. "A Study of John Donne's Sonnet XIV," *Anglican Theological Review*, XLI (1959), 10-12.

Peterson, Douglas L. "John Donne's *Holy Sonnets* and the Anglican Doctrine of Contrition," *Studies in Philology*, LVI (1959), 504-518.

Rooney, William J. " 'The Canonization'—the Language of Paradox Reconsidered," *ELH*, XXIII (1956), 36-47.

Simpson, Evelyn M. "The Text of Donne's 'Divine Poems,' " *ESEA*, XXVI (1941), 88-105.

Smith, A. J. *John Donne: The Songs and Sonets*. London, 1964.

Stein, Arnold. "Donne's Prosody," *PMLA* LIX (1944), 373-397.

——— *John Donne's Lyrics: The Eloquence of Action*. Minneapolis, 1962.

——— "Meter and Meaning in Donne's Verse," *Sewanee Review* LII (1944), 288-301.

Tillotson, Kathleen. "Donne's Poetry in the Nineteenth Century (1800-1872)," in *Elizabethan and Jacobean Studies*, pp. 307-326. Oxford, 1959.

Unger, Leonard. *Donne's Poetry and Modern Criticism*. New York, 1962. First published 1950.

Warren, Austin. "Donne's 'Extasie,' " *Studies in Philology*, LV (1958), 472-480.

Wiley, Margaret L. "The Poetry of Donne: Its Interest and Influence Today," *ESEA*, N. S. VII (1954), 78-104.

Williamson, George. "The Design of Donne's Anniversaries," *Modern Philology*, LX (1963), 183-191.

——— "Textual Difficulties in the Interpretation of Donne's Poetry," *Modern Philology*, XXXVIII (1940), 37-72.